FROM SLAVES TO SQUATTERS

From Slaves to Squatters

Plantation Labor and Agriculture in

Zanzibar and Coastal Kenya,

1890–1925

FREDERICK COOPER

New Haven and London   Yale University Press
Published in Kenya by Kenya Literature Bureau 1981

Designed by James J. Johnson
and set in VIP Baskerville type.
Printed in the United States of America by
The Vail-Ballou Press, Inc.,
Binghamton, New York

Library of Congress Cataloging in Publication Data

Cooper, Frederick, 1947-
    From slaves to squatters.

    Bibliography: p.
    Includes index.
    1. Agricultural laborers—Africa, East—History.
2. Slavery in East Africa—History.   3. Agriculture—
Economic aspects—Africa—East—History.   4. Planta-
tion life—Africa, East—History.   5. Africa, East—
Colonial influence—History.   I. Title.
HD1538.E22C66   331.7′63′0967623   80-5391
ISBN 0-300-02454-1

10 9 8 7 6 5 4 3 2 1

Contents

Tables

Figures

Preface

This study of labor and agriculture after the emancipation of slaves began as part of research into plantation slavery on the east coast of Africa. When I began, I thought of this aspect of the project as the closing of a parenthesis, the end of an archaic form of labor organization and social structure. If there were continuing effects of slavery on the economy and society of the coast, they were legacies of the past, and the colonial economy—whether more or less oppressive and constraining than what went on before it—was a new departure. This is a common viewpoint among historians of slavery. It is also, as my research eventually made clear to me, totally inadequate. Historical parentheses rarely close, and separating out legacies from past ways of organizing labor and production avoids the difficult problem of how modes of production actually are changed. So this book is not about the end of slavery. Nor is it a study of the colonial economy. It is a study of differing labor systems—of how they are conceived and operate—and above all a study of how they are transformed.

The years that bound this study are not overly precise, for my subject is bounded by processes rather than events: it begins with the actions the British colonial state took in its first decade of rule to undermine the independent economic, political, and social power of slaveowners in Zanzibar and coastal Kenya, a process that weakened the planters' control of labor and the organization of production far more than the colonial state intended. It ends at a time when the export crops emerging from the new organization of production were at a peak and just before a combination of local problems and worldwide depression led to a period of contraction, dislocation, and involution in coastal agriculture. My focus is on changes in how goods were produced at a time when external conditions for their export remained generally favorable.

The region this study covers was once part of a wider economic and political system centered on—although only loosely controlled by—the Sultanate of Zanzibar—and which later shared the experience of British rule, Zanzibar as a protectorate, the British portion of the mainland coast as a part of what became the colony of Kenya. I know parts of this large region better than others: fieldwork and quantitative analysis of landholding was undertaken in Malindi and Mombasa. Detailed archival material in England permitted close analysis of Zanzibar and Pemba, despite obstacles that have been placed in front of me and other re-

searchers to do research in Zanzibar itself. Similarly, some questions
have been relatively neglected—produce marketing for instance—but
such gaps are inevitable: the extent to which I have relied on the work of
at least a dozen other researchers who have studied the coast should
make it obvious that filling the merely apparent holes will require the
efforts of another dozen. My interest has above all been in understanding structures, processes, and interconnections within a wide, varied,
and changing region; I hope I have at least suggested why more local
studies will be of more than local interest.

My greatest debt is to the people who explained to me how they conceived of the problems of land and labor and who told me of their experiences and those of their parents. By talking to the children of slaves
and slaveowners, landlords and tenants, I was able to get a sense not only
of the variety of experiences, but also of the opposed conceptions of
economic order, conceptions that are deeply rooted in a sense of
morality and justice. I have tried to acknowledge information I was given
as I would any other historical source, but a document cannot patiently
explain a point or answer the questions of an inquisitive stranger. The
names of the people I spoke with on the coast of Kenya are listed in the
back of the book, and I have briefly stated why each is important. I am
very grateful to the people of Malindi and Mombasa, not just for their
help and patience, but for their interest.

The very different conceptions of the economy of British officials,
missionaries, and others, as well as a great variety of information on economic and social change, can be gleaned from documentary sources. I
want to thank the staffs of the archives where I worked and which are
listed in the Bibliography as well as the staffs of the libraries of Yale
University, Harvard University, Cambridge University, the University of
Nairobi, the Royal Commonwealth Society, and the Institute for Commonwealth Studies.

Oral information and land data on the coast of Kenya were gathered
in 1972-73 under the sponsorship of Yale University. Since then a fac-
ulty research grant from Harvard University has paid for computer
time to analyze some of these data, while additional research in England
was funded by the American Philosophical Society and the American
Economic History Association.

The data on land at Mombasa in this book come from collaborative
efforts with John Zarwan and Karim Janmohamed. The data were collected together, and Dr. Zarwan and I are continuing to work on a quantitative study of land and credit in Mombasa, while Dr. Janmohamed has
made use of this material in a way that complements my own in his il-
luminating study of land and urban development in Mombasa. The interpretations of results in this book are my responsibility, but my debt to

my collaborators and friends is a large one. Similarly, I am very grateful to Margaret Strobel for generously sharing with me information and ideas about Mombasa, as well as the experience of doing research in that city.

The process of rethinking my material and pondering approaches to the study of a changing economic and social order has been greatly assisted over the past several years by Carla Glassman. Drafts of the manuscript have been thoughtfully criticized by David Brion Davis, Stanley Engerman, William Freund, Carla Glassman, Molly Nolan, Rebecca Scott, Margaret Strobel, and John Zarwan. An early version of the sections on Zanzibar was presented to a conference on agrarian history, held at Columbia University in April 1977. I am grateful to the participants in the conference for their comments, and especially to Marcia Wright, who organized it. John Womack, Jr., also gave me valuable comments on the Zanzibar material, while the sections on Kenya benefitted from the reactions of Sara Berry, Margaret Jean Hay, Karim Janmohamed, John Lonsdale, and Sharon Stichter, and from seminars at Cambridge University and the University of Nairobi.

The first time I attempted to write about the coast of Kenya was in 1972, for a staff seminar at the Department of History of the University of Nairobi. It is appropriate that the final words of this book are being written in an office of that department, where I have been made welcome by the chairman, Godfrey Muriuki, and by the members of the staff. The experience of a shared pursuit of intellectual goals is a rare one, and I am glad that I have found it here.

F. C.

Nairobi
January 1979

Abbreviations Used in the Notes

a/c	Adjudication Cause: Records of hearings on applications for land titles on the coast of Kenya, 1912–24, Land Office, Mombasa
AgAR	Agriculture Department, Annual Report (Zanzibar or Kenya)
AgCom	Zanzibar, "Report of the Agricultural Commission," 1923
AR	Annual Report
ASP	Anti-Slavery Papers: records of the British and Foreign Anti-Slavery Society, Rhodes House, Oxford University
ASR	*Anti-Slavery Reporter,* series 4, unless otherwise specified
CMS	Church Missionary Society Archives, London
CO	Colonial Office files, Public Record Office, London
CocCom	East Africa Protectorate, "Report of the Coconut Commission," 1914
COCP	Colonial Office Confidential Prints, Public Record Office, London
CP	Coast Province Collection, Deposit 1, Kenya National Archives, Nairobi
DC	District Commissioner
D&C	Diplomatic and Consular Reports, Foreign Office, Annual Series
DO	District Officer
EAP	East Africa Protectorate
FA	Friends' Archives, London
FO	Foreign Office files, Public Record Office, London
FOCP	Foreign Office Confidential Prints, Public Record Office, London
HOR	Handing Over Reports, Kenya National Archives, Nairobi
JAH	*Journal of African History*
KNA	Kenya National Archives, Nairobi
LP	Frederick Lugard Papers, Rhodes House, Oxford University
MAL	Notes of interviews, Malindi, Kenya, 1972–73.
MSA	Notes of interviews, Mombasa, Kenya, 1972–73
NAD	Native Affairs Department, Kenya
NLC	Native Labour Commission, 1912–13, Report and Evidence (East Africa Protectorate)

P&A	Probate and Administration files, High Court, Nairobi
PC	Provincial Commissioner
PP	Parliamentary Papers
PRO	Public Record Office, London
PRB	Political Record Book, Kenya National Archives, Nairobi
QR	Quarterly Report
Reg., Mal	Registers of deeds pertaining to Malindi, 1903–20, Land Office, Mombasa
Reg., Msa	Registers of deeds pertaining to Mombasa, 1891–1919, Land Office, Mombasa
USCR	*United States Commercial Reports*

Swahili Terms

Most Swahili nouns add certain prefixes to denote singular and plural. For the names of ethnic groups, the prefix "M" refers to an individual, and "Wa" to more than one person or the collectivity. I have used these forms in referring to Swahili-speaking peoples, but in order to avoid the confusion of many languages have used simplified forms, without prefixes, for all peoples who do not speak Swahili. The following Swahili terms (plurals in parentheses) are also used:

haji (mahaji): a convert to Islam
hamali (mahamali): port worker, carrier
kibarua (vibarua): day-laborer
mzalia (wazalia): person of slave descent
shamba (mashamba): farm or plantation
sheha (masheha): headman
tembo: palm wine

Money and Weights

The units of currency employed here are either Sterling (£) or rupees (Rs, sing. Re). For most of the period, the currency conversion rate was Rs 15 to £ 1, but the pound fell around 1920 to Rs 10. In Zanzibar, rupees were the official currency throughout the period, but Kenya switched to shillings in 1921 (with a brief interlude when a unit called the florin was used), converting at the rate of Shs 2 to Re 1 (there are 20 shillings to the pound). There are 64 pice (or, alternatively, 100¢) to the rupee.

The local weight units used here are the frasila, equal to 35 pounds, and the pishi, about 4 pounds.

Map 1: British East Africa

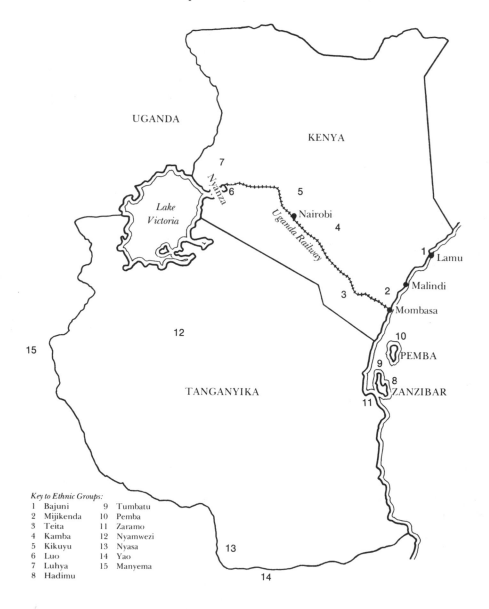

UGANDA

KENYA

7

Nyanza

6

5

Lake
Victoria

Nairobi

Uganda Railway

4

1 • Lamu

2 • Malindi

3

• Mombasa

12

10

15

• PEMBA

9

8

TANGANYIKA

ZANZIBAR

11

13

14

Key to Ethnic Groups:

1	Bajuni	9	Tumbatu
2	Mijikenda	10	Pemba
3	Teita	11	Zaramo
4	Kamba	12	Nyamwezi
5	Kikuyu	13	Nyasa
6	Luo	14	Yao
7	Luhya	15	Manyema
8	Hadimu		

Map 2: Zanzibar, Pemba, and the Coast of Kenya

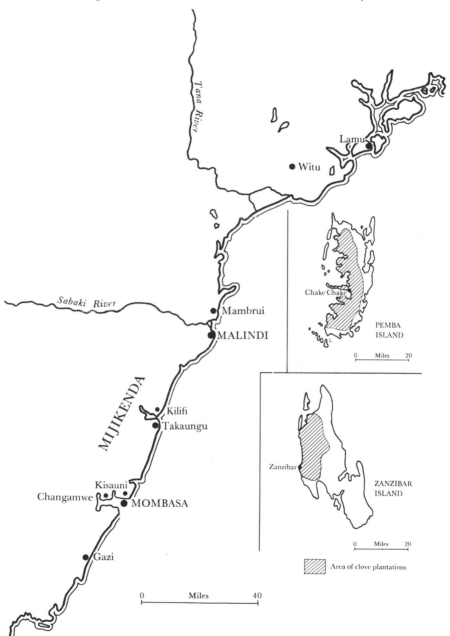

1   Introduction

For slaves in many places and at many times, emancipation has been a time of joy. No more would they work under their owners' eyes; no more would they live in fear that they or their children would be sold or sent away; no more would they be bound to a master who abused them; and no more would they be prevented from seeking even the most limited opportunities in neighboring farms or distant cities.

Never, as far as is known, has a slave community regretted its freedom; never, even in the face of the most dire poverty, has it wished to return to the security and oppression of slavery. But emancipation—in the southern United States, in the Caribbean, in Brazil, and in parts of Africa as well—has been a time of disillusionment as well as joy. The individual plantation owner may have ceased to be lord and master over his slaves, but the planter class did not lose its power. From the perspective of abolitionists, workers and employers in a free society interacted as individuals in the market place, selling and buying labor. But in case after case, a particular class—under the equally hallowed ideals of private property—kept land from the eager hands of ex-slaves and vigorously applied the instruments of the state and the law to block ex-slaves' access to resources and markets, to restrict their ability to move about, bargain, or refuse wage labor, and to undermine their attempts to become independent producers. At the same time, freed slaves fought hardest against the regimentation of gang labor and the efforts of planters to determine when and how any member of a laborer's family would work. The period after emancipation in the Americas, even more than the period before it, proved to be a time of struggle.

In most places, ex-slaves were able to some extent to force new labor arrangements on the planters in order to gain for themselves some improvement in standard of living, more leisure time, and limited control over how they worked. In a few instances where planters were weak or land abundant, ex-slaves built viable, independent agricultural communities. But more often planters and export-minded governments restructured the old plantation system and modified old patterns of dominance.[1]

1. The widespread nature of these problems is evident from the sketchy but useful survey in Wilemina Kloosterboer, *Involuntary Labour since the Abolition of Slavery* (Leiden, 1960), and the preliminary comparative analysis in C. Vann Woodward, "The Price of Freedom," in David S. Sansing, ed., *What Was Freedom's Price?* (Jackson, Miss., 1978), pp. 93–126. These issues have been explored most fully in the case of the West Indies, and the

In Africa, the emancipation of slaves who had served both African and immigrant masters was the act of colonial powers, undertaken in the decades after the conquest of African societies in the late nineteenth century. To the ruling class of Great Britain—more decisively than the other imperial powers—the abolition of slavery and the introduction of wage labor were seen in themselves to be an advance of civilization. That fact made it less necessary for colonial officials to dwell on the difficult question of what free labor actually meant. Ultimately, the experience of Great Britain made clear, free labor implied the submission of workers to a uniform code of laws, to the rigors of the market, and to internalized discipline, in contrast to the personal control and coercion of the slavemaster. But to Africa's new rulers, the time when such a concept of labor control could apply to the slaves they were freeing, as well as the cultivators they were conquering, lay in the dimly perceived future.

Colonial governments and businesses paid workers wages; they did not seek to create a wage labor system. They had little faith in the labor market, stripped of restrictive social relations and functioning through the self-regulating mechanism of supply and demand.

But the British colonial state in Zanzibar and coastal Kenya did not merely want more workers and greater output. The state sought to preserve a quite particular form of economic organization—the plantation—and to transform it by imposing a quite particular way of organizing labor. Indeed, the British seem to have followed the path of greatest resistance, propping up an aristocracy of ex-slaveowners whom their conquest had undermined and stifling the initiatives of the slaves they had supposedly set free.[2] The development of East Africa, officials

---

evolution of British policy and variations in local responses are analyzed in William Green, *British Slave Emancipation: The Sugar Colonies and the Great Experiment* (Oxford, 1976). For more references, see his "Caribbean Historiography, 1600–1900: The Recent Tide," *Journal of Interdisciplinary History* 7 (1977): 509–30, while the most penetrating analyses of this region can be found in the work of Sidney Mintz, notably "Slavery and the Rise of Peasantries," *Historical Reflections* 6, no. 1 (1979): 213–43, and *Caribbean Transformations* (Chicago, 1974). A model case-study is Alan Adamson, *Sugar without Slaves: The Political Economy of British Guiana, 1838–1904* (New Haven, 1972).

2. This argument is at variance with one made by Immanuel Wallerstein, who considers that the path of "least resistance"—encouraging production by African peasants—was more the norm and that deviations from it can be better explained by political than by economic factors. Clearly, colonial policies varied greatly, but Wallerstein and others are so taken by the distinction between African peasants and European capitalists that they have not probed the extent to which colonial policies were aimed at changing the relations of production *within* African societies, above all by fostering divisions between landowners and workers, or the extent to which the actions of Africans along the path of greatest resistance forced their colonial masters to find another one. "The Three Stages of African Involvement in the World-Economy," in Peter C. W. Gutkind and Immanuel Wallerstein, eds., *The Political Economy of Contemporary Africa* (Beverly Hills, Calif., 1976), esp. pp. 41–42.

believed, would not be well served by letting Africans work when, where, and how they chose. Development required that labor be steady, that it be under the direction of a property owner and the supervision of the state, and that laborers be made to learn and internalize new values and attitudes.

These policies were imposed on an economic and social structure that was very different from the image of unproductive agriculture, isolation from markets, and antieconomic cultural values that forms the implicit (if not explicit) backdrop for far too many discussions of "economic development."[3] On the coast of East Africa, a productive plantation economy had expanded enormously in the nineteenth century. The planters—immigrants from Arabia and Swahili-speaking, Muslim Africans from the coast itself—bought slaves, built plantations, and intensified the exploitation of labor in response to the growing demands of the Indian Ocean commercial system. Almost all the world's supply of cloves came from the islands of Zanzibar and Pemba, where Arabs from Oman established large clove plantations from the 1830s onward. On the adjacent mainland around mid-century, Swahili and Arabs developed vast plantations that exported grain to the food-poor regions of southern Arabia and to commercial centers, like Zanzibar itself. In both areas, coconuts were also grown for local consumption and to meet a modest demand for oils made from the dried fruit of the coconut. The trading mechanism that distributed goods around the Indian Ocean also extended deep into Africa and brought slaves to the coast, as well as ivory and other trade goods that fed the Indian Ocean trading system, which was in turn linked—via India and later Zanzibar itself—to European commerce.

The coast had thus long been a part of a world economy. What was new, above all, under colonial rule was the intervention of a European power in the productive process itself. The abolition of slavery seemed to entail such vast repercussions that colonial authorities hesitated for years and proceeded only when the power of the state had been consolidated: the legal status of slavery was abolished in 1897 in Zanzibar, seven years after the British had declared a protectorate, and it was not ended until 1907 in Kenya. Officials feared a rebellion of slaveowners less than the

3. This simplistic view of "traditional agriculture" is quite explicit in, for example, John C. H. Fei and Gustav Ranis, *Development of the Labor Surplus Economy: Theory and Policy* (Holmwood, Ill., 1964), p. 3; Theodore W. Schultz, *Transforming Traditional Agriculture* (New Haven, 1964), p. 4; Bruce F. Johnston and Peter Kilby, *Agriculture and Structural Transformation: Economic Strategies in Late-Developing Countries* (New York, 1975), pp. 26–27; and John M. Brewster, "Traditional Social Structures as Barriers to Change," in H. M. Southworth and B. F. Johnston, eds., *Agricultural Development and Economic Growth* (Ithaca, N.Y., 1967), pp. 66–98. The most valuable contribution of A. G. Hopkins has been to criticize tellingly such conceptions of precolonial Africa from within the neoclassical framework he shares with these authors. *An Economic History of West Africa* (London, 1973).

social and economic disruption that would follow the cutting of those
bonds of command which, they thought, were the sole foundation of
work discipline and social peace. The elimination of slave labor would
require more than changing slaves' legal status and paying them wages:
it required the reshaping of attitudes to work and mechanisms of social
control.

This book is an examination of the complex mechanisms of control
that the dichotomy of freedom and slavery has shrouded. It looks at
British ideas about slavery and wage labor not as a set of abstract principles, but as ways of articulating the social, economic, and moral bases of a
system of production, in opposition to other forms of labor organization
and agriculture and in the context of the extension of colonial rule and a
capitalist economy to Africa. It examines the means by which the colonial state buttressed, or failed to buttress, the domination of landowners,
while using the mechanisms of law and state power to redefine the basis
of the planters' control of labor. It stresses the contrasting ways in which
the plantation economy evolved in the two British colonies and the uneasy relationship of plantation labor to peasant production.

This is not the story of the imposition of an all-determining colonial
order—whether considered progressive or destructive—on hapless
people, but an examination of how both ex-slaves and ex-slaveowners
sought to redefine economic roles and relationships in their own ways.
For ex-slaves, the process of redefinition had two dimensions: refusal of
their ex-masters' demands for labor as colonial rule undercut the power
of the slaveowners, and rejection of the state's insistence that they were
people with no rights in land who must work—steadily—for wages. Ex-
slaves did not merely resist two conceptions of labor which they regarded
as oppressive. They used elements of each against the other: new kinds
of jobs created by the colonial economy enabled ex-slaves to escape the
plantation, while access to plantation land kept ex-slaves from becoming
too dependent on these jobs. This was not a dramatic struggle of rebellions and strikes, but a quiet and continuous one. Ex-slaves ignored demands for regular, year-round labor that the British expected of a working class; they would not leave plots of land to which they had had access
as slaves and which they regarded as their own; they moved onto other
land whenever they could; they put as much effort as possible into raising their own crops and as little as possible into their landlords'; they sold
produce that they did not consume but were careful to avoid too much
dependence for necessities on a marketing system they rightly felt was
rigged against them. They did not wish to be either slaves or proletarians.

These struggles took place in the fields, day after day, and the fundamental issues were the exact details of how people would work and how

they would obtain access to land. The different experiences of the Kenyan coast and Zanzibar (embracing, unless otherwise specified, the islands of Zanzibar and Pemba) reflect not simply variations in policy, but the relationship of the colonial state to the colonial economy. Both areas had viable plantation economies on the eve of the colonial takeover. In both cases, the continued supply of plantation labor involved intervention by the state: enforcement of owners' land titles, taxation, forced labor, assisted labor migration, vagrancy laws, and a variety of court-enforced tenancy systems. But similar laws were used in different ways.

To the Government of Zanzibar, the Arab aristocracy seemed to provide the only possibility for the continued production of a valuable crop and for the maintenance of order. On the mainland coast, the landowning aristocracy had already lost much of its ability to use land and control people by the time the state was ready to intervene directly in production, and in any case, grain and coconuts were not the stuff that imperialist dreams were made of: the price of these crops was too low relative to transport costs compared to a crop like cloves, and above all they were too fully integrated into local economies to profit sufficiently a regime that equated economic activity with exports. In Zanzibar, the state enforced the titles to land and trees held by Arab planters, and it directed labor and other resources to them. In the interior of Kenya, the state intervened even more vigorously to recruit and discipline labor for the white settlers it had enabled to obtain land. But on the coast of Kenya, the state only created the legal shell of a capitalist agricultural economy: it facilitated the commercialization of land, but in the absence of a corresponding effort to commercialize and control labor for the benefit of Arab and Swahili landowners, the concentration of land did not imply the control of production.

It required both state intervention in the control of labor and an export crop whose production and distribution could be readily supervised for the planters of Zanzibar to retain their economic and social dominance. Even there, efforts to create a disciplined plantation labor force were only partially successful. Ex-slaves did not become regular workers; they became squatters on plantation land and, most often, day or seasonal workers.

In both areas, ex-slaves and other Africans who migrated to plantation lands sought to combine agricultural work on their own with wage labor for others, hoping to obtain security and a cash income without losing control over the way they worked. In different ways, the disjunction between control of land and control of labor in Zanzibar and coastal Kenya helped produce rigid economic structures that neither provided workers and tenants with security or a chance to expand the productivity of the domestic unit nor gave landowners opportunities to accumulate capital or adopt new techniques and new crops. The British had not sought to create a more equitable economy through the abolition of slavery, but to fashion a more rational, controllable economy. Instead—largely owing to the efforts of ex-slaves themselves—the domination of an old elite was eroded; but officials, landowners, and ex-slaves alike became bound up in structures that made economic change both difficult and potentially dangerous.

Ex-slaves had to come to grips with the restrictive meaning of emancipation. Planters and governments could no more afford to ignore the precise meaning of free labor. But British abolitionists could, and largely did, avoid the question. Free labor for them did not imply an economic or social system. It meant the absence of personal and societal constraints on the labor market. By consigning slavery to the barbarous past, abolitionists emphasized the moral virtue of wage labor, however iniquitous the undermining of older economic values appeared to the workers of the Industrial Revolution.[4] Free labor was a marvelously vague notion, saving abolitionists from probing too far into what the ruling classes in both plantation and industrializing economies knew quite well: that the control of labor indeed required a system, embracing many aspects of society and depending on complex mechanisms of control from above.

Many scholars are still avoiding the same questions the abolitionists left vague. One frequently finds the same tendency to mistake particular structures for universal laws of behavior, to confuse "the economy" or "the society" with the interests of particular classes, and to portray the actions of specific classes taken within specific structures as part of a self-propelled movement toward development or modernity. These confusions are widespread and reflect the important role that scholars, like humanitarians several generations earlier, play in articulating the ideological and normative dimensions of the economic order in which they live.[5]

4. David Brion Davis, *The Problem of Slavery in the Age of Revolution, 1770–1823* (Ithaca, N.Y., 1975); Howard Temperley, "Capitalism, Slavery and Ideology," *Past and Present* 75 (1975), esp. p. 118. These questions are discussed further in chapter 2.

5. The common basis of antislavery ideology and neoclassical economics is clearest in the work of Adam Smith, and Davis (pp. 347–56) has perceptively analyzed his importance as a theorist and ideologue in debates over systems of labor. A growing number of critiques have pointed to the ideological functions of various branches of development studies and to their inability to analyze the importance of different kinds of economic, social, and political structures or to take account of the exercise of power. For the most germane example, see E. Wayne Nafziger, "A Critique of Development Economics in the U.S.," *Journal of Development Studies* 13 (1976): 18–34.

Similar biases emerge in studies of many aspects of labor and agriculture. Those of historians can be seen most clearly in the area which they have most fully covered, the southern United States. Although there are older traditions of Reconstruction history as well as valuable sociological studies of the rural South, the extraordinary burst of scholarship on slavery in the last two decades was accompanied by an equally striking hiatus—which is only just ending—in studies of labor following slavery. Scholars have found slavery pregnant with meaning for our times, yet they have had to abstract its legacy from all that fell in between. It is curious how fascinated scholars have been with a form of labor safely consigned to the past and how wary they have been of analyzing evolving forms of labor that fall under the rubric "free." Many studies that have been done are also curious: scholars of slavery—including conservatives, liberals, and radicals—have been willing to see slavery as a labor system, which in turn fostered certain kinds of social relations and ideologies, yet scholars of the post–Civil War United States generally focus on politics and race and treat the subordination of black labor as but one of many aspects of discrimination.[6] A leading textbook in Afro-American history reveals this difference in perspective in its title: *From Slavery to Freedom.* A specific labor system, historically defined, becomes a general and unrealized condition.[7]

These patterns are changing. A recent spurt of quantitative studies of the postwar South have focused on the relationship of economic growth to forms of labor and tenancy. Nevertheless, the econometricians, like abolitionists, have failed to analyze the organization of labor as the exercise of power or as a system of class control. They measure, in effect, aggregates of decisions made by individuals in markets. The structures

6. Historians have been insufficiently appreciative of the important field studies of labor and tenancy done in the South during the 1930s and, to a large extent, have dropped the questions of class analysis that were raised implicitly or explicitly in earlier works by W.E.B. DuBois and C. Vann Woodward. An equally critical assessment of studies of labor after slavery has been made by Harold Woodman, "Sequel to Slavery: The New History Views the Postbellum South," *Journal of Southern History* 43 (1977): 523–24. See also Charles S. Johnson, *Shadow of the Plantation* (Chicago, 1934); Arthur F. Raper, *Preface to Peasantry* (Chapel Hill, N.C., 1936); Hortense Powdermaker, *After Freedom* (New York, 1939); W.E.B. DuBois, *Black Reconstruction in America 1860–1880* (New York, 1935); C. Vann Woodward, *Origins of the New South, 1877–1913* (Baton Rouge, La., 1951). Among the best studies of particular states, although they fall short of a full analysis of the control of labor and economic power, are Joel Williamson, *After Slavery: The Negro in South Carolina During Reconstruction, 1861–1877* (Chapel Hill, N.C., 1965), and Peter Kolchin, *First Freedom: The Responses of Alabama's Blacks to Emancipation and Reconstruction* (Westport, Conn., 1972).

7. John Hope Franklin, *From Slavery to Freedom: A History of Negro Americans*, 5th ed. (New York, 1978). Another textbook transforms a socioeconomic unit into a residential one. August Meier and Elliot Rudwick, *From Plantation to Ghetto*, 3d ed. (New York, 1976).

that shaped the markets and the parameters of the decisions can only be treated as givens or invoked as exogenous factors to explain why optimizing behavior produced obviously nonoptimal results. Economic weaknesses turn out to be the products of flawed "institutions" and above all of the racism left over from the antebellum era: the problems of freedom lay in slavery.[8]

A further step, however, is being taken by scholars like Jonathan Wiener, who has looked at the planters of Alabama's black belt as a class seeking to reshape its control over a dependent labor force and defend its role in production against both the challenges of merchants and the efforts of freedmen to shape the way they would work. Violence, intimidation, and racial discrimination—as well as the use of state power—cannot be set off as "non-economic variables"; they were an intrinstic part of maintaining economic power.[9] In the South, the planter class of the late nineteenth century was relatively successful. Where planters' power was eroded and plantation laborers gained greater control over their labor conditions—as on the coast of East Africa—similar questions must still be asked.

8. Some quantitative historians have made the postwar South into a rational market economy performing as well as its resources allowed and not hampered greatly by racism, sharecropping, or the other familiar ills of the regions (Robert Higgs, *Competition and Coercion: Blacks in the American Economy, 1865–1914*, New York, 1977, and Stephen J. DeCanio, *Agriculture in the Postbellum South: The Economics of Production and Supply*, Cambridge, Mass., 1974). Roger Ransom and Richard Sutch have written a more critical and persuasive account; yet behind their work—as in that of Higgs and DeCanio—lies a pristine model of how an economy should grow through the optimal allocation of resources via competition, and the South's failure to do so is explained by monopoly and the legacy of slavery (*One Kind of Freedom: The Economic Consequences of Emancipation*, Cambridge, 1977). For more on this subject, see the special issues of *Explorations in Economic History*, vol. 16, no. 1 (1979) and of *Agricultural History*, vol. 53, no. 1 (1979), as well as Gavin Wright, *The Political Economy of the Cotton South: Households, Markets, and Wealth in the Nineteenth Century* (New York, 1978). For a penetrating, if occasionally oversimplified, critique of the theoretical and methodological limitations of this body of scholarship, see Woodman, pp. 527–43.

9. Jonathan M. Wiener, "Class Structure and Economic Development in the American South, 1865–1955," *American Historical Review* 84 (1979): 970–92, plus comments by Robert Higgs and Harold Woodman in ibid., pp. 993–1006. For a more detailed case study, see Jonathan M. Wiener, *Social Origins of the New South: Alabama, 1860–1885* (Baton Rouge, La., 1978). A related approach is pursued by Jay R. Mandle, *The Roots of Black Poverty: The Southern Plantation Economy after the Civil War* (Durham, N.C., 1978), and Dwight B. Billings, Jr., *Planters and the Making of a "New South": Class, Politics, and Development in North Carolina, 1865–1900* (Chapel Hill, N.C., 1979). The thinking of the planter class, faced with the need to modify how it controlled labor without losing its power, is thoughtfully analyzed by James L. Roark, *Masters without Slaves: Southern Planters in the Civil War and Reconstruction* (New York, 1977). The importance of the conflict over how labor would work in the first years after the war is emphasized by Ransom and Sutch, Wiener, Roark, Williamson, and Kolchin. This period is also emphasized in Leon Litwack, *Been in the Storm So Long: The Aftermath of Slavery* (New York, 1979).

Students of Latin America and the Caribbean have gone beyond views of the transformation of labor systems that stress either progress toward freedom or the steady and universal degradation of labor in the face of the advancement of world markets. Given that the era of formal emancipation generally coincided with or has been followed by a period of growing incentives for landowners to increase production, scholars have emphasized the variety of ways in which landowners and governments have sought to obtain and discipline labor, and the variety of ways in which workers and peasants resisted onerous conditions or took advantage of the high demand for labor. So many people in Latin America and the Caribbean have been driven into appalling poverty during the last century, that it is too easy to look at this process as inevitable, avoiding the question of how it happened, and the virtue of much of the recent literature has been its focus on the process of struggle itself.[10]

The question of how workers work is just one of many neglected aspects of the study of Africa. Yet Africanists have delved into certain aspects of labor in considerable detail. They have, however, largely skirted the most central issues. A recent textbook discussed the changes in labor at the advent of the colonial era under the heading, "From Slavery to Migratory Labor."[11] Why should migration be taken as the defining characteristic of labor at this time? Migration to seek wage labor implied an individual act, and most studies have treated it as a response to various "push" and "pull" factors impinging on the individual. At its worst, the migratory focus extends from geography to metahistory: as a movement from tradition to modernity. The movement of labor from an

10. Arnold Bauer emphasizes the contrast between ways of working in capitalist and precapitalist economies and the challenge this posed landowners and governments—a challenge that they did not always meet. (See "Rural Workers in Spanish America: Problems of Peonage and Oppression," *Hispanic American Historical Review* 59 [1979]: 34–63, and the wide range of studies which he reviews.) Similarly, Kenneth Duncan and Ian Rutledge argue that the impact of the growing market must be analyzed in terms of the particular modes of production that preceded it and that distinct patterns of capitalist development must be studied. The papers in the collection they edited provide fine examples of some of these patterns (*Land and Labour in Latin America: Essays in the Development of Agrarian Capitalism in the Nineteenth and Twentieth Centuries*, Cambridge, 1977). Also noteworthy are the stress on how rural people both resisted and used capitalist penetration in Juan Martinez-Alier, *Haciendas, Plantations and Collective Farms* (London, 1977) and the comparison of different directions that changes took in various parts of Mexico, in Friedrich Katz, "Labor Conditions on Haciendas in Porfirian Mexico: Some Trends and Tendencies," *Hispanic American Historical Review* 54 (1974): 1–47.

11. Philip D. Curtin, Steven Feierman, Leonard Thompson, and Jan Vansina, *African History* (Boston, 1978), pp. 555–57. There are numerous studies of labor migration, many of "traditional agriculture," a growing number of agricultural change, but few that focus specifically on agricultural labor. An exception is W. A. Warmington, E. Ardener, and S. Ardener, *Plantation and Village in the Cameroons* (London, 1960).

"overwhelmingly stagnant subsistence agricultural sector" to a "growing commercialized industrial center" becomes a teleological phenomenon, a step toward the modern world.[12] But who defined the form that progress would take?

The effects of the abolition of slavery on different parts of Africa have scarcely been studied.[13] Some scholars, however, have already defined the problem out of existence. A leading economic historian, A. G. Hopkins, insists that the transition from slave labor in West Africa was accomplished with "relative ease." What appears to Hopkins as the smooth adjustment of domestic units of production might instead reflect the collapse of very different ways of organizing production. Hopkins's stress on the market has led him to fail to analyze the specific structures that precolonial agriculture, in cases where slaveowners were able to amass

12. Fei and Ranis, p. 3. The classic statement of the surplus labor argument is in fact a more subtle and insightful piece than subsequent work along these lines (W. A. Lewis, "Economic Development with Unlimited Supplies of Labour," *The Manchester School* 22 [1954]: 139–91, and "Unlimited Labour: Further Notes," ibid. 26 [1958]: 1–32). Some scholars have modified Lewis without making any fundamental break with his paradigm (Michael P. Todaro, *Internal Migration in Developing Countries*, Geneva, 1976). More searching questions have been raised by Giovanni Arrighi, "Labor Supplies in Historical Perspective: A Study of the Proletarianization of the African Peasantry in Rhodesia," in Giovanni Arrighi and John Saul, eds., *Essays on the Political Economy of Africa* (New York, 1973), pp. 180–236, and Charles van Onselen, "Black Workers in Central African Industry: A Critical Essay on Historiography and Sociology of Rhodesia," *Journal of Southern African Studies* 1 (1975): 228–46.

13. The most useful studies are: William Derman, *Serfs, Peasants, and Socialists: A Former Serf Village in the Republic of Guinea* (Berkeley, 1973); Timothy C. Weiskel, "Labor in the Emergent Periphery: From Slavery to Migrant Labor among the Baule Peoples, 1880– 1925," in Walter L. Goldfrank, ed., *The World-System of Capitalism: Past and Present* (Beverly Hills, Calif., 1979), pp. 207–33; Denise Bouche, *Les Villages de liberté en Afrique noire française 1887–1910* (Paris 1968); Richard Roberts and Martin Klein, "The Banamba Slave Exodus of 1905 and the Decline of Slavery in the Western Sudan," *JAH*, forthcoming; and Martin Klein, "From Slave labor to Migrant Labor in Senegambia: Southern Saalum 1880–1930," paper presented to the African Studies Association Meeting, Boston, 1976. Abolition in a case where many slaveowners were Portuguese is discussed in W. G. Clarence-Smith, *Slaves, Peasants and Capitalists in Southern Angola 1840–1926* (Cambridge, 1979). Abolition is only touched on in Claude Meillassoux, ed., *L'Esclavage en Afrique pre-coloniale* (Paris, 1975), and Suzanne Miers and Igor Kopytoff, eds., *Slavery in Africa: Anthropological and Historical Perspectives* (Madison, Wis., 1977). Most work, however, has shed more light on colonial policies toward slavery than on anything that actually happened in Africa. François Renault, *L'Abolition de l'esclavage au Sénégal: l'attitude de l'administration française, 1848–1915* (Paris, 1972); François Renault, *Liberation d'esclaves et nouvelle servitude: les rachats de captifs africains pour le compte des colonies françaises après l'abolition de l'esclavage* (Abidjan, Ivory Coast, 1976); Jean Martin, "L'Affranchissement des esclaves de Mayotte, décembre 1846– juillet 1847," *Cahiers d'Etudes Africaines* 16 (1976): 207–33; Suzanne Miers, *Britain and the Ending of the Slave Trade* (London, 1975); and John Grace, *Domestic Slavery in West Africa* (London, 1975).

and control large bodies of slaves, entailed, and similarly to underplay the mechanisms that the colonial state and European firms erected to shape the ways domestic producers could and could not act.[14]

As with the study of labor, so with agricultural development. The most influential approaches—in international agencies as well as universities—center on how "individual productive units" move from "meager self-sufficiency" to "prosperous interdependence as producers . . . integrated into a national network of markets, information flows, and social institutions."[15] In some abstract sense, differentiation, specialization, and integration may be good for agricultural productivity, but such concepts tell the economic historian little. Through whose efforts, for whose benefit, and at whose expense did economies become differentiated, and why did differentiation take certain forms and not others?[16] The policy recommendations of scholars who have failed to ask such questions assume an air of unreality as politicians and entrepreneurs are asked to make decisions for "the society" without any cognizance being taken of the class interests that the decision-makers might have.[17]

14. Hopkins, p. 227. Miers and Kopytoff, whose approach is as narrowly kinship-based as that of Hopkins is market-centered, adopt an equally flat conclusion ("Introduction" to *Slavery in Africa*). Part of the problem is a failure to analyze slavery in African societies in terms of particular structures. See my "The Problem of Slavery in African Studies," *JAH* 20 (1979): 103–25. Most studies of abolition in French West Africa (see n. 13 above) stress the drastic consequences of slaveowners' loss of control over labor.

15. Johnston and Kilby, pp. 3, 34. The individualistic model is also clear in Fei and Ranis, p. 152, and Gerald K. Helleiner, "Smallholder Decision Making: Tropical African Evidence," in Lloyd G. Reynolds, ed., *Agricultural Development Theory* (New Haven, 1975), pp. 34–35, 50–51. The emphasis on making the individual specialize is at the heart of the assessment of economic progress in the 1960s done for the World Bank. The resistance of smallholders to such specialization is seen as irrational and primitive—largely a result of the unfortunate influence of women. That smallholders might have very good reasons to avoid specialization is considered below. See John C. de Wilde, *Experiences with Agricultural Development in Tropical Africa. Vol. I: The Synthesis* (Baltimore, 1967), esp pp. 53–55.

16. Some writers see agricultural development as a matter of improving technology and investment patterns. This argument has the great virtue of appearing to be value-free, but it is nothing of the sort. The most important technological improvement of recent decades, the "green revolution" in high-yielding seeds, has had a modest impact on improving productivity and a much greater impact on social structure. Capital intensive techniques have increased the wealth and power of large landowners while undermining smallholders and tenants and throwing agricultural laborers out of work. Keith Griffin, *The Political Economy of Agrarian Change: An Essay on the Green Revolution* (London, 1974), and T. J. Byres, "The Dialectic of India's Green Revolution," *South Asian Review* 5 (1972): 99–116.

17. Two leading development economists carry this naïveté to absurdity by presenting a list of prerequisites for balanced growth and then writing, "This list of requirements holds true irrespective of the choice of social system exercised by the under-developed economy." How does an economy choose a social system? (Fei and Ranis, p. 152).

This book will focus on specific classes and particular structures. It is about what happened to plantations; and the plantation is a specific kind of economic structure, a large, specialized unit producing for export markets and using low-skilled labor under central supervision and discipline.[18] Many economists now agree that large units offer few "economic" advantages over small ones, except for the cultivation of crops such as sugar and tea. Yet, historically, a large proportion of all plantations—including those of the East African coast—grew other crops. The genesis of such plantations and the strong efforts of the British to preserve them cannot be explained as natural responses to trends in world markets or the competition between efficient and less efficient producers, but must be understood in terms of the interests and power of particular groups—planters, merchants, and the colonial state.[19] The recruitment of plantation labor—in East Africa as in the Americas—can be only partly understood in terms of the flow of underemployed labor from subsistence economies to a more dynamic commercial sector, but can be analyzed more fully by examining the ways in which alternatives for laborers were narrowed and defined and access to resources was controlled.[20]

Peasants, it would seem, are very different from plantation workers. They work on their own, on small farms, with simple tools and the labor of their families. Most of what they grow they consume, but a portion of it is sold in markets or appropriated by the holders of political and eco-

18. On the concept of the plantation and its implications, see Jay R. Mandle, "The Plantation Economy: An Essay in Definition," in Eugene D. Genovese, ed., *The Slave Economies* (New York, 1973), 1: 214–28; P. P. Courtenay, *Plantation Agriculture* (London, 1965), p. 7; Pan American Union, *Plantation Systems of the New World* (Washington, 1959); Denis M. Benn, "The Theory of Plantation Economy and Society: A Methodological Critique," *Journal of Commonwealth and Comparative Politics* 12 (1974): 249–60; and George L. Beckford, *Persistent Poverty: Under-Development in Plantation Economies of the Third World* (New York, 1972). The opposite tendency to that criticized in these pages is found ·in Beckford, who overemphasizes the particularity of plantation agriculture to the exclusion of analyzing the broader mechanisms of economic domination of which the plantation is a part.

19. The lack of competitive advantage of plantations is stressed by W. A. Lewis, "The Export Stimulus," in Lewis, ed., *Tropical Development 1880–1913: Studies in Economic Progress* (London, 1970), p. 24.

20. Lewis has argued that government efforts to support plantation agriculture often depress surrounding areas. Yet his separation of the bad policies of governments from the generally good effects of export production is artificial. That governments frequently thwarted "development" does not mean that their performance "ranged from terrible to mediocre," only that the interests state policy was intended to promote must be examined carefully and that models which treat trade as an autonomous agent, neatly distinguishable from the interests of planters and the state, are misleading. Ibid., pp. 24, 38; and "Economic Development with Unlimited Supplies of Labour," p. 149.

nomic power.[21] Plantation and peasant agriculture have engendered great differences in kinship and community organization and in ethos and values. Some scholars, however, have pushed such distinctions too far, so that once a peasant is identified as such, his political ideas, his fears, and his ambitions are conclusively determined.[22] To some, the peasant is the hero of the marketplace, responding to incentives to grow new crops; to others, he is a drag on economic progress, too afraid of risks and change to transcend subsistence cultivation and simple techniques. Still others have debated whether the peasant is a revolutionary or a reactionary. All such monolithic views of the peasantry fail to appreciate the implications of the peasant's partial incorporation into markets and partial subordination to landlords, merchants, and the state, a form of subordination which extended to the appropriation of the surplus but not the manner in which labor was performed. Peasants did respond to market incentives, but their ability to provide for themselves meant that they—more so than plantation owners or capitalist farmers—could also *not* respond. Whether the peasant household embraced or resisted the world market and whether it was helped or hurt by the expansion of cash crop production depended very much on exactly how the penetration of commercial capital took place. There is no peasantry; there are peasantries.[23] And the politics of peasantries depends on their relations with other classes. In fact, a single peasant family could include people who at various times—each year or in the course of a lifetime—worked for wages in cities or on plantations. That peasantries can be differentiated and overlap proletariats presents no a priori reason for either quiescence or militancy, but it does mean that any analysis of class formation and class action will have to transcend static

21. This definition is based on Theodor Shanin, "Peasantry as a Political Factor," in Shanin, ed., *Peasants and Peasant Societies* (Harmondsworth, Eng., 1971), p. 240. See also John S. Saul and Roger Woods, "African Peasantries," in ibid., pp. 103–14, and Eric Wolf, *Peasants* (Englewood Cliffs, N.J., 1966).

22. Among the best treatments of the relationship of peasant and plantation production are: Mintz, "Slavery and the Rise of Peasantries," and *Caribbean Transformations;* Eric Wolf, "Specific Aspects of Plantation Systems in the New World: Community Sub-cultures and Social Classes," in Pan American Union, *Plantation Systems,* pp. 136–46; and Martinez-Alier. An overly specific view of what peasants are, detracts somewhat from two stimulating books: James C. Scott, *The Moral Economy of the Peasant: Rebellion and Subsistence in Southeast Asia* (New Haven, 1976), and Joel S. Migdal, *Peasants, Politics, and Revolution: Pressures toward Political and Social Change in the Third World* (Princeton, 1974).

23. Judith Ennew, Paul Hirst, and Keith Tribe argue that there is no peasant mode of production, and it is the range of responses to capitalist penetration by noncapitalist producers that defines a useful field of inquiry. "'Peasantry' as an Economic Category," *Journal of Peasant Studies* 4 (1977): 295–322. See also Henry Bernstein, "African Peasantries: A Theoretical Framework," ibid. 6 (1979): 421–43.

and homogeneous categories and explore a single, complex, and changing social field.[24]

The peasant producers of the East African coast were either ex-slaves
whose former owners could no longer make them work or people living
just outside the plantation region whose access to good land and markets
was made easier by the declining power of the planters. In either case,
cultivators had to come to grips with the fact that the ex-slaveowners still
dominated the ownership of land. Ex-slaves and the migrants to the
plantation region were becoming squatters—cultivators whose status was
an extralegal arrangement between landlord and tenant, with continu-
ally renegotiable rent and requirements, and with security dependent
mainly on the relationship of the two parties.

A lively debate is going on among economists about the economic rationality and impact on productivity of various forms of tenancy. Some
argue that tenancy is an "understandable market response" and that it
insures "the socially efficient employment of resources" by distributing
the risks of production and innovation between landlords and tenants.[25]
To see tenancy as a contract between equal individuals for mutual benefit
is to accept the mystifying nature of contract law at face value; and to
explain that tenancy, in the abstract, can distribute risks is not to explain
its origins. In fact, tenancy is a relationship between two classes. There
are many ways of sharing risks, and the role of the landowner was not
shaped so much by its intrinsic necessity as by the landowner's efforts to
make his role in production indispensable. Nor is there any way to show
that the landlord's rewards were commensurate with his contribution to
production except to define them as such. What a landlord received in
shares or rents had far more to do with his power to exclude people
from access to the means of production, a power that depended on the
actions of the state, the legitimacy of the law, and the press of popula-

24. The dangers of simplistic views of peasants are evident in a reference to "the apathet-
ic and quiescent state that normally characterizes their outlook on life" (George M. Foster,
"Introduction: What is a Peasant?" in Jack M. Potter, May N. Diaz, and George M. Foster,
eds., *Peasant Society: A Reader,* Boston, 1967, p. 8). A much more thoughtful view of the
political relationships of peasants and workers can be found in the work of Sidney Mintz,
especially "The Rural Proletariat and the Problem of the Rural Proletarian Consciousness,"
Journal of Peasant Studies 1 (1974): 291–325.

25. Joseph D. Reid, Jr., "Sharecropping and Agricultural Uncertainty," *Economic Development and Cultural Change* 24 (1976): 549–76, p. 571 quoted; idem, "Sharecropping as
an Understandable Market Response: The Post-Bellum South," *Journal of Economic History*
33 (1973): 106–30; Steven Cheung, *The Theory of Share Tenancy* (Chicago, 1969); and
D.M.G. Newbery, "Tenurial Obstacles to Innovation," *Journal of Development Studies* 11
(1975): 263–77. A better picture of sharecropping emerges from the autobiography of a
black cropper put together by Theodore Rosengarten, *All God's Dangers: The Life of Nate
Shaw* (New York, 1975).

tion.[26] In the southern United States, sharecropping arose from a struggle between landowners who wished to reconstitute plantation agriculture by using gangs of wage laborers and freedmen who wished to farm on their own, a struggle in which the planters employed all the methods of class domination and still did not obtain the degree of control they had sought. The coast of Kenya is a revealing instance of the consequences of the inability of a planter class to exclude.

The approaches to economic history and development economics which I have been criticizing are by no means lacking in complexity, variation, or self-criticism. But they have in common an artificial dichotomization of units of analysis into "the individual" and "the economy" and a vain and misleading tendency to make the operations of particular kinds of economic structures into the operations of universal and scientific laws.

More curious is the fact that some of the self-consciously radical alternatives being propounded by other scholars have quite similar limitations. One school of thought, most recently advanced by Immanuel Wallerstein, sees the colonial economy of Africa as a new stage in a longer process of subordinating the "periphery" to the European core of the capitalist world economy. Such a dimension is obviously indispensable to any analysis, but "dependency theory" approaches neoclassical economics in analyzing changes within Africa as direct reflections of changes in the world market. The processes by which exports were produced, however, remain in black boxes, and the complex ways that labor and surplus were extracted by colonial states and capital are seen to be mechanical derivatives of the structure of commerce. Most important, all the struggles over control of the means of production and the conflict over how people would work seem like nothing more than gasps in the face of the inevitable course of the world economy.[27]

Neither those who see development as a self-propelled process, nor

---

26. For a related argument about the rewards and functions of the capitalist farmer in general, see Robert Brenner, "The Origins of Capitalist Development: A Critique of Neo-Smithian Marxism," *New Left Review* 104 (1977): 59.

27. Wallerstein, "Three Stages of African Involvement," pp. 30–57. Influential books in this school include André Gunder Frank, *Capitalism and Underdevelopment in Latin America* (New York, 1969), and Walter Rodney, *How Europe Underdeveloped Africa* (Dar es Salaam, 1972), while Samir Amin puts a similar argument into more Marxist vocabulary (*Unequal Development: An Essay on the Social Formations of Peripheral Capitalism*, trans. Brian Pearce, New York, 1976). For critiques, see Brenner, pp. 25–92; Theda Skocpol, "Wallerstein's World Capitalist System: A Theoretical and Historical Critique," *American Journal of Sociology* 82 (1977): 1075–90; and Sidney W. Mintz, "The So-Called World System: Local Initiative and Local Response," *Dialectical Anthropology* 2 (1977): 253–70.

those who see "underdevelopment" in the same terms have entered what Marx called the "hidden abode of production."[28] The expansion of world markets, the penetration of capital, and the dominance of colonial states have sometimes undermined, sometimes intensified, slavery and other precapitalist modes of production, although these systems have rarely been left unchanged.[29] Some scholars see the distinctiveness of any form of labor organization as a direct consequence of the particular place it occupies in the world economy. Others have taken the important step of focusing on the "articulation" of expanding capitalism with the modes of production it encountered.[30] To make use of such a framework, one must avoid assuming that the form of articulation was entirely determined by the interest of capital in preserving precapitalist structures merely to enhance its own profits and examine as well the actions of landlords and peasants, slaveowners and slaves. In order to understand the directions and blockages of economic development, it is necessary to study both the class structures of precapitalist societies and the precise manner in which the extension of capitalism and colonial rule reshaped those structures.[31] Perhaps the continuing laments of development economists today—like those of colonial officials in the past—about the troublesome backwardness and intractability of Africans suggest that the system of capitalist exploitation has not been laid out as

28. Karl Marx, *Capital*, trans. Samuel Moore and Edward Aveling (New York, 1967), 1: 176.

29. The relationship of capitalism, slavery, and changing class structures in slave societies has been explored in the brilliant and controversial comparative study by Eugene D. Genovese, *The World the Slaveholders Made* (New York, 1969). See also Duncan and Rutledge, *Land and Labour in Latin America*.

30. Important contributions to this discussion include Ernesto LeClau, "Feudalism and Capitalism in Latin America," *New Left Review* 67 (1971): 19–38; Aidan Foster-Carter, "The Modes of Production Controversy," ibid. 107 (1978): 47–73; Brenner, pp. 25–92; Jairus Banaji, "Modes of Production in a Materialist Conception of History," *Capital and Class* 3 (1977): 1–44; Pierre-Phillipe Rey, *Les Alliances de classes* (Paris, 1973); and Claude Meillassoux, *Femmes, greniers et capitaux* (Paris, 1975). An important part of the analysis of articulation is the argument, emphasized for example by Meillassoux, that the continuing existence of precapitalist agriculture enables capitalists in Africa to pay sub-subsistence wages, so that the incomplete incorporation of Africans into the labor force seems like a stroke of genius. That is not how it appeared to officials at the time, a point that will be considered below.

31. Colin Leys makes the important point that what needs to be explained is not the tendencies of "capitalism in general," nor is it the drain of surplus from throughout the periphery to the core of a world economy; rather, it is the nature and limitations of the evolving class structures and modes of capital accumulation that develop in particular historical circumstances in the context of expanding and changing capitalism. "Capital Accumulation, Class Formation and Dependency—The Significance of the Kenyan Case," in Ralph Miliband and John Saville, eds., *The Socialist Register 1978* (London, 1978), esp. p. 263. See also the important discussion of these issues by Brenner.

neatly as it might seem, that the periphery has not been playing its proper role.

At the heart of the matter are the fundamentally different ways in which labor can be controlled and surplus extracted, and consequently, the complex and varied impact that the penetration of Africa by European governments and capital has had. While the debate on the theoretical approaches to these problems remains lively, local studies are becoming richer. Much research on South Africa, for example, has emphasized that the interrelated development of gold mines and large-scale farms, run as capitalist enterprises by white landowners, created an acute demand for a regular, disciplined labor force around the turn of the century. The demand for labor frequently brought capital into conflict with African peasants, who had taken advantage of earlier demands for produce. Between the African farmer on his own land, the farmer who obtained rights to cultivate white-owned land in exchange for limited labor, the landless farm worker, and the mine worker lay enormous gulfs in the nature of daily labor—in work rhythms and forms of discipline—and in the alternatives facing individuals and families over a lifetime. How Africans would work depended not simply on who owned land, but on how that land was used and controlled, on the way roads and railroads favored certain areas over others, on manipulations of produce marketing, on restrictions on labor mobility, and on the use of state power to obtain and discipline workers.[32] These were questions of class control, requiring action by individuals, firms, white farmers' organization, and the state, and complicated by the divergence of class interests among mine owners, capitalist farmers, and those farmers who preferred squatters to laborers, as well as from the bureaucratic interests of the state.[33]

32. Arrighi, "Labor Supplies"; Colin Bundy, *The Rise and Fall of the South African Peasantry* (Berkeley, 1979); M. L. Morris, "The Development of Capitalism in South African Agriculture: Class Struggle in the Countryside," *Economy and Society* 5 (1976): 292–343; Ian Phimister, "Peasant Production and Underdevelopment in Southern Rhodesia," *African Affairs* 73 (1974): 217–28; Robin Palmer and Neil Parsons, eds., *The Roots of Rural Poverty in Central and Southern Africa* (London, 1977); Charles van Onselen, *Chibaro: African Mine Labour in Southern Rhodesia, 1900–1933* (London, 1976); Charles Perrings, *Black Mineworkers in Central Africa* (London, 1979). The transformation of agrarian relations of production in South Africa during the same period covered by this book is being studied by several scholars under the direction of Stanley Trapido at Oxford University, and several valuable articles have also recently appeared in the *Journal of Southern African Studies*, esp. vol. 5, no. 1 (1978).

33. The combination of metropolitan and local interests added up differently in various parts of Africa and at various times, producing divergences in the extent to which peasants were encouraged or undermined, whether short or long periods of wage labor were encouraged, and so on. For an insightful look at these questions in relation to Kenya, see John Lonsdale and Bruce Berman, "Coping with the Contradictions: The Development of the Colonial State in Kenya, 1895–1914," *JAH* 20 (1979): 487–506.

The great virtue of much of the recent literature on southern Africa has been the historical specificity with which such problems have been studied. The most important question that remains is what the iniquitous methods of labor control actually did to social organization, culture, and values among African workers. It is not clear that southern African peasants as a whole—after their brief "rise" in response to demands for their produce—all "fell" in response to the demands for their labor, or that workers were driven into the state of abject subordination that the mine magnates had in mind for them.[34] Much of the story of the penetration of capitalism into Africa is a story of failure, of the inability of governments, settlers, and corporations to impose their conceptions of how labor and agriculture should be organized. If in parts of southern Africa, mining and agricultural capital did succeed in creating a severely exploited working class—leading to a society that was dynamic, productive, and brutal—the failure, or partial failure, of labor policy in Zanzibar and coastal Kenya resulted in a society of workers and peasants who were neither proletarianized nor impoverished.

But the standoff between the landed and the landless on the coast of British East Africa leads to another set of questions: did the unevenness with which capitalist relations of production penetrated African societies actually hinder capitalist exploitation or merely redirect the forms it took? Did the partial autonomy that cultivators retained allow them to do more than resist the demands of the colonial economy, and could their economies keep pace with mounting stresses resulting from their partial incorporation into a competitive world containing more dynamic and more oppressive regions? Did the continuation of class conflict itself prevent either landowners or squatters from expanding production or introducing new crops and new techniques?

To see that there was more than one side to the struggles over work and production, to examine the different outcomes of these struggles, and to see the implications of such conflict for further economic and social change is to strip away some of the layers of mystification that

34. For a penetrating critique of the idea that peasantries in central and southern Africa all rose and fell, see Terence Ranger, "Growing from the Roots: Reflections on Peasant Research in Central and Southern Africa," *Journal of Southern African Studies* 5 (1978): 99–133. Van Onselen's excellent study of the control of labor in gold-mining compounds is overly deterministic in its analysis of the compound system's effects on workers. Such African organizations as the Jehovah's Witnesses and Beni dance groups, while overtly accommodationist, may have helped to maintain the autonomy of the workers' values and social ties, thus avoiding the kind of accommodation to dominant cultural and social values that much of the "respectable" English working class eventually made. Van Onselen, *Chibaro*, and Gareth Stedman Jones, "Working-Class Culture and Working-Class Politics in London, 1870–1900: Notes on the Remaking of a Working Class," *Journal of Social History* 7 (1973–74): 460–508.

surround many discussions of "development" and "modernization" as well as of "underdevelopment" and "proletarianization."

The roots of conflicting concepts of labor and the social order within the coast of East Africa lie in the development of plantation agriculture in the nineteenth century.[35] Slaves had long served Arabs in Oman and Swahili on the African coast in a great variety of ways. They had been regarded as inferiors in social and religious terms. In the nineteenth century, they became laborers as well.

By the 1840s, clove plantations were well established on Zanzibar, and the work routine of slaves became regimented and rigorous. Five days of labor under a slave-overseer came to be the norm for year-round cultivation. During the harvest, slaves worked every day.

But the very success of the Omani Arabs of Zanzibar in producing cloves on a plantation scale drove down the price of this once rare spice. Commercially minded Omanis had thus been enticed into rural enterprises only to find the incentives for further intensifying production diminished, while lowered margins created an increasing need to make the plantation into a self-sustaining socioeconomic unit. Although slavery had become an essential economic institution, its evolution toward a brutally exploitative one—as in the sugar islands of the West Indies—went only partway. The rural isolation of the plantation helped recast older notions of slaves' social dependence in a new mold. Slaves were among the followers of a wealthy Omani, now tied to his plantation, providing for their own and part of the owner's subsistence, caring for the clove trees. The seasonality of clove production reinforced this pattern, for the year-round presence of slaves made possible the mobilization of labor for the harvest.

A second cycle of rising clove prices that led to booming plantations and then to falling prices and stagnation followed a hurricane in 1872 that destroyed most of Zanzibar's trees. The consequent jump in prices encouraged the transfer of many slaves to Pemba, which had been spared, and financed the importation of a large number of new slaves, who laboriously planted new trees on both islands. But by then Zanzibar was subject to steadily increasing British pressure to restrict the slave trade. None of the antislave trade measures stopped slaves from reaching Pemba, but the added complications and risk raised the prices which planters had to pay for smuggled slaves. When the price of cloves fell in the 1880s, Omanis were caught with enormous debts to Indian moneylenders. Indians, as British subjects, were not themselves allowed

35. What follows is taken from my *Plantation Slavery on the East Coast of Africa* (New Haven, 1977).

to employ slaves and in any case preferred commerce to agriculture. Omanis retained their clove plantations—many of them enormous—but the economy had become locked in a structure that could endure but not prosper.

On the mainland, members of the local Swahili population and Arab immigrants from Oman and the Hadramaut began to grow grain on a plantation scale in the 1840s, and plantation agriculture was still going strong on the eve of colonial rule.[36] The epitome of the system was reached in the area around Malindi—recently an abandoned town—in the 1870s and 1880s. Several planters acquired riches within a generation, and the largest holdings contained over 1,000 acres worked by over two hundred slaves. Slaves worked in gangs under the supervision of slave-overseers in fields that could yield three or four crops of millet and sesame each year. Making slaves work long hours was the key to the plantation system of Malindi, for there were no technical economies of scale in grain production. In Mombasa, however, a relatively large Arab and Swahili population and the presence of other African agriculturalists behind the town limited the amount of land that could be brought under grain—despite the extension of Mombasa's agricultural hinterland—and reduced the incentives to develop such forms of regimented labor. Coconuts, requiring less labor and producing a higher return per acre, came to be the favored crop.

On Zanzibar and Pemba, plantation development was largely an Omani enterprise. The Swahili-speaking peoples of Zanzibar Island, the Wahadimu, were pushed by Omani expansion into parts of the island where clove trees would not grow. In Pemba, there was no such separation between clove land and non-clove land, and the local Swahili group, the Wapemba, remained interspersed among Omani plantations and even took to clove cultivation on a small scale. Omani's privileged access to clove land and clove trees was to prove a lasting advantage.

On the mainland, however, members of local Swahili groups in all parts of the coast became major planters, even as Arabs acquired land. Common economic interests, however, did not end the importance of maintaining the identity and strength of communal groups for security

36. The term *Swahili,* as used here, is not a term for an ethnic group but a label for a number of groups that regard themselves as distinct yet live on the coast and consider it their home, speak Swahili as a first language, and practice Islam. The Wahadimu of Zanzibar, the Washella of Lamu Island and Malindi, and the Twelve Tribes of Mombasa are all Swahili groups, identified with particular localities. Despite variations in dialects and customs, plus the solidarity of local groups, the intense communications of the coast have brought about widely shared cultural patterns. For overviews, see A. H. J. Prins, *The Swahili-Speaking Peoples of Zanzibar and the East African Coast* (London, 1961), and A. I. Salim, *The Swahili-Speaking Peoples of Kenya's Coast, 1895–1965* (Nairobi, 1973).

and to protect those very interests.[37] The plantation economy of the mainland coast proved less open to Africans from the nearby hinterland, above all to Mijikenda living in the area from southern Kenya to just behind Malindi. The various Mijikenda subgroups traded actively with coastal ports, supplying ivory, cattle, and grain, but the combination of Arab-Swahili military strength and the extent of cultivation kept Mijikenda from settling on the rich coastal land, except for individuals who converted to Islam and became clients of coastal people. Although Mijikenda settlements expanded greatly in the nineteenth century and a group of "new men" acquired followers and wealth, they were only able to move coastward when Arab and Swahili cultivation and power were undermined.[38]

The plantation system was built with a captive labor force, and labor discipline was based on a combination of coercion and social dependence. The whip and the stocks were important instruments of the slaveholder's authority within his plantation. But the forces of the state backed him up only partially. The Sultan used troops and jails to catch runaways and punish other slave offenders, but the effectiveness of such measures was limited away from the capital of Zanzibar. Nevertheless, slaves could only escape from dependent relationships with great difficulty: they received a small plot of land from their masters, and the islands offered few alternative means of support. On the mainland as well, an individual who did not belong to a social group whose power was recognized was in an anomalous and dangerous position.

For slaves, taken from distant lands and torn from their own kinship and ethnic groups, accepting the protection of the slaveowner was virtually the only alternative to the vulnerability of the isolated individual in coastal society. At the same time, the slaveowner had little choice but to fulfill his role as protector if dependence was to be maintained.

The central image of the slaveholders' ideology was the Islamic patriarch. He had brought a slave from the world of war outside the Islamic

37. Units of analysis as broad as "Omani" or "Swahili" reveal little of group boundaries or patterns of conflict and alliance. Omani and Swahili communal groups—Al-Busaidi, Al-Mazrui, and Washella, for example—were relatively close-knit, but alliances were fluid and frequently crossed lines of race or origin. The maverick potentate, who built up a following from kinsmen, clients, slaves, freed slaves, and other detached persons, was also an important social type on the coast. The Zanzibari state never eclipsed such communal divisions, even among Omanis, and its power rested on its ability to provide security for trade and to make Zanzibar Island the focus of commercial relationships among Europeans, Indians, Arabs, Swahili, and Africans from the interior.

38. Thomas Spear, *The Kaya Complex: A History of the Mijikenda Peoples of the Kenya Coast to 1900* (Nairobi, 1979).

community, made him a Muslim, and generously looked after him, possibly even freeing him—of his own volition—to enter the Muslim community. The ideology did not take direct cognizance of plantation agriculture—for example, by justifying slavery through the need for labor—but assimilated the plantation order into older forms of dependence, all couched in religious terms. As with any ideology, Islamic norms did not in themselves make slaveowners generous or lenient, but they did lead them to regard what they had to do anyway as the will of God.[39]

In actuality, the customary limits on labor and the customary rights slaves came to have reflected the danger of slave resistance more than the masters' benevolence. Although the islands offered few places of refuge, some slaves fled to remote corners of them, and others stole boats to take risky voyages to the mainland. The coast of Kenya, especially behind Malindi, offered more space, and frequent flight put a brake on what was becoming the most rigid form of labor exploitation in East Africa. Outside of the plantation communities were a number of Swahili and Arab potentates who were willing to take in other people's slaves and use them as soldiers or henchmen in their conflicts with Zanzibari authority. Indeed, planters in the towns were also willing to arm their slaves and occasionally relied on their support in conflicts with each other. Needing the support of the men they wished to control, slaveowners had to acknowledge the limitations of their own power.

In day-to-day relationships with their owners, slaves also tested the limits of their exploitation by working poorly, disobeying orders, and withholding the deference that the slaveholders' self-image required. Slaves also resisted the cultural hegemony of their masters. Their own conversion to Islam could become a challenge to their owners' notions of religious superiority. At the same time, slaves could assert the validity of the culture of their homelands and challenge the slaveowners' ideology head-on. Both forms of cultural resistance were to become more important once the material basis of the slaveowners' domination was undermined by colonial rule.

Slaves did not overthrow or even threaten the system, but they did influence their reciprocal relations with their masters. Slaveowners could use the promise of a degree of acceptance of slaves who learned coastal customs and the promise of mobility or manumission to encourage obedience. They could decide which slaves would be allowed a modest improvement in position, but they had little choice but to allow some to

---

39. Frederick Cooper, "Islam and the Slaveholders' Ideology on the East Coast of Africa," paper presented to the Conference on "Islamic Africa: Slavery and Related Institutions," Princeton University, 1977.

rise. Above all, they had to insure that slaves did not develop stronger ties among themselves than they had with their owners. The forms of association that developed among slaves—such as the traditions of dance that originated in their homelands—represented a weak spot in the slaveowners' domination. Manumission helped prevent the crystalization of a self-conscious slave class, but it required the continual importation of slaves. Maintaining productivity and order at the same time became increasingly expensive in the late 1880s.

British officials thought they had taken over political authority from an Arab planter class that recalled the planter classes of the West Indies, even if they were, in British eyes, racially inferior and economically backward. The reality was more complex. In Zanzibar, the major clove planters were Arabs; on the mainland they were not ethnically or racially homogeneous. Throughout the coast, there was an enormous gulf in economic role and status between slaves and slaveowners. But political relationships were often closer between nonequals than among equals. The domination of slaveowners as a class had little basis in institutions which they collectively controlled. The state could not support the plantation economy in the way it did in the southern United States or the Caribbean. The colonial state itself was to play a crucial role in deciding whether a planter class, capable of acting as such, would come into being and how the organization of plantation agriculture would be transformed.

2 British Ideology and African Slavery

> Why Great Britain abolished slavery in its new African dominions is not an easy question to answer. Some scholars have seen abolition as one more step in the triumph of humanitarian sentiments and pressure groups in the nineteenth century. Yet the men who pushed for emancipation evinced little concern that abolition should improve the material welfare of slaves or raise their social status. Others have seen antislavery as a smokescreen for imperial ambitions or as a device by which an Arab-Indian commercial system was undermined for the benefit of a new colonial economy. Yet the men who abolished slavery did not expect England to profit from such a move, and—far from destroying the Arab-Indian economy—they sought initially to live off it.[1] To explain why abolitionists and administrators saw changes in the organization of production or in social structure as obstacles to emancipation, rather than reasons for it, requires looking beyond the artificial dichotomy of idealist and materialist explanations to an understanding of which aspects of humanity were and were not objects of concern and what the context and uses of those ideals were. At the same time, it is necessary to examine the widening gap between images and reality, as ex-slaves pushed faster than officials to alter the nature of agricultural labor.

CAPITALISM AND ANTISLAVERY

Urging that slavery be abolished in the newly established Protectorate of Zanzibar, a British official in 1891 advised the Foreign Secretary, "The disappearance of the status of slavery should be carried through with as little alteration as possible in the existing relations between master and slave."[2] This, to say the least, was a conservative approach to abolition. Yet other officials, notably Arthur Hardinge, Consul and Administrator-General from 1895 to 1901, were even more cautious, although they too regarded abolition as ultimately necessary. Antislavery organizations in London, missionaries in East Africa, much of the British

1. Compare Reginald Coupland, *The Exploitation of East Africa, 1856–1890: The Slave Trade and the Scramble* (London, 1939), with Richard Wolff, *The Economics of Colonialism: Britain and Kenya 1870–1930* (New Haven, 1974), pp. 30–46, and R.M.A. van Zwanenberg, "Anti-Slavery, the Ideology of 19th Century Imperialism in East Africa," in B. A. Ogot, ed., *Hadith 5* (Nairobi, 1975), pp. 108–27.

2. C. S. Smith to Salisbury, 3 April 1891, FO 84/2147.

press, and a few ex-officials urged prompt action, insisting that slavery was a stain on the British flag, but that the social impact of its abolition would be minimal. The most radical looked to the creation of a wage-labor market, through which ex-slaves would continue to labor on their ex-masters' plantations. The more conservative preferred a gradual amelioration in the lot of slaves, who would remain in a dependent status on the planters' estates. Neither the abolitionists nor the ameliorationists considered the possibility that ex-slaves might develop into an independent peasantry.

This conservatism was by no means a concession of the ideals of anti-slavery to the expediency of imperialism. To understand the limitations of antislavery ideology it is necessary to appreciate its meaning and functions in Britain in the course of the nineteenth century. David Brion Davis has cut through a debate, which has bored students of abolitionism for over three decades, between those who see the British decision to abolish the slave trade in 1807 and slavery in the British West Indies in 1834 as a triumph of humanitarian ideals and those who see the decision as a reflection of the economic interests of a capitalist class that had ceased to find slavery profitable.[3] The central question, Davis argues, is not whether abolitionists were humanitarians or hypocrites, but the relationship of their evolving ideals to the evolving social and economic structure of England. That slavery came to be the focus of their moral outrage was part of the ideological consequences of the development of capitalism.

By defining slavery as both wrong and archaic, abolitionists helped to emphasize a point which conditions among factory workers and the English poor made far from obvious—that the forms of labor control of the new economic order were morally unobjectionable. In precapitalist England, the personal power of the lord over his dependents had been intrinsic to the maintenance of order. Later, abolitionists came to see the evil of slavery in the absolute power of the master over his slaves, a power that usurped the law of God, the law of the state, and the law of the market.

The campaign against the slave trade and later against slavery itself

---

3. An ideology, as Davis uses the term, is "an integrated system of beliefs, assumptions, and values, not necessarily true or false, which reflects the needs and interests of a group or class at a particular time in history" (*Problem of Slavery in the Age of Revolution*, p. 14). The war-horses of the idealist-materialist debate are: Reginald Coupland, *The British Anti-Slavery Movement* (London, 1933); William L. Mathieson, *British Slavery and Its Abolition, 1823–1838* (London, 1926); and Eric Williams, *Capitalism and Slavery* (Chapel Hill, N.C., 1944). For another valuable commentary on this debate, see Temperley, "Capitalism, Slavery, and Ideology," pp. 94–118, and for an overview, see Michael Craton, *Sinews of Empire: A Short History of British Slavery* (Garden City, N.Y., 1974).

could hardly have succeeded if it had threatened to be an economic disaster for Britain or a blow to a vital segment of its ruling class. Still, abolition was not a move made by British capitalists to increase profits, but part of an effort to articulate and promote social and moral values necessary to the changing economic order.[4] Without a strong and consistent argument for the universal superiority—both economic and moral—of wage labor, an increasingly self-conscious capitalist class would be left without any meaningful ideology whatsoever. Abolitionism was part of an increasingly influential reform movement—concerned as much with England as with its slave-ridden colonies—that aimed, in Davis's words, "to inculcate the lower classes with various moral and economic virtues, so that workers would *want* to do what the emerging economy required.... [S]laves could be converted into sober, self-disciplined workers."[5]

These reforms did more to workers than *for* them. This is not to deny the sincerity of the reformers' belief that they were helping the lower orders or the religious framework in which they conceived of their actions. But even the growth of religious movements—from Quakers to Methodists—cannot be separated from the economic changes of the era, and the objects of their reformist zeal were quite particular: the roots of poverty and social dislocation lay more in the hearts of the poor than in society.[6] The years of growing influence of antislavery ideology were the years of growing powerlessness of the "free-born Englishman," of determined assaults on popular culture, on the independence of artisans, on the paternalistic relations that had partially characterized the countryside, and on many economic rights that Englishmen had long regarded as their own. The growing period of abolitionism, the end of the eighteenth century, was a period of counterrevolution, and its time of triumph, the early 1830s, occurred shortly after a widespread and bru-

4. Despite all the refutations of Williams's economic argument that are still pouring out, he has at least shown that changes in the structure of capitalism must be part of any explanation of the reasons for abolition of the slave trade, although narrowly defined economic interests are not in themselves a sufficient explanation. The continued profitability of the sugar economy of the Caribbean at the time when the abolition of slavery was being considered is stressed by Seymour Drescher, *Econocide: British Slavery in the Era of Abolition* (Pittsburgh, Pa., 1977). See also Roger Anstey, *The Atlantic Slave Trade and British Abolition* (Atlantic Highlands, N.J., 1975).

5. Davis, p. 242, emphasis added. Here, Davis is specifically referring to Quaker abolitionists.

6. Thus Wilberforce founded organizations like the Society for the Suppression of Vice, which made the amusements of the poor its major target (E. P. Thompson, *The Making of the English Working Class*, New York, 1963, p. 402). For the relationship of religion to the moral foundations of capitalism, see the trenchant and controversial discussion of Methodism in Thompson, pp. 350–400, and of the Quakers, in Davis, pp. 213–54.

tally repressed rebellion of the increasingly impoverished rural population and coincided with the infamous Poor Law.[7] If Wilberforce became a savior to oppressed black men in distant lands, he was detested as an oppressor by many of his fellow Englishmen.[8] The attack on the personal tyranny of the slaveowner and the attack on paternalism and traditional rights were two sides of the same coin.

Many abolitionists looked to a day when uniform and impersonal standards and objective authority would maintain the social order and when workers would internalize the necessary virtues of industry, thrift, and temperance. Nevertheless, some of them—Wilberforce included—had qualms about the dominance of the market and of self-interest and worried about the decline of "the grand law of subordination." But their vision of the ideal master-servant relationship required that superior authority be legitimate and that authority transcend self-interest; the slaveowner could not be the final arbiter of his own exercise of power.[9]

Antislavery ideology separated slavery from its economic context. It did not question the ownership of landed property that had been built up with slave labor, the social dominance of the property owners, the poverty and powerlessness of the workers, or the discipline and subordination of plantation labor, but it did seek to transform the mode of labor organization through law and state authority and to adapt it slowly to the demands and principles of a capitalist economy. Decades later, the Zanzibar Government remained true to these goals when it sought to restructure the personal subordination of the slaves into economic depen-

7. In the year 1834, there were, as Davis puts it, "two emancipations": slaves in the West Indies were freed from their masters, and workers in England were freed from public welfare by the harsh Poor Law (Davis, p. 357). This is not to romanticize the often harsh conditions preceding the Industrial Revolution. There is a long debate on the effects of the Industrial Revolution on the standard of living of the working class. Evidence of overall material improvement before the 1840s is far from clear, but the most important point is not what the workers earned but *how;* and the long period of erosion of the partial self-sufficiency and independence of rural tenants and farmers and urban artisans has been well studied. For farm laborers, the decline of the standard of living with the rise of agricultural capitalism was catastrophic. See Thompson, pp. 314–49; Eric Hobsbawm, *Labouring Men* (London, 1964), pp. 64–125; and Eric Hobsbawm and George Rudé, *Captain Swing: A Social History of the Great English Agricultural Uprising of 1830* (New York, 1968).

8. Thompson, pp. 56–57, 402; Williams, p. 155.

9. Thompson, p. 402; Davis, pp. 383–84. This ambivalence was crucial to the continuity of the English ruling class, enabling the reciprocal rights and obligations of lord and men to be replaced by impersonal and uniform standards upheld by the state, yet tempering this process by the personal mercy, power, and majesty of the lord. The changing relationship of older traditions of authority and newer concepts of the rule of law in eighteenth-century England is stressed in Douglas Hay et al., *Albion's Fatal Tree* (New York, 1975).

dence on landowners sanctioned by court-enforced contracts. The continuity of antislavery ideology was evident, too, in the Government's emphasis on transforming slaves more than masters, for it was the slaves who had been rendered incapable of working without compulsion and had to be taught new values. The Government's strong efforts to curb vagrancy and crime—and drinking and dancing as well—were all part of the abolitionist crusade and recall the similar effort directed at Englishmen and Irishmen: ex-slaves had to be made fit for their modified role. Only then could the wage-labor market operate on its own.

How the ideological content and functions of antislavery ideology evolved in the course of the industrial revolution and the overseas expansion of Britain has not been studied sufficiently. By treating abolitionism as an ideal detached from its socioeconomic context, historians have been unable to get beyond the largely pointless question of how well British policymakers lived up to these abstractions.[10] It is clear, however, that during the nineteenth century, antislavery ideology became increasingly conservative.

In part, the trend reflected changing conceptions of the lower orders that went along with the evolution of capitalism within Britain. In contrast to the pessimism of Ricardo, Malthus, and other political economists, their successors in the late nineteenth century acknowledged the evidence of increasing thrift, sobriety, and rationality within a segment of the working class: the moral virtues of capitalism were indeed being inculcated. The other side of this trend was to draw an ever sharper line between the respectable working class and what contemporaries called the "residuum": the vagrants, the casual laborers, the dangerous classes. Their poverty, degradation, and demoralization were, if not inherent, deeply rooted in their beings. The residuum threatened to contaminate the respectable working class, and its fate could no longer be left to the self-regulating mechanisms of the market. The casual poor of England had to be "Christianized" and "civilized," and above all contained and controlled by the state.[11]

Even earlier, abolitionists had believed that the stain of slavery colored the slave himself. But, in the debates over West Indian emancipation, they at least argued that emancipation, wage labor, and missionary ef-

10. Two recent studies of this period ably discuss how principles were set aside for expediency, how principles served as a cloak for expediency, and how expediency and principles sometimes coincided. But the two are kept distinct, and a discussion of changing ideology becomes impossible. Miers, *Britain and the Ending of the Slave Trade;* Grace, *Domestic Slavery in West Africa.*

11. Gareth Stedman Jones, *Outcast London: A Study in the Relationship between Classes in Victorian Society* (Oxford, 1971); idem, "Working-Class Culture and Working-Class Politics in London, 1870–1900," pp. 460–508; and Brian Harrison, *Drink and the Victorians: The Temperance Question in England 1815–1872* (Pittsburgh, Pa., 1971), esp. pp. 366–67, 394–95.

forts would make ex-slaves into respectable workers, if not independent peasants. By the late nineteenth century, such optimism was rare. A missionary on the coast of Kenya wrote of the dangers posed by freed slaves in terms remarkably similar to those used by contemporaries to describe the threat of the poor in East London: the liberation of slaves "would tend to produce a demoralized and dangerous class of people, such as would be sure in the future to embarrass the good government and to mar the prosperity of this country." The situation required caution in moving toward abolition, and above all the "overawing of the ill-disposed until the crisis shall be well over" and the education "into the ways of freedom of the irresponsible population to be freed."[12]

But even if a demoralized and dangerous class could be controlled, could it be made to work? The actual experience of abolition in the British West Indies, thanks in part to the terms in which abolitionists themselves defined the issues, contributed to increased skepticism. Abolitionists had been vague about the forms of economic organization that would follow slavery but confident that emancipation would be progressive economically as well as morally. Although few questioned the plantation system, there was a range of opinion. As high an official as the Permanent Undersecretary in the Colonial Office was "convinced that the inevitable tendency of things is toward the substitution of small holdings and a Peasantry living on detached Plots of land, for the old system of large Plantations." The advocates of plantations prevailed, however, and the Colonial Office approved vagrancy and other laws designed to make peasants into workers.[13] How they would perform in producing sugar became for abolitionists and sympathetic officials a crucial test of free labor.

In actuality, the effects of abolition on plantation labor were complex and varied. On densely populated islands, like Barbados and Antigua, ex-slaves had a few alternatives to wage labor, and the plantation structure remained intact. In Jamaica, many ex-slaves headed for the mountains, and the growing strength of a peasant economy undermined the plantation sector.[14] This process should have taught English observ-

---

12. W. E. Taylor to Henry Binns, 26 July 1895, PP 1896, LIX, 395, p. 18. See below for more evidence along these lines.

13. Sir James Stephen, 1840, quoted in Green, *British Slave Emancipation*, p. 85. Stephen was from a leading antislavery family. On Colonial Office policy, see Green, pp. 171–74, 191, and Temperley, *British Antislavery 1833–1870*, p. 113.

14. In Guiana, the plantation system remained alive but wages went up. However, as peasants were confined by the extent of the sugar estates to marginal lands without the vitally needed waterworks, and as immigrants brought in under indentures by the planters undermined the labor market, wages went down. The different patterns of change within the British West Indies are ably compared in Green, *British Slave Emancipation;* Mintz, "Slavery and the Rise of Peasantries"; and a variety of local studies.

ers a lesson about work; instead it taught them a lesson about workers. Sugar production fell substantially after abolition, and—irrespective of the efforts of ex-slaves to grow food on their own plots—that meant they were idle. Abolitionists had to explain away the drop in output or let ex-slaves take the blame.[15]

If trends in class relations in England and experience in the West Indies led a growing segment of English middle-class opinion to regard ex-slaves as incapable even of being a proper working class, the increasingly racist tenor of social thought within that milieu after the 1840s transformed the ex-slaves' inferiority into an immutable racial characteristic. Blacks came to be excluded from the optimistic side of reformism—the belief in individual improvement—and discipline and vigilance appeared to be the only way to keep them from idleness and disorder. These trends came together in British reactions to the disorders that broke out in Jamaica in 1865. Humanitarians were well aware of the oppression that lay behind the riots and vigorously denounced the brutality of the pro-planter administration that put them down and summarily executed many participants. Yet they now faced a strong counterargument: un-British as such measures might be, they were necessary against a class of ex-slaves and a race of blacks. The Governor was not prosecuted. The controversy clarified and reinforced the direction of social attitudes among the politically influential: being an ex-slave, being black, being lazy, and causing disorder became increasingly linked.[16] By the 1860s and 1870s, even the well-meaning were more and more likely to fear and loathe—and no more likely to understand—the people they were trying to help.

15. Sugar production in the British West Indies dropped by 36 percent between 1824-33 and 1839-46; in Jamaica, the drop was 50 percent (Temperley, "Capitalism," p. 103, and Drescher). On the abolitionists' ideological problems in explaining events, see Temperley, ibid., pp. 108-09, and Christine Bolt, *The Anti-Slavery Movement and Reconstruction: A Study in Anglo-American Co-operation 1833-77* (London, 1969), pp. 148-49. In the United States, abolitionists argued valiantly within the bounds of the free labor ideology that emancipation had proven "safe and practicable." James M. McPherson, "Was West Indian Emancipation a Success? The Abolitionist Argument in the American Civil War," *Caribbean Studies* 4 (1964): 28-34.

16. Douglas A. Lorimer connects changes in racial ideologies to changes in the English class system. *Colour, Class and the Victorians: English Attitudes to the Negro in the Mid-Nineteenth Century* (Leicester, 1978). On the evolution of racism, see Philip D. Curtin, *The Image of Africa: British Ideas and Action, 1780-1850* (Madison, Wis., 1964), and Christine Bolt, *Victorian Attitudes to Race* (London, 1971). The importance of the reaction to the Jamaica riots is stressed in ibid., pp. 75-108; Lorimer, pp. 178-200; Green, *British Slave Emancipation,* pp. 381-405; Philip D. Curtin, *Two Jamaicas: The Role of Ideas in a Tropical Colony 1830-1865* (Cambridge, Mass., 1955), pp. 101-203; and Bernard Semmel, *Jamaican Blood and Victorian Conscience: The Governor Eyre Controversy* (Boston, 1963).

British reactions to Reconstruction in the southern United States again revealed the narrowness of the options that were by then being considered in England—although American abolitionists propounded similar bourgeois ideologies—and the growing doubts about improvement and change.[17] After the Civil War, the American Congress thought seriously of distributing confiscated lands to ex-slaves, and it did establish schools, a Freedmen's Bank, and other institutions which suggest it envisioned that slaves might become at least a respectable working class. More important, ex-slaves were given the vote. These reforms were soon undermined, in part because even Radical Republicans were unwilling to compromise the idea of property, because the plantation system and the role of blacks as laborers were not seriously questioned, and because, by the 1870s, the economic and political reintegration of the United States required working with the older planter class that had reemerged in a new guise.[18] But in the extraordinary drama of Reconstruction there was a potential and a hope that was lacking in the colonies of Great Britain. The radical dimensions of Reconstruction, above all the suggestion of land redistribution and voting rights, struck even the more liberal English abolitionists as foolish, if not downright dangerous. The failure of Reconstruction confirmed their own experiences. Instead of coming to grips with the far-reaching social, political, and economic changes needed to make "free labor" more than an appealing image, the English middle class kept convincing itself of the dangers of change and the hopelessness of blacks. Even leading proponents of abolition expressed such attitudes when attention focused on slavery in East Africa in the 1890s.[19]

17. In England, slavery was less of an immediate problem, threatening the political system, and there was no strong equivalent to Garrisonian radicalism. But even the American radicals saw slavery more as a problem of sin than of class and had little more to offer free workers than the same injunctions to "economy, self-denial, temperance, education, and moral and religious character." Aileen S. Kraditor, *Means and Ends in American Abolitionism: Garrison and His Critics on Strategy and Tactics, 1834–1850* (New York, 1967), p. 250. On the relationship of capitalist ideology to less radical free labor views, see Eric Foner, *Free Soil, Free Labor, Free Men: The Ideology of the Republican Party before the Civil War* (New York, 1970).

18. James M. McPherson, *Struggle for Equality: Abolitionists and the Negro in the Civil War and Reconstruction* (Princeton, N.J., 1964); Willie Lee Rose, *Rehearsal for Reconstruction: The Port Royal Experiment* (Indianapolis, 1964); Louis Gerteis, *From Contraband to Freedmen: Federal Policy toward Southern Blacks, 1861–1865* (Westport, Conn., 1973); William S. McFeely, *Yankee Stepfather: General O. O. Howard and the Freedmen* (New Haven, 1968); Eric McKitrick, *Andrew Johnson and Reconstruction* (Chicago, 1960); Ransom and Sutch, *One Kind of Freedom;* Woodward, *Origins of the New South;* Litwack, *Been in the Storm So Long.*

19. Bolt, *Anti-Slavery Movement and Reconstruction,* pp. 161–70. The American experience is invoked as a lesson that not too much should be done for slaves in East Africa by Frederick Lugard, "Slavery under the British Flag," *The Nineteenth Century* 39 (1896): 353.

By the 1880s, antislavery had become entwined with the extension of British imperialism to new parts of Africa. The modern tendency to see colonial conquests as violent and bad, and emancipation as gentle and good, has obscured their ideological relationship. An important section of England's elite came to share an arrogance and sense of destiny that enabled it to think of the exploitativeness of the expanding capitalist system as the onward march of civilization and the exploitativeness of the precapitalist societies of Africa as chaos.[20] The much exaggerated abolitionist idea of Africa as a slave-ridden continent helped to dramatize this sense of disorder. Humanitarian organizations were sometimes ambivalent about conquest, exposing the vicious side of imperialism, but they still provided the routine exercise of power with a veneer of Christian concern.[21] Most curious was the willingness of the imperial powers to suspend, in the course of the crucial international conferences of 1884 and 1889–90, their deadly serious rivalries to discuss and articulate the standards which all civilized powers were to meet and impose. Not only the slave trade, but arms traffic and liquor exports elicited the ire of the imperialists, who saw in them images of violent and uncontrollable lower orders. An evolving imperialist ideology seemed to be transcending imperial competition.[22]

But if the destiny of European civilization provided a reason for doing something about African savagery, racism provided a reason for not doing too much. The process of conquest itself reinforced increasingly harsh views of Africans by the late nineteenth century, even among sympathetic missionaries.[23] On the one hand, not just conversion but a far-reaching transformation of African life was required. On the other hand, even such a transformation, many missionaries felt, could do no more than make Africans into respectful, diligent, and God-fearing subordinates. The implacable edifice of colonial rule had as an ideological concomitant a more rigid view of the permanent superiority of Euro-

20. A. P. Thornton describes the development of this sense of mission within the class that provided both Liberals and Tories with their leadership (*The Imperial Idea and Its Enemies: A Study in British Power*, London, 1959, esp. pp. 61–122). The connection of domestic class relations and imperialism is discussed in Bernard Semmel, *Imperialism and Social Reform* (London, 1960).

21. To find a fundamental critique of imperialism, one must look beyond the missionary and antislavery lobbies to, most impressively, J. A. Hobson, *A Study of Imperialism* (London, 1902). See Bernard Porter, *Critics of Empire: British Radical Attitudes to Colonialism in Africa 1895–1914* (London, 1968).

22. Miers, *Britain and the Ending of the Slave Trade*, provides a wealth of information but an inadequate analysis of the internationalization of antislavery.

23. Bolt, *Victorian Attitudes*, pp. 109–56; E. A. Ayandele, *The Missionary Impact on Modern Nigeria 1842–1914* (New York, 1966).

pean society to the decay of the pagan and Muslim world.[24] Some humanitarians plunged into their enormous task, but others—as well as more cautious government officials—came to think that to move slowly against archaic and immoral institutions was only to recognize reality: Africa was the dark continent.

Such was the context in which officials, missionaries, explorers, and others approached the problem of slavery on the east coast of Africa in the late nineteenth century. That the British Government acted cautiously and sought to keep slaves under economic and social constraints does not reflect the personal biases of local officials or the tempering of ideals by expediency so much as the conservative basis and direction of antislavery ideology itself.[25] Like all ideologies, abolitionism both obscured and illuminated. It exposed the violence of slavery and the personal tyranny of slaveowners, unchecked by societal constraints. But the notion of a free labor market left obscure the forces that made slaves or peasants into workers and maintained discipline within capitalist enterprises, while the image consigned the failures of the workers to their own lack of initiative in the face of impersonal and unbiased economic laws.

During the nineteenth century, reformers in England became increasingly unsure of the possibilities of slaves becoming self-disciplined workers and more fearful of the dangers of economic collapse and social unrest. When the issue of East African slavery came to the fore, some missionaries and members of antislavery societies were still content with the image of free labor and saw no reason to question its substance: freed slaves would simply become plantation laborers. Others, especially officials, were more fearful of the terrain of freedom and sought to postpone entering it until the state was strong enough to *make* slaves into workers. Earlier, a few reformers had thought ex-slaves might become peasants. By the end of the century, virtually all believed that slaves would either become an agricultural proletariat or remain dependent workers, tied to their former owners but watched over by a beneficient colonial state. Antislavery ideology, facing the idea of freedom, had begun with the vague and moved toward the restrictive.

---

24. Nancy Uhlar Murray, "Nineteenth Century Kenya and the 'Imperial Race for Christ, '" paper presented to the Historical Association of Kenya, Annual Conference, 1978, gives a stimulating interpretation of the changing meaning of conversion and civilization and their relationship to the need for labor, obedience, and order. On the link of Islam and heathenism to slavery and disorder, see Bolt, *Victorian Attitudes*, pp. 112–14.

25. Some abolitionists tried to blame the slowness of British action on the pro-Arab biases of the British Consul in Zanzibar, Arthur Hardinge. See below.

ADMINISTRATORS, ABOLITIONISTS, AND SLAVERY IN EAST AFRICA

In 1890, Zanzibar and Pemba became a British protectorate. The coast of Kenya, administered by a British chartered company since 1888, also became a protectorate in 1895.[26] Slavery, always an evil, had now become a taint on the British flag. The Foreign Office and the antislavery societies had long been concerned with the East African slave trade, especially since the dramatic voyages of David Livingstone in the 1860s, and British pressure had been instrumental in restricting the trade. Now the question was slavery itself, and the East African coast was the center of attention.

For all the controversy, the debates on British policy were conducted within a narrow ideological spectrum. By the 1890s, the British and Foreign Anti-Slavery Society was a fraction of its former self, diminished as much by its successes as by its failures. There is little evidence that a significant portion of the now much expanded voting public cared a whit about either slavery or Zanzibar.[27] The influence of abolitionists lay above all in the fact that within the narrow class from which England's rulers were drawn, they had no one to convince. That slave labor was both backward and wrong was intrinsic to that class's conception of work and economic order. Antislavery was a minor corollary to a major theorem.

The arguments that the advocates of prompt intervention in East Africa stressed point to the critical importance of disorder and personal tyranny to antislavery ideology. Missionaries and abolitionists put great weight on the argument that whatever the nature of slave society at Zanzibar, "throat-cutting, village-burning, slave raiding massacres . . . were the very cogs and wheels of the machinery which at last landed the slave at Zanzibar."[28] The *Anti-Slavery Reporter* dramatically publicized the occasional capture of a slave ship and gave preposterous figures for the magnitude of the trade at a time when it had at last begun to decline.[29]

26. Officials insisted that a protectorate was not a colony, and that Britain did not have the same obligations to end slavery that it would in British territory. Such fine points did little to assuage their critics. See the reprint of Parliamentary debates, 31 July and 1 Aug. 1890, in *ASR* 10 (1890): 154.

27. Temperley, *British Anti-Slavery*, pp. 228–32, 261. Miers's assertions about the influence of "public opinion" are based on evidence from a narrow elite. *Britain and the Ending of the Slave Trade*, pp. 315–16.

28. Horace Waller, *Heligoland for Zanzibar, or One Island Full of Free Men for Two Full of Slaves* (London, 1893), p. 43. It was also argued that the use of slaves as porters by Europeans, even when the slaves were paid and treated as free men, encouraged the slave trade, to which Hardinge replied weakly by invoking the paradox of uncivilized means being required for civilizing ends. Hardinge to Salisbury, 6 March 1896, FO 107/50.

29. In one calculation, 40,000 to 50,000 slaves were being exported from Zanzibar, a figure vastly in excess of the slave trade even at its height. Arbitrary figures on mortality in

At times, abolishing slavery was advanced as a means to the end of abolishing the slave trade.[30] So advocates of immediate abolition insisted that the slave trade remained rampant; the more cautious replied that it had already been curtailed.[31]

The slave trade—more so than slavery—created the kind of disorder that was irreconcilable with the advance of capitalism. Economic progress and civilization required the regularity, predictability, and absence of fear which only the Pax Britannica could provide. The ending of savage violence provided a unifying theme to humanitarians, traders, and other interventionists demanding action in "that Desolate Continent in the affairs of which we have been called by the Providence of God to interfere."[32]

With slavery itself, evil lay in the unchecked power of a person over his dependents. That was what the advocates of rapid abolition had in mind when they focused on the issue of "cruelty." The less enthusiastic claimed that the British presence and the Decree of 1890, which allowed slaves to claim freedom on the grounds of cruelty, already gave slaves recourse against the wanton exercise of power.[33] The *routine* exercise of

---

the slave trade—as high as 90 percent—were used in calculating the total impact of the trade as if they were quantitatively significant. *ASR* 13 (1893): 100, 317; 16 (1896), pp. 46, 97. See the numerous references to the continued slave trade in *ASR*, 1890–1897, and Joseph Pease, *How We Countenance Slavery* (London, 1895), pp. 4-5.

30. Charles Allen, letter to the *Friend*, reprinted in *ASR* 13 (1893): 349. See the same argument from various antislavery souces in *ASR* 13 (1893): 259, and 16 (1896): 44, 126, 211; and Lugard, "Slavery under the British Flag," p. 353.

31. For official views of the decline of the slave trade, see Rear-Adm. Bedford to Admiralty, 9 March 1895, FOCP 6717, p. 30, and Hardinge to Salisbury, 4 May 1896, PP 1896, LIX, 395, p. 34. By this time, the Government argument is the more plausible. See Carla Glassman, "The Illegal East African Slave Trade, 1873-1900," Unpublished paper, Cambridge University, 1977.

32. Horace Waller, speech to the Wesleyan Conference, 31 July 1894, in *ASR* 14 (1894): 212. See also Miers, *Britain and the Ending of the Slave Trade*, p. 291. In parts of central and southern Africa, the need that British interests had for peace and order if they were to establish commerce, labor recruitment, and mission stations, clashed more directly with continued slave-trading operations than it did in East Africa. Nevertheless, the underlying incompatibility of an advancing colonial regime and the slave trade was important even where the economic conflict was not so immediate. Louis Gann, "The End of the Slave Trade in British Central Africa: 1889-1912," *Rhodes-Livingstone Journal* 16 (1954): 40-50. The direct hope of some officials in South Africa in the 1870s that abolition of the East African slave trade would help to extend labor recruitment proved ephemeral. Norman Etherington, "Labour Supply and the Genesis of South African Confederation in the 1870s," *JAH* 20 (1979): 243-44, 249-53. Trevor Lloyd argues that the first investment made in Africa had to be in law and order. "Africa and Hobson's Imperialism," *Past and Present* 55 (1972): 130-53.

33. On brutality, above all British complicity in the situation that brought it about, see *ASR* 16 (1896): 11-12, 97; editorials from various newspapers reprinted in *ASR* 17 (1897): 94, 101, 172; Pease, p. 3. For the other side, see Euan-Smith to Anti-Slavery Society, 17

power, as well as the social and economic subordination of slaves, did not so acutely need to be curbed.

With the advent of the colonial state, the failure to end violence and restrain personal power had become an affront to British traditions and values. As a speaker to an antislavery rally invoked the image of "our British flag . . . floating over thousands of slaves," the audience cried "Shame!"[34] Whenever the Government, administering Islamic law as the protecting power, did anything to uphold the law of slavery, such as returning runaways, antislavery circles reacted vehemently. The problem could only be solved by inaction, avoiding the implications of the legality of slavery.[35]

Even the most cautious officials would not take issue with antislavery principles. Instead, they reminded critics that the East African coast was a "Mohammedan country," and therefore one must have lowered expectations of its people.[36] At the same time, with slave imports cut off and with cruelty punishable by law, the evils of slavery were diminishing and would soon die a "natural death."[37]

That the abolition of slavery might affect the economic position of slaves was to all concerned a cost and not a benefit. Officials, well aware of the West Indian experience, had no illusions that abolition would benefit the economy of Zanzibar, the mainland, or the British Empire.[38]

Dec. 1888, ASP, s22, 63; Rodd to Rosebery, 31 Dec. 1893, PP 1895, LXXI, 143, p. 16; George Curzon, statement to House of Commons, 24 June 1897, reprinted in *ASR* 17 (1897): 123–24.

34. *ASR* 14 (1894): 212. The message was rubbed in by editorials with titles like "Our Slaves in Zanzibar," and meetings about "Slavery under the British Flag." *ASR* 15 (1895): 147–83; Lugard, "Slavery under the British Flag," pp. 335–55.

35. The Foreign Office advised "discretion" in handling the problem of fugitive slaves, and Hardinge instructed his subordinates to "temporize on the fugitive slave question" (FO to Craufurd, 3 Dec. 1896, FOCP 6913, p. 218; Hardinge to Salisbury, 16 Jan. 1898, FOCP 7024, p. 122; Salisbury to Hardinge, 15 Dec. 1897, PP 1898, LX, 559, p. 26). See also the uproar over this issue in *ASR* throughout 1897. After that, officials decided not to return slaves forcibly at all. Hardinge to D. MacKenzie, 16 June 1898, ASP c59/134; Salisbury to Hardinge, 26 June 1897 (telegram), FOCP 6964, p. 148; statements in House of Commons, reprinted in *ASR* 17 (1897): 127–28; Hardinge to Craufurd, incl. Hardinge to Salisbury, 16 Jan. 1898, FOCP 7024, pp. 122–23.

36. Hardinge to Allen, 2 Sept. 1895, ASP, c59/130; Curzon, speeches to House of Commons, 27 March 1896, 10 Feb. 1898, reprinted in *ASR* 16 (1896): 100, and 18 (1898), p. 16; Salisbury to Hardinge, 29 June 1898, in *ASR* 18 (1898): 145.

37. See, for example, the statements of E. Grey to the House of Commons, 22 Aug. 1894, 7 March 1895, reprinted in *ASR* 14 (1894): 201, and 15 (1895): 23–25.

38. Even in Kenya, where the development of European plantations on the coast might conceivably have been aided by access to the labor of the slaves of Arabs and Swahili, the Adminstration did not abolish slavery until well after the laborers had effectively become detached from their owners. Before that, officials' fear of disorder made them careful "not to try to tempt slaves from their masters." Abolitionists criticized them for not doing enough to foster wage labor. EAP, AR, 1903–04, p. 28.

More likely, wrote the Foreign Secretary, Lord Salisbury, ending the legal status of slavery "will probably be injurious to the industry of the islands."[39] Hardinge, the strongest opponent of immediate action, was extremely pessimistic. Slaves, he felt, had been so conditioned by slavery that they would not work of their own accord: exports would drop drastically, damaging commerce and diminishing Government revenue by £26,500, while administrative and police costs would rise by £20,000 per year. Hardinge's estimates were vastly exaggerated, as another experienced official pointed out to the Foreign Office, but his fears were widely shared.[40]

In fact, Hardinge was better able than most to avoid reducing the problem to the inherent laziness of slaves. It was not that slaves were unwilling to work, he wrote in one despatch, but that left alone they would work *for themselves*. Zanzibar was so fertile that working for clove planters would be a poor alternative to growing their own crops. In order to give slaves legal freedom, their economic freedom had to be restricted. They should be made to pay rent; the tax burden on clove producers should be shifted to ex-slaves; movement of ex-slaves should be restricted; and labor during the harvest, although it would be paid, should be compulsory.[41]

The concept of work in nineteenth-century Britain was thus more exacting than that of East African plantation society: work had to be both steady and productive within a market economy. Hardinge at least partially understood that his notions of work were based on the assumption that workers had no direct access to the means of production and that special problems of control arose when they could get land. But in all cases, as E. P. Thompson and Michel Foucault have argued in different ways, the concept of work in a capitalist economy implied not just that needed tasks be performed, but that time, space, and action be

39. Memorandum by the Marquis of Salisbury respecting the abolition of slavery in Zanzibar, Dec. 1895, FOCP 6709.

40. Hardinge to Kimberley, 23 March 1895, FOCP 6717, pp. 17–18. His estimates were debunked in C. S. Smith to Kimberley, 26 May 1895, ibid., pp. 209–10, but there are further dire predictions in Rodd to Rosebery, 31 Dec. 1893, PP 1895, LXXI, 143, pp. 14–15, and Kimberley to India Office, 19 April 1895 (draft), FO 107/45.

41. Hardinge to Salisbury, 10 Jan. 1896, PP 1896, LIX, 395, pp. 24–25. Elsewhere, Hardinge railed on about the laziness of slaves, and other officials did the same. Even in retrospect, the belief that slaves would not work was maintained in official reports. Hardinge to Salisbury, 16 Jan. 1898, FOCP 7024, p. 121; Salisbury to Hardinge, 29 June 1898, FOCP 7077, p. 228; Report on Slavery and Free Labour by W. J. Monson, PP 1903, XLV, 745, p. 5; Kenya, NAD, AR, 1927, pp. 9–10; East Africa Commission, Report, 1925, p. 37. The belief that the premature freeing of slaves—before access to the means of production had been cut off from them—would lead to economic decline lay behind much of the restrictive legislation in postemancipation societies around the world. Kloosterboer, *Involuntary Labour*.

strictly controlled. That required hierarchy, authority, and discipline, which in the case of Zanzibar had to be assimilated to a preexisting social structure. Officials on the scene and in London described the Zanzibari class structure as "an Arab aristocracy"; a "trading class of British Indians"; "a middle and lower native trading and artisan element; and the residuum, estimated at 140,000 slaves." The residuum, to Victorians, was not capable of exercising an active role in the economy: "the Sultan, the Arabs, and the British Indians . . . are the only people directly interested in the production of cloves." If such people could not maintain control over production, "the bankruptcy of the State" would follow. The residuum, at best, could only obey.[42]

Indeed, missionaries and antislavery leaders widely shared these assumptions. "Centuries of oppression or of unbridled power" had left slaves—if not all Africans who had been touched by the slave trade—without self-reliance.[43] Donald MacKenzie, emissary of the Anti-Slavery Society to Zanzibar, agreed with Hardinge that the state must intervene to keep slaves at work for Arabs: he suggested that they be made to turn over half their produce to their former owner in exchange for access to land. The Quakers insisted that ex-slaves should work for wages, and most reformers simply assumed that plantations would go on as before. Despite the anti-Arab sentiments of the Christian missionaries, the acceptance of property ownership transcended dislike of particular property owners.[44]

42. George Curzon, "Slavery in Zanzibar," 29 Dec. 1896, CAB 37/40/58; Charles Euan-Smith to Salisbury, 3 Jan. 1891, FO 84/2146. Note also Curzon's emphasis on British responsibility to Arabs as "a class," in Speech to House of Commons, 27 March 1896, ASR 16 (1896): 101. On work and discipline, see E. P. Thompson, "Time, Work–Discipline and Industrial Capitalism," Past and Present 38 (1967): 56–97, and Michel Foucault, Discipline and Punish: The Birth of the Prison, trans. Alan Sheridan (London, 1977).

43. Lugard, "Slavery under the British Flag," p. 337; Taylor to Binns, 26 July 1895, PP 1896, LIX, 395, p. 18; editorials from the Daily News, 25 July 1897, and other newspapers, in ASR 17 (1897): 169, 171. The Quaker missionaries to Pemba believed that "slavery seem[ed] to destroy the moral character of boys," and careful supervision was needed to protect against "the slave instinct to sit down and 'rest.' " Letters of Herbert Armitage and Theodore Burtt, 18 Nov. 1891, 13 Feb. 1902, in ASR 22 (1902): 19–20, 47. The belief that slaves had been degraded beyond other Africans and therefore could only be given independence from their owners slowly was also important to the thinking of French colonial officials. Derman, Serfs, Peasants, and Socialists, p. 49, and Weiskel, "Labor in the Emergent Periphery," p. 216.

44. Donald MacKenzie, "A Report on Slavery and the Slave Trade in Zanzibar, Pemba, and the Mainland of the British Protectorates of East Africa," ASR 15 (1895): 95–96. On the Quakers, see below, pp. 44–45. Even an editorial that said of Arabs, "Let the scoundrels be ruined," was only arguing that they not be given compensation for their slaves, the general position of the Anti-Slavery Society and its friends (The Freeman, in ASR 17 [1897]: 96). The furthest any of these abolitionists would go was to suggest that the normal operation of the laws of the market would transfer plantations to more progressive landowners,

Given these assumptions, the economic argument left abolitionists on the defensive. They relied on the vaguest pieties about the greater efficiency of free labor but did not specify how a wage-labor economy would function, where the workers would come from, what kinds of wages and working conditions they expected to evolve, and what role the state would play. Some asserted that free labor would flock to the islands once slavery was abolished. At most, these abolitionists offered assurances that a free-labor market would produce a labor supply; they had little to say about the issue which obsessed Hardinge—the control of labor.[45]

Not only did the curtailment of the slaveowners' power risk economic decline, but it also endangered the social order of a hierarchical society. Officials and missionaries alike feared that any loosening of the bonds on the lower orders would lead to vagrancy, immorality, prostitution, crime, and drunkenness. With the "old restraints removed" from the slaves, only an "orderly evolution for them, from slavery to freedom, from license to law will save them from themselves."[46]

On Zanzibar, officials feared that freed slaves would foment popular disorders—"agrarian wars" as one put it. On the mainland, they feared both the resistance of slaveowners and the unruliness of slaves. As one leading official said, "if a large number of slaves are liberated at one time, they are apt to break loose, loot shops and shambas [farms or plantations] and commit all sorts of excesses."[47] To tamper with the delicate mechanisms of social control would produce, argued Salisbury, "much misery and some danger."[48]

---

still preserving property and the plantation system. One listed a variety of schemes to help landowners through the problem of abolition. Frederick Lugard, Memorandum to Chamberlain and Balfour re "non-recognition of slavery in courts of law," 22 Aug. 1895, LP, vol. 42; F. W. Fox to Kimberley, 5 June 1895, FOCP 6717, pp. 234–35.

45. John Kirk's contention that slave and free labor would not mix was quoted repeatedly by abolitionists. Kirk to Granville, 22 Nov. 1884, FOCP 5165, p. 263; Petitions of the Anti-Slavery Society to FO, 30 Dec. 1893, and 19 Aug. 1896, in ASR 13 (1893): 317, 16 (1896): 191; letters to the (London) Times, in ASR 15 (1895): 93, 17 (1897): 93. Officials did not think abolition would increase the supply of free labor. Hardinge to Salisbury, 4 May 1896, FOCP 6849, pp. 240–41; Curzon, reply to Anti-Slavery Society petition, 14 Nov. 1896, ASR 16 (1896): 262.

46. Report on Pemba by J. P. Farler, PP 1898, LX, 559, p. 60. See also Rodd to Rosebery, 31 Dec. 1893, PP 1895, LXXI, 143, pp. 14–15; Hardinge to Salisbury, 28 March 1898, PP 1898, LX, 559, p. 65; letters from the missionaries at Mombasa, 1896, in PP 1896, LIX, 395, pp. 18–19; Eliot to Lansdowne, 18 Feb. 1902, FOCP 7946, pp. 216–27; Lugard, "Slavery under the British Flag," p. 344.

47. Farler, Slavery Report, PP 1898, LX, 559, p. 64; Piggott to Hardinge, 1 Aug. 1895, FOCP 6761, p. 262. See also Curzon, "Slavery in Zanzibar," 29 Dec. 1896, CAB 37/40/58, p. 6; H. Percy Anderson, Memorandum on the abolition of the status of slavery in Zanzibar, 6 Feb. 1896, FOCP 6756, p. 1.

48. Salisbury, 1898, quoted in G. N. Uzoigwe, Britain and the Conquest of Africa: The Age of Salisbury (Ann Arbor, 1974), p. 167. For this reason, the argument that "Mohammedan

Finally, officials and missionaries alike realized that slavery encompassed a social welfare system of sorts, and they had no desire to do what was necessary to replace it. Islamic law and coastal customs, they felt (with some reason), required slaveowners to care for the young, the old, and the infirm. Abolishing the legal status of slavery might dissolve the reciprocal obligations of masters and slaves.[49]

Caution did not imply inaction, but only the postponement of abolition until the process of natural death and the consolidation of state power made the problems manageable. A large budgetary surplus in 1895 made the anticipated economic dislocation seem like less of a threat to Zanzibar's fiscal stability.[50] The succession of a docile Sultan and the quick suppression of a disgruntled Prince's attempted coup gave the Administration more confidence that it would not face rebellion on the islands (although the mainland was worrisome), while police could look after the crime and disorder expected from freed slaves. Meanwhile, Hardinge's claim that his policies were ameliorating slavery increasingly undermined his dire predictions about the impact of abolition. The time had come for abolition, argued the leading African expert in the Foreign Office in 1896, not because slaves needed help, but because their expectations had to be dampened by the state: "if the abolition of legal status is made immediate, the natives will, more or less, realize its limitation," although "stringent rule" was required while ex-slaves were learning this lesson.[51]

The Foreign Office, as it moved toward a decision during 1896, was seeking what Salisbury later called a "readjustment" of the plantation system that would bring the nature of labor into conformity with British ideology. The Government eventually decided that the "Arab aristoc-

---

society" had its own way of doing things was not merely an excuse for inaction but a reflection of very real fears of disorder. Even before emancipation, officials were convinced that slaves who were separated from their masters, by manumission or escape, were "the worst characters on the coast." Piggott to Hardinge, 1 Aug. 1895, FOCP 6761, p. 263.

49. These worries were one of the main reasons why the abolition decree of 1897 required that slaves ask for freedom and that slaveowners continue to care for slaves who had not done so. Earlier, as noted below, officials opposed the implementation of a decree issued in 1889 that declared all children born after 1890 to be free, claiming that it would cause slaveowners to turn out slave children. For continued concern over the welfare problem, see Memorandum by Mr. Cave on the Proposed Abolition of Slavery in the Islands of Zanzibar and Pemba, 1906, FOCP 9102, p. 21; Last to Cave, 29 Aug. 1907, FOCP 9215, pp. 39–40. For similar concerns expressed by a more ardent abolitionist, see Lugard, "Slavery under the British Flag," p. 344.

50. Even Hardinge admitted that the surplus would make abolition more feasible. Hardinge to Kimberley, 11 May 1895, FOCP 6717, pp. 224–25; Report on Customs by C. W. Strickland, incl. Hardinge to Salisbury, 12 March 1896, FOCP 6849, p. 33.

51. H. Percy Anderson, Memorandum, 1896, FOCP 6756, p. 3.

racy" must be supported not simply by recognition of its ownership of land but by compensation for slaves who were freed.[52] Plantation labor, moreover, could not be trusted to the labor market. George Curzon, a major policymaker in the Foreign Office, insisted that "free labour, paid labour, is not indigenous to the place—it is an exotic, it would have to be imported, it would have to be carefully tended and watered to enable it to grow."[53] "Tending"—it turned out—consisted of legal constraints to insure continued personal dependence of ex-slaves on planters, although such relations, as antislavery ideology made clear, must be mediated by the state. "Watering" meant enforcing the laws of property and forcibly preventing idleness and disorder. Only through pressure, vigilance, and time could ex-slaves internalize the discipline that had once been based on their masters' whips.

The antislavery lobby, despite its dramatic call for immediate abolition throughout British East Africa, was pushing for an equally conservative approach in 1896. The Anti-Slavery Society wrote to the Foreign Office that it favored proposals "for the abolition of the legal status of slavery with the least disturbance to the Arab and slave populations." The precedent that spokesmen invoked most often was not the West Indies—where the planter-worker relationship had changed considerably—but India, where the abolition of the legal status of slavery in 1843 had had little effect at all.[54]

The abolition of the legal status of slavery meant that no court would recognize any right or power over an individual by virtue of his being a

52. Salisbury to Hardinge, 29 June 1898, FOCP 7077, p. 229. The proponents of compensation stressed that it was both a way out of the moral commitment to Arabs to preserve Islamic law and a politically wise move to preserve a class upon which the Government depended for prosperity and stability. Compensation, however, was the most divisive issue in 1896. Opponents inside and outside the Foreign Office argued that the record of illegal importation of slaves since 1873 removed any moral commitments to Arabs and—most important—that simply to declare the legal status of slavery ended was a less disruptive move, while awarding compensation would make such an event out of abolition that slaves might notice that something was going on. See the summary of both positions in Curzon, Memorandum, 1896, CAB 37/40/58; Anderson, Memorandum, 1896, FOCP 6756; and Joseph Chamberlain, "Slavery in Zanzibar," 31 Dec. 1896, CAB 37/43/61. The arguments are discussed in Uzoigwe, pp. 155–71.

53. Curzon, speech to House of Commons, 27 March 1896, reprinted in ASR 16 (1896): 101.

54. Allen to Salisbury, 19 Aug. 1896, FOCP 6861, pp. 162–63. The Indian precedent showed that slavery could indeed be ended with "no disruption of the equilibrium or well-being of the country." Allen in ASR 13 (1893): 259; Petition of Anti-Slavery Society to FO, 30 Dec. 1893, ibid., p. 316; Kirk, memorandum, 19 June 1890, FOCP 6051, p. 266. Abolitionists were apparently correct that the Indian Act of 1843 made little difference to the slaves. Benedicte Hjejle, "Slavery and Agricultural Bondage in South India in the Nineteenth Century," Scandinavian Economic History Review 15 (1967): 98.

slave. The most prestigious advocate of this approach was John Kirk, long-time British consular agent in Zanzibar. He insisted that his plan was more conservative than Hardinge's.[55] The latter's wish to compensate slaveowners, which would require a court hearing, "implies active freeing to which I object." Above all, Kirk and his allies wanted to avoid "general emancipation."

Following the Indian precedent would allow "the slave and the master to work together as long as possible and so avoid a general upset of society."[56] Replying to Hardinge's contention that the wages of slaves who were hired out by their owners for urban labor would rise, Kirk argued that the Indian employers would simply reduce the wages by the proportion that had once gone to the slaveowner: "The labourer is just as well off, works the same, but the slave master loses."[57] The purpose of emancipation was clearly not to make the laborer *better* off. The main difference would be, as the abolitionists' Parliamentary spokesman, Joseph Pease, put it, "Slaves would be able to, so to speak, barter their labour to the masters who treated them best."[58] They would, it seems, still have masters. Slaves would be freed from the tyranny and violence of the individual slaveowner, but not from the subordination, poverty, and powerlessness of the plantation economy.

This approach assumed that it was the extraordinary power which legal ownership conferred on a slaveholder that made slavery what it was. In fact, abolishing the legal status of slavery implied little about social change. If the power of the planter was deeply rooted in his control over economic resources and in social and cultural hegemony, it would make little difference. If, however, the slaves had alternatives to the master, the slaveowner's loss of the legal power of restraint might be

---

55. Trying to pinpoint his differences with Hardinge—whom he called "a fool" and "a bit mad"—Kirk focused on differing prejudices: "Hardinge dislikes the Indians (who are my friends) and does love the Arabs whom I distrust as an agency for good." Their differing prejudices in fact reflect Kirk's identification with commercial as opposed to landowning interests. But if Kirk and Hardinge disagreed over who should be on top in Zanzibar, they did agree on who should remain on the bottom. Kirk's frequently vicious comments about Hardinge, Salisbury, and others conceal how many of their beliefs he shared. See Kirk's revealing private correspondence with Frederick Lugard, esp. letters of Oct. 1892, 13 Jan., 22 April, 10 June 1896, LP, vol. 40; 20 Aug., 9, 30 Oct. 1896, 10 March 1897, LP, vol. 41.

56. Kirk to Lugard, 9 Aug. 1896, LP, vol. 41; Kirk to Anti-Slavery Society, 17 Oct. 1896, ASP, s22, 67; Memorandum to FO, 12 Dec. 1896, FOCP 6847, pp. 1–5. Kirk advocated vagrancy restrictions on slaves analogous to those proposed by Hardinge.

57. Kirk to Lugard, 27 Aug. 1897, LP, vol. 41. Similarly, Lugard advocated abolishing the legal status of slavery because it would be cheap and cause little disruption. Memorandum, 1895, LP, vol. 42; "Slavery under the British Flag," esp. pp. 344, 353.

58. Speech to House of Commons, 1 June 1894, in *ASR* 14 (1894): 136–37.

his undoing. But the faith of abolitionists in the power of property and the workings of the labor market was such that this possibility was not discussed: "The freed slaves could not live on their freedom," and abolition would make slaves into an agricultural working class.[59]

But a more pessimistic belief in the need for state action—even if it meant compromising the free-market ideology—to create wage-labor plantations and avoid economic decline and social chaos was more consistent with the tide of opinion in the late nineteenth century.[60] Such views prevailed within the Foreign Office and Parliament.[61] The abolition decree of 1897 (see Appendix) and the measures taken to implement the decree were all designed to bolster Arab slaveowners, to tie ex-slaves to the plantations through contracts, to discourage the mobility and independence of workers, and to put down vagrancy, disorder, and immorality. The state would transform personal tyranny into orderly control of labor, not by replacing the property owner, but by supervising him.

The Decree of 1897 affected the islands, not the mainland. The difference points to the importance of the power of the state. In 1896 the British had put down a rebellion, which—fortunately for them—had not involved an issue like slavery that might have united Arabs and Swahili, and they hoped that coastal people had learned a lesson. But officials had themselves learned how difficult and costly defeating an Arab potentate could be, and they were well aware of the length of the Kenyan coastline, the independence of the coastal towns and peoples, and the ability of local leaders to mobilize diverse followers.[62] Not only was the Government less sure of its power over slaveowners than it was in the case of Zanzibar, but it also doubted that it was strong enough to bring

---

59. MacKenzie, *ASR* 15 (1895): 94.

60. The division of the opposed sides into optimists and pessimists was made by Anderson, Memorandum, 1896, FOCP 6756, pp. 2–3.

61. Kirk deluded himself into thinking, when the Foreign Office finally acted, that he had "won the day against them all...." He had fought hardest on the issue of compensation and lost, and the Decree of 1897 was only a partial reflection of his legal status approach. The Anti-Slavery Society, less interested in self-aggrandizement, regarded the Government's approach as a partial defeat. Kirk to Lugard, 6 May 1897, LP, vol. 41, and *ASR*, 1897–1902, for an often bitter attack on the inadequacies of Foreign Office policy.

62. Hardinge was particularly upset that the rebel Mbaruk bin Rashid had slaves and runaway slaves among his followers. The combination of independent slaves and independent potentates could produce chaos (Hardinge to Salisbury, 19 Jan. 1896, PP 1896, LIX, 41, p. 53). On the theme of British weakness on the mainland, see Hardinge to Kimberley, 24 June 1895 (telegram), FOCP 6717, p. 288; Anderson, Memorandum, 1896, FOCP 6756, p. 1; Balfour, speech to House of Commons, 24 June 1897, in *ASR* 17 (1897): 126; Hardinge, Administrative Report, 1896–97, PP 1898, LX, 199, p. 66; Salisbury, Memorandum, 1895, FOCP 6709.

about the kind of reformed agricultural dependence it sought or to prevent the "excesses" of liberated slaves.[63] At the same time, it insisted that slaveowners—however independent—were losing control over their slaves more rapidly than in Zanzibar; the process of natural death was rapid. Only in 1907, a full decade later, was slavery in coastal Kenya abolished, and by then both the experience of Zanzibar and the extent of change in Kenya made officials think that it would cause minimal disruption.[64] Even cautious action against slavery had to follow the secure establishment of the colonial state.

For all their conservatism, abolitionists were vigilant in pressuring the Government to implement its policies vigorously and fairly. They were appalled that the Decree of 1897 did not include concubines, excluded the mainland, and contained provisions that restricted ex-slaves' access to the labor market. They were obsessed with the modest number of slaves that were being freed. The taint on the British flag was not being removed fast enough or completely.[65]

The strongest pressure for the vigorous implementation of one of Britain's last programs to free slaves came from a group that had been active from the first, the Quakers. The mission station they had established in Pemba in 1896 became a watching-post on Government action and an example of a more thorough approach.[66] Just as Quakers had once led other members of the middle class to see the sanctity of the labor market, they stuck to this belief when others had become increas-

63. High Commissioner Eliot in EAP, AR, 1900–01, FOCP 7867, p. 33; C. Hill, Minute on Question of Annexing the British Protectorates of Africa, 7 April 1901, FOCP 7716, pp. 12–13.

64. On the natural death argument, see Curzon, speech to House of Commons, 18 May 1897, *ASR* 17 (1897): 123; EAP, AR, 1900–01, FOCP 7867, p. 33; Lansdowne to Eliot, 31 July 1901, ibid., p. 145, and the statements of various officials on the coast in FOCP 8932 (1906), pp. 77E–77I. Antislavery advocates did not buy this argument. See letter of Bishop Tucker to the (London) *Times,* reprinted in *ASR* 17 (1897): 91–92, and many other commentaries during the period between abolition in Zanzibar and in Kenya. For more on abolition on the mainland, see chapter 5.

65. These criticisms were raised in the annotations that accompanied the reprinting of Salisbury's instructions to Hardinge in *ASR* 17 (1897): 74–75. But the editors of the *ASR* had nothing whatsoever to say about the two points on which Salisbury placed the most emphasis: the danger of "violence or excess" by freed slaves and the threat of economic dislocation because slaves were "naturally improvident and adverse to labour." On these points there was no disagreement, although the question of whether the state should respond to these dangers by placing constraints on freed slaves or leaving the labor market unfettered was debated for years. See the *ASR* in the years after 1897 for a record of abolitionists' continuing concern, and chapter 3 for more discussion of the issue of labor control.

66. Hardinge contrasted the Quakers to the less critical Anglican and Catholic missionaries on Zanzibar. Hardinge to Salisbury, 13 Jan. 1898, FOCP 7024, p. 141.

ingly conscious of the inadequacies of a laissez-faire ideology in the face of the problems of controlling a labor force. They opposed any obstacles to slaves being freed, such as requirements that they be able to prove they had a job or a place to live before leaving their master. They opposed contracts that would "bind the people to the soil," and did not like the idea of ex-slaves paying rent in labor for the plots they received from the planters. Contract labor, like slave labor, provided no incentives to self-discipline. Their notion of free labor was a rigorous one: "Not for one moment do I suggest that it is a desirable goal for the slave to be able thus to work or not as he chooses, or to wander about working a few days here and there." Only through steady, well-supervised work would slaves overcome what Quakers, along with Salisbury and Hardinge, felt to be a deep-rooted "slave instinct" to be idle and thriftless.[67]

On their own model plantation, the Quakers kept a close watch over their charges, setting them to work on clove trees. The work-load, eight hours per day, five and a half days per week, was greater than was customary in the days of slavery, but the worker-converts were paid wages, taught "to work and become independent," and helped to live "pure, moral, and Christian lives."[68] The Quakers' concern for slaves and their belief in the social values of capitalism were inseparable, and they brooked no compromise because of centuries of degradation under slavery. As the Quakers' continuing efforts at implementing abolition and building a new kind of plantation community made clear, theirs was a pure vision of a free-labor economy, demanding a new kind of worker, a new kind of discipline.

Despite their differences, both the Administrators and the Quakers conceived of work in terms of regularity, discipline, and control from above. They had similar prejudices about slaves, whose experience of a different sort of discipline had left a legacy that had to be overcome, and they often extended their fears of idleness and disorder to all

67. Herbert Armitage, Comments on the White Book, 16 Feb. 1903, ASP, c73/101; Armitage to Buxton, 31 July 1901, 9 Sept. 1902, ASP, c73/90, 96; Theodore Burtt to Buxton, 3 Dec. 1900, *ASR* 21 (1901): 14-15; Armitage, letter, 18 Nov. 1901, *ASR* 22 (1902): 18-20; excerpts from a letter from Burtt, 4 April 1902, ibid., pp. 45-47. In the association of casual labor—"working a few days here and there"—with idleness another parallel with middle-class beliefs about the English poor clearly emerges. Armitage felt that slaves were so "thriftless" that they could not make good use of the money earned by working seasonally; they had to be kept at work full time. *ASR* 22 (1902): p. 18.

68. Armitage, "Comments," 16 Feb. 1903, ASP, c73/101; Alderman J. Duckworth, "Slavery in East Africa," *ASR* 22 (1902): 24; Report of Yearly Meetings, 1901, p. 136, 1906, p. 172, 1911, p. 101, FA. On the Pemba mission, see also Henry S. Newman, *Banani: The Transition from Slavery to Freedom in Zanzibar and Pemba* (London, 1898). The severity of discipline at the missions of the Church Missionary Society near Mombasa is discussed by Murray, "Nineteenth Century Kenya and the 'Imperial Race for Christ,'" pp. 33-35.

Africans—indeed to all preindustrial peoples. English racial prejudices predate the development of capitalism, but their content and significance were altered by the changing roles that the lower orders were being forced to play. Faced with a society of nonwhites, British officials in East Africa decided that only some of them were supposed to work. Others might be a dubious aristocracy and ineffective managers, but aristocrats and managers they would remain.[69] With their rigid dichotomy between owners and workers, between labor and idleness, officials and missionaries had little basis on which to build an understanding of what ex-slaves would want and how ex-slaves would act.

The Control of Labor and Agriculture, 1890–1907

The abolitionists were quite right to stress the element of personal power in slavery, but they were unable to see that power in context. In the 1890s, as people in London debated abolishing the legal status of slavery, the complex and delicate bases of the slaveowners' control were being slowly eroded.

The plantations had survived a series of measures undertaken since the 1870s by the Sultan of Zanzibar, under strong British pressure, to curtail the slave trade. Imports of slaves continued, but prices rose, encouraging diversification of sources and the concentration of supplies on coastal plantations, while cutting into the planters' profits. Although grain prices on the mainland remained buoyant in the late 1880s, the sharp decline in clove prices caught planters in Zanzibar and Pemba in a squeeze. But creditors had no desire to foreclose; the slave population could, if necessary, feed (although not reproduce) itself; and the plantation system remained economically and socially viable on the eve of colonial rule.[70]

The end of the slave trade came in the 1890s, above all through the gradual destruction of the African polities that had maintained the long and complex networks that gathered and distributed slaves.[71] As early as

69. The attitudes of officials in London toward white and nonwhite planter classes were actually more similar than one might expect. In the 1890s, comments from the Colonial Office about the planters of Guiana were similar to those about Arabs in Zanzibar: neither group was quite civilized. But in both cases, "contempt for the planters was more than mitigated by the fear" of the plantation laborers. Adamson, p. 256.

70. Cooper, *Plantation Slavery*, chapter 4.

71. Slaves continued to dribble in, but European penetration inland did what blockades had failed to do. Moreover, the uncertain future of slavery made plantation owners less willing to risk the now enormous costs and risks of buying slaves. Vice-Consul O'Sullivan, Report on Pemba, 1896, PP 1896, LIX, 395, p. 41.

1893, the naval officers who patrolled Pemba were complaining that they had "little to do."[72]

Shortly after establishing its Protectorate over Zanzibar in 1890, the British Administration passed in the Sultan's name a new decree that banned all sales of slaves, even within the islands and the coast of Kenya; ruled that all slaves who were cruelly treated would be freed and their owners punished; allowed slaves to buy their freedom; and permitted only the children of a dead slaveowner to inherit his slaves. This decree pointed to a cautious intervention in the institution of slavery itself.[73] But the Sultan, with Consul Euan-Smith's approval, quickly issued a decree clarifying that slaves who misbehaved would "be punished as before." Euan-Smith insisted that "moderate reasonable punishment" was needed to prevent slaves from getting "big heads." A second decree stipulated that a slaveowner need not accept a slave's offer of money for self-purchase, and the Administration quietly decided to ignore an earlier agreement with the Sultan that granted freedom to all slaves born after 1 January 1890. Officials feared that slaveowners would cast loose slave children and discourage childbearing.[74] All together, these limitations reflected the concern of officials that slavery was an integrated social system in which discipline and paternalism were inseparable, and that any tampering with it would risk social disruption.

The decree was enforced, above all, in the towns. Some 3,000 slaves on the coast of Kenya were freed between 1888 and 1895, although half of them had freed themselves by running away and were simply benefitting

72. Summary of Annual Report on the Slave Trade on the East Indies Station, incl. MacGregor to FO, 24 April 1893, FOCP 6454, p. 95. Officials at Malindi—which had once had the most voracious appetite for labor—thought the slave trade was "now stamped out" (J. Bell-Smith, Report on Malindi and Takaungu Districts, Dec. 1892. incl. I.B.E.A. Co. to FO, 18 March 1893, FO 2/57). There is also evidence of a pattern previously found before the caravan trade adjusted to the closing of coastal ports to slave exports: the redirection of slave-trading networks to dispose of slaves (although a reduced number of them) inland instead of sending them to coastal plantation areas. Hardinge, Report, PP 1898, LX, 199, p. 59.

73. The boldness of this step so overwhelmed Consul Euan-Smith that he urged that Arabs be given some "rest" for a considerable time. Officials of the I.B.E.A. Co. wanted to do even less. Euan-Smith to Salisbury, 14 Aug. 1890, FOCP 6105, pp. 150-51; Euan-Smith to de Winton, 2 Aug. 1890, ASP s22/65.

74. Proclamations of 9 and 20 Aug. 1890 by Ali bin Said, in PP 1890-91, LVII, 1099, p. 31. The original decree, dated 1 Aug. 1890, is in ibid., p. 3. On punishment, see Euan-Smith to de Winton, 4 Aug. 1890 (telegram), FOCP 6105, p. 140. On the decision to ignore the decree about slave children, see Euan-Smith to Salisbury, 9 Jan. 1890, FO 84/2059; FO to Euan-Smith, 23 Jan. 1890, telegram, FOCP 6039, p. 72. The decree was resurrected, without attention being called to it, in 1898. Hardinge to Craufurd and MacDougall, 17 Oct. 1898, FOCP 7159, p. 113.

by having their former owners paid off.[75] But the social system of the coast was being altered not so much by the antislavery measures themselves as by the overall transformation of the political economy of the coastal region. Slavery is not a thing, and it makes little sense to say "it" got better or worse, harsher or more benign.[76] Rather, it is necessary to examine the slow weakening of coercion and dependence through which slaveowners had controlled their slaves.

First, the Decree of 1890, plus growing British intervention in courts, compulsory registration of documents, and other means of regulating economic transactions dislocated the rationality of a system under which people could be property. When all exchanges of slaves were banned, the property value of slaves could no longer be realized; mortgages on the most valuable form of property could not be enforced; estates could not be liquidated.[77]

Second, the degree to which slaves could be coerced was undermined, jeopardizing the authority of the master within his plantation. Although punishment short of cruelty was still allowed, the slaveowner was no longer the final arbiter. Slaves, among whom an effective communications network seems to have flourished, made use of this check and brought complaints of brutality before officials.[78] Most important, the restraints on punishment reduced the slaveowners' principal deterrent to escape, while raids against the fugitive slave settlements became im-

---

75. Hardinge insisted that the decree was enforced "systematically" in the towns, but admitted that it did not do much outside of them. But on both islands and the mainland there was a steady trickle of slaves freed each year under its provisions: for example, 411 in Zanzibar in 1894, 533 in Kenya in 1897–98. Hardinge to Salisbury, 12 April 1896, PP 1896, LIX, 41, p. 91; Resumé of the operations of the I.B.E.A. Co. in repression of slavery, 1888–93, 28 March 1893, FO 2/57; P. L. McDermott, *British East Africa or IBEA* (London, 1895), pp. 407–08; Zanzibar, AR, 1894, p. 2; Hardinge, Report, 1897–98, PP 1899, LXIII, 269, pp. 23–24.

76. This problem mars the detailed account of the 1890s in Rodger Frederic Morton, "Slaves, Fugitives, and Freedmen on the Kenya Coast, 1873–1907" (Ph.D. diss., Syracuse University, 1976), pp. 341–88.

77. Hardinge to Salisbury, 12 April 1896, LIX, 41, p. 91; de Winton to Euan-Smith, 4 Oct. 1890, incl. Euan-Smith to Salisbury, 15 Oct. 1890, FO 84/2065; Balfour to Hardinge, 25 Aug. 1898, FOCP 7090, pp. 204–05; Hardinge, Report, 1897–98, PP 1899, LXIII, 269, p. 24. Even the perceived imminence of abolition made the value of slaves as capital unsure and could thus undermine the long-term stability of slavery. Jaime Reis, "The Impact of Abolitionism in Northeast Brazil: A Quantitative Approach," *Annals of the New York Academy of Sciences* 292 (1977): 119.

78. Rodd to Rosebery, 31 Dec. 1893, PP 1895, LXXI, 143, p. 16; Hardinge to Kimberley, 26 Feb. 1895, ibid., p. 31; MacLennan to Hardinge, 16 Aug. 1895, PP 1896, LIX, 395, p. 21. In the most notorious case of cruelty, one of Pemba's richest slaveowners was sentenced to seven years in jail, a fine of Rs 5,000, and subsequent deportation. Cave to Salisbury, 28 Feb. 1896, FOCP 6827, p. 295; *ASR* 16 (1896): 48–50.

possible. The 1890s elicited a plethora of runaways, above all on the mainland coast.[79]

The extent of the exodus from plantations put the Imperial British East Africa Company (I.B.E.A. Co.) in an awkward situation soon after it took over administration of the coastal strip in 1888. Afraid to alienate local slaveowners who threatened to storm those missions that harbored runaways and dependent on the production of the plantations for revenue, the Company was inclined to argue that it had to enforce the law as it stood. It was willing to countenance the use of force to return escaped slaves and prevent mission stations near Mombasa from sheltering runaways. That Englishmen should take such actions brought vehement protests from London, forcing the I.B.E.A. Co. to make involved arrangements to placate slaveowners without returning slaves.[80] After it took over in 1895, the Foreign Office solved the dilemma by doing nothing: it said slaveowners could sue their escaped slaves for loss of services but it would not force slaves to return. It also tried to use what later became a favorite tactic: threatening runaway slaves at the missions with prosecution for vagrancy unless they went to work or rented a plot of land.[81]

The "runaway problem" did not merely consist of hapless refugees, but of viable local communities, some attached to missions, some independent and dating at least to the 1870s. The I.B.E.A. Co. looked to these communities as a possible labor pool, but they in fact presaged

79. The files of correspondence between officials in coastal towns of Kenya and headquarters in Mombasa are filled with letters on runaways. See files CP 67/14, 67/15, 68/20, 75/46, and Hardinge to Salisbury, 17 Feb., 12 April 1896, PP 1896, LIX, 41, pp. 62–63; Piggott to Asst. DC, Rabai, 20 April 1896, CP 91/187; MacDougall to Craufurd, 1, 25 March 1897, CP 75/46; W. W. A. Fitzgerald, *Travels in the Coastlands of British East Africa and the Islands of Zanzibar and Pemba* (London, 1898), pp. 119, 121, 124. Because of its extensive hinterland, the mainland coast offered the best possibilities for escape, but slaves left Pemba in canoes seeking refuge on the mainland or asylum with British naval vessels. DO, Vanga, to Craufurd, 21 April 1897, and Tritton to Rogers, 30 Oct. 1897, CP 97/183; O'Sullivan, Report, 1896, PP 1896, LIX, 395, p. 41; C. S. Smith to Salisbury, 3 April 1891, FOCP 6127, p. 65. See also Cooper, *Plantation Slavery*, pp. 200–10, and Morton, pp. 183–229.

80. In the early days, the company lent its flag to Malindi slaveowners searching for runaways, G. MacKenzie to Euan-Smith, 18 Oct. 1888, FOCP 5770, p. 158; de Winton to Malindi Sheikhs, 28 Sept. 1890, FOCP 6805, pp. 174–75; Hardinge to Kemball, 26 Nov. 1896, ASP, s28/65. See also Morton, pp. 230–82, and Norman R. Bennett, "The Church Missionary Society in Mombasa, 1873–1894," in Jeffrey Butler, ed., *Boston University Papers in African History* (Boston, 1965), 1: 159–94.

81. Hardinge to Salisbury, 13 Nov. 1895, FOCP 6805, pp. 173–74; Salisbury to Hardinge, 26 Jan. 1897 (telegram), FOCP 6964, p. 148; W. H. Hamilton, Memorandum, 15 May 1905, FOCP 8932, p. 77F; Minute by Hardinge on Hollis to Craufurd, 31 Dec. 1897, FOCP 7024, pp. 122–23; Suggestions by Sir R. W. Webster, 6 Feb. 1899, FOCP 7400, p. 156.

quite a different kind of economic transformation.[82] Lugard, while serving the Company, tried to organize a scheme whereby the villagers
would work for the Company and earn money to buy freedom from
their owners. Leaders of the runaways went partway along with the
plans, but their followers did not do the required work.[83] The idea that
the I.B.E.A. Co. would redeem slaves—indeed the entire debate in England over fugitive slaves—was acquiring an air of unreality. Slaves
could leave without English blessings and with little fear of recapture.
Behind Malindi and Takaungu, runaway slave villages were cultivating
"marvelous" fields of grain and were becoming "well-to-do."[84] By 1903,
the villages as such began to decline, for the runaways no longer needed
the protection of a community but could move around and find a place
to farm.[85] The increasing ability to escape the labor discipline and social
subordination of the plantation was what mattered to the runaways, and
most were "quite indifferent as to whether they receive[d] their freedom
papers."[86]

In 1890, the coast had been seething with tension over the runaway
problem. Slavery was not quietly winding down; rather conflict was
mounting as the domination of the slaveowners was called into question.
By the early 1900s, the transformation had taken place to a significant

82. G. MacKenzie to Euan-Smith, 12 Feb. 1890, FOCP 6039, p. 174.

83. Lugard's self-righteousness in the cause of abolition did not give him any sympathy
for slaves who had liberated themselves. He held back earlier plans of the I.B.E.A. Co. to
recognize certain runaway communities in order to develop his plan to have the runaways
work for their freedom for the Company: "Those willing to work out their freedom will be
worthy of it." Margery Perham, ed., *The Diaries of Lord Lugard* (London, 1959), entry for 29
Dec. 1889, vol. 1, pp. 56–57. See also I.B.E.A. Co. to Lugard, 21 Aug. 1892, LP, vol. 42,
and the summary of this project in Morton, pp. 220–26.

84. Lugard. *Diaries*, entry for 16 Jan. 1890, vol. 1, p. 71; Fitzgerald, pp. 119, 121, 124;
Collector, Malindi, to Tritton, 22 Aug. 1899, CP 74/43; Report by Mr. A. Whyte on His
Recent Travels along the Sea-Coast Belt of the British East Africa Protectorate, PP 1903,
XLV, 759 p. 8. The worst restriction on the villagers was that they might be retaken if they
traveled to coastal towns. But Lugard reports the case of a runaway from the village of
Fulladoyo who had the mischance of running into his owner on a visit to Mombasa. When a
kind-hearted official of the I.B.E.A. Co. offered to redeem the slave for $25, the runaway
"remarked to his master that he had better take it as he must assuredly run away again,
since his possessions were all at Fulladoyo." *Diaries*, entry for 30 Jan. 1890, vol. 1, p. 89.

85. Monson, PP 1903, XLV, 745, p. 4. The resident official at Malindi noted that
runaways were not interfered with after the Mazrui rebellion, while some of them took so
much palm wine from trees owned by Mazrui who had once raided their villages that the
trees became worthless. MacDougall to Piggott, 8 Jan. 1896, CP 75/46; MacDougall, Notes
on the History of the Wanyika, 31 March 1914, PRB, Kilifi, KFI/11.

86. EAP, AR, 1903–04, p. 28. Similarly, slaves in parts of French West Africa left their
owners without waiting for the French to act, Roberts and Klein, "The Banamba Slave
Exodus of 1905."

extent, and the line between a slave's escaping and simply farming had become blurred. The slaves had moved faster than the law.

A third dimension of the changes in the 1890s was the weakening of the political and social dimension of slavery. The complexities of this process are most clearly revealed in the so-called Mazrui rebellion of 1895–96, which was in fact a battle between two factions of this Omani communal group of the Kenyan coast, one backed by the Sultan of Zanzibar and the British, the other led by Mbaruk bin Rashid, long an independent power on the coast. Mbaruk's followers included a subgroup of the Mazrui, Mijikenda converts to Islam, slaves who had run away from other planters, freed slaves, slaves Mbaruk had bought, and others. The reactions of slaves—Mbaruk's and his rivals'—were varied. Many fought alongside their masters, and some of Mbaruk's war leaders were of slave origin, while a number of Mbaruk's slaves followed him into exile after his defeat. Some runaways joined Mbaruk; others were coerced into doing so; and still others were pressured into opposing him. Many slaves, throughout a wide area, were caught up in the disruption. A large number drifted away after the fighting, but some of them drifted back.

There is an underlying consistency behind the varied responses of slaves: their loyalty had never been blind and their willingness to fill the role of personal follower reflected the actual ability of the master to provide protection, livelihood, and membership in a community. As Anglo-Zanzibari power finally wore Mbaruk down, the basis of his slaves' loyalty was undermined. Mbaruk was no longer an adequate protector, nor were the other slaveowners from Mombasa to Malindi who had failed to insulate their slaves from the raids and battles.[87] But the defeat of Mbaruk—the last of the independent magnates who had often troubled the coast—had a further implication: slaveowners had not only been poor protectors, they were no longer necessary. The individual who walked to Mombasa or set up a farm in an abandoned area had less to fear from his isolation.[88] The image of an ordered plantation life with which some British officials were comfortable had depended on the cli-

---

87. There is a wealth of evidence on the responses of slaves and runaways in Correspondence respecting the Recent Rebellion in British East Africa, PP 1896, LIX, 41. The breakdown of protection also emerges in MacDougall to Piggott, 17 Oct. 1895, ibid., pp. 41–42; same to same, 3 Feb. 1896, CP 75/46; CMS Mission Book, 21 Oct. 1895, KNA, CMS/1/624. See also Morton, pp. 341–88, and Peter Koffsky, "History of Takaungu, East Africa, 1830–1896" (Ph.D. diss., University of Wisconsin, 1977). An even longer period of disorder weakened plantation owners and production in the hinterland of Lamu. Marguerite Ylvisaker, *Lamu in the Nineteenth Century: Land, Trade, and Politics* (Boston, 1979).

88. The importance of the colonial peace to an ex-slave in Zanzibar is emphasized in "The Story of Rashid bin Hassani of the Bisa Tribe, Northern Rhodesia," recorded by W. F. Baldock, in Margery Perham, ed., *Ten Africans* (London, 1963), p. 118.

mate of fear surrounding it. The steps taken against the outside disorder had shaken the order within.

If dependence was weakened so too was reciprocity. Assimilation and upward mobility for slaves were less practicable as rewards for accommodation, since replacements for the slaves so rewarded could no longer be obtained. But so important were manumission and mobility to the structures of dependency that voluntary manumissions under Islamic law continued even after slaveowners were given the possibility of receiving compensation under British law. Slaveowners could try to maintain the gradations of a hierarchical society and the idea of their own benevolence, but such values could no longer be part of a self-perpetuating system.[89]

Finally, slaves acquired a few more alternatives to their economic dependence on landowners. The expansion of imperial activity increased the demand for caravan porters, and Zanzibar was the center of recruitment. Supposedly, slave-porters owed half their pay to their owners. In reality, masters had little control over what their slaves did, and in the 1890s were complaining that slaves left on caravans without permission and failed to turn over the required money. Officials even feared that slaves might leave Zanzibar altogether and settle along the caravan routes in the interior.[90] Mombasa was also a staging area for caravans to Uganda, while the early railroad surveys in Kenya—and after 1896 railroad construction itself—created new demands for workers. There was a "great exodus" of slaves from coastal towns as far away as Lamu to Mombasa and the railroad camps. Railroad wages were above the going rate for hired labor on the coast, and although the work was menial and often dangerous, a slave who deserted his master in the late 1890s could survive.[91]

It would still be a distortion to see this process as a transformation of laborers who had been tied to an individual into a labor pool freely cir-

89. There is also evidence of the ideological crumbling of the system, as well as the loss of economic viability, in the panic selling of slaves to Arabia. O'Sullivan, Report on Pemba, 1896–97, FOCP 7032, p. 114. On the significance of manumission and its continuation beyond abolition, see Cooper, *Plantation Slavery*, pp. 242–52.

90. Cave to Lansdowne, 15 April 1901, FO 2/454; Hardinge to Salisbury, 29 Jan. 1896, PP 1896, LIX, 395, p. 32.

91. Constant complaints of labor shortages in Mombasa suggest that these options were quite real. Binns to Lang, 10 Nov. 1890, CMS G3/A5/o/1890/304; Frederick Jackson, *Early Days in East Africa* (London, 1930), p. 354; Craufurd to Weaver, 24 July 1896, CP 86/118; Hardinge, Report, 1896–97, PP 1898, LX, 199, p. 6; Hardinge to Salisbury, 20 April 1898, FO 107/92; Rogers to Hardinge, 3 Feb. 1898, CP 69/22; Hardinge to Binns, 9 Feb. 1899, PP 1899, LXIII, 303, p. 25; Monson, PP 1903, XLV, 745, p. 4; Steward to Lansdowne, 9 Jan. 1905, FO 2/914. See also Karim K. Janmohamed, "African Labourers in Mombasa, c. 1895–1940," in B. A. Ogot, ed., *Hadith 5*, pp. 155–60, and chapter 5, below.

culating among a new class of employers. Under the slave system, the practice of hiring out slaves, common in Zanzibar town and Mombasa, had provided flexibility. In the colonial era, neither the Administration nor private employers put much faith in labor pools; a tighter structure of control was needed. Many African workers were also reluctant to throw themselves into a labor pool: they sought to transform or develop economic and social relationships that could provide security, cash income, and choice, structures that combined casual labor with long-term tenancy. But even the option of urban and caravan labor altered the nature of rural work, providing slaves with more effective means of resisting punishment, humiliation, and grueling work routines. Dependence and security slowly came to mean something much more positive than they had when slaveowners had more power.

The above is a schematic view of a complex and varied process taking place over seven years in Zanzibar and nearly twenty on the coast of Kenya. By focusing on the bases of slaveholders' hegemony and the way they were undermined, it is possible to understand the diversity of the process. Malindi had been the epitome of the regimented labor system of the nineteenth century; it became the epitome of the plantation system's decline. While slaves continued to produce grain, evidence points to the decline of "cruel" punishments, to many instances of slaves refusing to work and helping themselves to coconuts, to the ability of slaves to cultivate land for their own benefit, and to the inability of slaveowners to replace slaves whose labor they had lost.[92]

The islands posed a slightly different problem. Because they were smaller, more fully cultivated, and less politically volatile, the colonial peace made less of a difference and economic options for slaves were more narrow. But Pemba—like Malindi a purely agricultural region—experienced some of the conflict between slaveowner and slave that characterized the uncertain period before abolition in Brazil and the West Indies.[93] British administration was remote, but the shortage of slaves, increasing the planters' need for intense labor and decreasing their ability to get it, appears to have led to a period of confrontation as

92. "Bishop Peel in East Africa: Visit to Jilore and Malindi," *Church Mission Intelligencer,* n.s. 26 (1901): 32; MacDougall, Memorandum, 26 May 1905, FOCP 8932, pp. 77H-I; Monson, PP 1903, XLV, 745, pp. 1-4; Piggott to Anti-Slavery Society, 29 Aug. 1895, *ASR* 15 (1895): 186. Much of the data on the period after abolition (chapter 5) suggests that the drifting off of slaves did not begin suddenly in 1907. For example, some slaves testitied that they had set up their own village near Malindi long before; a slaveowner at Mombasa noted that he once had nine to ten slaves but only had three in 1907. A/c 111D of 1914 and 42N of 1918 (Nine Tribes Case).

93. Green, *British Slave Emancipation,* pp. 113-15; Robert Conrad, *The Destruction of Brazilian Slavery, 1850-1888* (Berkeley, 1972), pp. 184-90; Mary Reckord, "The Jamaica Slave Rebellion of 1831," *Past and Present* 40 (1968): 108-25.

slaveowners and slaves sought to bend and redefine their relationship. On the eve of abolition, the Administration feared it was not in control: "cruel" slaveowners and "savage" slaves faced each other, and the long-term stability that Arab planters had once sought seemed to have broken down. Slaves fled to British cruisers or to the mainland. Instances of brutal punishment were exposed. But at the same time, slaves often successfully refused to work; routine cultivation declined; and slaveowners had to provide higher monetary inducements to laborers during the harvest.[94] The problems of the 1890s point to the conflict that underlay an unstable balance of power.

Urban slaves had long lived and worked with the most independence, and the shortage of porters and port workers in the 1890s meant that the owners' control over how much a slave worked and how much of the wages were turned over to them diminished.[95] Officials in Zanzibar thought that rural slaves preferred to live near the city so that they could have access to the Government if they were mistreated, but proximity probably conferred the more important benefit of movement into a fluid urban society, involving slaves, freed slaves, and migrants from throughout the Western Indian Ocean region. Casual labor in the port, in Indian and European households, and in commercial enterprises provided income and flexibility. The quarter of town where this diverse population congregated provided shelter and a set of networks for activities that the Government came to define as crime: small-scale slave trading, for example, took place within this milieu, carried on by slaves, freed slaves, and a wide range of other inhabitants.[96]

Mombasa also attracted slaves from all along the coast. Real estate registers beginning in 1891 point to significant levels of economic activity—from house buying to ivory trading—among slaves and ex-slaves. Lists of

94. O'Sullivan, Report, 1896, PP 1896, LIX, 395, pp. 41, 45-46; Hardinge to Salisbury, 23 April 1898, PP 1898, LX, 559, p. 72; Capt. MacGill, "Further Report on the Detention of a Canoe and 5 Slaves by H.M.S. *Phoebe* on 14 April 1895," FO 107/46; DO, Vanga, to Craufurd, 21 April 1897, and Tritton to Rogers, 30 Oct. 1897, CP 97/183. In the early years after abolition, officials in Pemba observed that slaves had drifted off over a long period. Farler to Mathews, 13 March 1899, PP 1899, LXIII, 303, p. 48. Similarly, increased demand for slave-produced crops induced Lozi slaveowners to push their slaves harder in the 1890s, but the demand for migrant labor in mines, towns, and railways gave slaves a means of resistance. W. G. Clarence-Smith, "Slaves, Commoners and Landlords in Bulozi, c. 1875 to 1906," *JAH* 20 (1979): 231-33.

95. Many slaves did not pay their owner at all but retained whatever wages they earned. Hinde, Minute, 19 Oct. 1906, CP 94/166.

96. Rodd to Rosebery, 31 Dec. 1893, PP 1895, LXXI, 143, p. 17; Last, Report, 1898, PP 1898, LX, 559, p. 47. On the nature of social and economic relationships in Malindi Quarter of Zanzibar town, see Glassman. For the involvement of slaves with peoples of various origins in slave dealing, see the list of 174 such cases in *Documents relatifs à la repression de la traite des esclaves* (Brussels, 1897), pp. 220-50.

rentals indicate that slaves were able to live independently in certain quarters of the city—notably "New Town"—again in conjunction with a great variety of people without deep roots in the Swahili society of "Old Town."[97] The Administration's fear of the "floating population" of Mombasa suggests that a fluid urban society was emerging in Mombasa similar to that of Zanzibar, not to mention the dangerous habitats of the "residuum" of East London.[98]

New alternatives and the breakdown of old forms of dependence did not constitute a revolution in economic and social power. Above all, the new situation gave slaves an increasing ability to leave plantations, while it subtly altered relations of slaves with their *own* masters. But it did not redefine slaves' status within their community, and it did not allow slaves to bargain readily with different landowners. To do so would have involved the landlords in a violation of the laws and norms on which their status as slaveholders were based. It was in this regard that the abolition of the legal status of slavery had considerable impact. The acceptance of compensation by slaveowners made socially legitimate what declining control over labor was making economically necessary: that planters, using the land which was their one remaining asset, compete for labor on whatever terms they could offer. The symbolic importance of compensation helps to account for the fact that folk-memories on the Kenyan coast telescope the vast changes of the nearly twenty years before 1907 into the result of what people call "iwatha," the payment of compensation. In a sense, formal abolition freed the slaveowners; the slaves had been slowly freeing themselves for quite some time.

Planters' control over labor weakened at differing paces and in differing ways, but weaken it did. This is not the same as saying that the planters, as a group, lost their political, economic, and social position, and this distinction partly explains why the planters, who were losing so much, resisted the imperial takeover and the undermining of their labor so little.[99]

The Zanzibari state that was taken over in 1890 was less an effective institution than a nodal point in a widespread network of commercial relationships. The Sultan's power base consisted of his own personal de-

97. Cooper, *Plantation Slavery*, pp. 229–30. On the emergence of different social networks and distinct cultural patterns in the new neighborhoods of Mombasa, see Margaret Strobel, *Muslim Women in Mombasa, 1890–1975* (New Haven, 1979).

98. Hardinge to Salisbury, 16 Jan. 1898, FOCP 7024, p. 122; Stedman Jones, *Outcast London*.

99. The evolving relationships described below were not part of the history of Germany's involvement on the coast of Tanganyika, and this difference may be related to the serious rebellion which Germany faced in 1888. Fritz Ferdinand Müller, *Deutschland-Zanzibar-Ostafrika: Geschichte einer deutschen Kolonialeroberung, 1884–1890* (Berlin, 1959).

pendents and slaves, leadership of the Al-Busaidi communal group (which itself divided over succession disputes), uneasy ties with certain factions of Omanis, and pragmatic relationships with people of diverse origins—from Swahili to Indians—who benefitted from the security and commercial opportunities which the Sultan's control of the entrepôt of Zanzibar provided.

British involvement with the state structure goes back to the aftermath of the death of the Sultan who had built up Zanzibar, Seyyid Said, in 1856. British assistance had forestalled the rebellious intentions of two brothers of the new Sultan and had helped overcome challenges from rival Omani groups in Zanzibar and the depredations of traders and privateers from the Persian Gulf. Such outside support changed the character of the state and explains the often contradictory position the Sultan took on the slave trade from the 1860s onward. His power base depended on his own slaves and his relationship with other slaveowners, but British assistance was now vital to maintain his partial autonomy from those very subjects.[100] While the British used the Sultan, he also used them, above all to strengthen himself against Omani and Swahili opposition. To a large extent, the antislave trade patrols winked at the activities of the royal family while they damaged—not altogether by coincidence—the economic base of his rivals. The antislave trade campaign was no simple opposition of "British" to "Arabs," but a more complex, pragmatic, and shifting pattern of alliances. Even before Zanzibar became a protectorate, its army was trained and commanded by an Englishman.[101]

The state's dependence on an external ally to insure partial independence from coastal society affected the mainland coast as well. Coastal towns like Mombasa, Malindi, and Lamu were administered by officials, Liwalis, appointed by the Sultan, mostly from among his Al-Busaidi communal group. The exceptional wealth that these men—above all Salim bin Khalfan of Malindi and later Mombasa—acquired, owed much to the advantages of political and commercial connections in Zanzibar, but their riches ultimately depended on the same means of production as those of other planters: slaves. By the 1880s, the Liwalis were playing the same game as the Sultan, profiting from their slaves while supporting the Anglo-Zanzibari attack on the slave trade. These men were

100. Cooper, *Plantation Slavery*, pp. 115–20; Coupland, *Exploitation of East Africa 1856–1890*, pp. 14–37, 62–101, 152–70; Abdul Mohamed Hussein Sheriff, "The Rise of a Commercial Empire: An Aspect of the Economic History of Zanzibar, 1770–1873" (Ph.D. diss., University of London, 1971); Norman R. Bennett, *A History of the Arab State of Zanzibar* (London, 1978).

101. For an analysis of the political uses of the antislave trade treaties, see Glassman. See also Coupland, pp. 237–70.

neither pro-slave trade nor anti-slave trade; they were skillfully balancing their twin sources of power.[102]

The advent of colonial rule was thus not a European conquest of an Arab state. The people whom the new regime fought were the old enemies of the Zanzibari Sultanate, such as Mbaruk bin Rashid Al-Mazrui. The British once again settled a succession dispute in Zanzibar, linking their own interests to those of a faction of the dynasty.[103] But gradually one pillar of the Sultan's power base, and that of his supporters and officials, was eroded, while the other became more essential. Even so, the state did not wholly subordinate these men, for economically it was dependent on duties on the cloves and grain that their slaves grew.[104]

The origins of the colonial state thus lay in an alliance with a particular segment of the old elite that slowly and subtly changed its nature. As later sections of this book will make clear, the links between the state and planters were subsequently generalized beyond this small circle to embrace the leading landowners as a whole. The state's role in organizing labor in Zanzibar and enforcing land titles in Kenya—both of which involved personal contacts between officials and planters—slowly created a new kind of dependence. From a weak Sultanate amid strong planters, the state became a strong force amid weakening planters. This process, beginning in 1856, took place in slow stages—and it is far from obvious that the British themselves envisioned it as a grand strategy with clear objectives—so that the Arab and Swahili leaders who had the most to lose were already intertwined with the Anglo-Zanzibari Sultanate by the time that planters as a whole began to lose the basis of their economic power. A new relationship between the state and the planters emerged without uniting the elites of the islands or the mainland coast in a fight for survival.[105]

The effects of these changes on agriculture were not quite what they

102. On the relationship of the Liwalis to the British, see Morton, pp. 118–20, and on Salim bin Khalfan as a planter, see Cooper, *Plantation Slavery*, pp. 90–91.

103. "The Sultan does recognize his dependent position," noted an official. H. W. de Sausmarez to FO, 23 Dec. 1895, CAB 37/40/66. For general histories of this period, see Salim, *Swahili-Speaking Peoples of Kenya's Coast,* and L. W. Hollingsworth, *Zanzibar under the Foreign Office, 1890–1913* (London, 1953).

104. Marie de Kiewiet, "History of the Imperial British East Africa Company, 1876–1895" (Ph.D. diss., University of London, 1955); John S. Galbraith, *Mackinnon and East Africa 1878–1895: A Study in the "New Imperialism"* (Cambridge, 1972).

105. Conflict over who should benefit from the labor of slaves was an important cause of the resistance of Baule to the French in the Ivory Coast. Weiskel, "Labor on the Emergent Periphery," pp. 214–15. Genovese argues that whether abolition threatened the survival of a class rather than one component of class power was crucial in determining the nature of resistance to emancipation (*The World the Slaveholders Made*).

seemed to worried British officials at the time. On both the islands and the mainland, many officials claimed that the population of slaves was declining, that land was reverting to bush, and that crops were going unharvested.[106] Yet in 1895 Zanzibar and Pemba recorded the largest harvest in the history of the clove tree—537,460 frasilas. In 1901, Commissioner Eliot described Malindi in almost the same terms that had been used in the 1870s: the "granary of the Protectorate." Amid reports of idle slaves come simultaneous reports of "splendid crops" and "very fruitful" grain harvests.[107]

The plantation structure was being shaken more than the production of crops. On Zanzibar and Pemba, routine weeding and cultivation on clove estates—done exclusively by resident slaves—was suffering, but for the few months of the harvest, labor was mobilized on new terms. In 1896, free workers in Pemba were picking cloves and receiving between a third and half of the crop. Such incentives had been given slaves before, but they were much smaller and limited to the additional days slaves worked beyond their customary five.[108] Free labor was still scarce, but it could be found. The problem was that it was expensive and undisciplined: slaveowners believed their own slaves were more reliable.[109] A substantial portion of the surplus generated by labor was being shifted to the laborers.

In Malindi, a District Officer followed his ritualistic railing against the laziness of slaves by complaining of their "independent attitude." Because of it, labor was short, although the district as a whole had brought in a good crop and agriculture was in "a satisfactory condition."[110]

Grain, unlike cloves, requires continuous labor. Available customs statistics indicate that around 1897 the coast as a whole was exporting

106. Gerald Portal to Chappel, n.d. [1892], Portal Papers, Rhodes House, s108, no. 17; O'Sullivan, Report, 1896, and Hardinge to Salisbury, 10 Jan. 1896, PP 1896, LIX, 395, pp. 23, 41; Henry S. Newman, "Narrative of Visit to East Africa, 1897." FA, MS vol. 204, p. 51; Monson, Report, PP 1903, XLV, 745, p. 3.

107. Fitzgerald, p. 560; EAP, AR, 1900–01, FOCP 7867, p. 12; *Gazette for Zanzibar and East Africa*, no. 16, 18 May 1892; Weaver to Craufurd, 25 July 1896, CP 75/46; MacDougall, Quarterly Report on Malindi District, 8 April 1901, incl. Eliot to Lansdowne, 5 May 1901, FOCP 7823, p. 168; Whyte, Report, PP 1903, XLV, 759, pp. 3–7.

108. O'Sullivan, PP 1896, LIX, 395, pp. 45–46. O'Sullivan does not make it clear whether slaves got these high payments in kind as well. Fitzgerald claims that free labor was used to only a limited extent in 1891 (p. 524). See also Cooper, *Plantation Slavery*, pp. 133–34, 156–61.

109. Fitzgerald, pp. 549–59.

110. Murray to Sub-Commissioner, 9 Jan. 1902, CP 71/25. A similar contradiction of prejudices against slaves and observations about agriculture occurs in Monson, PP 1903, XLV, 745, p. 5.

TABLE 2:1

EXPORTS FROM KENYA, 1895–1906 (IN RUPEES)

	Grain	Copra	Rubber (wild)
1895–96	242,000	—	146,000
1896–97	271,000	—	194,000
1897–98	286,000	—	131,000
1898–99	80,000	—	192,000
1899–1900	145,160	—	261,000
1900–01	—	—	—
1901–02	336,000	81,000	77,000
1902–03	293,000	229,000	117,000
1903–04	309,000	166,000	162,000
1904–05	307,000	141,000	324,000
1905–06	406,000	141,000	284,000

SOURCES: EAP, AR, 1899–1900, p. 8, 1905–06, p. 16.

NOTE: Although these figures are for the Eastern African Protectorate as a whole, these products were basically coastal, at least—with grain—until railroad subsidies were introduced at a later date.

about a third of the grain, by value, that Malindi alone exported in 1887. This decline may reflect disorganization of markets and incompetent collection of duties, as well as wishful thinking in the 1887 estimates; but it may also reflect the fact that the success of Malindi's grain plantations came from the tight control and continual inputs of slave labor.[111]

The export figures from Kenya, shown in Table 2.1, suggest more than the breakdown of grain as a plantation crop. The bad years of 1898–99 and 1899–1900 resulted from a drought that hit the area immediately behind the coast, and the precipitous decline in exports probably stemmed from the diversion of grain to regional consumption, as the coastal plain became more intimately tied to its hinterland than be-

111. Between 1887 and 1891–92, export duties collected at Malindi dropped precipitously, from over Rs 90,000 to Rs 13,000, but that may partly reflect poor collection. Thereafter, export duties do not indicate a steady decline but fluctuate. Mambrui's contribution to export duties did decline by half between 1891–92 and 1903–04. Officials stress that the coastal economy revived after the Mazrui rebellion. Weaver to Craufurd, 24 July 1896, CP 75/46. For statistics on the 1890s, see table 2.1 and Hardinge, Report, PP 1898, LX, 199, pp. 9, 11–12; EAP, AR, 1903–04, pp. 33–34. For the 1887 estimates, see Fredric Holmwood "Estimate of present Customs duty upon the trade of His Highness the Sultan's dominions between Wanga to Kipini inclusive," William Mackinnon Papers, Africa, I.B.E.A., no. 943, School of Oriental and African Studies, London. See also Cooper, Plantation Slavery, pp. 80–113.

fore.[112] The increase in rubber exports—and this was wild rubber from the coast—reflects the efforts of people to obtain a marketable product which they could exchange for food. That rubber exports fell after the famine and then rose again may suggest a modest redirection of activity toward an exportable product that could be gathered rather than grown, and hence did not require continual disciplined labor.[113] But grain exports revived strongly after the drought. The progressive decline of labor control evident in the period 1890–1907 was not paralleled by a corresponding decline in agricultural output. Grain production itself may well have been in the process of being restructured.

But exports are not the only, or the best, measure of an economy's health. Indeed, Eliot noted in 1901 the "singular paradox that it is better for the Protectorate revenues that the natives should be in distressed circumstances than that they should be prosperous, because when they are distressed they are obliged to work and live on imported dutiable articles, whereas when they are prosperous they pay no taxes."[114] Too much of the negative evidence on coastal agriculture refers to plantations and to exports, while too many observers saw bountiful crops to accept a picture of agricultural decline. The crux of Eliot's worries was that, as one of his officials put it, "all the coast peasantry, however, are well-fed and well-to-do," living off their crops supplemented by fish.[115] Coastal people may not have been prosperous, but they were getting by, and their neighbors, the Mijikenda, were at this time selling surplus grain from their hinterland farms and beginning to move onto more fertile coastal lands that the landlords were no longer able to utilize themselves. The area behind and north of Malindi, above all, was being increasingly used by "industrious and intelligent" Giriama, the northernmost Mijikenda subgroup. The Indian grain-dealers of Malindi were adapting to this new organization of production, collecting and bringing

112. In the previous devastating famine in the hinterland in 1884, many children were pawned to coastal slaveowners, but this time Mijikenda came to the coast to obtain food through work, credit, charity, and helping themselves to land. The famine nevertheless caused many deaths. Weaver to Craufurd, 18, 22 July 1898, CP 75/46; Rogers to Craufurd, 22 July 1899, CP 69/22; Craufurd to Salisbury, 12 June 1899, FO 2/197.

113. Free people as well as slaves gathered wild rubber, and an extensive network of Arab, Swahili, and Indian rubber traders developed. Rogers to Craufurd, 17 Aug. 1896, CP 68/20; Weaver to Craufurd, 24 July 1896, CP 75/46.

114. EAP, AR, 1900–01, p. 12. On the revival in 1901, see also Marsden to Eliot, 24 Dec. 1901, FOCP 7946, p. 126, and MacDougall to Tritton, 14 Jan. 1901, CP 71/25.

115. Whyte, PP 1903, XLV, 759, p. 4. Much of the picture of declining plantations is based on one estate, Magarini, which the I.B.E.A. Co. had taken over from its owner: masterless plantations are prone to undercultivation. Some reports mention that other, smaller plantations were doing better. Ibid., pp. 6–7; Eliot, Report on Native Tribes of East Africa, incl. Eliot to Lansdowne, 9 April 1902, FO 2/570.

to town the many small loads of grain and selling cloth, sugar, and beads. As early as 1902, Giriama organized a grain hold-up to drive up prices.[116] Palm wine from coastal coconut trees was being sent to Mombasa for cash or to Mijikenda in the hinterland for grain or fowls.[117] All this was occurring at a time when the Government—in Zanzibar and the mainland—was doing virtually nothing to promote communications and marketing on the coast or to aid agriculture itself.[118]

The decline of the mainland's grain exports may thus have been a sign of economic improvement for the bulk of the coast's people, a redistribution of produce and a flexibility in economic activities that the plantation system had suppressed. The continuity in clove exports from Zanzibar suggests that clove cultivation may have been more compatible with the increasing autonomy of cultivators than was the plantation production of grain, and that capital in trees gave planters a basis for continued control over production, even if they had to share more of the surplus with their laborers. Slaves and immigrant Africans, although they did not own land, were taking advantage of a changing situation to transform the balance among a set of economic activities: production for their own use, for regional exchange, and for export, as well as labor for others. But the colonial state in both Kenya and Zanzibar was to act on the basis of Eliot's paradox. The people who had suffered under slavery had to struggle against new forms of labor control and new restraints on their opportunities to farm that went under the name of freedom.

Persistence and Evolution in Antislavery Ideology: Forced Labor under the British Flag

The idea of freedom in antislavery ideology embodied a very particular—and narrow—concept of economic and social morality. The

116. MacDougall to Tritton, 14 Jan., 8 April 1901 CP 71/25; "Description of the Province, 1899–1900," CP 98/191; Monson, PP 1903, XLV, 745, p. 7; Whyte, PP 1903, XLV, 759, p. 7; Hardinge, Report, PP 1898, LX, 199, p. 3. On the holdup, see Murray to Gilkison, 27 Oct. 1902, CP 71/25.

117. Hardinge, PP 1898, LX, 199, p. 67; Lugard, *Diaries*, entry for 30 Dec. 1889, vol. 1, p. 57; Rabai Dist., QR, 1st quarter, 1902, FOCP 7954, p. 52; Whyte, PP 1903, XLV, 759, pp. 10–11. This trade was building on earlier patterns of exchange. See Spear, *The Kaya Complex.*

118. The British Consul admitted that "not a rupee of the Government money is spent outside the limits of the town of Zanzibar" except for a few low-paid officials. Pemba's agricultural development was frustrated by prohibitions against exporting directly to Mombasa and Tanga, which would have eased transport but reduced Government control. Nothing was done, officials admitted, to assist maize marketing on the Kenyan coast. Portal to Rosebery, 2 Oct. 1892, FO 84/2233; Armitage to Anti-Slavery Society, 31 July, 18 Nov. 1901, *ASR* 21 (1901): 137, *ASR* 22 (1902): 19; EAP, AR, 1903, PP 1907, XL, 697, p. 15.

humanitarian lobby remained both steadfast and strait in its assessment of the rights and wrongs of labor systems as it continued to argue with colonial officials in Kenya and Zanzibar in the first decades of the twentieth century. But the controversy over forced labor that erupted in East Africa in the 1920s offers the best illustration of the continuing importance not only of the image of slavery, but of the basic tenets of antislavery ideology and their relationship to changing economic interests. And the controversies of the 1920s hint at the ideological connections between antislavery and the beginnings of a new and still flourishing humanitarian ideal—economic development.

Antislavery circles had, in the aftermath of abolition, kept a vigilant lookout for Government policies that were "slavery by another name."[119] Then a crisis over forced labor erupted in 1919, provoked by the order of the Government of Kenya for official "encouragement" of African labor for settler farms. All concerned knew quite well that "encouragement" was a euphemism for coercion, pressure brought to bear by District Officers and African headmen. The labor circular came after heavy-handed wartime labor recruitment for both the military and the settlers had caused considerable suffering and mortality, and it was part of a far-reaching campaign to step up and regularize the recruitment of a labor force in Kenya. At the same time, officials in Zanzibar assumed new powers to compel labor for public purposes and pressure people into picking cloves.[120]

The campaign against forced labor involved missionaries, Christian organizations in England, the still-surviving Anti-Slavery Society, and a maverick ex-Kenya hand, Dr. Norman Leys. In almost all their broadsides the image of slavery abounded. Compulsory labor for private gain was slave labor, and its resurrection under the British flag was a terrible evil. The remedy was the same as that advocated by the Quaker missionaries of Pemba: a totally free labor market.[121]

The criticism of the missionaries in Kenya—the "Bishops' Memorandum"—was the most cautious, containing the usual Victorian pieties about the virtues of work and admitting that some forms of compulsion, for public benefit only, might be needed to instill in Africans the

119. See the *ASR* throughout the four or five years after abolition in Zanzibar.

120. Kenya, Labour Circular no. 1, 23 Oct. 1919, PP 1920, XXXIII. 81, pp. 6–7. For the context of this controversy, see Anthony Clayton and Donald Savage, *Government and Labour in Kenya, 1895–1963* (London, 1974).

121. John H. Harris, "Back to Slavery?" *Contemporary Review* 120 (1921): 190–97; John H. Harris, *Africa: Slave or Free?* (London, 1919); Frank Weston, *The Serfs of Great Britain* (London, 1920); letter of Anti-Slavery Society to CO, in *ASR*, ser. 5, 10 (1920): 52.

proper attitudes for a work force.[122] The influential J. H. Oldham—seeing himself as a Christian conscience of empire—invoked the memory of Wilberforce, criticized the harsher sides of colonial profiteering, but looked to empire to bring the higher side of Christian civilization to Africa and did not question an economy in which Africans served as laborers to a "vigorous and enterprising European community." The Anti-Slavery Society's memorials also stuck narrowly to the issue of the use of official coercion for private profit.[123]

But in labelling as slavery—and hence archaic and un-British—the policy of "encouragement," the Christian critics were making the underlying structure of the settler economy appear all the more British and moral. The encouragement issue was easily papered over by better-phrased memoranda. As the crisis passed, more and more Kenyans were going to work.[124]

Leys invoked the memory of the abolition of the slave trade and compared the Kenyan system of labor recruitment to slavery. He resurrected the old argument that free labor worked better than slave.[125] His solution was to remove Government agents from recruitment and thus make "labour entirely and universally free."[126]

---

122. The memorandum is in PP 1920, XXXIII, 81, pp. 8-10. See Robert L. Tignor, *The Colonial Transformation of Kenya: The Kamba, Kikuyu, and Maasai from 1900 to 1939* (Princeton, 1976), pp. 167-69, for a perceptive discussion of the limitations of humanitarian opinion on this subject.

123. Joseph H. Oldham, *Christianity and the Race Problem* (London, 1925), p. 101; Anti-Slavery Society to CO, in *ASR*, ser. 5, 10 (1920): 52-55.

124. When the Colonial Secretary, Lord Milner, replied to charges in the House of Lords by insisting that he was trying to steer "a middle course between allowing the natives to live in idleness and vice and using improper means to get them to work," his critics had little to say, for they shared his assumptions. The appropriate despatches from the Colonial Office undid the damages of the 1919 circular without changing labor recruitment, and the Anti-Slavery Society was able to congratulate itself on its "useful work." House of Lords debate, 14 July 1920, in *ASR*, ser 5, 10 (1920): 73; Annual Meeting of the Anti-Slavery Society, 27 April 1921, *ASR* 11 (1921): 54-55; Tignor, p. 181. See the cautious modification of the original circular in PP 1921, XXIV, 433, pp. 3-4.

125. Leys added a new twist to this argument, asserting that when a man worked involuntarily, the money he earned bore no relation to his needs and the income had little more effect than inflating the price of cattle or brideprice in the Reserves. Only if labor were free to respond to its wants would employment and consumption have an economically rational relationship to one another. (Norman Leys to CO, 7 Feb. 1918, in John W. Cell, ed., *By Kenya Possessed: The Correspondence of Norman Leys and J. H. Oldham 1918-1926* [Chicago, 1976], pp. 92-97; Norman Leys, *Kenya*, 4th ed. [London, 1973; 1st ed., 1924], pp. 310-11). For a revealing analysis of the difference between the views of Leys and Oldham, see Cell's introduction to their correspondence.

126. Leys, 7 Feb. 1918, in Cell, p. 92.

Leys took a step beyond the laissez-faire of the abolitionists toward a kind of welfare capitalism in keeping with trends in Great Britain.[127] He saw more clearly than any other observer the irreversible and devastating effects on African social life that land grabbing and pressure on labor were having, and he recognized that such tendencies would lead to disorder. He also saw that the Native Reserves were paying the costs of welfare and child-rearing for the benefit of employers and that the Government's labor policy risked undermining itself by damaging African agriculture. He favored positive measures in the countryside and cities to restore them to viability, and he was frank enough to admit—as the Bishops were not—that improvement in African economic welfare would make labor more expensive. Leys also regarded the extension of political rights to Africans as essential to their economic welfare. However, like the earlier abolitionists, he did not want to dismantle the property relations that had grown up under a coercive and greedy regime. The basic mechanism that would balance African cultivators and European planters was the marketplace, free from the distortions of official compulsion.[128]

Ley's liberal critique of the Kenyan Government presaged a shift in imperialist ideology and colonial policy in the direction of "development," a gradually growing belief that governments should coerce less and do more to foster education, infrastructure, new techniques, and better commercial institutions. Such action would facilitate the ultimate means that would incorporate peasants and workers into an export economy—the market.[129]

Development economics, as both a scientific description of an ongoing process and as a guideline to action, has had a mixed record. However, it

127. Leys believed that Kenya represented "capitalism at its worst, grown rankly into an unnatural monstrosity," and his solution was to make capitalism more natural, more in tune with the market. It is difficult to call Leys's position socialist, as Cell does. N. Leys, p. 379, and Cell, pp. 32–33.

128. Leys, in Cell, pp. 91–102, and N. Leys, Kenya, pp. 314–40, 394–95. See also William McGregor Ross, Kenya from Within (London, 1968; orig. 1927).

129. D. A. Low and John Lonsdale aptly refer to the new wave of British efforts at developing her African colonies in the 1940s as "the second colonial occupation." "Introduction" to Oxford History of East Africa (Oxford, 1976), 3:12. For the slow evolution of these ideas among the "official classes," see J. M. Lee, Colonial Development and Good Government: A Study of the Ideas Expressed by the British Official Classes in Planning Decolonization 1939–1964 (Oxford, 1967). E. A. Brett links the economic problems within Great Britain to an increasing willingness of the Colonial Office to consider long-term improvements in African economies, beginning in the depression after World War I. Colonialism and Underdevelopment in East Africa: The Politics of Economic Change 1919–1939 (New York, 1973), pp. 115–40.

should not simply be assessed on its technocratic self-image, but also in terms of ideology. If civilization and order—plus the frankly arrogant assumption that Europeans had the right to make use of whatever resources they found—provided the ideological basis for the process of colonization, the idea of development provided the vital ideological foundation of the transition from colonial rule to political independence and the neocolonial economy.[130]

The ideology of development viewed the poverty of Africa, compared to the rest of the world, in terms of the workings of the market principle: poor resources, backward technology, low participation of workers and cultivators in economically valuable activities, low investment rates, and other concrete, measurable, impersonal failings in a competitive system. The developers, like the abolitionists, continued to see the poverty of the laborer in terms of his own failings, but these inadequacies were now perceived as social rather than moral—lack of skills, lack of tools, lack of the desire to achieve, and lack of the other objective and universal components of modernity. In placing this emphasis on the universal principles of economy and social structure, the ideology has questioned the abilities of the players far more than the rules of the game: the institutions and structures of a capitalist world economy.

The ideology of development—unlike the more overtly racist idea of civilization—has had the great virtue of appealing as much to the leaders of independent states as to European governments, international agencies, and corporations. It is simplistic to see such leaders as neocolonial lackies or as cynics, but developmentalism placed the particular interests of such leaders—and their mutually beneficial relationship with foreign capital—in the light of broad and obviously desirable goals and apparently universal scientific principles.[131] Like antislavery ideology, including its later manifestations, the ideology of development has illuminated

130. This paragraph should be another book, and I do not mean to belittle the work done in any of the branches of development studies. I am only trying to suggest ways of looking at the continuing relationship of ideology and economic change that will be useful in the more specific analysis that follows.

131. Colin Leys has referred to rulers and officials in Africa as an "auxiliary bourgeoisie," suggesting that their class position is based less on control of production than on mediating between international capital and local producers. He stressed that this class is by no means wholly subordinate to overseas capital but is acting in its own interests and has a considerable degree of autonomy in thought and action. In a more recent article, he argues that indigenous capital has become increasingly oriented toward production. An African bourgeoisie did take over the state and in turn used it to enhance and transform its own accumulation of capital, developing itself in the guise of developing the nation. *Underdevelopment in Kenya: The Political Economy of Neo-Colonialism* (Berkeley, 1974), and "Capital Accumulation, Class Formation and Dependency."

some dimensions of economic change, but it has left the meaning of economic power in darkness.[132]

The debates over slavery in the nineteenth century, over forced labor in the 1920s, over colonial rule in the 1950s and 1960s, and over racial domination and exploitation in southern Africa today all reflect a deep tension within capitalism between the drive for profits and the accumulation of capital, which often shows little respect for the means by which that accumulation takes place, and the principles of the capitalist system itself, defined by the dominance of wage labor and the market mechanism. Deviations from the principle of a free-labor market have, one after another, come to be challenged within the English ruling class itself, as violations of liberal norms and as self-defeating and backward. Such criticisms have in themselves reinforced those norms, at times when capitalist ideology itself has been under challenge.

The rooting out of evil, from slavery and savagery to apartheid and poverty, cannot simply be seen as the continuing forward march of humanitarian ideals. There is continuity not only in the particularity of the issues raised by the friends of the African, but also in the purposes which their ideology has served. And while the kinds of tasks the state has been asked to undertake have changed considerably, continuity is striking in the way humanitarians have accepted as givens the structures created under economic policies that are now perceived to be exploitative and reactionary. Just as the abolition of slavery often left intact a plantation system, so colonial rule in parts of Africa helped create patterns of landholding, dependence on export crops and imported products, narrow marketing networks, and vested interests among certain classes of the indigenous peoples that have made the further use of the methods of the colonial state no longer necessary to capitalist interests overseas. That segments of capitalist classes—white settlers in Rhodesia for instance—still insist, and often depend, on overt coercion to maintain their economic position, has posed a threat to interests that now regard such forms of economic power as both superfluous and dangerous.[133]

132. After its failures in the 1960s, development theory became more skeptical and complex and more willing to acknowledge equity as a goal along with growth. But because the underlying model of development is independent of any analysis of the exercise of economic power, the developers' calls for equity appear tacked-on and naïve. The most influential document in this new approach, the International Labour Office study of Kenya, politely asks Kenya's rulers to redistribute their own incomes and reform the structures on which their privileges are based. See International Labour Office, *Employment, Incomes, and Equality* (Geneva, 1972), and C. Leys, pp. 258–71.

133. Recently, several British governments have tried both to get rid of the white regime in Rhodesia and to insure that nothing drastic was done to the structure of property ownership—itself the result of decades of white supremacist policies and the likely cause of

The relationship of universal principles and particular interests continues to evolve.

An understanding of that relationship helps to explain the connections between the campaign against slavery in the 1890s, the critique of forced labor in the 1920s, and the gradual assimilation of many of the ideas and limitations of Leys's critique into the policy of development in Kenya. The evolution of the mechanisms that tied Africans to the colonial economy rendered the controversy over "encouragement"—in the narrow terms of the latter-day abolitionists—irrelevant soon after it began.[134] But the issue was part of a wider tension within Kenyan capitalism, in which the settlers represented the more blatantly rapacious side of the controversy, while Leys and the Bishops were the purists. The state oscillated between the two extremes, trapped by the expensive support-system already erected for the settlers, too easily coopted or pressured by settlers to undermine their position, too narrow-minded to promote vigorously any alternatives, yet put off by the expense and inefficiency of settler agriculture, dependent on taxes and duties on Africans for a disproportionate share of its revenue, and rightly fearful that intense exploitation would one day lead to conflict.[135] In the 1920s, the purist view was too weak to do more than prevent the triumph of the settlers, as happened in Rhodesia.[136] That side became stronger when its economic benefits became more concrete, and the purists acquired some none-too-pure allies. To international import-export houses, to owners of plantations which were more competitive than settler farms with Afri-

---

future inequality. Something like this was successfully done in Kenya. See Duncan G. Clarke, "Land Inequality and Income Distribution in Rhodesia," *African Studies Review* 18, no. 1 (1975): 1–8.

134. During the 1920s, the number of Kenyans pulled into the wage-labor force expanded greatly, while in many places working conditions deteriorated (Clayton and Savage, pp. 151–53; Tignor, pp. 182–83; Frank Furedi, "The Kikuyu Squatters in the Rift Valley, 1918–1929," in B. A. Ogot, ed., *Hadith 5*, pp. 177–94). Nevertheless, avoiding the appearance of forced labor—whatever the realities of labor recruitment—was very important to the Colonial Office in this period and led to much careful phraseology in other instances as well. Roger G. Thomas, "Forced Labour in British West Africa: The Case of the Northern Territories of the Gold Coast 1906–1927," *JAH* 14 (1973): 79–103, and Elliot J. Berg, "The Development of a Labor Force in Sub-Saharan Africa," *Economic Development and Cultural Change* 13 (1965): 409–10.

135. Especially in periods of bad prices for settler crops, the state leaned on the less costly, less volatile African cash crop economy. The "Dual Policy" of the 1920s, stressing both African and European agriculture, was a half-hearted attempt to have it both ways. See I. R. G. Spencer, "The Development of Production and Trade in the Reserve Areas of Kenya, 1895–1929" (Ph.D. diss., Simon Fraser University, 1974), and for a fuller discussion of the Kenyan state, Lonsdale and Berman, "Coping with the Contradictions."

136. Diana Wylie, "Confrontation over Kenya: The Colonial Office and Its Critics, 1918–1940," *JAH* 18 (1977): 427–48.

can peasants, and to economic interests in Great Britain, the settlers became more dispensible than the mechanisms that tied all producers, African and white, to imperial markets.[137] But only decades later, after a
violent rebellion had exposed the costs of settler power and colonial
domination, and only after the emergence of a Kenyan elite that was
becoming closely tied to a capitalist economy, could the direct control by
European producers, under a European state, be relinquished.[138]

In the recruitment of an African labor force in Kenya—and in Zanzibar as well—the invisible hand took over only when the visible one had
done its work. The ideology of imperialism would only stop defining the
lower orders of African societies as a residuum that had to be carefully
watched and made to work and start conceiving of them as people who
should be helped to develop, once it was clear what direction development would take. The following chapters will try to examine what anti-
slavery ideology and its successors have obscured: the mechanisms of
making men work and controlling their performance, the building and
reshaping of structures that would continue to define the parameters of
economic activity and change, and the efforts of workers and cultivators
to shape those structures themselves.

137. Such views were pushed by the leading businessman Sir Humphrey Leggett, but
with only gradual success. Leggett argued that African production could be profitable for
Kenya if suitably encouraged and channelled through appropriate marketing
institutions—presumably like those he owned—as could plantations in which there were
technical economies of scale. White colonists, however, were an expensive failure. In effect,
Leggett's dispute with the settlers and the Kenyan Government reveals the contradiction
between different modes of capital accumulation, one based on the crude and forceful
exploitation of labor, the other on the increasing importance of capital investment and
improved productivity. This difference is related to Marx's distinction between absolute
and relative surplus value. See Leggett to Masterton Smith, 26 Jan., 28 March 1922, CO
533/1291, and his testimony and memorandum to the East Africa Commission, 1931, PP
1930–31, VII, 1, vol. 2, pp. 338–39, and vol. 3, pp. 44–60.

138. The state's efforts to shape a class of landowning Africans that would cut across the
old racial divisions involved it in sharp contradictions within African societies and between
African laborers and white employers in the large-farm sector, especially when the boom in
tropical produce after World War II increased the profitability of the latter. Both sets of
contradictions helped lead to the so-called Mau Mau rebellion and to a period of intense
state intervention aimed at creating a stable class structure. See M. P. A. Sorrenson, *Land
Reform in Kikuyu Country* (Nairobi, 1967); Gary Wasserman, *The Politics of Decolonisation:
Kenya Europeans and the Land Issue 1960–1965* (Cambridge, 1976); Apolo Njonjo, "The
Africanization of the White Highlands" (Ph.D. diss., Princeton University, 1977); and C.
Leys, *Underdevelopment in Kenya.*

3 Labor and the Colonial State: Zanzibar, 1897–1925

The labor policies of the Zanzibar Administration in the aftermath of abolition were more than a series of ad hoc measures to pressure ex-slaves to work on clove plantations. The state was trying to instill new social values and new attitudes toward work; but meanwhile it sought to maintain control through the only means it believed ex-slaves would understand: dependent relations with ex-masters. The means by which the Administration sought to effect this transformation recall directly the postemancipation policies in the West Indies and indirectly the extended effort to break the rural poor of England and Ireland of their irregular and unruly habits.

The idea of educating a working class was put forward quite explicitly at the time of abolition: "the slaves have to be taught that not only is indolence a vice, but that they will never be able to estimate justly the true value of freedom or independence until they understand the value of their labour, and are willing to apply themselves to it."[1] Colonial education did not take place primarily in schools, but in fields, courts, and jails. Unlike the arbitrary authority of the slaveowner, the authority of the state would embody general principles and regular procedures. An ex-slave who ate a coconut that was not his would not simply be punished but would be put through a ritual process that would demonstrate the power of the state over him and specify the notions of property that the state was trying to define.

Two inseparable concepts were at the core of colonial education: property and work. The idea of property, as applied by the state, emphasized a rigid dichotomy between ownership and nonownership rather than a complex of shared rights in land or produce. The idea of work—taught to those who lacked property—emphasized regularity, the organization of time and human energy around the work routine, and the necessity of discipline. It was a moral and cultural concept, very different from the task orientation characteristic of preindustrial societies.[2]

1. Arabs also had to be taught the value of free labor and their own roles as employers and managers. J. T. Last, Report, 1898, PP 1898, LX 559, pp. 51–52, 54.

2. Foucault emphasizes that the new ways of controlling the body and time permeated all social institutions from the eighteenth century onward—schools, the military, hospitals, and prisons, as well as factories (*Discipline and Punish*, pp. 135–230). See also Thompson, "Time, Work-Discipline, and Industrial Capitalism."

Prohibitions against drinking and dancing—as in England—were as much a part of changing concepts of labor as forced recruitment, vagrancy laws, and the insistence that workers put in regular hours.

In terms of British ideology, the new labor system was progressive because the workers were paid wages. However, the idea of a free-labor market was largely irrelevant to officials' plans: the state wished to tie workers down on the estates and to bring others in, to direct the flow of labor to particular places, and to control wages, hours, and the pattern of the workingman's life. The state did not think of the problem of work as distinct from its mission to preserve order, but dealt with both issues through court-enforced contracts and the criminal law. The state wanted not simply workers but hegemony, not simply output but control over the production process. It needed, above all, to get workers to internalize cultural values and behavior patterns that would define their role in the economy and society.

To a large extent, the Government succeeded in obtaining labor. It did not succeed in extracting steady labor from each worker, in controlling wages or hours, in arresting mobility, or in inducing laborers to internalize new attitudes. The bitter lamentations in official reports about the idleness of ex-slaves, and officials' persistent obsession with controlling labor, point to a failure of social and economic policy that the continuing viability of clove production would appear to belie.

The ex-slaves of Zanzibar and Pemba, far from being a feckless lot, had their own ideas about work and property. Under the demeaning conditions of slavery, they had had access to small plots and houses and saw little reason why "freedom" should mean losing them. They sought to establish some kind of land rights that would provide economic security, as well as a chance to sell small quantities of produce from these plots, as they had done as slaves. Ex-slaves also had no difficulty with the concept of wage labor, but they wished to control the conditions under which they would work, to make cash earnings part of their economic lives rather than to subordinate their lives to the regularity of plantation labor. What the British regarded as a conflict between work and idleness was to the ex-slaves a question of *how* they would work and for whom.

Control of production required supervision; law and order required authority and hierarchy. The planter class had to be preserved. Yet the planters had their own concepts of work and property. The slaveowner's self-image as protector and benefactor had, of course, concealed the element of reciprocity in the master-slave relationship: the slaveholder's need to fulfill certain obligations if he was to get slaves to fulfill theirs. Nevertheless, the idea that both the service of slaves and the beneficence of masters came out of a long-term, multifaceted relationship—as opposed to the contractual and specific relationships characteristic of capitalist society—was deeply rooted in the ideology of the planter class.[3] These values did not persist merely because they were religious and traditional. They allowed a planter class to adjust to its loss of power without wholly losing the sense of being socially superior persons generously providing for dependents while accepting their services. What planters would give and receive was very much in question, but the planters' ideology gave them a normative basis on which to respond to the pressures of ex-slaves and others for long-term commitments to provide them with land and security. The importance of planters' conceptions of labor and their paternalistic self-image lay in how these notions were used, from above and from below.

The divergence of the planter class from the state is a special instance of a much-discussed problem, the "semi-autonomy" of the state. In advanced capitalist society, one argument goes, the state must stay one step above the immediate interests of the capitalist class. Otherwise, it would be unable to reconcile the often conflicting imperatives of maintaining order and accumulating capital; it could not arbitrate conflicts between factions of the capitalist class; and it could not provide the nation with any legitimacy that transcended the interests of a single class. A colonial state must also confront the differences between capitalist interests in the colony and in the metropole and the problem of integrating precapitalist modes of production with the capitalist one whose dominance of state is trying to foster. Nevertheless, white settlers in Rhodesia, Kenya, and elsewhere have shown themselves remarkably able to subvert the semiautonomy of the state, even where London was supposedly in command. Their success reflected not simply the close social and cultural ties that develop among whites in a colonial outpost or the weakness of local administrations; it also reflected the shared conceptions of work, land, and economic order that transcended the periodic divergences of imperial and settler interests.[4]

Such was not the case in Zanzibar. Although the state accepted the plantation system and Arab predominance as givens,[5] Arabs could not exert influence as effectively as could white settlers, with their intimate

3. Cooper, "Islam and the Slaveholders' Ideology."

4. For different views of this question, see: Ralph Miliband, *The State in Capitalist Society* (London, 1969); Nicos Poulantzas, *Political Power and Social Classes*, trans. Timothy O'Hagan (London, 1973); and the debate between the two in *New Left Review* 58 (1969): 67–78, ibid., 59 (1970): 53–60, ibid., 82 (1973): 83–93, and ibid., 95 (1976), pp. 63–83. See also John Holloway and Sol Piciotto, eds., *State and Capital: A Marxist Debate* (London, 1978), and the stimulating application of some of these ideas to Kenya in Lonsdale and Berman, "Coping with the Contradictions."

5. Just as new officials in Kenya were often coopted by settlers, so new officials in Zanzibar were soon transfixed by the status quo. When Edward Clarke arrived to become British Consul-General, he thought that white settlers might improve the sluggish econ-

ties to officials and connections back home. More important, the approaches of the state and the planters to the crucial problems of controlling land and labor were often at cross-purposes. The differences surfaced frequently in officials' complaints about the ineptitude of Arabs as managers and the state's efforts to exercise direct control over labor. The measures which the state took, supposedly in the interests of the planters, were often ignored or undermined by the planters themselves. The distinction between state and capital is everywhere essential, but the extent of the divergence in Zanzibar emphasizes how necessary it is to specify the mechanisms that connect state power and class power. In the gap between the two, ex-slaves fought for their own autonomy.

By the 1920s, the state had not succeeded in creating an agricultural proletariat committed to steady labor; the Arab landowners had failed to keep ex-slaves as personal dependents tied to their estates; and the ex-slaves had not acquired the security they desired. All the compromises led to a structure that was neither equitable nor harshly exploitative, but it was above all brittle and unadaptable. One day, when the role of the colonial state came into question, the structure would be transformed by revolution.

The Master-Slave Relationship Redefined

On 5 April 1897 the slaves of Zanzibar and Pemba got their chance to be free. They could ask a court—presided over by an Arab or English official—to give them a certificate of freedom. Slaves were not obliged to do so, and their owners remained responsible for those who did not. Owners were compensated for slaves freed in court. The freed slaves, under Article 4 of the decree (see Appendix), could be declared vagrants if they could not prove that they had a place to stay and a means of support. The decree specified that rent—in kind or in labor—would have to be paid for an ex-slave to retain his house and garden plot. Even more restrictive measures had been considered: prohibiting slaves from leaving the islands for five years, compelling them to stay and pay rent on the estates of their own masters, and requiring participation in the harvest.[6]

---

omy, but he quickly came around to the viewpoint that the system should stand as it was. Even Kenya's pro-settler Governor Belfield, doubling as High Commissioner of Zanzibar, thought that white settlers would be too much trouble in Zanzibar and that the existing system should be maintained. Clarke to Grey, 28 Sept. 1912, FO 367/295; Belfield to Law, 25 Oct. 1915, CO 618/12.

6. O'Sullivan, Report on Pemba, 1896, PP 1896, LIX, 395, p. 45; Salisbury to Hardinge, 10 Feb. 1897, PP 1897, LXII, 97, p. 4.

TABLE 3:1

SLAVES FREED IN ZANZIBAR AND PEMBA, 1897–1907

	Zanzibar			Pemba				
	Men	Women	Total	Men	Women	Children	Total	Grand Totals
1897	—	—	240	—	—	—	478	718
1898	243	261	504	610	751	200	1,561	2,065
1899	705	722	1,427	980	1,102	148	2,230	3,657
1900	580	546	1,126	230	329	24	583	1,709
1901	273	313	586	92	148	15	255	841
1902	516	397	913	260	286	36	582	1,495
1903	14	40	54	196	226	25	447	501
1904	37	80	117	60	72	4	136	253
1905	26	83	109	—	—	—	226	335
1906	10	35	45	59	74	—	133	178
1907	—	—	20	—	—	—	65	85
	(2,404)	(2,477)	5,141	(2,487)	(2,988)	(452)	6,696	11,837

SOURCES: Farler to Mathews, 26 Jan. 1900, FOCP 7405, pp. 112–13; Hardinge to Salisbury, 9 April 1900. PP 1901, XLVIII, 173, p. 2; Cave to Lansdowne, 15 April 1901, FOCP 7823, p. 131; Farler, Report, 1901, PP 1903, XLV, 955, p. 16; Last, Report, 1902, incl. Cave to FO, 18 March 1902, FO 2/728; Farler to Rogers, 12 Jan. 1904, FOCP 8349, pp. 41–42; O'Sullivan to Cave, 31 Dec. 1904, FOCP 8435, p. 145; Cave to Grey, 26 July 1906, FOCP 8882, p. 90; Last and Farler, Reports, 1906, FOCP 9132, pp. 120, 124; AR, 1909, p. 50.

NOTE: Zanzibar figures through 1906 come from a summary (Last, Report, 1906), and differ only slightly from the incomplete returns in yearly reports. The summary figures for Pemba (AR, 1909) are about 600 short of the sum of the figures in the annual reports, which are used here. Breakdowns according to sex are not available for all years, and the totals (in parentheses) are thus partial.

In the ensuing decade, over 11,000 slaves were freed under these provisions, and nearly Rs 500,000 in compensation was paid to the former slaveowners. The average compensation was about what slaves had cost when they were abundant, but was well under their cost in the 1890s and equivalent to less than five months' wages. The courts relied on the opinions of "Arabs of good position" to insure that claims were genuine; the Administration was trying to help a particular social group.[7]

As Table 3.1 suggests, the years 1898–1900 were the time when slaves were most likely to claim freedom. Thereafter, applications dwindled, a

7. Farler to Mathews, 26 Jan. 1900, FOCP 7405, p. 111.

reflection of the impact of the actions of those who had obtained freedom on the lives of those who had not.[8] The fact of having gone before a court quickly ceased to define the actual relations between slaveowner and slave: a new basis of interaction had to be developed irrespective of legal action. At one time, there were probably over 100,000 slaves in the islands, although this had been reduced by 1897. The majority of slaves drifted off before or after the decree, without stopping in court.[9] Some slave-owners may even have pressured their slaves into seeking freedom so their obligations would be dissolved and they could collect compensation. Other slaveowners freed their slaves under Islamic law, preferring a heavenly reward to a monetary one. Few of such slaveowners were in the principal clove-growing area, however: only 12 percent of the over 6,000 slaves freed under Islamic law were from Pemba.[10]

Among the slaves who freed themselves in court, the opposite was true: over half were from Pemba. The more exploitative basis of slavery in Pemba made emancipation a very significant factor on that island, however great the changes since 1890. Of the slaves freed in Zanzibar Island, 64 percent were city dwellers, and they were likely to free themselves for a different reason: long accustomed to a degree of independence, such slaves had to turn over half their earnings to their owners, a duty they had often evaded but could now dissolve.[11] The incomplete data on freed slaves also suggest how full a part women had played in the plantation economy. Indeed, they were a majority among rural freed slaves—59 percent in Pemba—and their prominence may reflect the lesser degree of mobility that female slaves had. Concubines, however,

8. A new decree in 1909 finally declared slavery dead and put an end to compensation claims. It allowed concubines to claim freedom but otherwise had little impact (PP 1909, LIX, 57, pp. 2–3). Although the Quaker missionaries in Pemba initially criticized local officials for obstructing the abolition process, by 1900 they were admitting that slaves were losing interest because Arabs had to treat them "as free men to retain them on their plantations." Burtt to Buxton, 3 Dec. 1900, ASP c77/105; Burtt, letter, 11 Sept. 1900, Friends Yearly Meeting, 1901, p. 132, FA; Armitage to Buxton, 27 May 1900, ASP c75/88.

9. Population estimates are unreliable, but categories that included a large proportion of ex-slaves numbered 90,000 in the 1924 census. Estimates from the nineteenth century range from 140,000 upward but are probably inflated. Perhaps 10,000 died of smallpox in 1898–99, and annual attrition rates are unknown. It is hard to be more precise than to say that the 11,000 slaves freed by law must have been well under the number who drifted off from 1890 onward. See Zanzibar, Report on the Native Census, 1924.

10. AR, 1909, p. 12; Robert Nunez Lyne, Zanzibar in Contemporary Times (London, 1905), p. 185; J. E. E. Craster, Pemba: The Spice Island of Zanzibar (London, 1913), p. 142.

11. See the statistics on slaves freed in 1900 and 1901 in Last to Mathews, 10 Jan. 1901, PP 1901, XLVIII, 173, pp. 29–30, and Last to Raikes, 5 Feb. 1902, PP 1903, XLV, 955, pp. 8–9. See aso Hardinge to Salisbury, 4 July 1897, PP 1898, LX, 559, p. 7, and Cyril Frewer, "The Natives of Zanzibar and Pemba," Central Africa 25 (1907): 75.

were excluded from the decree altogether, and were only allowed to leave the harem after 1909.[12]

Slaves, in responding to the Decree of 1897, were not choosing between "slavery" and "freedom," but were assessing their economic options. They had to weigh the opportunities they would have if they left their masters—by going to court or walking away—against the possibility that the process of abolition would improve conditions on the plantations.[13]

To stay meant continued access to the land and homes they had used as slaves. Some slaves came to court seeking freedom but changed their minds when informed that they would be turned off the land unless they paid rent. Some delayed their trips to court until after the crops they had carefully tended were harvested. Others continued to pay their masters a portion of the wages they earned—as slaves who were hired out had long done—in order to insure that they would have a place to go if taken ill. Old slaves were particularly reluctant to forfeit their right to be fed by their owner.[14]

The Administration interpreted the slaves' rights to property strictly. Although Islamic law specified that property amassed by a slave belonged to his master, coastal custom had been more flexible, and slaves had been able to trade and buy land on a modest scale. The British courts were not so generous. In one case, a slave who had lived on his master's property for several years without being asked to leave or pay rent was held liable for rent for past access to the property and lost both land and goats as an assumed debt.[15] Such actions illustrated the danger

12. Women comprised 53 percent of the plantation slaves freed on Zanzibar Island but 49 percent of those in other occupations. See the statistics cited above and further discussion of them in Cooper, *Plantation Slavery*, pp. 222–23. Under the 1909 decree, concubines could leave the harem and forfeit rights to material support and to custody of their children by their masters, or else they could stay (PP 1909, LIX, 57, pp. 2–3).

13. Douglas Hall argues that the exodus of Jamaican slaves from plantations after abolition was not so much a flight from bad memories of slavery as a more gradual and selective withdrawal of labor in the face of the bad conditions being imposed on "free" labor on the estates and the frequent attempts of landowners to impose rent on the slaves' own provision grounds, which ex-slaves regarded as a betrayal. "The Flight from the Estates Reconsidered: The British West Indies 1838-42," *Journal of Caribbean History* 10-11 (1978): 7-24. One of the most important episodes of migration from plantations in the southern United States also occurred only after a long and trying experience on them. Nell Irvin Painter, *Exodusters: Black Migration to Kansas after Reconstruction* (New York, 1976).

14. Lyne, *Zanzibar in Contemporary Times*, p. 105; Hardinge to Salisbury, 8 Sept. 1897, PP 1898, LX, 559, p. 12; AgAR, 1898, p. 32; Farler to Mathews, 16 June 1899, PP 1900, LVI, 839, p. 7; Last to Mathews, 22 Feb. 1900, PP 1901, XLVIII, 173, p. 61; Last to Raikes, 6 Feb. 1902, PP 1903, XLV, 955, p. 6.

15. This case, involving a slave called Mshangama, upset the Quakers, who feared the

of losing hard-earned property and much-needed security and created incentives for ex-slaves to retain a dependent relationship with their former master. It remained uncertain whether this rigid concept of property ownership would make slaves into workers.

Some slaves believed that waiting for their master to manumit them would improve their social status more than the piece of paper provided by an alien authority. Indeed, slaves freed in court were referred to as "slaves of the government," as if the authorities had bought them with the compensation money.[16] Slaves, although no colonial official appreciated this point, had also developed a stake in the places they lived that did not derive from their masters. They had families, neighbors, and friends. As in Jamaica, slaves might have to choose between "hatred of the estate and love of home on the estate."[17]

Slaves were less likely to leave an extremely wealthy slaveowner than one of middling means, for they had more to lose.[18] If a slaveowner failed to offer slaves wages or reasonable terms, ex-slaves left. There took place, wrote an official, a "shuffling of the cards as a result of which certain Arabs have gained in labour what others have lost." Many slaves went to the immense plantations of the Sultan which the Government had taken over and where squatters were welcome if they would do some work. The Government's supervisory staff was meager, and ex-slaves could live and farm relatively independently, performing plantation work from time to time for wages.[19] Some labor-starved plantations went out of cultivation and could be used by squatters. In remote parts of Pemba, where conflict between slaves and landlords had recently been

decision would discourage hard work and thrift among slaves. Eventually, kind souls paid off Mshangama's debts, but not before the Foreign Office affirmed the important verdict of the local court. Armitage to Anti-Slavery Society, 13 July 1904, Armitage to Lansdowne, 26 July 1904, and Armitage to Brooks, 3 Oct. 1904, in ASP s22/G2, and *ASR* 24 (1904): 64-67, 125-26. The judgments are in *Zanzibar Gazette*, 8 June 1904, and FO to Armitage, 14 Sept. 1904, ASP s22/G2.

16. Last to Grain, 3 May 1908, FOCP 9331, p. 38; Cave to Lansdowne, 24 Sept. 1902, PP 1903, XLV, 955, p. 22. In Swahili, such ex-slaves were known as *mateka*, a word also used to refer to captives freed from slave ships in an earlier period and settled at missions on the Kenyan coast. Hardinge to Salisbury, 9 April 1900, FOCP 7403, p. 102; Morton, pp. 283-340.

17. Cooper, *Plantation Slavery*, chap. 6; Hall, p. 24.

18. Hardinge to Salisbury, 23 April 1898, PP 1898, LX, 559, p. 72; Lyne, *Zanzibar in Contemporary Times*, pp. 184, 186.

19. D&C, Pemba, 1900, p. 11, quoted. There were only one to three white supervisors for over a score of Government plantations (AgAR, 1910, p. 141). See also AgAR, 1899, p. 20; Farler to Mathews, 2 Aug. 1897, PP 1898, LX, 559, p. 11; same to same, 31 Jan. 1899, PP 1899, LXIII, 303, p. 34; Farler to Rogers, 12 Jan. 1904, FOCP 8349, p. 42. Other ex-slaves went to missions, where wages were higher but supervision stricter. Farler, Report, 1901, PP 1903, XLV, 955, p. 14.

the most severe, ex-slaves could often find land and grow rice unhindered.[20] Such options created a competitive situation: up to twenty Arabs, Indians, and others attended court in Pemba hoping to obtain recently freed slaves as workers and tenants.[21]

Whether slaves and ex-slaves could move about, whether there was any place worth moving to, and whether the state could stop them were among the most important questions that shaped the evolution of labor systems after slavery throughout the world.[22] Because slaves in Zanzibar and Pemba could leave their plantations, those who stayed could insist on better conditions.

The commonly accepted workweek in the first years after abolition came to be three days, compared with five at the height of slavery. A survey of some of the major plantations of Pemba in 1902 revealed a variety of workers and of arrangements within a broad pattern. The enormous estate of Suliman bin Mbarak—with 10,000 clove trees—had 200 laborers, of whom 150 were freed slaves. All had verbal agreements with the owner, requiring them to work for three days per week in exchange for as much land as they needed and rights to fruit and coconuts on the estate. During the harvest, they were paid 4 pice per pishi of cloves picked (64 pice = Re 1; 1 pishi = 4 lbs). Outside of the harvest, they could also work for wages on their free days. Another plantation, with 3,000 trees, had proportionally fewer workers: 15 slaves and 25 freed slaves. They had written contracts but similar terms. Another estate had a small number of slaves, but they were supplemented by Wapemba who worked for two or three days at a time.[23]

The harvest created the greatest pressure and gave slaves and ex-slaves their best bargaining position. The clove is a bud, appearing at the tips of the tree's branches. There are two annual harvests, one of which is by far the larger. Cloves must be picked at precisely the right time, and

20. Last, Collectorate of Zanzibar AR, 1905, FO 367/29; Craster, Report on Pemba, 29 Feb. 1913, FOCP 10239, p. 11; Last to Cave, 23 May 1908, FOCP 9401, p. 80. A missionary who saw the remote settlements in Pemba asked that his letter not be published so that the Government would not try to collect taxes or rent from the ex-slaves. Burtt to Buxton, 5 Aug. 1904, ASP, c77/115.

21. Cave to Salisbury, 9 Aug. 1899, PP 1900, LVI, 839, p. 3.

22. The different outcomes of the struggle to move are stressed in Adamson, *Sugar without Slaves;* Mintz, "Slavery and the Rise of Peasantries"; Green, *British Slave Emancipation;* Mandle, *Roots of Black Poverty;* Higgs, *Competition and Coercion;* Wiener, "Class Structure and Economic Development in the American South"; and Roberts and Klein, "The Banamba Slave Exodus of 1905."

23. Cave to Lansdowne, 24 Sept. 1902, PP 1903, XLV, 955, pp. 20–21. A few years earlier, in Zanzibar, the workweek was four days of six hours each. Farler claimed that the work done each day was reduced. Last, Report, 1898, PP 1898, LX, 559, p. 52; Farler, Report, 1898, ibid., p. 59.

not all cloves on a tree ripen simultaneously, so that a single tree should be picked two or three times. Men climb ladders to pick mature trees, and children, women, and old people help with the lower branches. The picking itself is a delicate task, and trees can be damaged, especially when hasty pickers break off high branches in order to work on them on the ground. Cloves must then be separated from stems—a task often done in the evenings—and dried in the sun for three days before being bagged and sent to town or to clove merchants. All this must be done with care.[24]

The skill required, as well as the intensity of labor, had made Zanzibar's planters distrustful of anyone but their own slaves and willing to give pickers a share of the cloves harvested on the two days that slaves ordinarily had off. In the course of the 1890s and more decisively after abolition, planters ceased to be able to rely on tied workers but had to compete with each other for labor. Whether legally freed or not, whether subject to labor obligations as part of rent or working for the harvest alone, pickers were paid by the pishi of green cloves that they picked. Slaves and ex-slaves took little time to take advantage of the tight labor market during the harvest. Employers who paid low wages or used false measures lost their labor, and wages were driven up during the course of each harvest.[25]

Slaves were willing to work on an estate, wrote an official in 1900, only if two conditions were fulfilled: a settled home and settled wages. Although obtaining security required some continuity in relations of dependence, the fact that an estate provided both land and employment gave ex-slaves flexibility. With a cash income from picking, they could buy meat, rice, clothing, and other provisions for which they had once relied on their owner. The fertile soil of Zanzibar made it possible for a small plot to produce not only enough crops for a family's subsistence, but a small surplus for sale. Some slaves kept goats as well. One official wrote of the "comparative affluence" of slaves on the Sultan's old plantations, which enabled them to refuse wage labor (beyond the expected three days) when they so desired.[26] To many owners, the situation

24. Hardinge to Salisbury, 10 Jan. 1896, FO 107/49; D&C, Zanzibar, 1900, p. 9; G. E. Tidbury, *The Clove Tree* (London, 1949), pp. 112–18.

25. Farler to Mathews, 31 Jan. 1899, PP 1899, LXIII, 303, p. 34; same to same, 26 Jan. 1900, PP 1901, XLVIII, 173, p. 1; Arthur Hardinge, *A Diplomatist in the East* (London, 1923), p. 207; Lister to Grain, 31 Jan. 1908, FOCP 9401, pp. 108–09; Burtt to Buxton, 3 Dec. 1900, ASP, c77/105.

26. Farler to Rogers, 12 Jan. 1904, FOCP 8344, p. 42; Letter of T. Burtt, 11 Sept. 1901, Friends Yearly Meeting, 1901, p. 132, FA; Last, Collectorate Report, 1905, FO 367/29; Lister, Collectorate Report, ibid.; J. Blais, "Les Anciens Esclaves à Zanzibar," *Anthropos* 10–11 (1915–16): 510.

seemed to leave them with old obligations to provide land and none of the control they had once enjoyed.[27]

As early as 1898, officials were realizing that their predictions of disaster in the clove harvest had been wrong. There was "no acute labour crisis." When ex-slaves were offered a good wage, they were "delighted" to pick cloves. With piecework, productivity jumped from 7 to 8 pishis per man-day to 10 or more. But slaveowners had to pay 3 or 4 pice per pishi for wage labor or else make arrangements to share the harvest with the pickers, often half and half.[28] Such observations should have undermined the myth of slave laziness, but they did not. Vice-Consul O'Sullivan in Pemba, the one official whom the Anti-Slavery Society believed to be orthodox on wage labor, wrote that "steady, regular work is just what your slave or free slave dislikes very much." Looking back on this period, another official termed ex-slaves "the most unproductive members of the community." A leading Indian businessman decided that "liberated slaves became like animals suddenly freed from lifelong bondage, leading an irresponsible, easy existence."[29]

The crux of the problem was not that ex-slaves did not work, but that they did not work steadily or predictably. Harvest labor was a burst of effort at a particular point in the agricultural cycle; this pattern was characteristic of preindustrial labor. Piecework provided incentives for ex-slaves to increase their productivity, but it also allowed the pickers to work as long and as fast as they wished. Officials believed more discipline was needed: on Government plantations a staff of "hustlers" with "a commanding voice and a red braided coat" urged ex-slaves onward after they had earned all they wanted and were quitting. This experiment was only tried briefly, but a hierarchy of supervisors continued to keep watch over the harvest. Arab estates, the Administration felt, suffered from lackadaisical supervision, often by paid overseers rather than the planter himself.[30]

27. Grain to Cave, 5 March 1908; FOCP 9331, p. 36; Lyne, *Zanzibar in Contemporary Times*, p. 185; Craster, *Pemba*, p. 142.

28. O'Sullivan-Beare, Report on Pemba, 1898, PP 1899, LXIII, 303, pp. 50–51, 55; Farler to Mathews, 31 Jan. 1898, ibid., p. 35; Hardinge to Salisbury, 23 April 1898, PP 1898, LX, 559, p. 74; Farler to Mathews, 26 Jan. 1900, PP 1901, XLVIII, 173, p. 8; Hardinge to Salisbury, Report on Visit to Pemba, 6 Jan. 1900, PP 1900, LVI, 839, p. 21. Quaker missionaries reported the feeling of "excitement" when a clove harvest began. Burtt to Brooks, 6 Jan. 1906, FA, PZ(F)/1.

29. D&C, Pemba, 1900, p. 12; Hollis to Amery, 19 March 1927, CO 618/41; Yusufali Esmailjee Jivanji, *Memorandum on the Report of the Commission on Agriculture, 1923* (Poina, India, 1924), p. 6. The Agricultural Commission was equally negative in its views of slaves. AgCom., 1923, p. 20.

30. Report of the Director of Agriculture, 1908, FOCP 9330, p. 77; BB, 1913, p. V–3. On Arabs' failures at supervision, see AgAR, 1919, p. 29; Last, Abolition of Slavery and Hut Tax, Report, 8 Feb. 1903, incl. Cave to Lansdowne, 18 March 1903, FO 2/728.

The problem ran deeper. Work discipline is part of a structure, not a habit. Ex-slaves' access to the means of production enabled them to resist the control of work which officials wished to impose and which in fact was imposed on other plantation economies. Officials knew that ex-slaves also cultivated small plots for themselves; but far from interpreting the labor that was put into them as a sign of industry, they looked upon such agricultural activity as part of the easy life that kept ex-slaves away from genuine work. Slaves might sometimes put in an acceptable working day, but not an acceptable working year. Officials were viewing agricultural labor through the lens of industrial capitalism: unless the laborers devoted their lives to wage labor, they were not working at all.[31]

But this conception of work, applied to situations where labor demands were variable or seasonal, created a dilemma: the state wanted continuous command of labor but not to pay wages continuously. Ideologically, the contradictory imperatives of minimizing costs and making wage labor into a way of life conjured up the specter of disorder, as it did in the dockyards of East London. Practically, the requirement that workers be able to survive on their own for part of the year, yet respond with alacrity when called upon, meant that their access to resources had to be so marginal that they would be happy with whatever work they could get or else that workers be so caught up in a web of coercive relationships that they would work on command. In the British West Indies, creating this marginality and control had not always been easy.[32] In Zanzibar, officials faced the obstacles of unusually fertile land, a weak landlord class, and a government as parsimonious in regard to the costs of repression as it was with everything else. Requiring slaves to pay a rent in labor in exchange for the use of subsistence plots neither solved the contradictions inherent in seasonal labor nor guaranteed that the stipulated labor would be forthcoming when wanted. The question came back to the exercise of power on the plantation. Ex-slaves were working, but their ability to exercise choice was quickly proving to be a severe obstacle to the state's control of labor.

In addition to this blending of independent cultivation and intense but short periods of wage labor, ex-slaves had a few other options. A considerable number migrated to Zanzibar town, where an open and

---

31. Last, Report, 1898, PP 1898, LX, 559, p. 51; O'Sullivan-Beare, D&C, Pemba, 1900, p. 12; and R. N. Lyne, Report on Agriculture, 1902, in FOCP 8177, p. 66.

32. The importance of regular work to capitalism is stressed in Thompson, "Time, Work-Discipline, and Industrial Capitalism," while the difficulties of imposing such conceptions on precapitalist societies is discussed in Bauer, "Rural Workers in Spanish America." The contradictions of regularity and casual labor in Victorian England emerge in Stedman Jones, *Outcast London*, and the problems of the continual control of intermittent plantation labor are discussed by Curtin, *Two Jamaicas*, p. 127.

heterogeneous African quarter offered a contrast to the dependent social relations of the plantation. The port and import-export houses employed casual labor year round, while domestic service and government jobs were also to be had. The influx of ex-slaves into the town produced a large "floating population," so that from the time of abolition onward labor was relatively abundant. Urban wages, however, were generally higher than rural and were driven upward by periodic demands for labor for road building and military labor during World War I. Urban residents sometimes took to the fields, but only, officials complained, when an unusually heavy crop made picking easy and wages high.[33] The Administration felt that the coincidence of ample labor with high daily wages was being maintained by the preferences of the laborers to work only half a month. This was a simplistic view of casual labor, but in the official mind, the desertion of the plantations by ex-slaves, the "floating" urban mass, idleness, and criminality were inexorably linked.[34] For ex-slaves, however, urban labor offered flexibility and choice, as well as wages that compared favorably with alternatives.

The urban alternatives were particularly important in breaking the domination of planters over their ex-slaves in the years after abolition. But even before World War I, Zanzibar was declining as an entrepôt, and with the narrowness of the islands' economy, urban employment could hardly remain a dynamic force. In 1925, 81 percent of the recorded wage-labor force was in agriculture, even though rural workers were almost certainly underestimated. By the 1930s, urban employment was to become scarcer, and the unsteady nature of casual labor more a source of poverty than of flexibility.[35]

Similarly, slaves—whether legally freed or not—could leave the islands

33. Raikes to Cave, 18 Feb. 1903, FOCP 8177, p. 5; Last to Raikes 6 Feb. 1902, PP 1903, XLV, 955; p. 6; AR, 1909, p. 6; R. Armstrong, "Agriculture," in *Zanzibar: An Account of Its People, Industries and History* (Zanzibar, 1924), p. 29. In 1911 Public Works labor was paid Rs 18 per month, compared with Rs 12 for weeding labor on Government plantations. In 1898, wages had been Rs 10 in town, Rs 8 in the country. AgAR, 1911, p. 151; F. C. McClellan, "Agricultural Resources of the Zanzibar Protectorate," *Bulletin of the Imperial Institute* 12 (1914): 414; Hardinge to Salisbury, 23 April 1898, PP 1898, LX, 559, p. 74. See the Blue Books for more details on wages.

34. One official commented that he did not know how freed slaves in town supported themselves, but when the tax man came around, they had money. Another noted that public works drove up agricultural wages. Raikes to Cave, 18 Feb. 1903, FOCP 8177, p. 58; Cave to Lansdowne, 20 Dec. 1904, FOCP 8438, p. 35; Report on the Administration and General Condition of the Zanzibar Protectorate, incl. Cave to Grey, 2 Nov. 1908, FOCP 9459, p. 78; Sinclair to Belfield, 28 March 1917, incl. Pearce to Long, 9 May 1917, CO 618/17. On crime, see below, pp. 111–20.

35. BB, 1925, p. 126. On the deterioration of labor conditions, see Epilogue. The importance of the unavailability of alternative forms of employment to maintaining the economic power of a planter class is stressed by Mandle, Adamson, and others.

for Kenya and find work on the railroad. This alternative was important around the turn of the century but evaporated as stiffening taxation and labor policies in Kenya reversed the predominant direction of migration.[36] All in all, one official estimated, 10,000 slaves had wandered away from the plantations by 1901, seeking work, land, or a new home.[37]

Within a few years of 1897, the laws that gave slaves freedom and narrowed their property rights were losing significance to a more basic change in actual economic relations. Ex-slaves were taking for themselves—with the acquiescence of their ex-masters—a combination of rights in land and access to wage labor. An aged ex-slave told a visitor of the reality of the changes: "I spent all my strength working for the Arabs and now I am too old to work for myself. I was born too soon."[38]

Slaves and ex-slaves had more economic options because their former owners had lost their ability to mobilize labor via the slave trade and had less control over the laborers they had. Part of the problem was demographic. New laborers were not arriving, and a smallpox epidemic— part of a pattern of disease that disrupted African societies at the dawn of the colonial era in much of Africa—struck the slave population of Pemba with particular force in 1898–99, killing perhaps 10,000 people.[39] Officials and missionaries, however, saw the decline in slave population as a long-term problem attributable to the slave character. Promiscuity and venereal disease reduced fertility, and slave women—lacking family values—practiced abortion. Population decline, they felt, was a major cause of labor shortage.[40]

36. Rogers to FO, 26 Feb. 1903, FOCP 8098, pp. 214–15; Last to Raikes, 6 Feb. 1902, PP 1903, XLV, 955, p. 5.

37. Cave to Lansdowne, 15 April 1901, FO 2/454.

38. Craster, *Pemba*, p. 213.

39. O'Sullivan, Report, 1899, FOCP 7405, pp. 117–18. Helge Kjekshus stresses the importance of the combination of epidemics of rinderpest, smallpox, and other diseases with the devastation of colonial wars and labor recruitment in undermining the structure of African economies and contributing to a period of demographic and economic disaster in the early colonial period (*Ecology Control and Economic Development in East African History: The Case of Tanganyika 1850–1950*, Berkeley, 1977). For a more balanced account that still gives much weight to these issues, see John Iliffe, *A Modern History of Tanganyika* (Cambridge, 1979).

40. One official compared the immorality and decline in population of ex-slaves, who lacked "ancient customs or traditions to maintain or to control them," and the social solidarity and growing population of the Wahadimu. However, the relative population changes may reflect social redefinition, not demographic trends (Notes by Mr. Last on the Decrease of the Population of the Island of Zanzibar, 10 April 1907, FOCP 9331, pp. 27–28). See also AgAR, 1899, p. 20; Cyril Frewer, "Industrial Work in Zanzibar and Pemba," *Central Africa* 23 (1905): 8–9; Cave to Grey, 3 March 1908, FOCP 9331, p. 24; Godfrey Dale, *The Peoples of Zanzibar* (London, 1920), pp. 16–17; AgCom, 1923, p. 20. For more on demographic issues, see J. G. C. Blacker, "Population Growth and Differential Fertility in Zanzibar Protectorate," *Population Studies* 5 (1962): 258–66.

However, the reports of population loss are not based on demographic data, and the view of slave degeneracy reflects little more than Victorian race and class prejudice. The first remotely accurate population count, in 1924, revealed that Zanzibar and Pemba had a population that was unusually dense by African standards—nearly 200 people per square mile. There were over 180,000 "natives" in the islands, and 90,000 of them were listed in social categories that suggest slave descent.[41] The question remains whether ex-slaves were dying out or doing less work or being redefined socially. The problem was not simply one of the ratio of labor to land, but of the ability of planters to control both resources.[42]

The problem with ex-slaves was not that decades of degradation had made them unfit for a wage economy, but that their ability to manipulate the changing economic order was being used not only to increase their income but also to enhance their control over the rhythm of their economic lives. Their bargaining position, however, had narrow limits. They had access to land, but they did not own it. Only by reconstituting older forms of dependent relationships or isolating themselves from both planters and Government could ex-slaves get land. In the years following abolition, landowners had little choice but to grant rights in land they could not otherwise use. However, Zanzibar provided no homogeneous community to protect such rights, and the law was not on the side of ex-slaves. At the same time, ex-slaves' ability to obtain cash was constrained by the same factor that constrained other Zanzibaris: the utter dependence of the islands on cloves (and to a lesser extent coconuts) as an export commodity. Even if a patch of ground could be found, it might not provide a cash income. The very importance of avoiding excessive dependence on their own landlord meant seeking opportunities for wage labor elsewhere, and for most people that meant picking cloves. While unable to control land tightly, landowners—aided in a variety of ways by the state—held on to their trees. Ex-slaves came to balance two types of relationships to the planters: a personal, if not very exacting, dependence on a landowner and a flexible but largely unavoidable pattern of participation in harvest labor. Ex-slaves now had more

41. Native Census, 1924, pp. 8, 11. In the southern United States, as Kolchin argues, the myth of a decline in the population of ex-slaves after emancipation reflected the withdrawal of work time from plantations, not demographic decline. (*First Freedom*, p. 8). On the redefinition of social identity, see chapter 4.

42. The attempt to explain why some societies adopted slavery and later invented other repressive mechanisms to replace it, by distinguishing between cases of "open resources," where coercion is necessary to maintain a labor force, and "closed resources," where high population relative to resources forces people to seek work, is at best a partial explanation. For this argument, see H. J. Nieboer, *Slavery as an Industrial System* (The Hague, 1910), and W. Kloosterboer.

choice of which planter they were to be dependent upon and means of limiting the extent of their dependence, but they had not found a basis for ending it altogether.

THE CONTRACT SYSTEM

The British Government was not simply sitting by and watching while new economic relationships evolved. The Administration deplored the slaves' and ex-slaves' "feeling of independence" and sought to tame it. That ex-slaves could work for wages or not as they chose required intervention.[43] Officials sought to establish—through the predictable and enforceable mechanisms of the law—a modified kind of bond between landowner and ex-slave. Meanwhile, they hoped to undermine the conditions that gave workers a relatively strong bargaining position. The Government's response was typical of postemancipation regimes as well as of colonial governments faced with the substantial economic independence that most African cultivators enjoyed.[44]

The foundation of Government policy was so obvious that officials scarcely commented on it at the time. The Administration accepted the land titles of the planters. Decades later, one of the Empire's leading agricultural experts commented that Zanzibar's land policy was based "on the assumption, apparently, that the system of land tenure in Zanzibar is identical with that in England."[45] Land sales and mortgages were registered, and the supposition was that such deeds conveyed the same rights over land and trees as freehold. Later, the Government became more conservative in its association of land titles with what it perceived of as a landowning class. It took no measures—such as those taken in Kenya—to facilitate the sale of land, and in the 1930s it sponsored various schemes to maintain the Arab planters' hold over land when mount-

43. Last to Hardinge, 25 Jan. 1898, PP 1898, LX, 559, p. 5; Farler, Report on Pemba, 1898, ibid., p. 60; Hardinge to Salisbury, 23 April 1898, ibid., p. 71.

44. The unsuccessful apprenticeship scheme that constituted the transition from slave labor in the British West Indies, the contract system pushed by the Freedman's Bureau after the American Civil War, and the contract labor that generated considerable conflict as Portuguese Angola moved away from slavery were among a variety of mechanisms in postemancipation societies designed to tie ex-slaves, in some legally sanctioned manner, to individual landowners. Kloosterboer; Green, *British Slave Emancipation;* Wiener, "Class Structure and Economic Development"; Clarence-Smith, *Slaves, Peasants and Capitalists in Southern Angola.* The troublesome implications for colonial states of Africans' access to land is stressed by Arrighi, "Labor Supplies in Historical Perspective."

45. Sir Alan Pim, "Report of the Commission appointed by the Secretary of State for the Colonies to consider and report on the Financial Position and Policy of the Zanzibar Government in relation to its Economic Resources," 1932, p. 89. For an example of this simplification, see the statements of Agriculture Director McClellan, "Agricultural Resources," p. 413.

ing debts to Indian financiers threatened large-scale transfers of plantations to a different social group. Although the Government recognized that outside of the plantation area, Wahadimu and Wapemba "natives" had certain rights to land that differed from freehold, it made no such concessions to ex-slaves and none to anyone in the plantation areas.[46] A landless people was being created.

But rights in land had to be enforced, not by the personal power of the property owner, but by the regular and seemingly unbiased operation of the law.[47] To insure that the landed would maintain their property rights and the landless would work for them, the state first turned to a contract system. Drawn up in court, enforced by penal sanctions, contracts were based on the patently false but ideologically necessary premise that landlord and worker were equals, with different commodities to exchange. The reality was an attempt to use both the legitimacy and coercive ability of the state to maintain class power.

This approach was implemented at the same time as the Decree of 1897. The Sultan set an example by freeing his slaves (without compensation) and offering them the right to keep their huts and plots in exchange for four days of labor per week. Other slave-owners were encouraged to do the same, regardless of whether their slaves were formally freed. The courts took the initiative in establishing such arrangements, so that—in addition to the 2,000 slaves freed the first year—2,278 contracts were drawn up. J. P. Farler, Slavery Commissioner in Pemba, toured the large estates in the company of the Liwali (Arab local administrator), drawing up contracts between landowners and the slaves on their estates.[48]

Hardinge noted that slaveowners, faced with the "slaves' new spirit of independence," were making verbal agreements along the lines of the Sultan's example, sometimes in the presence of an official, most often just between master and slave. He ordered that such agreements be made in writing and registered before the courts, specifying all the conditions and the time-limit, which he thought should be two years.[49] The master-slave relationship was to be brought under the purview of the law.

---

46. Registration of sales, transfers, and mortgages was made compulsory in 1892, but the process of survey and adjudication undertaken in Kenya after 1908—and designed to facilitate sales by clearing up questionable titles—was put off for decades. Portal to Rosebery, 27 Dec. 1892, FOCP 6403, p. 39; Hollis to Coryndon, 2 Aug. 1924, incl. Coryndon to Thomas, 1 Sept. 1924, CO 618/33; Pim, p. 90.

47. On the importance of this distinction, see Foucault, pp. 84–85, 89–90, 137.

48. Hardinge to Salisbury, 23 April 1898, PP 1898, LX, 599, pp. 69, 71; Newman, p. 123; letter of Farler, in *ASR* 19 (1899): 34.

49. Hardinge to Salisbury, 23 April 1898, PP 1898, LX, 599, p. 71.

For slaves on the verge of freedom, the pressures to enter into a contract, particularly with their own masters, were strong. The compensation procedure required that the master and slave appear together in court, where the master "may hold out to him inducements to return to the land as a free labourer," while the Magistrate would instruct the slave "that his freedom does not mean that he can squat on his master's land, and at the same time refuse him all payment either in rent, in produce, or in labour."[50] The Pemba missionaries complained that the procedures were so coercive that they discouraged slaves from seeking freedom, and even Hardinge admitted that the Arab Magistrates in Pemba were so zealous in enforcing the masters' rights that slaves were initially reluctant to use the courts.[51]

However, officials, particularly Farler in Pemba, were not satisfied with pressure, and they had an instrument in the Vagrancy Article of the Decree of 1897. In 1899, Farler began to insist that a slave, in order to be freed, had to bring to court the person on whose land he intended to settle. Having a landowner as a patron—one willing to appear in court—became a prerequisite for freedom. The Friends missionaries in Pemba found this to be an appalling restriction on slaves' ability to seek work. They took their views to London, and Salisbury agreed that such conditions could not be imposed *before* freeing a slave. But he pointed out that slaves could still be prosecuted for vagrancy *after* they were freed. In fact, the Government was already making liberal use of the vagrancy statute.[52]

Salisbury's action did not reduce the pressure on slaves, whether legally freed or not, to enter into contracts. Nor did it alter the restrictive nature of the contracts. The Slavery Commissioners were insisting that ex-slaves sign contracts with people whom the officials though needed the labor, the owners of large clove plantations. The contracts prevented workers from changing plantations without a court's permission. The court could punish workers for failing to perform a "reasonable amount of work."[53] The worker was thus bound to a relationship with one landowner, and coercion—this time by a court—was the primary means of labor discipline. Consul-General Cave argued that such a system was bet-

50. Ibid.; Farler to Mathews, 26 Jan. 1900, PP 1901, XLVIII, 173, p. 90; D&C, Pemba, 1900, p. 13.

51. The missionaries felt that the Pemba authorities, both British and Arab, at first harassed slaves who sought freedom, but that this problem ceased and was followed by a period when slaves were reluctant to come forward owing to the severity of the contract system itself. Burtt to Newman, 13 March 1898, FA, MS 212; Burtt to Buxton, 3 Dec. 1900, ASP, c77/105; Burtt, speech to Society of Friends, 26 May 1903, in *ASR* 23 (1903): 94.

52. Farler to Mathews, 16 June 1899, PP 1900, LVI, 839, p. 7; letters of Armitage and Cave, and Salisbury to Cave, 18 Nov. 1903, in PP 1903, LVI, 839, pp. 2–4, 17.

53. D&C, Pemba, 1900, p. 11; Cave to Lansdowne, 21 Feb. 1903, PP 1903, XLV, 955, p. 3; letter of Armitage, 18 Nov. 1903, in *ASR* 22 (1902): 20.

ter for the slaves than turning them loose on the labor market, for it provided "a fixed residence, a settled occupation, a methodical life, and a contented mind."[54]

The Quakers also wanted ex-slaves to live a methodical life, but their purist view of the labor market clashed with the Administration's stress on dependence. A fixed week's work in lieu of wages was "utterly bad," for it provided no incentives to do more than minimal work in the three days and so fostered "shiftless, idle ways." As a system of labor discipline, contract labor was too similar to slavery, and only unrestricted and regular wage labor would teach slaves the proper lessons.[55] With equally condescending views of slaves, the Quakers emphasized discipline, the administrators stability.

But it took more than contracts to recreate dependent conditions analagous to slavery. In some cases, the state could bring power to bear. In the town of Zanzibar, shortly after abolition, Hardinge observed a "mutinous spirit" among day laborers, who refused to carry out the contracts they had with port merchants. The Government sent the police to make it clear that workers would be punished for breach of contract. The display of force drove two points home: acceptable conduct was defined by law, and the one institution now capable of exerting power would not hesitate to do so.[56]

However, as Hardinge recognized, it was more difficult to exercise power in the remote plantation districts than in the small city. Landowners had trouble making slaves do the work specified in the contracts: slaves could leave plantations without being caught; and squatters could not be dislodged from the land they were cultivating. Farler complained that slaves in the remote northern part of Pemba would not work. Hardinge reported a "strike" among slaves on a rice farm that ended only when the landowner gave the slaves a "present." Even on its own plantations, the Government found that laborers wanted to work by the day, but not enough days to satisfy the Administration. Attempts to enforce the three day's compulsory labor failed; workers simply did not do the work.[57]

The Administration was particularly eager to include a picking requirement—10 to 12 pishi per day—in the contracts, and ex-slaves were particularly eager to evade it. Landowners wanted to have a resident picking force not only because their year-round presence was one way being sure of having them on the plantation during the harvest, espe-

54. Cave to Lansdowne, 24 Sept. 1902, FOCP 8040, p. 57.

55. Letters from Armitage, 18 Nov. 1901, and Burtt, 4 April 1902, in *ASR* 22 (1902): 18–20, 45–47, plus the comments of Armitage, 16 Feb. 1903, in FOCP 8177, p. 53.

56. Hardinge to Salisbury, 23 April 1898, PP 1898, LX, 599, p. 73.

57. Ibid., p. 72; Farler, Report, ibid., p. 60; Hardinge, Report, 1898, PP 1898, LX, 361, p. 6; AgAR, 1899, pp. 22, 28.

cially in the early days of each harvest as trees gradually reached the picking stage, but also because long-term dependents were less likely than strangers to damage trees. However, the keen competition for labor during the harvest meant that ex-slaves were scarcely confined by the contracts, but would go wherever the piecework wages were highest. Nevertheless, planters remained anxious to keep resident laborers, hoping that—with competitive wages—the squatters would at least pick their patrons' cloves first.[58]

This weakness in the planters' control left the problem of tree damage by pickers unsolved, and the Government—consistent with its overall approach—looked to penal sanctions for a solution. As pickers, paid by the amount of cloves they gathered, broke off branches in order to pick them more rapidly, the Agriculture Department sent in the police to do what planters once had done—punish bad work. The punitive approach had some effect, but branch breaking and other shortcuts remained problems that the police could not solve.[59]

By 1904, the entire contract system was coming apart. In Pemba, 448 contracts had been approved by courts in 1902, 664 in 1903, but in 1904 the number fell to 91, and then to 14 the year after. Ex-slaves had been breaking contracts and, if a court tried to enforce them, leaving the area. The Government was unable to keep track of ex-slaves, and the landowners needed resident laborers too desperately to turn away someone who had reneged on a previous contract. Landowners soon came to see little advantage in court-enforced contracts, and they sought to make their own arrangements with ex-slaves.[60]

58. Fitzgerald, pp. 601–02; Farler to Mathews, 29 Aug. 1897, FOCP 7032, p. 8; McClellan, p. 415; Farler to Mathews, 31 Jan. 1899, PP 1899, LIII, 303, p. 34; same to same, 26 Jan. 1900, PP 1901, XLVIII, 173, p. 8; Burtt to Buxton, 3 Dec. 1900, ASP, c77/105; AR, 1900, p. 12; Report of Mr. C. E. Akers on the General, Financial, Commercial and Economic Situation in Zanzibar, 1908, FOCP 9330, p. 77; F. C. McClellan, Memorandum on Labour Conditions in the Zanzibar Protectorate, 21 Nov. 1921, incl. Sinclair to Churchill, 28 Dec. 1921, CO 618/26; Hardinge, *A Diplomatist in the East*, p. 207.

59. Careless pickers also omitted going over trees more than once, and so failed to pick all cloves at the proper time. AgAR, 1897, p. 8; D&C, Zanzibar, 1900, p. 9; AgAR, 1902, in FOCP 8177, pp. 66–67; AgAR, 1905, incl. Cave to Grey, 10 Aug. 1906, FO 367/29; USCR, 284 (1911), p. 1157; Sinclair to Long, 11 April 1917, incl. Pearce to Long, 3 May 1917, CO 618/17.

60. Figures on contracts are from Consul Cave, cited in *ASR* 26 (1906): 97–98. The failure of the system is also described in Burtt, letter of 3 March 1905, *ASR* 25 (1905): 48; Cave to Grey, 26 July 1906, FOCP 8882, pp. 89–96; Lister, Report on Pemba, 1905, incl. Cave to Grey, 10 Aug. 1906, FO 367/29. Afterward, the approach to labor contracts taken by the Kenyan Government—the Masters and Servants Ordinance (in its many versions), which places a series of standardized although discriminatory obligations on employers and employees—was not implemented in Zanzibar until 1925 and then had little effect. Hollis to Amery, 30 Oct. 1925, CO 618/37; Pim, 1932, p. 22.

The contract system had appeared to the British as a practical and gradual way of changing the organization of labor. It converted a resource which landowners seemingly controlled but did not directly exploit, non-clove land, into labor, while putting only minimal strain on the resource they lacked most, money. It induced people who were inclined to work occasionally to work regularly, reducing their options to three days of labor per week for an entire year or nothing at all. It accorded well with British desires to avoid precipitous change in what they regarded as a stable hierarchical social structure. Yet ideologies that underplay the importance of power and overplay the importance of the force of law or the legitimacy of authority can deceive the rulers far more than the ruled. Ex-slaves proved to be unawed by planters or the state and quite unwilling to regard the amelioration of the conditions of slavery as the limits of their aspirations. Mobility and flexibility were precisely what ex-slaves wanted, and shirking labor obligations and breaking contracts were—as the Quakers rightly argued—the type of resistance that a system of tied labor engendered.[61] What the contract system required was firm discipline on the plantations and a realistic threat that shirkers would be evicted and deserters prosecuted, plus— ideally—a shortage of land and an excess of people outside the plantations. In other parts of the world, vigorous action by planters and the state, as well as the narrowing of resources outside the plantations, have been necessary to make labor tenancy into an effective source of labor, and planters have often had to accede to the demands of tenants.[62] Experience has also shown that severe actions against

61. The relationship of desertion to long-term contracts is stressed in Charles van Onselen, "Worker Consciousness in Black Miners: Southern Rhodesia, 1900-1920," *JAH* 14 (1973): 245, and Thomas, "Forced Labour in British West Africa," pp. 80-85.

62. Even a firm policy of evictions could merely drive away the potential labor force if workers had someplace to go (Curtin, *Two Jamaicas*, pp. 128-30). Thus contracts had to be part of a "web of coercive labour legislation," as well as a web of implementation for it to work as effectively as it did in extracting agricultural and mine labor in South Africa and Rhodesia. Van Onselen, "Worker Consciousness," p. 245, discusses mine labor, while the implications of a new resolve by the state to make tenancy into an effective source of labor are stressed by Stanley Trapido, "Landlord and Tenant in a Colonial Economy: The Transvaal 1880-1910," *Journal of Southern African Studies* 5 (1978): 26-58; Tim Keegan, "The Restructuring of Agrarian Class Relations in a Colonial Economy: the Orange River Colony, 1902-1910," ibid., pp. 234-54; and Morris, "The Development of Capitalism in South African Agriculture." The relationship of such pressures on plantation residents to external constraints—absence of land and the bringing in of new workers—is stressed by Cristobal Kay, "The Development of the Chilean *hacienda* system, 1850-1973," in Duncan and Rutledge, *Land and Labour in Latin America*, p. 121, as well as in other studies in that volume, and by Adamson. On the other hand, as Bauer and Martinez-Alier insist, tenancy arrangements emerged from a two-sided struggle, not just the imposition of mounting exactions on a hapless peasantry.

plantation residents can indeed provoke resistance, and the thrust of the Zanzibar Government's policy from the beginning was to preserve social order and avoid the expenses of tight administration. Budget deficits in most years between 1896 and 1902 hardly made this the time to implement the kind of system that could register workers, trace deserters, and evict contract violators on a scale as massive as the breakdown of plantation discipline. Such measures lay so far beyond a Civil Service with under thirty Europeans that they were never even considered. The colonial state had not faced the extent to which a transition from slave labor to labor tenancy implied a transformation in relations of power, any more than the Quakers were ready to admit the coercive dimensions of a wage-labor system.[63]

What the law could not do by itself, Arab landowners had to do for themselves—namely, find some way to induce slaves to work on clove plantations. The failure of the contract system left a squatter system that had been evolving all along. It was based on personal ties and verbal understandings and was remote from the operations of the state. It reflected the actual—and potentially changing—balance of interests and economic power between landlords and tenants rather than abstract notions of regular work and rigid definitions of property. The ex-slaves who stayed on their former owners' estates or moved to new plantations formed the core of the squatter population that was to be an essential element of rural economic structure throughout the colonial era. In addition, some of the migrant laborers became squatters. Squatting, wrote the British Resident in 1917, had become "universal."[64]

Squatting was a long-term relationship. For landless people, it provided much-needed security, and their ability to grow subsistence crops—and even a modest marketable surplus—enabled ex-slaves to exercise considerable choice over when and under what conditions they would work for wages. Because slaves had a choice of landlords, they could influence the reciprocal relations with the patron. The labor rent of three or four days that had been part of the contract system withered

---

63. Slaves who had not agreed to contracts resisted eviction directly after abolition, and the Government seems to have dropped further attempts (Hardinge to Salisbury, 23 April 1898, PP 1898, LX, 559, p. 72). The weakness of the Civil Service and the Swahili police—which itself had to be punished and reorganized after a strike in 1906—is obvious in Zanzibar, AR, 1909, esp. pp. 7, 10, and administration and the judiciary remained weak (W. H. Ingrams, "Memorandum on Native Organization and Administration in Zanzibar," 1926). Administrative weakness and parsimony are underestimated as factors shaping the history of labor in Africa. The danger of resistance to increased burdens on labor tenants in two African cases is mentioned by Morris (pp. 323-28) and stressed by Frank Furedi, "The Social Composition of the Mau Mau Movement in the White Highlands," *Journal of Peasant Studies* 1 (1974): 486-505.

64. Sinclair to Long, 11 April, 1917, CO 618/17.

away; and money-rent was collected only where land was unusually productive, with rice land, for example. Even the Government had to strike
a bargain with its tenants. A large number of squatters had occupied its
plantations rent-free until 1911, with the sole expectation that they
would pick cloves for wages. When rent was imposed, clove pickers were
exempted, as were the old and sick.[65]

Such arrangements, on both Government and private plantations, became customary throughout Zanzibar and Pemba. No rent was generally
charged, although picking and sometimes weeding were expected, for
which the squatter was usually paid the going wage. The squatter could
plant ground crops but usually not tree crops such as cloves or coconuts.
Sometimes the only formality was that the squatter ask the owner's permission before settling; in other cases, a squatter had written permission
to stay, countersigned in court and valid throughout his lifetime. Ex-
slave squatters were often involved in a set of social relationships as well;
for example, the landlord would act as the guardian of a squatter's
daughter in Islamic marriage rites. Such interaction reaffirmed, for the
landlord, the patriarchal nature of his position and, for the ex-slave, the
long-term, personal nature of the landlord's commitment to give him
land.[66]

As the squatting system became entrenched, officials looked on it as a
hangover from days gone by, an irrational preference of landowners to
have personal dependents and of slaves to remain idle and dependent.[67]
They complained that squatters were growing crops for their own needs
instead of "economic crops" that could be exported and taxed. They
were afraid that giving squatters effective occupation rights was compromising the value of land titles. Officials thought of requiring Arabs to
make tenants perform a certain amount of labor, as the contracts had
vainly insisted. Failing that, they reminded Arabs that ground rent
"formed an important item of revenue on all landed properties."[68] The

65. AgAR, 1910, p. 141, 1911, p. 166, 1919, p. 25, and 1920, p. 10. The absence of rent
continued throughout most of the colonial era. C. K. Meek, Land Law and Custom in the
Colonies, 2d ed. (London, 1949), p. 73.

66. For the continuing importance of such customs, see W. R. McGeach and William
Addis, "A Review of the System of Land Tenure in the Islands of Zanzibar and Pemba,"
1945, pp. 11, 20; William H. Ingrams, Zanzibar: Its History and Peoples (London, 1931), p.
205; Tidbury, p. 111.

67. Last, Report, 1898, PP 1898, LX, 559, p. 51; AgAR, 1911, p. 165, and 1920, p. 10;
AgCom, 1923, p. 20. On the other hand, the American consul waxed eloquent on the
ability of the "Arab race" to supervise the African. USCR 135 (1917): 959.

68. McClellan, Memorandum on the Coconut Industry of the Zanzibar Protectorate,
incl. McClellan to CO, 25 March 1916, CO 618/16; Memorandum of a meeting with Arabs
and the Director of Agriculture, incl. Sinclair to CO, 10 Oct. 1913, CO 618/2; Sinclair to
Long, 11 April 1917, incl. Pearce to Long, 3 May 1917, CO 618/17.

Administration wanted Arab clove planters to behave like good capitalists and were frustrated when they did not.

The eagerness of planters to obtain residents on their land was by no means economically irrational, but it did reflect the intertwining of social values and economic needs over many decades. The prestige value of slaves was a social manifestation of the nature of Zanzibari plantation agriculture, of the seasonal nature of clove cultivation, and the need for plantations to be partially insulated communities. In the twentieth century, harvest labor—so vitally needed at so precisely defined a time—did not suddenly spring from a rationalized and efficient labor market. Labor recruitment required the mobilization of social ties. Landowners sought to redefine their relations with their ex-slaves and to attract new residents, and land was the best inducement they had to offer. Long-term relations were a basis for obtaining short-term labor, but the weakness of the planters' position meant that wages paid to residents still had to be competitive with those paid to outsiders.[69]

As before abolition, resident workers fitted into the seasonal pattern of the clove tree. During the harvest they pitched in, while the plots they cultivated year-round for their own benefit helped to keep the plantation from becoming overrun by the bush. But when it came to weeding around the trees themselves, wages had to be paid, and ex-slaves, who had other sources of modest cash income, were not always willing to do the work.[70] Having a well-peopled plantation would keep out thieves as well as weeds, and in a society where police forces were weak, personal dependents were essential to preventing theft of produce by outsiders. The residents, however, would be given a share of the coconuts that the thieves otherwise would have stolen.[71]

The state failed to create a regular, controllable labor force through legally enforceable contracts, and the planters had to cede much of their control over non-clove land and the rhythm of labor in order to obtain any labor from ex-slaves at all. While still straining to discipline labor within the plantation, the state began searching for new laborers outside the area of privately owned land.

RECRUITING PICKERS

British experience in the West Indies had shown that large-scale, carefully controlled immigration could, over time, force down wages and

---

69. In general, as Alan Richards argues, agrarian systems that relied on settled workers with access to land should not be regarded as throw-backs to antiquated forms of production. "The Political Economy of *Gutswirtschaft:* A Comparative Analysis of East Elbian Germany, Egypt, and Chile," *Comparative Studies in Society and History* 21 (1979): 488.

70. Mainland migrants ended up doing much of the weeding. AgAR, 1919, p. 25; McGeach and Addis, "System of Land Tenure," p. 10. On the mainlanders, see below, pp. 104–11.

71. AgAR, 1920, p. 11; McGeach and Addis, p. 10. On crime, see below.

undercut the independence of all laborers, ex-slaves and immigrants alike. India—that great reservoir of labor for the British Empire—was considered once again, but the profit margin of clove production was too narrow for such an undertaking, and officials in India had misgivings about providing cheap labor for non-English planters.[72]

The Government turned to a target closer to home, three groups, all Swahili-speaking Muslims, who were the oldest inhabitants of the islands. The Wahadimu of Zanzibar, living in the south and east of the island, where clove trees would not grow, had been largely excluded from the clove industry. They had probably been pushed off fertile land by the advance of clove plantations, while their number, proximity, and communal strength made it inopportune for plantation owners to force them into plantation labor. The Wapemba of Pemba Island remained interspersed throughout the island as clove planting expanded, living on the lowlands between the ridges where the cloves grew. Some grew cloves on a small scale. The Watumbatu lived on a small island and on the adjacent parts of Zanzibar Island. They supplemented farming with fishing and crafts but had little direct connection with the plantation economy or with cash-producing exports in general.[73]

The British were undoubtedly correct that the predominance of slave labor in nineteenth-century Zanzibar and Pemba made the expansion of "free" labor by people outside the plantation most unlikely. It was not simply that slavery debased the social value of work, but plantation discipline made working conditions unattractive for anyone who had a choice.[74] Indeed, the gradual breakdown of that discipline in the 1890s

72. Mass recruitment of laborers in India for plantations in Fiji, Ceylon, and Malaya went on as late as the 1930s. Beckford, *Persistent Poverty*, p. 57; Hugh Tinker, *A New System of Slavery: The Export of Indian Labour Overseas 1830–1920* (London, 1974). For a fine analysis of the effects of immigration on labor in Guiana, see Adamson.

73. There are some traditions of a communal labor obligation placed on Wahadimu during the nineteenth century, but there is little evidence that it was a significant factor in plantation labor. Most likely these traditions reflect wishful thinking about the extent of the Sultan's power. In 1891, when the clove industry had expanded enormously and slaves were becoming expensive, Fitzgerald's references to Wahadimu labor suggest that it was both voluntary and scarce. Later sources claim that Wahadimu labor was negligible (Fitzgerald, *Travels*, pp. 539, 549–50; AgAR, 1898, p. 33; Lyne, *Zanzibar in Contemporary Times*, p. 240). The British eagerly cited the precedent of the Sultan's corvée, but the principal evidence for it—vague as it is—pertains to the period before 1856. AgAR, 1901, pp. 27–28; Raikes to Cave, 18 Feb. 1903, incl. Cave to Lansdowne, 18 March 1903, FO 2/728; Lansdowne to Cave, 3 Dec. 1902, FOCP 8040, p. 218. On the actual evidence, see John Gray, *A History of Zanzibar from the Middle Ages to 1856* (London, 1962), pp. 161–63. See also Cooper, *Plantation Slavery*, pp. 57–59, 71, and John Middleton, *Land Tenure in Zanzibar* (London, 1961).

74. What slaves in the southern United States hated above all about their working conditions was the gang system, and this organization of labor prevented the emergence of "wage-labor plantations" both before and after abolition. Eugene D. Genovese, *Roll, Jordan, Roll: The World the Slaves Made* (New York, 1975), p. 313; Ransom and Sutch, *One Kind of Freedom*, pp. 65–71.

led to a modest introduction of voluntary labor during the harvest, some by Wapemba, some possibly by freed slaves. But slaveowners had to pay dearly for such labor: as much as half the crop for harvest labor alone. As of 1900, Wapemba (and Watumbatu and Wahadimu as well) participation in the Arab plantation economy was small, and local officials complained that Wapemba were far too attached to their own farms.[75]

The Administration attempted to expand the contribution of Swahili to the clove harvest by creating two labor bureaus in 1901, one for each island. Plantation owners were asked to report before the harvest the number of workers they would need. The bureaus fixed wages at four pice per pishi of cloves. In 1901, the Pemba bureau alone distributed 8,000 laborers for the harvest.[76]

The basis of the British effort to mobilize new plantation workers was forced labor. The Vice-Consul in Pemba had proposed in 1900 that "every able bodied negro in the island, not himself possessed of a clove shamba, would be liable under penalties to give his services in connection with the harvesting of the annual clove crop, upon such terms as regards payment as would be fixed by His Highness [the Sultan]." Race and landlessness were to determine who the working population would be; the state would set the terms. In 1901 the Sultan wrote to the *masheha* (singular *sheha,* headman) of the Wapemba asking them to help Slavery Commissioner Farler "make all their young men who were not otherwise engaged go into the plantations and pick cloves at the market rate of pay." The masheha agreed, provided that Wapemba who had their own clove trees be allowed to pick them first.[77]

The methods used to obtain Wapemba pickers were hardly subtle. Each sheha had to provide a list of his subjects and supply a set number of men. If a sheha complained that his men would not obey orders to pick cloves, Farler would send the police to bring his followers before the bureau: "After a good talking to, they generally agreed to work without further trouble." Apparently they did, for Farler announced in 1902 that "the labour question, as far as Pemba is concerned, has been solved."[78]

But the methods were too blatant. The Foreign Office decided in 1904 that the corvée labor in the harvest was "dangerously akin to the form of

75. D&C, Pemba, 1900, p. 13. In comparison, tenants in the southern United States more typically worked all year for a half-share of the harvest.

76. Farler, Report, 1901, PP 1903, XLV, 955, pp. 10–11.

77. Ibid., p. 11. Farler did not take Wapemba clove estates seriously. They were small, and the only exemption allowed Wapemba was to pick their own cloves first, not to avoid picking other people's cloves. The British did not consider that owning a little property made one part of the propertied class. Farler to Rogers, 15 Aug. 1904, FOCP 8382, p. 108.

78. Farler, Report, 1901, PP 1903, XLV, 955, p. 11; ibid., 1902, FOCP 8177, p. 108; Farler to Rogers, 15 Aug. 1904, FOCP 8382, p. 108.

compulsion against which it was the intention of the Decree of 1897 to safeguard the native population of the islands." Such qualms changed little. The line between organizing labor recruitment and compulsion was a fine one, particularly where the recruiters were local authorities and where the scene of the action was conveniently remote. "Constant pressure and personal visits" continued, but the Government was satisfied with its ideological purity by the fact that corvée laborers received the same pay as volunteers.[79]

On Zanzibar Island, forced labor began with the harvest of 1904–05, and it soon fed a transportation system that provided pickers to the heavy growing areas of Pemba. After suffering losses for want of labor in recent harvests and finding that exhortation by touring officials produced no volunteers among Wahadimu, the Administration took a firmer line as soon as the 1905 crop appeared to be promising. Officials—the police chief among them—made the rounds of masheha and told them to get their people ready for the harvest. Each Wahadimu village was assigned a quota, and the sheha was supposed to send half of that number for fifteen days' picking and then the second half to relieve them. The Agriculture Department estimated that 5,000 Wahadimu were involved. The harvest of 1905 was a good one. Officials did even better two years later: 639,185 frasilas, the largest harvest ever.[80]

In the successful harvest of 1907, as one official put it, "every possible forcible method was used. The people were driven from their houses, the Assistant Collectors were ordered to go about the villages and drive them in, the masheha were suspended or made to go and pick cloves themselves till they produced a certain number of laborers."[81]

In that year, the Government also began less heavy-handed ways of bringing forth labor, above all moving men from Zanzibar to Pemba. A ground tax of Rs 2/2 had been in effect since the days of the Sultanate. The tax was not high—perhaps two days' picking wages—or effectively collected, and it produced little revenue, but the Administration hoped it would encourage labor. In 1907 the Government offered to refund the Rs 2/2 to anyone who picked cloves for over thirty days, as well as to Wahadimu and Wapemba who owned over 1,000 clove trees (which hardly any did). In 1908, Rs 13,629 of the Rs 37,419 collected in Zanzibar and Pemba were refunded. Neither revenues nor the number of

79. FO to Cave, 31 Aug. 1904, FOCP 8357, p. 214; Cave to Lansdowne, 26 Oct. 1904, FOCP 8382, p. 31; AR, 1909, p. 27; AgAR, 1911, p. 144.

80. AgAR, 1905, incl. Cave to Grey, 10 Aug. 1906, FO 367/29; Last to Cave, 23 May 1908, FOCP 9401, pp. 85–86; AR, 1909, p. 23. On the vain attempt at persuasion, see AgAR, 1901, p. 27.

81. Collector of Zanzibar to First Minister, 15 May 1912, in AR, 1911, pp. 30–31. See also AgAR, 1910, p. 146, and Last to Cave, 23 May 1908, FOCP 9401, pp. 85–86.

laborers that taxes brought forth were worth the trouble they caused, and hut taxes were dropped in 1912.[82]

In addition, the Government began to offer free passage to Zanzibari pickers sailing to Pemba. In 1907, 3,700 of them used the free passes, while an estimated 2,000 went on their own. The program fluctuated greatly into the 1920s, but in some years over 8,000 pickers were sent to the island where they were most needed.[83]

The use of forced labor was much more than a prod given a reluctant people to enter the labor market. As Consul Cave said in 1904, "the Government should exercise a certain amount of control with respect to both the manner in which the available labour is to be utilized and the rate at which it is to be paid for."[84] The Government did not simply want labor, but subordinate and cheap labor, and it was not going to trust a labor market to supply it.

However, the fact that the Government was so successful in obtaining the labor—although not the control or the low cost—has much to do with the fact that the workers were not so reluctant after all. Wapemba had picked to a limited extent in the 1890s; Watumbatu took especially quick advantage of the rising demand for labor after abolition, perhaps because they could come and go quite easily to Pemba and had fewer clove trees themselves than the Wapemba. But the trend was general and common to much of Africa. Cheap manufactured goods were becoming more available and certain patterns of consumption were becoming important parts of daily life.[85] For the Swahili groups, growing food was not a problem but acquiring cash was. Their land was not the best, and the export economy was geared to clove trees, few of which they owned (see chapter 4).

The participation of these peoples in the clove harvest cannot be

82. A. Gunning to Clarke, 25 March 1907, FO 367/56; Lyne to Akers, 4 Dec. 1907 and 8 Jan. 1908, incl. Cave to Grey, 25 Jan. 1908, FO 367/94; AR, 1911, p. 11. The introduction of tax rebates involved some bungling that underlines government weakness. One official, without proper authorization, promised Wapemba and Wahadimu tax relief for picking. The Foreign Office was annoyed but felt unable to pull back for fear that the Swahili "would certainly refuse to have anything to do with the picking of cloves." FO Minute (n.d.) to Cave to FO, 9 Dec. 1907 (telegram), FO 367/56. The figures cited suggest that well under 20,000 people paid the tax; there were 70,000 adult male "natives" in the Native Census, 1924.

83. AgAR, 1911, p. 150; G. D. Kirsopp, "Memorandum on Certain Aspects of the Zanzibar Clove Industry," 1926, p. 40.

84. Cave to Lansdowne, 26 Oct. 1904, FOCP 8382, p. 31.

85. Farler, Report, 1901, PP 1903, XLV, 955, p. 11; Lyne, *Zanzibar in Contemporary Times*, p. 211. On the spread of shops and the expanding desire for cash to spend in them, see McClellan, p. 412. Arrighi emphasizes the importance of consumption patterns to locking Africans into wage labor, although this subject requires much more study. See chapter 4 on the dearth of opportunities for earning cash.

studied simply in terms of their responsiveness to wage incentives. Dependence on planters was no more appealing than shortage of cash. Swahili would undoubtedly have been welcome as wage laborers or tenants on Arab clove plantations, but that would have meant breaking the ties with their own villages that not only provided secure access to land for coconuts and subsistence crops, but made them part of a community.[86] Clove picking gave them a chance to earn money without disrupting their entire way of life.

By the harvest of 1911, it was becoming clear that Wapemba, Watumbatu, and Wahadimu were responding more to incentives than to force. In that harvest—breaking yet another record—the masheha were still "persuading" people to pick cloves, but the Agriculture Department believed their influence was on the wane and plantation owners were bargaining directly with pickers. The relief gang system in Zanzibar was dropped, and officials believed that the pickers recruited by masheha were more likely than others to desert. Although the refunding of the hut tax was ended, over 8,000 Wahadimu still took the steamer to Pemba, and more went by local vessels. Many Wahadimu villages were "almost deserted" during the harvest season.[87]

Clove picking had become a part of Wahadimu life, but only for a few months each year. From 10,000 to 15,000 people went each year to Pemba, and an equal number often picked in Zanzibar. Women and children joined the migration, and workers moved into crude huts on the owners' estates or built their own temporary shelters. All soon learned the techniques, so that the quality of work improved.[88] But if pickers did not like the working conditions, they went back home. Many returned from Pemba within ten days; most did not bother to wait for their free trip home. When workers in Zanzibar felt they were being cheated by the use of an oversized pishi to measure their output, or when they felt they were being assigned more difficult branches to pick than the resident laborers, they would not work. Lacking the power to police the plantations or the routes home thoroughly, the Government

86. Efforts to get Wapemba to become sharecroppers on Arab estates—even on good terms—were fruitless. Hardinge to Salisbury, 2 April 1897, FOCP 6964, p. 31. On the relationship of community to land tenure, see Middleton.

87. See the reports of Collectors and Assistant Collectors from Zanzibar Island in AR, 1911, pp. 31, 46, 51, 145, 150, and Ingrams, *Zanzibar, Its History and Peoples*, p. 254. By the 1920s, masheha had lost most of their authority. AR, Pemba, 1923, pp. 198–99; Ingrams, "Memorandum on Native Organization," 1926, pp. 2–4.

88. Robert Nunez Lyne, "Causes Contributing to the Success of the Zanzibar Clove Industry," *Bulletin of the Imperial Institute* 8 (1910): 144; Craster, p. 187; McClellan, p. 412; McClellan, Memorandum on Labour, 21 Nov. 1921, incl. Sinclair to Churchill, 28 Dec. 1921, CO 618/26; AgCom, 1923, p. 11. Participation of women and children in picking continued. Labour Department, AR, 1959, p. 8.

could do little to prevent this. Confronted one time by a group of Wahadimu upset with conditions they had found in Pemba, an official had to promise to help out and assure the workers that if they chose to leave an employer, nothing would be done to them.[89]

Wapemba—through choice and compulsion—had become wage-labor pickers at a slightly earlier date, and before 1910 officials believed that Pemba was ahead of Zanzibar in terms of the availability and organization of labor. But Wapemba also had more flexibility. Their homes were nearby the largest clove-growing areas, and Wapemba often worked for only a few days at a time. If wages were low, they went home.[90] As early as 1904, Wapemba were negotiating directly with landowners. Sometimes Wapemba, like most Wahadimu, worked under Arab supervision and were paid wages daily. Others, however, made agreements that gave them more control over the picking process itself. Sometimes they picked in exchange for half the produce. At other times, a group of Wapemba—as many as thirty—agreed to harvest an entire estate for a lump sum. These procedures provided strong incentives to Wapemba to work without disrupting the agricultural cycle or village life, but they did not produce the kind of labor force the Administration desired: the workers had too much choice about when and how to work, and planters had too little disciplinary power. The poor quality of work, especially the old problem of branch breaking, and the casual basis of employment were two aspects of one problem: the lack of regularity and discipline.[91]

In the next decade, officials' early assessments of the performance of Wapemba and Wahadimu were reversed. Wahadimu, once mobilized, came forth predictably each year; Wapemba were independent and resentful, all too ready to return to their villages. In 1920, the Agriculture Department claimed that picking wages were about 11 percent higher in

---

89. Rivers-Smith, Report on Mkokotoni Dist., AR, 1910, p. 171; Collector of Zanzibar to First Minister, 15 May 1912, AR, 1911, p. 30; AgAR, 1915, p. 47. The importance of governmental weakness is noted by a man in the field in Acting Asst. Collector, Mwera, to Acting Collector, Zanzibar, 31 Dec. 1910, AR, 1910, p. 172.

90. Raikes to Cave, 18 Feb. 1903, FOCP 8177, p. 58; Cave to Lansdowne, 28 Sept. 1904, FOCP 8382, p. 114; same to same, 26 Oct. 1904, FOCP 8383, p. 32; Last to Cave, 23 May 1908, FOCP 9401, p. 85; Lister to Grain, 31 Jan. 1908, FOCP 9401, pp. 108–09; Akers, Report, 1908, FOCP 9330, pp. 85–86; Asst. Collector, Chwaka, to Collector, 31 Dec. 1911, and Asst. Collector, Weti, to First Minister, 21 Feb. 1912, in AR, 1911, pp. 46, 65; AgAR, 1914, p. 2.

91. Cave to Lansdowne, 26 Oct. 1904, FOCP 8383, p. 32; Lister to Grain, 31 Jan. 1908, FOCP 9401, pp. 108–09; Sinclair to Long, 11 April 1917, incl. Pearce to Long, 3 May 1917, CO 618/17; Kirsopp, "Zanzibar Clove Industry," p. 10. On poor quality of work, see Raikes to Cave, 18 Feb. 1903, FOCP 8177, pp. 66–67; Belfield to Harcourt, 21 Nov. 1913, CO 618/3; Sinclair to Long (cited above); AgAR, 1919, p. 29; AR, 1920, p. 7; AgCom, pp. 20–21.

Pemba than in Zanzibar. Four years later, it insisted the differential was 40 percent.[92]

Part of the difference was that there were nearly twice as many clove trees in Pemba as in Zanzibar, while Zanzibar had a higher non-Arab population. Laborers who went to Pemba, instead of to nearby plantations in Zanzibar, would demand a higher wage to cover their migration costs and would be likely to work for longer periods. However, if one looks exclusively at Arab-owned plantations, the ones to which wage labor was directed, Pemba had only 20 percent more trees to be picked than Zanzibar.[93] And Wapemba were insisting as much as the migrants on a high wage. That they could do so is best explained by the slow extension of clove planting to Wapemba that had clearly emerged by the 1920s (see chapter 4). Selling cloves, for a substantial minority of Wapemba, became an alternative to selling labor, although the relative self-sufficiency of agriculture shielded Wapemba from too much reliance on either. Zanzibar, however, reflected the classic plantation model of a dichotomy between one social group that controlled large properties and a second group, on marginal land, with marginal access to markets, that had few alternatives to wage labor to meet cash needs. Yet even in Zanzibar Island, the disadvantages the Wahadimu faced were more those of owning land unusable for export crops and having market facilities too undeveloped to sell what surplus they did produce rather than an insufficiency of food. Thus, even in the 1940s and 1950s—when cash was more necessary than ever—pickers were still quick to leave Pemba if wages in a particular harvest turned out to be too low or if their own farms required attention earlier than usual.[94]

This relative independence lay at the root of the Government's continued unhappiness with the state of labor organization, even though Wahadimu, Watumbatu, and Wapemba remained the mainstay of the harvest and continued to bring in ever larger crops. The Agricultural

92. AgAR, 1911, pp. 144-45; Asst. Collector, Weti, to First Minister, 21 Feb. 1912, AR, 1911, p. 65. On wage differentials, see AgAR, 1920, pp. 13-14, 1924, p. 4; Kirsopp, p. 10.

93. On tree ownership, see AgAR, 1922, p. 99, and further discussion in chapter 4. In 1924, there were 32 percent more Wahadimu than Wapemba, while the "native" population of Zanzibar as a whole was 40 percent larger than that of Pemba, although the town accounts for some of the difference (Native Census, 1924). Expenses of the trip from Zanzibar to Pemba were reduced by the subsidized travel and by the provision of housing by plantation owners. Tidbury, pp. 111-12.

94. When rains came early in 1947, pickers went home to plant rice, despite high wages. In 1959, low wages sent pickers home early (Zanzibar, Labour Report, 1947, p. 7, 1959, p. 9). In other places, where workers lacked this kind of access to crop land, they had no such flexibility in seasonal labor. Adamson; Kay, p. 121; Peter Eisenberg, *The Sugar Industry in Pernambuco, 1840-1910: Modernization without Change* (Berkeley, 1974); Mintz, "The Rural Proletariat and the Problem of the Rural Proletarian Consciousness."

Commission of 1923 complained about the lack of "systematised control of labour." Pickers moved from plantation to plantation seeking higher wages; the price of labor was bid up during the course of each harvest; contracts could not be enforced and pickers suddenly deserted; malefactors could not be found.[95]

Periodically, the Government moved to reduce choice. During World War I, when demands for labor outside the islands added to the usual strain, a new labor control decree was passed; and it continued in force, with amendments in 1921 and 1923. The decrees allowed the Government to require any "native" who could not prove he had worked for wages for 60 days to be set to work for a public purpose, and officials made the dubious argument that clove picking was a public purpose because cloves were taxed.[96] A missionary charged that in some harvests labor recruitment amounted to a "man gang" approach—men were simply rounded up. But the Government claimed that the decrees were only used against recognized riff-raff and that in the 1920–21 harvest only 500 of the 24,000 people employed were recruited that way.[97] The Colonial Office did not believe clove picking was a public enterprise; Zanzibar was caught in the controversy over forced labor in Kenya; missionaries made a fuss; and cloves were getting picked anyway. The Administration backed down, and even dropped using forced labor for road building.[98] Nevertheless, the laws remained on the books. Worded so vaguely that they could apply to almost any "native," the labor control decrees reaffirmed the Government's power to use the corvée, and

95. AgAR, 1918, p. 44, 1920, p. 14; AgCom, pp. 20–21; AR, Zanzibar Dist., 1924, pp. 197–99; McClellan, Memorandum on Labour Conditions, 21 Nov. 1921, incl. Sinclair to Churchill, 28 Dec. 1921, CO 618/26. Complaints about lack of control over the flow of labor and the bidding up of wages continued. Labour Department, AR, 1947, p. 7.

96. Even the Colonial Office thought this argument made no sense. Minute by A. C. C. Parkinson, 18 July 1921, to Pearce to Churchill, 6 June 1921, CO 618/25. The 1923 version of the decree, after pained exchanges between Zanzibar and London, defined Government powers more narrowly. See Northey to Churchill, 9 Jan. 1922, CO 618/29, and the attached drafts and minutes.

97. Weston to Travers, 24 Oct. 1921, Universities Mission to Central Africa Archives, C2, fols. 76–77; Weston to Chairman, 1 Aug. 1921, ibid., fols. 65–66; Weston, Memorandum, 1 Sept. 1921, incl. Oldham to Wood, 1 Nov. 1921, CO 618/28; Weston, *Serfs of Great Britain*. For the Zanzibar Administration's reply, see Pearce to Churchill, 6 June 1921, CO 618/25; Sinclair to Churchill, 28 Dec. 1921, CO 618/26.

98. On Colonial Office caution, see Minutes to Northey to Churchill, 9 Jan. 1922, CO 618/29; Coryndon to Thomas, 7 Aug 1924, and Minutes, CO 618/33; CO to High Commissioner, 29 Nov. 1923, CO 618/30; Minutes to Hollis to Amery, 19 March 1927, CO 618/41. The Administration had to give in to Wapemba preferences to work a few days at a time on its Pemba road construction project, since the necessary Colonial Office approval for compulsory labor was not forthcoming. Hollis to Amery, 4 Sept. 1925, CO 618/36; Costley-White to Amery, 26 June 1926, CO 618/40.

TABLE 3:2
WAGES FOR CLOVE PICKING, ZANZIBAR

Wages: Pice/Pishi

Year	Start of Harvest	End of Harvest	Harvest Labor Cost Rs/Frasila (Dried)	Harvest Labor Cost % of Export Price
1897	3	—	—	—
1907	3	10–12	3.5	36
1913	5	12	—	—
1914	4	9	—	—
1914 (Arab)	4–5	10–12	—	—
1920 (Govt.)	4	9	—	—
1920 (Arab)	5	15	1.4–4.3	8–23
1921	8	15	—	—
1922	5	10	—	—
1923	5	12–14	5	25
1924	6	16	2.7–7.3	14–36
1926	5	14	—	—
1927	5	not hold	—	—
1929	6	9–10	—	—

SOURCES: AgAR, 1898, p. 12, 1913, p. 10, 1920, p. 12, 1921, p. 128, 1922, p. 83, 1924, p. 4, 1927, p. 245; AgCom, p. 21; Kirsopp, Report, 1926, p. 9; AR, Pemba, 1925, p. 64, 1926, p. 34, 1929, p. 300.

forced labor remained at one pole of the mechanisms of labor recruitment.

In 1920, the Administration also tried to restrict mobility and bargaining through a new contract system for the harvest. Wahadimu and Wapemba were advanced money if they signed a labor contract. But even the Agriculture Department admitted that the terms were unfair, and the pickers simply broke the contracts. Police and courts could not find the violators, and even if they did, the clove harvest was by then long over. What continued to work was the personal touch: local officials and masheha sought out workers, leaned on them a bit, and directed them where they were needed.[99]

Planters continued to bid for workers by paying competitive wages and agreeing to the pickers' preference for daily labor. As Table 3.2 shows, picking wages—continuing on a piecework basis—rose substantially until the 1920s and were bid up in the course of each harvest. According to Government figures, the cost of picking labor, per frasila

99. McClellan, Memorandum on Labour, incl. Sinclair to Churchill, 28 Dec. 1921, CO 618/26; AgAR, 1920, pp. 11, 13.

of cloves, rose 50 percent between 1914 and 1919, a total of 150 percent between the 1880s and 1920. The cost spurted again in 1919–21. What this meant in real terms is hard to say. Prices in England and India rose sharply during World War I and only went part way down in the early 1920s, so that wages fell slightly compared to the price of imports, although the workers' real net earnings—thanks to more bountiful harvests—may have risen. However, there is some evidence (chap. 4) that prices of items like fish and cassava, which laborers often bought, did not go up nearly as much as those of rice and the luxuries of the wealthy. On the other hand, there was a large, though unsteady, rise in the world price of cloves, especially between 1918 and 1924, that was roughly equivalent to the rising cost of harvest labor.[100] The planters could afford the consequences of a competitive labor market, but they could not keep the benefits of high export prices to themselves.

In 1920, a clove picker in Pemba—where wages and productivity were higher than in Zanzibar—could reportedly earn nearly Rs 2 per day. In a fifty-day harvest, a worker could thus earn almost Rs 100, equivalent to five months' labor at the current monthly rate.[101] Most pickers, above all Wapemba, did not work throughout the harvest, and the withdrawal of so much labor power helped to keep wages up.

In the 1920s, harvest wages stabilized and fell somewhat, partly because the harvest had become a regular and essential part of the lives of the pickers, above all of Wahadimu, and they could no longer easily withdraw their labor to force wages up. The limitations posed by the narrowness of the Zanzibari economy were compounded in 1924, when clove prices began to fall and the threat of British industrial purchasers of cloves to turn to synthetics brought a new resolve to the Government's old concern to lower wages (chapter 4). The free labor market had become "ruinous."[102] In 1927, the Government moved firmly to fix and lower wages. It used a tax rebate scheme in which planters—themselves unwilling to arrange a cartel—participated to pressure them into forming district committees that would fix wages at five pice per pishi. The scheme had a little success, but as early as the 1927 harvest, pickers in Pemba were returning to Zanzibar when faced with the low wage. Plant-

100. As of 1920, the price of cloves had risen 127 percent since 1894. AgAR, 1920, p. 12; AgAR, 1919, p. 36, 1921, p. 128, 1924, p. 4; Kirsopp, "Memorandum on Certain Aspects of the Zanzibar Clove Industry," p. 9; AgCom, p. 20. There are no price indices for Zanzibar, let alone one geared to laborers. But see the British and Indian indices in R. H. Crofton, "Statistics of the Zanzibar Protectorate," 1933, p. 28.

101. On Zanzibar Island wages were as much as Rs 1⅛ per day (AgAR, 1920, pp. 13–14). These estimates seem high, but other officials claimed that pickers could earn Rs 3 per day. Hollis to Amery, 30 Oct. 1925, CO 618/37.

102. Report of the Labour Committee, incl. Hollis to Amery, 13 April 1927, CO 618/41.

ers started paying higher wages surreptitiously, and the bidding up process resumed. The spread between the start and the end of the harvest had been narrowed but not eliminated. Overall, labor costs were driven down by 20 percent by 1929, but the price of cloves had fallen even more. Government wage fixing did little more than help planters survive.[103]

Although the Government had only moderate success in cutting wages and less in shaping the way pickers worked, it remained obsessed with the need to "control and regularize" the flow of labor. Officials worked through masheha to try to assure that people would be recruited in certain places, and labor officers of the Department of Agriculture arranged for them to be sent to others. Workers were brought to collecting stations, registered, and sent out.[104]

From the first years of the labor bureaus and forced labor, many Arabs came to depend on the Government for their workers. It was imperative, therefore, that planters cooperate with the state. In 1909–10, the 2,000 clove pickers given free passes to Pemba were sent to a mere 86 private plantations, plus 15 Government ones, an average of about 20 workers per plantation. In 1920, the Government had 632 requisitions for labor, and sent no labor at all in 323 cases. Although it granted 49 percent of the requisitions, it supplied 70 percent of the total number of laborers requested by the successful applicants. The Government preferred to send many workers to a few plantations rather than spread the labor over a wider number of planters. The larger applications seem to have been favored.[105] Planters had to be sure that the Administration accepted them as legitimate and sound. The labor distribution process was contributing to the creation of a dependent planter class.

Such dependence was far from complete, however, thanks to the workers' independence of the state. Plantation owners therefore sought to develop a network of personal contacts. Because the timing of the picking season was more precise than the organization of the labor market, social relations had to be mobilized. Just as the relationship of owner

103. On the origins of the wage-fixing scheme, see Memorandum of Agriculture Director, 15 Dec. 1926, incl. Hollis to Amery, 13 April 1927, CO 618/41. On its partial success, see AgAR, 1927, p. 245, 1929, p. 290, 1933, pp. 4–5; AR, Pemba, 1929, pp. 4, 300, 1931, p. 64.

104. Farler, Report, 1901, PP 1903, XLV, 955, p. 11; AgAR, 1913, p. 10, 1918, pp. 44–45, 1919, p. 29, 1920, pp. 13–14; Pearce to Churchill, 6 June 1921, CO 618/25; Sinclair to Churchill, 28 Dec. 1921, CO 618/26; Northey to Churchill, 9 Jan. 1922, CO 618/29. Organizing the harvest was not inexpensive. In 1913, for example, the Agriculture Department spent Rs 15,850, including Rs 7,000 on "gratuities" for masheha, on the harvest. AgAR, 1913, p. 10.

105. On all the requests, an average of 36 laborers each were asked for. On the successful ones, 51 each were granted. AR, 1909, p. 66; AgAR, 1920, p. 13.

to resident worker was used to establish a special claim to their services during the harvest, so relations established with Wahadimu and Wapemba headmen *before* the hiring period were important to the harvest process. The wealthier clove growers gave presents to the masheha. Many traveled to the villages to make prior arrangements for the harvest. Some advanced money to individuals whose food crops had not yet matured, hoping that indebtedness could be used to mobilize labor. But pickers could always desert and contracts could be broken: landowners had to bargain continuously with individual pickers. Personal networks and responsiveness to a competitive situation were both essential in order for a plantation owner to harvest his crop, and in either case the planter with substanital cash resources available before the crop came in had the advantage.[106]

Plantations, several writers have argued, are incompatible with viable peasant economies in the same region; the plantation must subordinate its hinterland and reduce the population to dependence on it.[107] In Zanzibar and Pemba, largely independent farming and fishing communities did coexist with plantations, but at a high cost to the planters. Harvest labor proved compatible with village life in ways that year-round plantation labor was not, but the villages weakened the ability of planters to control even harvest labor. The continual help of the state allowed planters to continue to profit from their clove trees, but all the coercion and subsidies did not break the independence of the clove pickers and only belatedly and to a limited extent reduced their wages.

RECRUITING WEEDERS

The people whose labor enabled the harvest to go forward—taking up the slack caused by the decline in labor extracted from slaves—were not interested in sacrificing secure land tenure and community life for year-round work on the plantations. Weeding around the clove trees and other continual tasks on the plantations were performed mainly by ex-slaves who were too few and too interested in their own plots. Although by 1905 large harvests were being brought in, plantations were

106. AgAR, 1918, pp. 44–45; McClellan, Labour Memorandum, incl. Sinclair to Churchill, 28 Dec. 1921, CO 618/26; AgAR, 1910, p. 145; C. Frewer, "Clove Harvest, 1904," *Central Africa* 23 (1905):155; Tidbury, p. 111.

107. Beckford; Adamson; Ramiro Guerra y Sanchez, *Sugar and Society in the Caribbean: An Economic History of Cuban Agriculture* (New Haven, 1964). The response of Swahili to plantation employment is what Eric Wolf calls "double adaptation . . . one foot into the plantation way of life, while keeping the other foot on the peasant holding." The footstep onto the plantation in Zanzibar is rather smaller than that in Wolf's example of Jamaica. "Specific Aspects of Plantation Systems in the New World."

becoming overrun with weeds. New sources of labor were desperately needed.[108]

Zanzibar, however, had long been part of a vast and complex regional economy. That economy had been disrupted by the violence of the colonial conquest, above all in German Tanganyika, and by epidemics and famines. Colonial boundaries and the undermining of ivory and slave-trading networks affected the region's commercial structure and eliminated opportunities that had been seized by peoples like the Nyamwezi of Tanganyika. After having become committed to a pattern of trade linked to a world economy, they found their old avenues to wealth and power shut off. Chiefs could no longer collect numerous henchmen with the promise of a share of the spoils of hunting and caravan operations, while ordinary people could no longer gain a dry-season income from porterage or a harvest bonanza from sales to passing caravans. For such groups, labor migration was neither a response to new enticements nor a desperate strategy for survival, but an effort to maintain the economic advantages that a differentiated economy had once given them. Experience had acquainted Nyamwezi with much of East Africa, and the conditions of employment in Tanganyika made it advisable that they use this knowledge. Throughout East Africa, however, the pressures to seek work were varied, from coercion to land shortage to increased availability of imported goods. In many places neighboring Zanzibar the pressures to seek work were becoming more intense than they were in Zanzibar in the first two decades of the twentieth century.[109]

It was to this wide region that the Zanzibar Government turned for help. It first tried to recruit pickers on three-month contracts, mostly from Kenya, and obtained 819 workers in 1905 and 1,600 in 1907. However, the pickers did not harvest as many cloves as their contracts specified; they were dissatisfied with living conditions and became "riotous" when there were delays in repatriations; and the transport costs were high.[110]

108. AR, Pemba, 1905, incl. Cave to Grey, 10. Aug. 1906, FO 367/29.

109. The term *Nyamwezi* applies to a number of related peoples from western Tanganyika. They dominated the labor market in Tanganyika before the 1920s. Andrew Roberts, "Nyamwezi Trade," in R. Gray and D. Birmingham, eds., *Pre-Colonial African Trade* (London, 1970), pp. 39–74; Iliffe, pp. 160–62; Kjekshus, pp. 157–60. Nyamwezi were notable for their participation in wage labor in Tanganyika and Kenya as well as Zanzibar. My argument follows one given in another context by W. G. Clarence-Smith and R. Moorsom, "Underdevelopment and Class Formation in Ovamboland, 1845–1915," *JAH* 16 (1975):365–82. On the pressures exerted on people in Kenya to seek wage labor, see Clayton and Savage.

110. The mainland pickers cost the planters Rs 38,000 and the Government Rs 34,000 in 1907, while the cloves they picked fetched only Rs 160,000. On the failure of this scheme, see Sinclair to Lansdowne, 3 May 1904, FOCP 8356, p. 89; Cave to Lansdowne, 26

To bring workers so far for so short a time was not the way to bring costs down. But at the same time—and without much fanfare—mainland migrants were beginning to find a niche where Wapemba and Wahadimu had no desire to go. The year-round task of weeding around clove trees came to be the specialty of mainland laborers, above all of Nyamwezi.

In 1908, 187 Nyamwezi were working on Government plantations. They quickly became "our principal weeders," and officials rejoiced in the improved appearance of the clove plantations. By 1909, they were "an established feature in Zanzibar plantation life." They were paid Rs 10 per month plus Rs 2 for food, and they were expected to weed the areas around six clove trees each day. Some soon grew cassava for their own consumption, plus a little for sale.[111]

Migrants kept coming, and their importance to plantation cultivation increased. They came without official recruitment—thanks, no doubt, to a Nyamwezi communications network that officials knew nothing about.[112] Later, when a registration ordinance was in effect from 1917 to 1921, 8,000 men passed through the office and many others were missed. The 1924 census—not a paragon of thoroughness—uncovered 5,741 weeders from mainland ethnic groups, including 2,608 Nyamwezi. Over half the weeders listed by occupation in the census were Nyamwezi. Another 30 percent came from other mainland ethnic groups that had supplied Zanzibar with slaves; many of them undoubtedly were ex-slaves. The increasing importance of the mainlanders, however, did not end the migratory nature of their services. In the three years 1924–26, 13,546 mainlanders arrived, but 9,233 left. In later years numbers fluctuated in response to economic conditions in Zanzibar and wages on the mainland.[113] As with harvest labor, the Government sought to control

Oct. 1904, and Cave to Stewart, 1 Oct. 1904, FOCP 8383, pp. 32–33; Memorandum by O'Sullivan-Beare on Mainland Labour recruited for the 1904–05 clove crop in Pemba, 31 Dec. 1904, FO 2/923; AgAR, 1905, incl. Cave to Grey, 10 Aug. 1906, FO 367/29; Reports by Farler and McClellan on the 1907 harvest, FOCP 9641, pp. 123, 127; Akers Report, 1908, and enclosures from the Director of Agriculture, 1908, FOCP 9330, pp. 41–44, 79; AR, 1909, p. 27. In addition, the Kenyan Government did not like to see labor leave its shores, although casual laborers continued to go to Zanzibar for the clove harvest on their own. CO to FO, 28 May 1907, FOCP 9132, p. 76; QR, Malindi, 4th quart. 1911, CP 1/37; Akers Report, 1908, FOCP 9330, p. 78.

111. Director of Agriculture, Report, in Akers Report, 1908, FOCP 9330, p. 74; AR, 1909, pp. 65–66.

112. The Germans were not keen on Nyamwezi leaving the country, but they kept coming. Cave to Grey, 23 Feb. 1908, FOCP 9331, p. 7; McClellan, pp. 412, 414; AgCom, p. 21; Armstrong, p. 29.

113. For more on occupations and ethnic classifications, see chapter 4. Native Census, 1924, pp. 8, 11; AgAR, 1920, p. 4; Kirsopp, "Memorandum," p. 11, AgCom, p. 21; Hollis to Amery, 19 March 1927, CO 618/41, AR, Zanzibar Dist., 1930, pp. 135–36, 1931, p. 134;

the distribution of the migrants, arranging contracts between Arabs and weeders.[114]

Many migrants stayed two or three seasons, although some stayed less than six months. While Wapemba and Wahadimu invariably preferred daily labor or piecework, immigrants insisted on monthly wages and needed quarters and cooking utensils. Some brought their wives, and many grew their own food. A number settled permanently as tenants on the land of planters eager to acquire resident laborers. Only a few bought clove estates.[115]

Officials exempted Nyamwezi from their scorn of African laborers. One official from a later period said that a Nyamwezi with a hoe was like Yehudi Menuhin with a violin. The contrast with ex-slaves and other Swahili laborers was paramount in official minds and was seen in racial terms: the Swahili was "physically inferior and less amenable to discipline than the mainland visitor." Some mainlanders, wrote an official in 1915, worked on a Government plantation in the morning and for an Arab in the afternoon. The Nyamwezi work ethic, he felt, should be rewarded with increased tasks.[116]

This amenability to discipline was less a matter of character than of the structure of work within a regional economy. In fact, demands on weeders had been increasing all along. While the wages of weeders, like those of pickers, rose until the early 1920s, so too did productivity, as Table 3.3 reveals. Picking costs rose steadily from the 1890s and spurted 50 percent between 1914 and 1925, but weeding costs actually fell after 1909.[117] The contrast reflects the different basis on which mainland immigrants entered plantation labor. Having invested in a long journey, migratory laborers wanted to make as much money as quickly as possible, but they were less concerned with the amount and pace of labor than were the clove pickers. Wartime inflation and the alternative of military pay caused mainland laborers to desert the Government plantations

---

Anthony Clayton, "The General Strike in Zanzibar, 1948," *JAH* 17 (1976):420. Migrants, as Clayton describes, were important in urban labor in Zanzibar town.

114. AgAR, 1920, p. 4.

115. Cave to Grey, 28 Feb. 1908, FOCP 9331, p. 7; Report on the Island of Pemba by Capt. Craster, 29 Feb. 1912, and comments by McClellan and Clarke, in FOCP 10239, pp. 3, 13, 17; AgAR, 1919, p. 25; Armstrong, p. 29; AR, Zanzibar Dist., 1925, p. 53; Memorandum by Senior Commissioner, 15 Oct. 1925, incl. Hollis to Amery, 30 Oct. 1925, CO 618/37. The 1924 Native Census (pp. 8, 11) lists only 135 Nyamwezi shamba owners.

116. F. B. Wilson, interview, Cambridge, Eng., 16 Sept. 1977. Wilson's sensitivity to the particular agricultural skills of different peoples is not found in the crude racial interpretations of most officials. Ingrams, *Zanzibar, Its History and Peoples*, pp. 32–33; Craster, p. 74, AR, Pemba Dist., 1926, p. 34.

117. In addition to table 3.3, see the comparisions of picking and cultivation costs in AgCom, p. 21, and Kirsopp, "Memorandum," p. 9.

TABLE 3:3
WEEDING WAGES, ZANZIBAR

	Required Task Pengeles	Wage Rs/mo.	Labor Cost Rs/Pengele
1897	—	8–9	—
1909	6	10+2 for food	2
1910	—	12	—
1913 (Govt.)	7	12	1.7
1913 (Arab)	6	12	2
1917	—	16	—
1920–21	10	21	2.1
1922	10	18	1.8
1924 (Govt.)	10	18	1.8
1924 (Arab)	8	12–15+rice	1.5–1.9
1925 (New rules)	15	18	1.2
or	10	12	1.2

SOURCES: AgAR, 1897, p. 25, 1917, p. 119, 1924, pp. 2–3; AR, 1909, pp. 65–66; McClellan, memorandum, 17 July 1913, incl. Sinclair to CO, 10 Oct. 1913, CO 618/2; McClellan, "Agricultural Resources," p. 415; AgCom, p. 21; Armstrong, "Agriculture," p. 29; Hollis to Amery, 30 Oct. 1925, CO 618/37.

NOTE: A pengele is the square bounded by four clove trees, each separated by 21 feet, namely, 441 square feet. A month is 26 working days.

until a 30 percent increase in wages was implemented. Earlier, however, the Government's attempt to increase daily tasks for six to eight pengeles (the area bounded by four clove trees) resulted in a compromise at seven, and the Government had no difficulty keeping workers, even though Arab planters were less demanding. This pattern of response was a contrast not only to clove pickers but to coastal people in Kenya, who shunned the higher-paying European plantations, with their demanding work routines, in favor of Arab and Swahili estates, where the manner and duration of their labor were more to their own choosing.[118]

The situation became clearer when the Government—as clove prices fell after 1924—tried with new vigor to cut wages. By then, increased immigration had already reduced wages somewhat, although they were still 50 percent above prewar levels.[119] Officials decided in 1924 to fix wages at a lower level and got Arab planters to agree not to hire workers

118. AR, 1909, pp. 65–66; AgAR, 1917, p. 119, 1919, p. 36. For comparisons with the coast of Kenya, see chapter 5.

119. The connection between increased immigration and declining wages after 1920 is made in AR, 1920, p. 8; AgAR, 1922, p. 85.

who left Government plantations. But when the Government informed Nyamwezi headmen of this plan, it was warned that their men would leave if wages were reduced but that they would be willing to do more work. So officials agreed to keep wages at Rs 18, but raise the daily task to 15 pengeles instead of 10, or else to pay Rs 12 for 10 pengeles instead of the Rs 12 to 15 for 8 pengeles that was more typical of Arab estates. This system worked far better than the cuts in picking wages that officials were also trying to ram through, and the Government believed it was getting five to six hours of labor per day instead of three, although both figures are probably low. Nyamwezi preferred a speedup to a wage cut, and officials were doubtful enough of their own power to try for both. The labor supply for weeding remained adequate.[120] Given the economic situation on the mainland, Nyamwezi had to look farther afield than Zanzibaris, and were consequently more vulnerable to the fluctuations and manipulations of plantation labor. To save the income they needed so much, they had to confine their struggle to the parameters of a wage economy, conceding more work for the same pay. They could not, like the pickers, struggle over *how* they would work.

Before the wage fixing of 1924, the Agricultural Commission complained that wages were high in comparison to the mainland. Weeders could return home with as much as Rs 300 to Rs 500, a substantial sum by official conceptions of African labor. Even in 1931, a report complained that wages were still, in real terms, considerably above prewar levels. Despite increased productivity, labor costs made it impossible to follow the planting methods of the days of slavery. Then, for example, young clove plants were carefully watered, but now such care would cost too much.[121]

As usual, officials complained about the lack of control over the migrants: they would break contracts, move about, or go to town at will. At first, mainland weeders refused to help with the harvest, apparently content with the weeding wages and the access to land they had year-round. In the 1924 season, mainlanders were doing some picking, but not to the same extent as Swahili, for the opportunity of earning

---

120. AgAR, 1924, pp. 2–3; Hollis to Amery 19 Feb. 1925, CO 618/35; same to same, 16 June 1925, CO 618/36. Migration later went down somewhat when conditions in Tanganyika improved. AgAR, 1933, p. 23.

121. To earn over Rs 300 would require two years' work if the worker was able to grow all his own food. More likely, officials felt, he could save half his earnings. AgCom, p. 21; AgAR, 1920, pp. 4, 24; C. F. Strickland, "Report on Cooperation and the Economic Condition of the Agriculturalists in Zanzibar," incl. Strickland to Acheson, 12 June 1931, CO 618/49; R. S. Troup, "Report on Clove Cultivation in the Zanzibar Protectorate," 1931, p. 29. Earlier, the Agriculture Department observed that if Zanzibar had tried to start a clove industry at that time, it would not have been able to do so. AgAR, 1909.

money for a short period of intense labor was not what appealed to people who had migrated hundreds of miles.[122]

Mainland labor did not displace or threaten the ex-slaves still resident on plantations in the same way that the labor of indentured immigrants in, for example, Guiana drove down wages and undermined the partial independence of ex-slaves. Officials continued to complain of the "utter hopelessness of the freed slave labour," and they remained unable to enforce labor obligations on the ex-slaves. Clove trees had to be weeded at the same time as the ex-slaves' crops, and it was the ex-slaves' own fields that came first. The official views may have been exaggerated, but the ex-slaves could use their plots and the earnings from seasonal labor to maintain some control over their conditions of wage labor. The Government—always eager to set an example for other landlords— could do little more than make the best of it: on Government planta- tions, freed slaves still squatted rent-free, provided only that they helped out in the harvest.[123] Nyamwezi weeded the Government's clove trees.

Initially, the state had tried to create an agricultural proletariat out of ex-slaves. Instead, from its failure to control ex-slaves, its use of coercion to recruit and channel labor, and the constraints and incentives that im- pinged on various peoples on and off the island, a more complex pattern of labor emerged in which mainland laborers, Wapemba, Wahadimu, and Watumbatu, and freed slaves all came to occupy different niches of plantation labor, coming from different situations and having differ- ent objectives. To the state, this was an undesirable compromise, forced upon it by the fact that the laborers had access—in different ways— to land. Yet the separation of distinct roles in clove production— weeding, picking, resident labor—among different peoples had the effect of making each niche dependent on the others. No one worker, no one group of workers, saw the process of clove production through from seedling to dried clove. While all were only partially dependent on plantation labor for their livelihood, the lack of development of alternative economic activities—itself accentuated by the drawing out of labor from local economies—meant that most had little alter- native to wage labor for part of the time to meet their cash needs.[124]

122. AgCom, p. 21; Memorandum on Labour by McClellan, 1921, incl. Sinclair to Churchill, 28 Dec. 1921, CO 618/26; AR, Zanzibar Dist., 1924, p. 197; AR, Pemba Dist., 1926, p. 34.

123. McClellan, p. 414; AgAR, 1911, p. 151, 1920, p. 10; Blais, p. 510. However, Wapemba disliked Nyamwezi immigrants and at times refused to sell them food. Craster, pp. 102–03. On Guiana, see Adamson.

124. In parts of the Americas, the cultivation of plantations by resident slaves also gave way to a complex blend of labor by plantation residents, several laborers from nearby vil- lages, and immigrants—often indentured. Whether or not cheap and subordinate labor

Islanders had little alternative to plantation labor. Only Wapemba, to any significant extent, were able to move into clove production themselves, despite the fact that clove trees required little capital and offered few advantages to the large producer. The atomization of plantation labor was thus a result of the laborers' economic strength and a cause of their weakness.

WORK, PROPERTY, AND THE CRIMINAL LAW

In 1901, the Slavery Commissioner of Pemba ordered the police to round up "all vagrants and masterless men" and send them to pick cloves.[125] Being masterless in a society where masters had been abolished had become a crime. The police and the criminal law were being used to force people into dependent relationships and into labor that was regarded as productive, even as court-enforced contracts and a variety of techniques of recruitment were being used to effect the same ends.

The crackdown in Pemba was part of a wider pattern. Beginning in 1897, police forces were augmented and a large number of arrests were made for categories of crime that were invariably, in official minds, linked: vagrancy, theft—especially of farm produce—adultery, assault, and drunkenness. Social scientists who have moved beyond regarding crime as the result of the criminal's villainy have often seen in crime statistics the reflection of a society's pathology: crime reflects social dislocation or deprivation. Yet crime statistics often reveal more about the people who define crimes than about those who commit them.

Such was the case in Zanzibar. Vagrancy is invariably an ill-defined crime, let alone in a case where social structure and labor organization are changing. Property crimes are hardly easier to specify when rights of access to farm products are changing and where the extent and legitimacy of landowners' control of land is anything but clear and universally

---

could be obtained depended upon the ability of the state and the planter class to narrow alternatives available to local workers, to control immigration, and to prevent competition for labor among planters; and the extent to which seasonal labor was a desirable supplement to independent cultivation or a job on which workers relied for a great proportion of their meager incomes depended on how this power was exercised. Among the studies of this transition process are Adamson; Curtin, *Two Jamaicas*; Michael Craton, *Searching for the Invisible Man: Slaves and Plantation Life in Jamaica* (Cambridge, Mass., 1978), esp. p. 293; Eisenberg, *Sugar Industry in Pernambuco*; and a forthcoming study of Cuba by Rebecca Scott. See also Mintz, "Slavery and the Rise of Peasantries."

125. Farler, Slavery Report, 1901, PP 1903, XLV, 955, p. 11. The phrase "masterless men" suggests an ideological throwback to precapitalist England, an indication that colonial rulers were in some ways conservative by eighteenth-century standards. See Christopher Hill's chapter, "Masterless Men," in his book on seventeenth-century England, *The World Turned Upside Down* (London, 1972), pp. 32–45.

accepted. Indeed, the Administration was trying to effect a change in property rights that parallels the gradual erosion of the rights which European cottagers and tenants once had to common land and hunting. Once the complex rights of different classes became submerged beneath the absolute ownership of property, rights became crimes and had to be punished.[126] Coercion would be part of the process of redefinition, but it would be done by the state, under established procedures, and in the name of society as a whole.

Although crime statistics were rarely reported in a consistent fashion, the convictions for what officials called "petty crimes"—those listed in Table 3.4—were numerous just at the time that slaves were being freed. There was no doubt in official minds that the crime problem and the slave problem were closely related. Salisbury observed that the high incidence of crime "may not be regarded with any surprise by those who had, from local experience, awaited with some apprehension the prospect of a sudden relaxation of the bonds of compulsory toil." Without such bonds, Farler insisted, crime was to be expected, for slaves had the "bodily strength and passions of full-grown men and women, yet without any power of self-restraint."[127]

It is neither important nor accurate to argue that officials prosecuted such crimes with the specific intention of forcing ex-slaves into the labor market. Rather, crimes reflected the kind of society the British wanted to end and the kind they wanted to create. Property crimes followed directly from the Government's decision to recognize title to land and houses: if theft was not prosecuted, property rights meant little. Adultery, assault, and drunkenness were all aspects of disorder, all part of a pattern of living that industrial capitalism could not tolerate. In the aftermath of abolition, officials had feared that slaves would "sweep in a great wave of disorder across the surface of the two Islands of Zanzibar and Pemba," and the officials had, in a sense, created their own wave of petty crime. The crime figures—a rate of over one conviction per twenty people in Zanzibar town in 1906, about one per fifty "natives" (let alone ex-slaves) overall—suggest a turbulent population that the almost total absence of less ambiguously defined crimes, like murder, would seem to belie.[128]

126. Hay et al.; E. P. Thompson, *Whigs and Hunters: The Origins of the Black Act* (London, 1975); Foucault, pp. 84–85.

127. Salisbury to Hardinge, 29 June 1898, FOCP 7077, p. 229; Farler, Report, 1898, PP 1898, LX, 559, p. 61; Hardinge to Salisbury, 23 April 1898, ibid., pp. 70. 72; O'Sullivan-Beare, Report, 1898, PP 1898, LXIII, 303, p. 53.

128. Curzon to House of Commons, 10 Feb. 1898, in *ASR* 18 (1898):14. Farler feared not only "unrest among the slaves," but "terrible agrarian wars between slaves and their masters." He claimed that armed bands of slaves had roamed Pemba shortly after abolition

TABLE 3:4
CONVICTIONS FOR PETTY OFFENSES

Year	Population	Vagrancy	Theft, Burglary	Assault	Adultery	Intoxication	All Convictions Reported
1897	Zanzibar: slaves and ex-slaves	325	627	—	—	461	—
1898	Zanzibar and Pemba: total	912	666	312	—	666	—
1899	Pemba: slaves and ex-slaves	472	365	94	43	19	—
1901	Pemba: total	451	473	276	166	16	—
1901	Zanzibar: total	46	267	151	74	58	657
1902	Pemba: slaves and ex-slaves	142	390	287	73	41	934
1902	Zanzibar: total	23	203	133	28	74	505
1904	Zanzibar: urban	3	449	94	8	852	1,752
1905	Zanzibar: urban	0	380	87	6	444	1,343
1906	Zanzibar: urban	40	469	218	10	563	1,593
1906	Zanzibar: rural	2	395	225	28	74	859
1906	Pemba: total	96	287	179	54	37	1,110
1907	Zanzibar: rural	17	373	230	1	164	989
1907	Zanzibar: urban	—	—	—	—	—	1,068
1907	Pemba: total	2	424	232	18	103	903

SOURCES: Hardinge to Salisbury, 23 April 1898, PP 1898, LX, 559, pp. 68, 70; Mathews to Hardinge, 17 March 1899, PP 1899, LXIII, 303, p. 32; Farler to Mathews, 26 Jan. 1900, and Cave to Lansdowne, 19 April 1901, PP 1901, XLVIII, 173, pp. 14, 36; Cave to Lansdowne, 21 Feb. 1903, and Farler, Report, 1901, PP 1903, XLV, 955, p. 16; Farler, Report, 1902, FOCP 8177, p. 107; Last to Raikes, 8 Feb. 1903, FOCP 8177, pp. 74–75; Farler, Report, 1906, and Taubman, Report, 1906, FOCP 9132, pp. 111–12, 122; Last to Cave, 23 May 1908, and Durand to Grain, 1 Jan. 1908, FOCP 9401, pp. 91, 100–01; Report on Pemba, incl. Cave to Grey, 2 Nov. 1908, FOCP 9459, p. 97; AR, 1909, p. 46.

NOTE: Not all cases under the 1905 Vagrancy Act are included, notably 138 convictions in 1907.

This particular assortment of crimes—as well as excessive dancing—formed a unified whole, and it was closely linked to the problem of work. One official lumped these related attitudes and fears together:

> The slaves, especially in the northern part of Pemba, won't work. . . . They are often dancing day and night. The cocoanut trees are cut for toddy in defiance of the masters, and much drunkenness and quarrelling ensues. The Walis and Jemedars have many cases of cutting and wounding brought before them, and the immorality is frightful. House-breaking and stealing are the natural consequences of the excess and have been numerous.[129]

Freed slaves, officials claimed, committed the most petty crime in the islands; most prostitutes were freed slaves. The idle and disorderly "floating population" of Zanzibar town was largely made up of ex-slaves who flocked to town.[130]

The conjuncture of resistance to work, disorder, crime, dissipation, and immorality was implicit in antislavery ideology: slaves were rootless people, incapable of working or upholding any standards of conduct. The problem of crime was part of the emancipation process: slaves had to be made fit for an orderly society and taught self-discipline. The attack on crime was not a direct attempt to make people work: it was an assault on the social complex of idleness.

So too was the attack on drinking and dancing, enforced by criminal law. Hardinge clearly saw dances (*ngomas*) and the drinking of palm wine (*tembo*) as alternatives to work. Unable to restrain themselves, ex-slaves and other "natives" would drink and dance all night and sleep all day. Edward Clarke, Consul-General in 1912, was particularly eager to "prevent a number of childish savages from wasting their money and their very small stock of energy in a demoralising dance" that was also likely to lead to a "dangerous state of sexual excitement," as well as

---

but had been stopped by the police. Report, 1898, PP 1898, LX, 559, p. 64; Farler to Mathews, 26 Jan. 1900, FOCP 7405, pp. 106–07. The estimates of crime rates are based on the very rough census of total native population in 1910. See Kuczynski, pp. 652, 680–81.

129. Farler, Report, 1898, PP 1898, LX, 559, p. 60. These associations are also evident in Hardinge to Salisbury, 23 April 1898, ibid., p. 70; O'Sullivan-Beare, Report, 1898, PP 1898, LXIII, 303, pp. 53–54; AgAR, 1914, p. 2.

130. Cave to Lansdowne 20 Dec. 1904, FOCP 8435, p. 35; Last, Report, 1906, FOCP 9132, p. 117; Farler, Report, 1906, ibid., p. 122; Report by Drs. MacDonald and Curwen upon the question of a Decrease in the Native Population of Zanzibar, its Causes, and any suggested Remedies, 1908, FOCP 9331, p. 32; Last to Raikes, 23 June 1908, incl. Cave to Grey, 13 Aug. 1908, FO 367/99; AgAR, 1914, p. 2. The connections for the English middle class between urban life, casual labor, prostitution, crime, and disorder is stressed by Stedman Jones, *Outcast London*.

crime.[131] The Government banned all ngomas in public places and required a permit for dances in private homes, for which a small fee had to be paid. Even this allowed too much room for dissipation for Clarke, who, prodded by his Agriculture Department, sent numerous despatches on the subject to the Foreign Office. That the dignified gentlemen who formed British foreign policy should be concerned with the fact that one Athman Abdulla, an ex-slave from the Lake Nyasa region, was holding a dance called "Lelemama" from 8 P.M. to 2 A.M. one night may seem excessive, but Clarke was sending them weekly lists of ngomas. Foreign Office officials thought Clarke was a bit carried away, but they were not amused.[132] Indeed, the assault on popular amusements in England dated to the rise of capitalism in the eighteenth century, and the cause was by no means neglected by the reformers of the Victorian and Edwardian eras.

The problem of drink had so concerned European powers that a ban on importing spirits for Africans was tacked onto the prohibitions on slave trading and arms sales in the Brussels Agreement of 1890.[133] The new order would be a sober one. The Zanzibar Government went beyond that, prohibiting all sales, possession, and consumption of "native" liquors as well as imported ones. A violator could get up to a year in jail plus a Rs 1,000 fine. Such draconian legislation was based on the grounds that Zanzibaris "possess no self control and are thus seldom able to take intoxicants in moderation." Selling tembo was prosecuted—there were 103 convictions in Zanzibar Island in 1907—and drunks were thrown in jail, especially in Zanzibar town.[134] The moral virtues of a work-oriented society were being forcibly taught.

If the assault on petty crime, dancing, and drinking struck at the social

131. Hardinge to Salisbury, 23 April 1898, PP 1898, LX, 559, p. 72; Clarke to Grey, 11 Dec. 1912, FO 367/345. See also O'Sullivan-Beare, Report, 1898, PP 1898, LXIII, 303, p. 54; Craster, p. 310; AgAR, 1911, p. 30.

132. Clarke to Grey, 6, 20 Aug. 1912, FO 367/304; same to same, 11 Dec. 1912, FO 367/345; AgAR, 1911, p. 30; Sinclair to Grey, 3 April 1913, FO 367/345. Various complications prevented Clarke's total ban from being implemented, but permits were still required for private ngomas. On the connection of capitalism and popular amusements in England, see Thompson, *Making of the English Working Class;* Stedman Jones, "Working-Class Culture."

133. Miers, *Britain and the Ending of the Slave Trade.* The application of such principles revealed a certain ambivalence. South African industrialists at first found that making and selling liquor to Africans brought in profits and created a consumer demand that brought forth wage labor. But as industrial discipline became an increasing concern to the magnates, drinking became a problem and the owners came into conflict with the liquor interests they had helped to create. Charles van Onselen, "Randlords and Rotgut, 1886–1903," *History Workshop Journal* 2 (1976): 33–89.

134. Sinclair to Harcourt, 27 Nov. 1913, CO 618/3; Durand to Grain, 1 Jan. 1908, FOCP 9401, pp. 100–01; AgAR, 1911, p. 30.

complex of idleness, the prosecution of vagrancy was a *direct* attempt to make people work and to define work in terms of the plantation system. Shortly after abolition, Liwalis were instructed to impose terms of imprisonment or hard labor, from a few days to a week, on anyone found "wandering about without a home or visible means of subsistence."[135]

But a "great deal of vagrancy" continued to be prevalent, particularly among ex-slaves, in the face of the high number of prosecutions in 1897 and 1898.[136] In 1899, as noted earlier, officials in Pemba briefly tried to make a home and a means of support a precondition for freedom. At the same time, all slaves found in town—the principal refuge for people who wanted to avoid plantations—without a house or work were arrested and sent to the plantations. Allegations were made, through antislavery circles, that officials were simply rounding up people and sending them to Arab plantations even when they already had a job.[137]

The Foreign Office rejected house and job as a precondition for freedom, but saw nothing wrong with the pursuit of "masterless men." In fact, authorities made it more and more unpleasant to be caught without an employer-landlord-patron: a first vagrancy offense in Pemba was punishable by seven days in jail, with the proviso that the court would find work for the offender. The sentence for a second offense was a month in jail, for a third, three months. The jails of Pemba were soon crowded, mostly with vagrants. "Inveterate vagrants," along with prisoners serving long sentences, were used in roadwork.[138]

A new vagrancy decree in 1905 regularized all these practices: anyone who neglected or refused to maintain himself or his family *or* who was found asking for alms *or* who was without visible means of subsistence (except, in all cases, the infirm) was deemed a vagrant. He could be committed to up to three months in jail, and the Government was instructed to provide him employment at a very low wage. If a person refused such work, another two months would be tacked onto the sentence. The long-range aim of this harsh decree was "inducing the freed slave to work and . . . keeping [him] from a criminal life." Meanwhile, as a judge noticed, "if much labour were required, it would be General

135. Hardinge to Salisbury, 23 April 1898, PP 1898, LX, 559, p. 70.

136. Farler to Mathews, 26 Jan. 1900, and O'Sullivan, Report, 1899, FOCP 7405, pp. 107, 120. Conviction statistics are in table 3.4.

137. Farler to Mathews, 31 Jan., 16 June 1899, PP 1900, LVI, 839, pp. 7, 34; Edib to Pease, 17 April 1899, FO 107/108. It is impossible to verify these allegations.

138. O'Sullivan-Beare, Report, 1899, PP 1901, XLVIII, 173, p. 16; Farler to Mathews, 26 Jan. 1900, ibid., p. 101; D&C, Pemba, 1900, p. 4. In England, an increasingly harsh distinction was made between inveterate vagrants and people who were temporarily out of luck. Rachel Vorspan, "Vagrancy and the New Poor Law in Late-Victorian and Edwardian England," *English Historical Review* 92 (1977):59–81.

Raikes' duty, as Head of Police, to instruct his men to arrest as many men as possible."[139] In 1910, the requirement that the Government pay arrested vagrants for their labor was dropped, and mashcha were empowered to arrest vagrants in rural areas. But even before then, as the falling conviction figures indicate (except for 1906), the laws were not being vigorously enforced. The problem, officials found, was the fact that though vagrants could be sent someplace to work, it did not necessarily mean they would stay there.[140]

But the Administration remained concerned with its need to control idleness and work. When World War I added to the strain on the labor supply, new measures were added. The Native Labour Control Decree of 1917 was aimed at the able-bodied "native" without "regular employment," and was designed to channel him into Government-approved work. Not surprisingly, work on a private clove plantation was considered to be of a "public nature," although the Colonial Office, once it was criticized on such an issue in Kenya, disagreed.[141] Bishop Weston charged in 1921 that this decree was being used in an arbitrary manner to recruit harvest labor. However, the Government claimed that Weston's charges were based on a single incident caused by an overzealous official; that a tiny portion of harvest labor was recruited this way; and—above all—that those who were rounded up were all vagrants and loafers "well known to the police."[142] However exaggerated Weston's account may be, the decrees delineated a certain concept of idleness and gave officials power to transform such notions into labor. The decrees were ambiguous about "natives" who owned clove trees; but they clearly did not apply to Arabs, who constituted, in official eyes, a planter class. Behind British conceptions of work and idleness was the idea that one either was a planter or worked—regularly—for a planter.[143]

139. Cave to Lansdowne, 22 July 1905, and FO to Cave, 24 Aug. 1905, FOCP 8692, pp. 54, 68; Report by Judge Smith respecting Efficiency of Sultan's Courts of Zanzibar, 2 June 1905, FOCP 8691, p. 78; AR, 1909, p. 46.

140. Clarke to Grey, 10 May, 20 Sept. 1910, and Langley to Clarke, 2 Aug. 1910, FO 367/200; Cave, Memorandum, 16 Oct. 1906, FOCP 9102, pp. 20–22.

141. Sinclair to Belfield, 22 March 1917, incl. Pearce to Long, 9 May 1917, CO 618/17; Long to Pearce, 5 July 1917, CO 618/17.

142. Weston to Oldham, incl. Oldham to Wood, 12 Sept. 1921, CO 618/28; Weston to Chairman, 1 Aug. 1921, and Weston to Travers, 24 Oct. 1921, Universities' Mission to Central Africa Archives, C2, fols. 65–66, 76–77; Sinclair to Churchill, 28 Dec. 1921, CO 618/26. The decree was used to pick up 500 men for the clove harvest in 1920–21. Pearce to Churchill, 7 June 1921, CO 618/25.

143. One official's reply to Weston's charge that *anyone* was subject to the roundup was to insist that the Government wanted to encourage the owners of small clove estates. That left the position of the African smallholder ambiguous but did make clear the position of anyone who did not own property. Sinclair to Churchill, 28 Dec. 1921, CO 618/26.

The second most important element in the attack on idleness and disorder was the Government's attempt to stop the theft of agricultural
produce, praedial larceny as it was called. Squatting on unused land or
on an Arab plantation, no matter how hard one toiled on food crops, was
seen by officials as idleness. This logic easily took a further step: officials
saw squatting as crime. As the Director of Agriculture put it in 1902, the
Zanzibari native "can settle on anybody's land, cultivate a small vegetable
patch at his leisure and help himself, under cover of darkness, to cocoa-
nuts and fruit in his vicinity." Others saw produce theft and labor as
alternatives: ex-slaves "would rather steal than work."[144]

What one man regards as theft, another may regard as his right. The
appropriation of produce, by masters and by slaves, had long been in
question. Slaves had sold cloves to passing brokers behind their owners'
backs and for their personal profit. But officials believed that abolition,
by turning loose the idle and the unrestrained, had vastly increased the
incidence of produce theft just at a time when they were seeking to impose a more rigid definition of property. Sometimes crops were appropriated for sale, sometimes for consumption. At times, fruit was taken by
squatters' from their landlord's trees; at other times it was taken by passing strangers.[145] To the Government, all this was simply theft.

Yet in the social context of Zanzibar, rights to produce were part of the
struggle for economic power, part of efforts by planters and squatters to
determine what rights tenancy conferred. Taking coconuts or other
produce was the other side of not fulfilling the labor demands of a contract. Slaves had no more reason to accept the planter's rights to the
produce of the trees he owned than to accept his rights to the people he
owned. They had even less reason to acknowledge that rights they had
long held as slaves were no longer honored.[146] The Government's arrests were an attempt to establish its own conception of property, and
therefore, it hoped, the landowners' effective control over land, its
fruits, and—in turn—the labor of the people who stayed on it.

But what went on in the remote plantations of Zanzibar and Pemba is
difficult to ascertain. Despite the Government's long battle against theft,
praedial larceny was still rampant in 1907. A new enactment—The
Praedial Larceny and Agricultural Produce Decree of 1909—reversed
the normal English standards of proof and made it incumbent on a "na-

144. Lyne, Agricultural Report, 1902, FOCP 8177, p. 66; Last, Report, 1898, PP 1898,
LX, 559, p. 53; Farler to Mathews, 2 Aug. 1897, ibid., p. 11; Pearce to Long, 24 May 1908,
CO 618/19.

145. Farler to Mathews, 26 Jan. 1900, FOCP 7405, p. 107; Lyne, *Zanzibar in Contemporary Times*, p. 250; Collector of Zanzibar to First Minister, 15 May 1912, in AR, 1911, p. 33;
Craster, p. 194. On theft in the time of slavery, see Cooper, *Plantation Slavery*, p. 232.

146. Slaves resisted early attempts at eviction from land they had used. Hardinge to
Salisbury, 23 April 1898, PP 1898, LX, 559, p. 72.

tive" carrying produce to prove he had not stolen it. But the campaign against produce theft ran into the same obstacle as the attempt to introduce labor contracts: rural police forces were as weak as the law was severe. In 1912, officials claimed that produce theft was on the increase.[147] Landlords' control over the produce of their estates—especially coconuts—remained tenuous.

The vagrancy decrees and efforts to stop theft and other crimes did not have their intended effect. Bishop Weston's vision of widespread impressment came closer to what officials might have wished they could do than to what they actually did. The Government could only act selectively, and mainly against those people with the weakest social roots. The vagrancy and labor control decrees were used most effectively in periodic roundups of the urban poor.[148]

The Government's campaign to redefine concepts of work was doomed to failure, for it was divorced from actual patterns of social relations, the ability to use force, and ideology. For a ruling class to attain hegemony, as Antonio Gramsci has argued, the exercise of repressive power by the state must operate in conjunction with the redefinition and control of culture and social norms by the dominant class.[149] In Zanzibar, the state tried to exercise power through the police and the courts, but the concepts of social order that it wished to instill were remote from the actual exercise of power on the plantations.

The plantation owners could no more accept British conceptions of work and property than could the ex-slaves, Wapemba, and Wahadimu. The planters' behavior undermined the vagrancy decrees, and the kind of relations they sought to establish with their workers—as much as the kind of relations the workers sought to establish with them—helped to render the official conceptions irrelevant. Officials complained that the decrees did not work because estate owners were willing to let people occupy their property. The owners' did not deny their tenants access to the coconuts on their estates, whether within the tenants' own plots or not. Permission to squat, without extracting a substantial payment in labor or money, made the concept of vagrancy inoperable.[150]

Because plantation owners needed protection against theft by outsid-

147. Police Chief Taubman to Gen. Raikes, 1 Jan. 1907, FOCP 9122, p. 16K; Cave to Grey, 19 Aug. 1908, FO 367/99; AR, 1909, p. 10; Collector of Zanzibar to First Minister, 15 May 1912, AR, 1911, p. 33; AgAR, 1911, p. 169; Sinclair to Harcourt, 28 Nov. 1913, CO 618/3. In Jamaica, authorities also fought against praedial larceny, and also failed. Curtin, *Two Jamaicas*, p. 130.

148. AgAR, 1920, p. 14; Pearce to Churchill, 6 June 1921, CO 618/25.

149. Antonio Gramsci, *Selections from the Prison Notebooks*, trans. and ed. Q. Hoare and G. N. Smith (New York, 1971).

150. Hardinge to Salisbury, 23 April 1898, PP 1898, LX, 559, p. 72; AgAR, 1910, p. 146, 1920, p. 11; McClellan, Labour Memorandum, incl. Sinclair to Churchill, 28 Dec. 1921, CO 618/26.

ers, they were all the more eager to acquire resident workers. The residents, of course, got a share of the produce that would have been stolen.[151] That negated much of the impact of the laws against theft: they neither reinforced the ownership of property nor pushed the propertyless into labor.

It is difficult to see what happened to the Government's campaign to redefine the law of property and work, for the statistics are sparse and inconsistent. The crusade against the "petty crimes" of indiscipline and disorder was still going on in 1914 through the use of a punishment often employed to beat sense into preindustrial peoples and dropped for the civilized ones—flogging. In a record of floggings sent to the Colonial Office—there were 365 cases in 1914—offenses included theft, drunkenness, fighting, disorder, and refusal to work. Many of the offenders had characteristic slave names. A number of them were African policemen being flogged for neglect of duty, an indication of how difficult it was for a colonial state to impose its own concepts of work.[152]

In the 1920s, thefts continued to be prosecuted, although only a small percentage of the incidents reported were solved. Produce theft was being combatted through the Agricultural Produce Decree, under which there were 135 convictions in 1925, 98 in 1926. The Native Liquor Decrees produced 149 convictions in 1925, 221 the following year.[153] But all the complaints about crime and disorder among freed slaves had trailed off rapidly after abolition, and the tendency to treat theft, vagrancy, assault, adultery, and drunkenness as a single complex faded. The Administration's approach to crime in the 1920s had become less of a crusade directed against the values and habits of the lower orders than a routine response to reports of crimes: the police reports contain parallel charts of crimes reported and convictions obtained. Vagrancy had ceased to be a problem for the courts and had become a matter of recruitment for public works, and the severity of the legislation was not paralleled by severity of enforcement. The new criminals were mainland immigrants who got drunk and caused minor disturbances; these were the same mainlanders whose industriousness was being praised. By the 1920s and 1930s even these problems were considered minor, and reports indicated that there was little for the police to do.[154] The state had not remade patterns of work or notions of property; it had settled for a more modest concept of law and order.

151. Lyne, *Zanzibar in Contemporary Times,* p. 245.

152. Flogging Return, incl. Pearce to Harcourt, 21 Jan. 1915, CO 618/11. By this time, the Colonial Office had doubts about flogging and complained that the Zanzibar Government was overdoing things. Harcourt to Pearce, 22 March 1915, ibid.

153. AR, Police, 1926, pp. 59–60.

154. AR, Zanzibar Dist., 1923, p. 191; Pemba Dist., 1923, p. 200, 1925, p. 65; Police, 1927, p. 79, Police, 1931, pp. 39–40; Pim, "Report," 1932, pp. 35–36.

At most, the long campaign against vagrancy, produce theft, and petty crime added somewhat to the risks of wandering around and helping oneself to coconuts. The campaign may have made an ex-slave more likely to seek a plantation on which to squat but no more likely to work. In 1920, officials were still voicing their old plaint: ex-slaves "live a life of vagrancy and indolency on the Arabs' plantations."[155] Twenty-three years of fighting crime and vagrancy had helped induce ex-slaves to lead such a life *on* Arab plantations rather than *off* them. The social reality of Zanzibar and Pemba in 1920 was that of a squatter society, in which owners and tenants shared rights in land and in produce in a complex fashion. In the end, the Government's attempts to create a society divided into owners and workers amounted to periodic and ineffective harassment. The state had failed to redefine norms and expectations.

CONCLUSIONS

Wage labor was not, as George Curzon of the Foreign Office had asserted in 1891, an "exotic" that had to be tended and watered. The colonial state had tried to make slaves into an agrarian working class by changing their legal status, educating them in new values, pressuring them into accepting obligations to work for wages, and punishing them for their idle and disorderly ways. Such plans were aimed not simply at getting the most cloves picked for the least money, but at creating a fully committed wage-labor force. Officials' thinking was no mere reflection of irrational Victorian class prejudices but a conviction that a labor system in which workers had little choice about when and how to work was more controllable and predictable—and in the long run more profitable—than a more flexible labor system. Their plans foundered on the one essential aspect of capitalism that few of them were willing to confront directly: that the origins of a working class lie in its alienation from the means of production. In England, all the efforts to awe, subdue, and punish the rural poor had been concomitants of a fundamental transformation of the way in which an agrarian population obtained access to land. In Zanzibar, ex-slaves and other cultivators were harassed, cajoled, and imprisoned, but not chased off the land.

Migratory labor systems, some scholars argue, form the basis of an especially profitable form of capitalism in colonial areas. By preserving, in stunted form, precapitalist forms of production—in which farmers have direct access to land—capitalist firms can pay wages that are below the cost of reproducing the work force: raising children and supporting people not actually at work. This is an important argument, and at the very least points to the structural conditions that make a low-wage econ-

155. AgAR, 1920, p. 10.

omy viable. Nevertheless, care must be taken to avoid making the seemingly symbiotic relationship of capitalist and precapitalist modes of production appear to be an organic, smoothly functioning system, and it should be kept in mind that this argument is a structural, not a causal one, and does not explain how migratory labor systems arose. Juan Martinez-Alier wonders if colonial officials and capitalists came to espouse the preservation of precapitalist economies as "a rationalization of their own misgivings when confronted with the herculean and dangerous tasks of depriving the whole indigenous population of access to land."[156] In Zanzibar, ex-slaves—struggling to avoid dependence on wage labor—made migrant labor into a necessity. The state first tried in earnest to recruit migrant clove pickers after nearly eight years of striving to make resident workers the mainstay of plantation labor. The advent of the Nyamwezi weeders, following the even greater failure of planters and the state to extract year-round labor from residents, illustrates the structural relationship of wage-labor sectors to distant economies, and also the need to analyze how workers, the state, and employers tried to control economic choices and the nature of work across a wide geographical and social field.[157]

Martinez-Alier also points out that the juxtaposition of capitalist and precapitalist structures is only one of several ways to minimize the costs of reproduction (or production) and not necessarily the best one. Indeed, the initial efforts of the Zanzibar Government represent a common variant in situations of high demand for produce, concentration of landholdings, and relatively weak state power: settling a population *on* estates.[158] The reproduction of the labor force then took place outside of the nexus of supervised wage labor, but within the estate. Compared to a

156. Martinez-Alier, p. 13. For Marxist analyses of the "super-exploitative" profits that derive from these structures, see Meillassoux, *Femmes, greniers et capitaux;* Rey, *Alliances des classes;* and Michael Burawoy, "The Functions and Reproduction of Migrant Labor: Comparative Material from Southern Africa and the United States," *American Journal of Sociology* 81 (1976): 1050–87.

157. If one examines labor recruitment in a regional perspective and over time, one sees that it depends on the *active* exercise of class and state power, not just to collect workers, but to define and limit their access to resources. In some cases, creation of an area in which the only opportunities were labor migration stemmed from attempts at exploitation and administrative control that went awry. Van Onselen, *Chibaro,* Leroy Vail, "Ecology and History: The Example of Eastern Zambia," *Journal of Southern African Studies* 3 (1976): 129–55.

158. Martinez-Alier, p. 13. In such a system, migratory labor would be supplementary, used mainly to handle seasonal peaks and to keep the settled laborers anxious about their security. Estate agriculture could develop through the expansion of demand on a less market-oriented system of large landholdings or through transitions away from slave labor. See the suggestive article of Alan Richards, "The Political Economy of *Gutswirtschaft.*"

plantation solely relying on wage labor, this system required less supervision and less repression, but compared to migrant labor, it vastly narrowed the autonomy accorded precapitalist social structures. But what went on inside these estates—how much laborers worked, the mixture of wages and resources with which they were remunerated, the nature of discipline—and the way the labor system evolved, depended very much on the struggles of tenants and workers against planters and the state.[159] The squatters of Zanzibar had fewer legal rights than tenants in many other places, but they acquired access to land on relatively favorable terms and relatively substantial control over when they performed plantation labor, as well as daily wages for work actually performed. Yet the danger that the economic position of the squatters might erode or that the state might play a different role lent an element of uncertainty and tension to the situation.

Slowly and grudgingly, officials came to accept the fact that they would not build a class committed to plantation labor with values and expectations appropriate to such a role. They increasingly sought to manipulate and control a far more complex system, in which different groups, each only partially dependent on plantation work, entered specific niches of the plantation system. The new workers, like the old, tried to manipulate the system as well, in ways that varied with the nature of their involvement with the plantation system. Meanwhile, officials concealed their frustrations and protected themselves from seeing the mystifying nature of their own ideology by explaining the deviations from expected patterns through creating and perpetuating an enduring stereotype of the strange and primitive work habits of slaves, or indeed of all Africans.[160]

At the heart of these frustrations lay the contradiction between the fundamental changes in labor organizations which the state envisioned and its anxiety to avoid social change and disorder. Arab slaveowners were, perhaps, odd agents for transforming a slave society. They were,

159. The initiatives of tenants toward shaping forms of labor tenancy are stressed by Morris, pp. 310–11. The other side of this process are the varied mechanisms of discipline and control—from the sanction of the "sack" to physical punishment—that can be used against tenants. Richards, esp. pp. 484, 495–97.

160. A leading luminary on colonial labor questions later wrote of "the disinclination of the freed slaves to work for wages, or even to take adequate steps to support themselves." The ex-slave was "an irresponsible and reluctant worker who was most inefficient unless closely supervised.... Slave mentality has thus injuriously affected not only the freeman but also the employer and society generally." G. St. J. Orde Browne, *The African Labourer* (London, 1933), pp. 25, 28. See also East Africa Commission, Report, 1925, p. 37. Similarly, Jamaican officials and landowners resorted to theories that ex-slaves were not economic men in order to explain their "perverse working habits." Curtin, *Two Jamaicas*, pp. 142–43.

in British eyes, tainted by oriental indolence; they had carried on a cruel slave trade long after Englishmen had learned better; and they were not even white. But they did own land, and they were accustomed to having command over people. It was easier to admit that Arab slaveowners could be made into landowners and managers than to acknowledge that landowners and managers could be dispensed with altogether. But it was the planters who had to come to grips each year with unweeded plantations and unpicked cloves, and with the immediate need of bargaining and adapting to the demands of ex-slaves and migrant workers. The concessions they made were based on realistic assessments of their economic power; they were also much more readily subsumed under the planters' patriarchal ideology than the rigid conceptions of land and labor held by officials. Having failed to penetrate to the heart of the plantation—and having been forced to follow Arab practices on the Government's plantations to a greater extent than Arabs had to follow theirs—the officials' attempts to harass and discipline workers merely pushed them more deeply into the kind of agrarian social relationships the Government had hoped gradually to undermine. The only other way the plantation system could have been made to work would have been for planters and officials to unite in a more brutal campaign against squatters, independent cultivators, and the supposedly idle than either group could envision.

The cloves of Zanzibar and Pemba were picked; the trees were weeded; and the planters retained their land and at least some aspects of their way of life. The long, intense, and expensive effort of the colonial state to recruit, channel, and control labor had helped to preserve the plantation structure and the planter class. But it had not created a landless working class. Ex-slaves, mainland migrants, Wapemba, Wahadimu, and Watumbatu threw themselves—in quite different ways—into the wage-labor market and bargained effectively; but they also kept themselves partly removed from it. Ex-slaves were also willing to develop relations of dependence to gain access to land, but they struggled to define the terms. What officials regarded as idleness, stealing, contract breaking, or stubborn resistance to cultivating "economic crops," was part of this struggle, undramatic but not unsuccessful.

4 Planters, Squatters, and Clove Trees: Agriculture in Zanzibar, 1897–1925

The clove planters survived the decline of their power over labor and the readjustments of the abolition era largely because the world market in cloves was so favorable in the period before 1925. The export statistics that economists often stress make Zanzibar appear a rousing success, and officials in 1925 were congratulating themselves on the health of the plantation economy. The growth of clove exports was part of a worldwide trend in markets for tropical produce and a typical response of agriculturalists to price incentives.

But Zanzibar was undone as much by the boom before 1925 as by the depression which followed. Investments in slow-maturing trees committed Zanzibar's planters and their creditors to an organization of agriculture and a choice of crops that could not be adjusted. The squatters on plantation lands and the small-scale cultivators in outlying areas were squeezed by the expansion of the plantation sector, especially on Zanzibar Island. Official policies and market pressures which drained labor away to the plantations checked smallholders further. As in many parts of the world where plantations eventually faltered, the planters' retention of resources, the rigidities of marketing systems, and government favoritism still forced the rest of the population into a choice between labor for planters ever more conscious of minimizing costs and peasant production on marginal land remote from markets. The acute vulnerability of Zanzibar to the pressures of the world market in cloves was a consequence of the interests of particular groups—planters, moneylenders, and the state—that had become wedded to the plantation economy and the ongoing conflict between them and the squatters, workers, and independent cultivators.

CLOVES IN THE EXPORT ECONOMY

To chart the exact course of the clove industry is difficult, for there are no time series of trees or acres planted, no indications of how much of the export price went to producers. The only accounts of receipts and expenditures are atypical, for they apply to Government plantations, which were managed in their own way, paid no interest charges, and were not subject to the 25 percent duty on clove exports.[1] Only from the 1920s are scattered data on the ownership of trees and indebtedness available.

But the most important fact is obvious from the data from the Customs Department shown in figures 4.1–4.5. Price and output were both rising until 1925. The rapid fluctuations were normal for clove cultivation, a consequence of changing weather and the damage caused by picking a large crop from the delicate trees. Given Zanzibar's near monopoly of the world's cloves, changes in clove production had drastic effects on price. In the early 1920s, the rise in average clove prices over prewar levels was slightly ahead of the rise of the price index in India and England, but then the rapid decline in clove prices preceded the world Depression by some five years.[2]

The overall trend makes it clear that, whatever the problems of finding, disciplining, and paying labor, cloves were getting picked. The 58 percent jump in the clove production of Zanzibar Island in 1905–14, compared with the previous decade, almost certainly can be attributed to the mobilization of labor to pick existing clove trees. There was little new planting in the uncertain decade before 1905, and clove trees take ten years to become fully productive.[3] But there was new planting after that, which sent clove production to a new level in the 1920s, and a further spurt in planting in the wake of the jump in prices at the end of World War I.[4]

1. Government plantations produced only 2 percent of Zanzibar's crop in the late 1920s. R. S. Troup, "Report on Clove Cultivation in the Zanzibar Protectorate," 1931, p. 10.

2. The world market for tropical products was generally favorable up to 1913, and the dip that affected a number of commodities in 1920–23 did not affect cloves. The timing of the end of this favorable period, 1925, was peculiar to cloves, but its cause—competition from synthetics—was not unique, and the world depression of 1929 hit Zanzibar as it did other tropical regions (Lewis, *Tropical Development 1880–1913*, esp. p. 33). Issues like inflation and terms of trade deserve specific attention, but some idea of price changes that affected Zanzibar's imports come from the Indian (Calcutta) price index: 100 (1914), 126 (1916), 178 (1918), 201 (1920), 176 (1922), 178 (1924), 148 (1926). R. J. Crofton, "Statistics of the Zanzibar Protectorate, 1892–1932," 1933, p. 28.

3. Pemba—by far the larger producer—was not expanding so rapidly; output grew by 13.6 percent in this period (Kirsopp, "Report," 1926, p. 46). The uncertainties of the time of abolition were reflected in low land values and low investments in trees. Clove prices, land values, and planting all increased in 1918, as observers noted, and both the favorable conditions around 1910–12 and the rise in production ten years later suggest a similar increase in planting before the war. O'Sullivan, Report on Pemba, 1896–97, PP 1898, LX, 361, pp. 8–9; AgAR, 1905, incl. Cave to Grey, 10 Aug. 1906, FO 367/29; Extract from Dr. Andrade's Report for 1909, incl. Clarke to Grey, 17 May 1910, FO 367/200; D&C, Zanzibar, 1911–12, p. 11; Pearce to Long, 24 May 1918, CO 618/19.

4. On postwar planting, see AR, Pemba Dist., 1925, pp. 63–64; Hollis to Amery, 15 Jan. 1926, CO 618/39.

FIGURE 4:1
CLOVE PRICES, RS/FRASILA

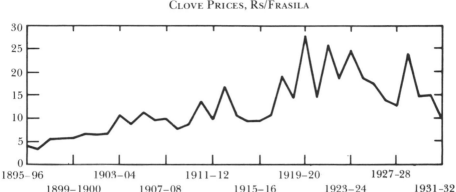

Zanzibar's old standby—the spice market of India—still contributed much to the clove industry's growth, absorbing around 45 percent of the expanding crop each decade until 1930. But from the late nineteenth century, European markets had become quite important. Clove oil, distilled in Europe from cloves and (with much lower yields) clove stems, was used in toothpaste, topical anesthetics, and above all vanillin, the artificial vanilla used in confectionery. From 1906, Germany's growing chemical industry absorbed a large quantity of cloves, averaging £75,000 per year or 23 percent of the total, and Germany became the world's principal producer of clove oil.[5] The war cut off Germany from its clove supply, and British firms quickly moved in to establish a virtual monopoly, sharing it only with an American firm with strong British ties, Graesser-Monsanto. With a few firms dominating the market in a valuable product, the rising price in Zanzibar was not then a crucial issue. Zanzibar's planters responded with a wave of planting. The stage was set for a textbook case of the relationship of an imperial power, metropolitan industry, and colonial agriculture, a sequence of events that was to leave Zanzibar saddled with too many clove trees, too many debts, and too little room for change.

The new pattern of demand also brought about increased reliance of Zanzibar on markets in the United States and, above all, Great Britain for its expanded output. The British share of exports had been 12 to 16 percent, by value, before the war; it averaged 32 percent between 1919 and 1923. The American market, lagging slightly, doubled its proportionate take to 29 percent in 1920–26.[6]

5. Crofton, "Statistics," p. 17; Tidbury, *The Clove Tree,* pp. 199–205.
6. Crofton, "Statistics," p. 17.

FIGURE 4:2
QUANTITY OF CLOVES EXPORTED, 1,000S OF FRASILAS

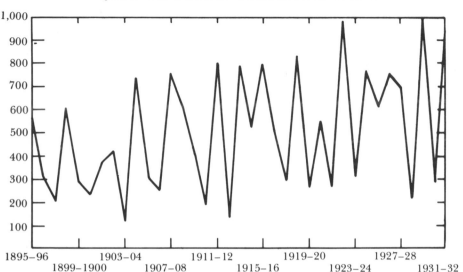

Officials were well aware of the stimulus that the expansion of vanillin production had provided. Now that the manufacturers were predominantly British, the Colonial Office became increasingly involved in their relationship to the colonial plantations.[7]

The firms did not hesitate to use their economic muscles. Five corporations, the most important of which was W. J. Bush and Co., dominated the industry and coordinated efforts through the Association of British Chemical Manufacturers. Some Zanzibari officials were soon apprehensive over what they saw as a "powerful combination," and the Colonial Office and the local officials handled the companies carefully.[8] Although several chemical companies—one French, one Zanzibari Indian, and later one British—proposed to establish clove oil distilleries in Zanzibar, which might have saved on freight and labor costs, the Government stalled and alerted Bush to the proposals. The Association of British Chemical Manufacturers opposed granting licenses for local distillation, arguing that it would jeopardize a British industry "of very old standing," which British clove oil distillation in fact was not.[9] The

7. The concern with British manufacturing interests is made explicit in CO to Ministry of Shipping, 1 Aug. 1918, CO 618/26; AgCom, 1923, p. 1.

8. AgCom, Minority Report by R. H. Crofton, pp. 39-40; J. M. Bush to CO, 4 July 1918, CO 618/20.

9. Sinclair to Milner, 22 Sept. 1919, CO 618/21; W. J. V. Woolcock, Manager of the Association of British Chemical Manufacturers, to Board of Trade, 18 Sept. 1922, incl.

FIGURE 4:3
EXPORT EARNINGS FROM CLOVES, MILLIONS OF RUPEES

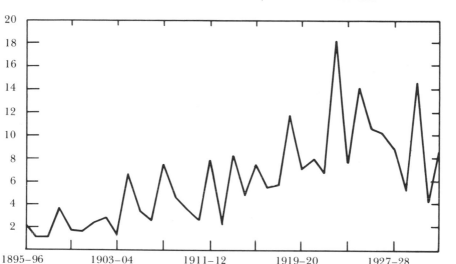

Government-appointed Agricultural Commission in Zanzibar agreed: "Distillation of oil of cloves in the United Kingdom is in the hands of a few old established firms and it would appear undesirable to substitute plantation distillation of so valuable a product for that undertaken at home by firms long experienced in the technical matter."[10] The Colonial Office affirmed that it would refuse permits for local distillation "because of the desire to avoid competition with the old-established firms in England."[11]

Having protected English firms from the challenge of the colonial periphery, the Colonial Office was soon beset by agitation from the companies about the high price of cloves. Technology gave the companies a strong new argument, a still more artificial form of vanilla, this one made from coal tar. Zanzibar's one strong point, its virtual monopoly of cloves, could be undercut. In 1925, Bush demanded that

Dept. of Overseas Trade to CO, 3 Jan. 1923, CO 618/31. Under the Manufacture of Oil of Cloves Decree of 1918, a license was required to distill cloves in Zanzibar. The authorities had reacted promptly to the industry coming into British hands. Tidbury, p. 191.

10. AgCom, p. 4.

11. This phrase was inserted into a minute that contained the usual Colonial Office rationale for restricting economic activities in Africa, "the danger of export of cloves being adulterated." Quality control was a rationale; control of manufacture was a reason. Minute by C. J. Jeffries, 3 Dec. 1925, to Hollis to Amery, 7 Nov. 1925, CO 618/37.

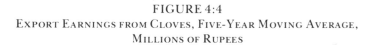

FIGURE 4:4
EXPORT EARNINGS FROM CLOVES, FIVE-YEAR MOVING AVERAGE,
MILLIONS OF RUPEES

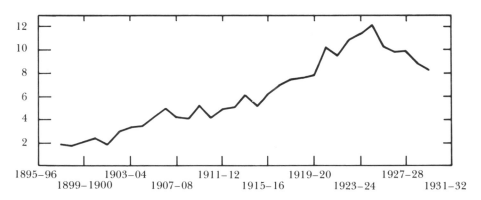

the Government give it a refund whenever the price of cloves went above an agreed-upon figure.[12]

At first, Zanzibari officials thought the demand a "preposterous and immoral" infringement on their territory. Still thinking in terms of the spice trade, some officials thought the threat to cut off a market was a bluff. The Colonial Office went along with the men on the scene, but—less committed to local habits and more sensitive to commercial pressures—it remained worried.[13]

Within two years, Zanzibar and London had caved in. "The Clove Oil Industry can no longer compete in the open market unless the cost of production of cloves can be very materially reduced."[14] Production costs would be lowered—at the expense of the workers' wages—and the clove manufacturers would be subsidized—at the expense of Zanzibar's treasury. Working closely with Bush and Graesser-Monsanto, the Colonial Office devised a drawback scheme, under which manufacturers paid the market price but received a remission of all or part of the 20 percent duty on cloves depending on how much the price exceeded 5d per pound. Such a scheme would keep spice prices high—Indians would pay the cost of Zanzibar's monopoly. At the current price of 8d per pound

12. J. M. Bush to CO, 27 April 1925, CO 618/38; Costley-White to CO, Oct. 1924, incl. Hollis to Amery, 9 Feb. 1925, CO 618/35.

13. Hollis to High Commissioner, 5 Feb. 1925, incl. Hollis to Amery, 9 Feb. 1925, CO 618/35; Kirkham (Director of Agriculture) to CO, 3 Feb. 1925, incl. in above; Minutes by C. J. Jeffries and C. W. Bottomley, 31 Dec. 1925 and 13 Jan. 1926, to Hollis to Amery, 7 Nov. 1925 CO 618/37; Amery to Hollis, 23 June 1925, filed with Bush to CO, 27 April 1925, CO 618/38.

14. Kirkham, Memorandum, 7 Jan. 1925, incl. Hollis to Amery, 5 Feb. 1927, CO 618/41.

when the regulations went into effect in 1928, the full drawback would be granted. Only approved firms, which had to promise not to switch to synthetics, qualified, and six made the list. Bush and Graesser-Monsanto bought 69 percent of the drawback cloves and received most of the Rs 133,615 that was remitted the first year.[15]

By 1929, the drawback scheme was failing. Clove prices, although declining sharply since 1925, were not stable, and a small harvest in 1928–29 sent them up. The price of coal tar derivatives was dependable. Monsanto pulled out of the scheme in 1929, while the British firms were forced to rely on the protected home market to sell clove oil, losing exports to new vanillin manufacturers who used synthetics. Desperate, the Zanzibari officials now tried to encourage local distillation, but the companies with the capital and the technology were investing in synthetics. By 1931, only one company was accepting drawbacks; all the British firms had abandoned the scheme. At one time, 33 percent of the clove exports had gone into distillation, in 1931 only 9 percent.[16]

Subsidizing the chemical firms had been the result of the British commitment to keep Zanzibar an island of cloves. The effort accomplished nothing. Even before it went into effect, the British share of clove exports had fallen from 41 percent in the boom year of 1923 to 6 percent in 1926. It stayed below 10 percent. The American share peaked at 29 percent in 1926 and in three years fell to 13 percent, despite the drawback. But the Dutch East Indies began to import more cloves. India and East Asia together increased their share of Zanzibar's export market from below 50 percent before 1926 to 73 percent in 1930. After a period of expanded European markets in the early colonial era, the Indian Ocean markets had once again come to the fore. For the ensuing decades, the welfare of Zanzibar's clove producers was to depend on the taste which Indonesians had developed for putting cloves in their cigarettes.[17]

15. Correspondence on the drafting of the decree is in CO 618/43/2. See also Hollis to Amery, 5 Feb. 1927, CO 618/41; H. M.'s Trade Commission to East Africa to Commissioner of East African Dependencies, London, 7 Nov. 1929, CO 618/45; Kirsopp, Report, 28 June 1929, incl. Hollis to Passfield, CO 618/45.

16. Minute of A. B. Acheson, 28 Aug. 1929, to Resident, Zanzibar, to CO, 4 Aug. 1929, CO 618/46; Resident to Passfield, 9 Jan. 1931, CO 618/49; Pim, "Report," 1932, pp. 64–65.

17. In absolute terms, the fall in British and American purchases was equally precipitous (Crofton, "Statistics," p. 13; Resident to Passfield, 9 Jan. 1931, CO 613/49). Officials blamed synthetics for the drop in prices after 1924. Memorandum on "The Clove Industry and Vanillin," prepared for the Hilton Young Commission, incl. Hollis to Bottomley, 13 March 1928, CO 618/44. The Java clove cigarette industry began around 1916, and the dependence of Zanzibar on this market, and the old spice market of India, is clear from the desperate commissions that visited the East. G. D. Kirsopp and C. A. Bartlett, "Report of a mission appointed to investigate the clove trade in India and Burma, Ceylon, British Malaya and the Dutch East Indies," London, 1933; "Report of the Zanzibar Clove Mission to India, Jan. 6–20th 1958," 1958. See also Tidbury, pp. 197–98.

FIGURE 4:5
CLOVE PRODUCTION, BY FIVE-YEAR PERIODS

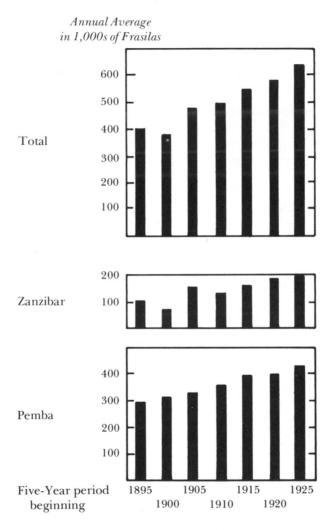

*Annual Average
in 1,000s of Frasilas*

SOURCES FOR FIGURES 4.1–4.5:   R. H. Crofton, "Statistics of the Zanzibar Protectorate,"
1933, p. 15; G. D. Kirsopp, "Memorandum on Certain Aspects of the Zanzibar Clove Industry," 1926, p. 46.

In 1925, officials in Zanzibar thought they had put the clove industry
"in a sounder position and on a better footing than it [had] been since
the abolition of slavery." Arab planters were "more prosperous than they
[had] been for years." In fact, expansion had prepared the way for a
crisis. The downslide had already begun in 1925, and within a few years,

officials—still hoping for better markets—had taken to composing variations on children's rhymes: "A clove a day keeps the dentist away."[18]

The only significant complement to cloves in the export economy was copra (dried coconut), Zanzibar's standby in times of falling clove prices. It was a good counterfoil to cloves, for its price—dependent on a world market of which Zanzibar was only a tiny part—did not fluctuate wildly, and it required little labor outside of the harvest itself. On the other hand, the market did not produce the spectacular rise of clove demand, and copra consistently yielded lower profits than cloves, according to figures from Government plantations.[19] Especially before the 1920s, plantation owners did not plant coconut trees nearly as systematically as they did cloves. Coconut trees were often planted in gaps in clove plantations or on the edges of clove land. Wahadimu and Wapemba had small holdings. The Government set an example by planting coconuts as a plantation crop on its own estates, but did not direct resources toward coconut trees as it did with cloves. But a large price rise after the war—39 percent above prewar levels in the period 1919-22—encouraged plantation owners, especially in Zanzibar Island, to pick coconuts more thoroughly as well as plant more trees. The effects of such incentives, unfortunately, paralleled those of the extension of clove-tree planting, now that coconuts were more of a plantation crop. Planters were stuck with more trees and larger harvests as the price fell after 1922 to prewar levels. The depression of 1929 made things worse.[20] But even the brief period of encouragement—coming at a time when cloves were also commanding more resources—did not provide incentives to do what the copra industry needed most: investments in drying equipment, improved marketing, and grading of produce. Ever since, bad drying and low quality have bedeviled the copra industry.[21]

18. AR, Pemba Dist., 1925, pp. 63-64; Hollis to Amery, 19 Feb. 1925, CO 618/35; AgAR, 1928, pp. 272-73.

19. Over the period 1915-26, Government plantations showed a 17 percent higher return on capital in cloves trees than in coconut trees. In the peak period for clove prices, when copra prices had already somewhat declined, the difference was 40 percent. "Report of the Retrenchment Committee," 1927; Crofton, "Statistics," pp. 18-19. In the 1860s, a period of falling clove prices, the value of coconut product exports had briefly approached that of cloves, but once Pemba's posthurricane trees began to produce, cloves were worth 2.3 times as much as coconut products in the export market (1890s). This gap increased by the 1920s. Crofton, pp. 18-19, and Cooper, *Plantation Slavery*, pp. 62-65, 138.

20. Even as prices declined by 1929 to the same level as in 1910-14, output—by volume—was 45 percent higher (Crofton, p. 18). On the rise and fall of copra after the war, see Memorandum on the Cocoanut Industry of the Zanzibar Protectorate, by McClellan, March 1916, incl. McClellan to CO, 25 March 1916, CO 618/16; AgCom, 1923, p. 7; AgAR, 1926, p. 174; Armstrong, "Agriculture," p. 32; AgAR, 1929, p. 283, 1930, p. 307; 1932, p. 6.

21. Zanzibar's copra was sun-dried, and the climate was so wet that the copra often turned moldy. A small number of Indians did most of the drying; Arab planters generally

In any case, coconuts were too useful locally to be a good plantation crop. Ripe nuts were used for cooking and unripe nuts for drinking, while trees could be tapped for palm wine. All these uses were alternatives to producing copra, and the tree owner was not always the one to make the choice, for coconuts were easy to appropriate.[22] Because neither middlemen nor landowners could be sure that expansion or improvement of the coconut industry would benefit them, the potential for a complement to cloves as a plantation crop was not exploited. In the 1920s, cloves were contributing over three times as much as copra to Zanzibar's export earnings. The versatility of the coconut tree actually hurt the planters, making smallholders who had trees and squatters who took nuts less dependent on wage labor.[23]

In the first years of British rule, some officials and merchants had quickly realized that Zanzibar was producing too many cloves and not enough of anything else.[24] After thirty years of colonial development, monoculture had become still more pronounced: 65 percent of Zanzibar's export income came from cloves in the 1890s, 70 percent in the 1920s. In the first plateau of the clove industry, the 1850s, annual production had been on the order of 200,000 frasilas; in the posthurricane cycle, that mark was hit in the mid-1880s and passed in the 1890s. By the 1920s, 300,000 frasilas was a bad harvest; the peak was 990,000.[25] Expansion was a rational response to conditions in the world market, but it

did not, although smallholders in Pemba dried their own copra. Rural shopkeepers—mainly the same Indians who sold imported goods—collected nuts for copra. A European cartel controlled exporting in Zanzibar port, where local copra was bulked with imports from the mainland (McClellan, "Agricultural Resources," pp. 420–22; McClellan, Cocoanut Memorandum, incl. McClellan to CO, 25 March 1916, CO 618/16; Director, Imperial Institute, to CO, 24 June 1915, CO 618/13; AgCom, pp. 6–7, 43; USCR, 107 [1917], pp. 505–06; Belfield to Law, 25 Oct. 1915, CO 618/12). On the continuing problem of low quality, see J. D. Acland, *East African Crops* (London, 1971), p. 49, while the poor state of Zanzibar's coconut industry in comparison with other parts of the world is clear in Reginald Child, *Coconuts* (London, 1964).

22. The Administration was firmer than its Kenyan counterpart in combatting palm wine as an alternative to copra; it banned tapping and selling altogether in 1912. It is not clear if this measure was effective. Government efforts to prevent "coconut theft" clearly did not work. Agriculture Director to Holm, in Kenya, 19 Jan. 1923, CP 56/1525; AgAR, 1926, p. 155, and chapter 3, above. For comparison with Kenya, see chapter 5.

23. The Government occasionally commented on how useful coconuts would be as a complement to cloves, but it did little more than develop its own plantations, issue seedlings, ponder new drying techniques, and wax romantic: coconuts were the "sheet-anchor which enables the country to keep head on the storms of the clove industry." AgAR, 1926, p. 152.

24. O'Sullivan, Report on Pemba, 1896, PP 1896, LIX, 395, p. 43; Hardinge to Salisbury, 10 Jan. 1896, ibid., pp. 23–24; Gray Dawes & Co. to Smith MacKenzie & Co., forwarded to FO, 21 Nov. 1895, FO 107/46.

25. Cooper, *Plantation Slavery*, pp. 52, 61, 131; figure 4.2 above.

left planters with a large investment that was, literally, rooted in the soil. While some Zanzibaris, as discussed below, ate imported grains, land and labor that could have been used for food were tied up with cloves; planters were in debt and their creditors' capital was also tied up. Planters, under pressure from their creditors, could only react to falling prices as they reacted to rising ones: by harvesting more cloves.[26]

The Government had helped to perpetuate monoculture. Its own plantations stuck to cloves and coconuts; its labor policies were designed around the clove cycle; it built roads to bring cloves out; it was handing out seedlings to planters and paying bonuses on young trees at the very time when clove prices were collapsing; and it did very little for any other sector of agriculture.[27] Meanwhile, the Colonial Office was making sure that the classic division of labor between colony and metropole would be preserved, and when the British firms moved away from cloves, it paid them to keep buying. The commitment to monoculture and the plantation structure meant that workers would have to bear much of the brunt of the problems which expansion accentuated. The speedups in weeding that the Government began on its own plantations in 1924 and the wage-fixing agreements that it implemented throughout the islands in 1927 were important ways of meeting a price squeeze. In 1929, the Agriculture Department thought it had succeeded in cutting production costs by 20 percent.[28] Other ways of responding to the problems of clove production had already been foreclosed by expansion or lay outside the realm of Colonial Office thinking.

PLANTATIONS, PEASANTS, AND THE CONTROL OF PRODUCTION

The colonial state did not simply encourage monoculture; it helped preserve a particular structure of production. Its support of the clove industry was based on the concept of ownership, and its policies were intended to perpetuate the dominance of what officials perceived to be an Arab upper class and to link that class to the state.

Almost all Government reports throughout these years equated the owners of clove trees with an Arab upper class, and they identified the role of that class with the control of labor. "No other class," wrote the

26. This "perverse response," as economists call the increase of production after a price fall, was urged upon planters by at least one expert, although he knew full well that, given Zanzibar's near-monopoly, more production would send the price down still further. Kirsopp, "Report," 1926.

27. AR, Pemba Dist., 1925, pp. 63–64, 87. For more on Government supports to clove plantations, see below.

28. AgAR, 1929, p. 290. The need to own plantations was strongly emphasized in "Report of the Committee on Retrenchment," 1927, p. 34.

Resident in 1913, "is so capable of the successful cultivation of cloves or in the management of native labour."[29] Complaints about Arabs focused on their failure to live up to that role.[30] But whatever the Arab's defects, the only real alternative was to put new people into the old structure, and neither Europeans nor Indians were considered promising.[31] Alternatives to the plantation system were rarely mentioned and never seriously considered. One minor official in the Colonial Office observed in 1919 that the Zanzibar Government had supported the "plantation principle" over the "garden principle" and had sought "to compel the natives to work as labourers for the Arabs and to warn the Arabs not to let the native squatters acquire proprietary rights. The more long-sighted policy would probably have been to assist those natives who showed evidenced willingness to work a small area of clove trees to acquire proprietary rights." In 1926, a local official claimed, correctly, that the small-scale "native" clove grower was becoming more important and that Government policy should foster this process instead of hinder it. Suggestions such as these were dismissed on the dogmatic assertion that the clove was a plantation crop.[32] Even when Arab planters were on the verge of bankruptcy in the 1930s, the state took action to preserve them as owners of clove plantations and managers of labor.[33]

The mobilization of labor was the crux of Government policy: labor went only to the owners of clove trees and primarily to respectable

29. Sinclair to CO, 10 Oct. 1913, CO 618/2. See also Lyne, "Causes Contributing to the Success of the Zanzibar Clove Industry," p. 144; Pearce to Churchill, 6 June 1921, CO 618/21; and Sinclair to Devonshire, 27 March 1923, CO 618/30.

30. Last to Raikes, 8 Feb. 1903, FOCP 8177; AgAR, 1912, p. 140; Coryndon to Thomas, 26 Aug. 1924, CO 618/33; Hollis to Coryndon, 2 Aug. 1924, incl. Coryndon to Thomas, 5 Sept. 1924, ibid.; Kirsopp, "Report," 1926.

31. Indians were "entirely unsuited by temperament and training for an agricultural career," thought officials. Europeans posed a dual problem: they clashed with established landed interests and with the existing arrangements with tenants, and they were likely to make demands on an administration that was getting accustomed to its own way of doing things. AgCom, p. 17; Clarke to Grey, 28 Sept. 1912, FO 367/295; Belfield to Law, 25 Oct. 1915, CO 618/12; Pearce to Law, 10 Nov. 1915, CO 618/11.

32. Minute by J. A. Calder, 10 Feb. 1919, to Pearce to Long, 24 May 1918, CO 618/19; Kirsopp, "Report," 1926, pp. 4–5. Cloves as a smallholder crop were quickly dismissed in AgAR, 1926, p. 152. The options that commissions and officials actually considered were far narrower: bonus schemes vs. cuts in the duty, government intervention in marketing to get around Indian middlemen, more loans to Arabs. Officials themselves described their decisions as "conservative"—for example, after the Agricultural Commission of 1923 made its report. AgCom; Amery to Acting High Commissioner, 21 July 1924, CO 618/33.

33. One of the more critical outside experts who later visited Zanzibar rued the absence of a "large homogeneous body of substantial growers" who would act like a real planter class. His less critical colleagues simply assumed that such a class existed (Pim, p. 84). On British policy in the 1930s, see Michael F. Lofchie, Zanzibar: Background to Revolution (Princeton, 1965), pp. 101–26.

Arabs. Similar principles affected other agricultural schemes. Beginning in 1907, interest-free advances were made to planters to help them pay clove pickers. Such loans, made against the crop that was about to be picked, went "only to persons of known reliability." In the mid-1920s, these loans were directed to the large plantations of Zanzibar. In 1925, an average of Rs 496 went to a mere 117 planters in Zanzibar, an average of Rs 81 to 216 proprietors in Pemba.[34]

The most important encouragement to plant more clove trees in the period of expansion in the 1920s was the Bonus Scheme. Fiscal conservatism had kept the 25 percent export tax on cloves—paid in kind at the Zanzibar Customs House—intact, although officials had long discussed lowering it to "ameliorate" the position of the Arabs. In 1922, as revenues soared, the Administration decided to insure that any benefits of tax reform would go directly to the planters and not to middlemen. A fifth of the clove duty would be returned to the planters through an annual bonus proportional to the number of clove trees owned. The Bonus Scheme reached far more growers than the harvest loans but still rewarded the larger planter more than the smallholder.[35]

Table 4.1 shows the disbursements under the Bonus Scheme. It lasted until 1928, when it was replaced by a reduction of duty—from 25 percent to 20 percent—that was far easier to administer.[36] Other policies supported clove cultivation and the planters. Seedlings were given away to encourage new planting—80,000 in 1925 alone. Extra bonuses were paid (for a time) on newly planted trees and for plantations meeting certain standards of maintenance. Facilities were offered to store cloves until the low price of the peak harvest season had risen, and money was advanced on these cloves; like the harvest loans, this plan reached only a few planters. Not quite trusting the planters it supported, the Government issued legal requirements for weeding, clearing, and controlling pests, to be verified by Government inspectors.[37]

The Agriculture Director particularly liked the Bonus Scheme be-

34. Pearce to Harcourt, 11 July 1914, CO 618/7; AgCom, p. 11, and Minority Report, p. 51; AgAR, 1924, p. 10, 1925, p. 91. At first, the Government put most of the loan funds into Pemba, which produced the most cloves, but by the 1920s, the generally smaller plantations of Pemba were being discriminated against.

35. Pearce to Harcourt, 7 June 1914, CO 618/14; Memorandum on Clove Industry by Sinclair, 22 Dec. 1922, CO 618/29. The bonus began at Rs 10 per 100 trees and rose to Rs 15. AgAR, 1925, pp. 87, 91.

36. Kirkham, Memorandum on the Maintenance of the Clove Industry in Zanzibar, incl. Resident to CO, 11 June 1930, CO 618/48.

37. The storage plan provided an average of Rs 2,809 to only 27 planters in 1925 (AgAR, 1925, pp. 87, 91). See the AgAR throughout the 1920s for reports on these support schemes. See also the Plantation Preservation Decrees of 1913 and 1918, Sinclair to Grey, 1 May 1913, FO 367/351; Pearce to Long, 24 May 1918, CO 618/19.

TABLE 4:1

DISPERSEMENTS UNDER BONUS SCHEME, 1922–1926

	Owners	Properties	Bearing Trees	Amount—Rs
1922	18,320	32,479	3,000,953	155,766
1923	—	—	3,620,420	543,064
1924	—	26,629	—	354,526
1925	—	—	—	474,533
1926	—	—	—	498,032

SOURCES: Zanzibar, AgAR, 1922, p. 99, 1923, p. 41, 1924, 1925, pp. 87, 91; memorandum incl. Hollis to Bottomley, 13 March 1928, CO 618/144.

cause it "gave him a valuable hold over producers in his effort to promote cooperation." So much did the Administration equate clove production with an Arab planter class that its policies toward the "native" who had trees were quite ambiguous. The corvée laws from the early 1900s merely gave Wapemba tree owners the right to pick their own cloves before they picked Arabs'; the Native Labour Control decrees simply referred to "natives."[38]

Social policy also divided the Arab planter class from the "native" population. Hoping to make Zanzibar's "principal Arabs" identify their interests with those of the state, Hardinge and his successors recruited Arabs to positions in the Administration. Some of the Sultan's relatives and retainers remained on the Civil List and received stipends, albeit at reduced levels.[39] Educational institutions, such as they were, sought to modify and update the terms on which this same group maintained its dominance: the state school system began as an Arab school, and even as it grew, it brought few Africans beyond the early grades.[40] Economic and social policy combined to rigidify a dependent aristocracy, defined by the ownership of clove trees and its relationship to the state.

If the world clove market and state policy encouraged planters to di-

38. Momorandum prepared for Hilton Young Commission, incl. Hollis to Bottomley, 31 March 1928, CO 618/44. See also AgCom, p. 11, and chapter 3 on the Labour Control Decrees.

39. This policy is laid out in Hardinge to Salisbury, 23 April 1898, PP 1898, LX, 559, p. 78, and it was reaffirmed and strengthened in 1924 on the grounds that Arabs should serve the Administration because they had "wider capacities for ruling than the local native." W. H. Ingrams, "Memorandum on Native Organization and Administration in Zanzibar," 1926, p. 5. Prominent Arab names are found on the Government Staff List; other senior officials were Indians. Sultan Ali bin Hamood to Grey, 11 March 1906, FOCP 8753, p. 103; AgCom, p. 16; Staff List, 1924, pp. 1–49; Report on the Zanzibar Protectorate, 1911–23, p. 3. The Civil List, as of 1913, provided various relatives of the Sultan with annual stipends of Rs 1,200 to Rs 15,000. BB, 1913, J 4–6.

40. AR, 1910, pp. 191–92, 1911, p. 69, argues specifically for Arab education. See also Hollingsworth, Zanzibar under the Foreign Office, pp. 198–202; Lofchie, pp. 92–93.

rect their energies toward growing ever more cloves, the planters' indebtedness cemented their dependence on cloves. Like the cycles of overplanting and overproduction, indebtedness was not a new problem. As early as 1860, observers noted that many estates were being mortgaged to Indian merchants and financiers. The problem became more acute when the price of slaves rose after 1873 and grew worse still when the price of cloves fell in the 1880s, just as the heavy investments came to fruition. Yet foreclosure did not result. Indian moneylenders, forbidden by British law to run slave plantations themselves and wary of the risks of holding or reselling property whose productive capacity could be lost by further action against slavery, generally preferred to rewrite mortgages and collect as much of the interest and principal as the owner could afford while retaining a lien on the property. The system had a fragile stability: Arabs remained on the land and Indians kept to their successful roles as brokers and moneylenders. But capital was tied up; inefficient producers were not eliminated; and innovations or changes were avoided for fear of upsetting a delicate arrangement.[41]

The need to pay for labor did not make the situation easier. Indians could compete for labor on an equal footing with Arabs—and some did—but most continued to rewrite mortgages. Indian economic success was based on the commercial networks linking different sectors of East African economies with other areas of the Indian Ocean system, of which western India had long been a crucial focus. The advantages Indians had over Arabs and Africans in commerce depended, above all, on the use of communal and kinship ties to link different locations and to channel information, goods, and capital.[42] But Indians had no advantages as producers. With land values uncertain in the years following abolition, it remained more profitable and prudent for Indian financiers to collect what they could rather than take over plantations.[43]

Emerging from a period of heavy indebtedness, Arabs faced abolition

41. Cooper, *Plantation Slavery*, pp. 139–44.

42. This topic needs much more work. But see Edward A. Alpers, "Gujarat and the Trade of East Africa, c. 1500–1800," *International Journal of African Historical Studies* 9 (1976): 22–44; John Zarwan, "Indian Businessmen in Kenya: A Case Study" (Ph.D. diss., Yale University, 1976); P. A. Memon, "Mercantile Intermediaries in a Colonial Spatial System: Wholesaling in Kenya, 1830–1940" (Ph.D. diss., University of Western Ontario, 1974).

43. Hardinge, Report, 1898, PP 1898, LX, 361, p. 89; Clarke to Grey, 17 May 1910, FO 367/200; Lyne *Zanzibar in Contemporary Times*, pp. 271–72; Craster, *Pemba*, p. 246; D&C, Zanzibar, 1911–12; p. 11; Sinclair to Harcourt, 10 Oct. 1913, CO 618/2. By rewriting mortgages at below market value, a creditor could eventually foreclose and resell at a profit. This, of course, depressed property values and made it less likely for other investors to make permanent investments with long-term risks. D&C, Pemba, 1900, p. 5; Extract of Report of Dr. Andrade, incl. Clarke to Grey, 17 May 1910, FO 367/200; Sinclair to Devonshire 17 July 1923, CO 618/30.

with little unencumbered capital. Compensation money was a fraction of the often unrepaid cost of slaves, and planters sometimes used it to try to clear themselves of old debts.[44] Plantation owners had little money to pay their labor and had to borrow. All the British efforts to supply Arab planters with labor could not spare them the bill, and the Administration's inability to lower picking wages until the mid-1920s meant that harvest labor rose in cost slightly faster—and far more steadily—than harvest income. Cultivation labor had to be paid over the entire season. Since many planters began the period of wage labor already in debt, the terms of new loans—especially in the early years—were not favorable.[45] Labor recruitment perpetuated Arab planters as a landed elite, and perpetuated their indebtedness as well.

Interest charges appear to have made the profitability of a clove plantation before the war doubtful, although data on costs and revenue are so scanty that no firm conclusions can be reached. A calculation extrapolated from Government plantations over a five-year period ending in 1913 (and allowing for payment of the clove tax) indicated that a plantation would realize only a 3.7 percent return on capital. Accounts from a European clove estate in 1915 showed an 8 percent return, but they were based on the Zanzibar clove price, not the producer price of cloves. But interest rates were 10 to 15 percent. So a heavily mortgaged plantation might make less than the interest rate on its capital.[46]

The short-term fluctuations of clove production exacerbated the problem. A tree had to be picked over even if the crop was poor, so labor costs did not decrease proportionately in a bad year.[47] Loans could not be paid back. When a good year followed, the creditor could insist on immediate payment in kind and then hold the cloves for a more favorable price: the benefits of speculation in a volatile market largely went to the moneylenders.[48]

44. D&C, Pemba, 1900, p. 11. Compensation money, under the 1897 decree, was not seizable for debt, but some landowners used it to rid themselves of the lien on their land.

45. Interest rates did go down, but from an extremely high starting point after emancipation. Some estimates (perhaps exaggerated) are: 30 percent (1900), 20 percent (1905), 10 to 15 percent (1913). D&C, Pemba, 1900, p. 5; Lyne, *Zanzibar in Contemporary Times*, p. 271; Sinclair to Harcourt, 10 Oct. 1913, CO 618/2. See also Hardinge to Salisbury, 10 Jan. 1896, LIX, 395, p. 27; AgAR, 1899, p. 21; Craster, pp. 207–08; AgCom, p. 4.

46. Even in 1924, when clove prices were very high, government plantations were only making a 6 percent profit. For the calculations, see Sinclair to Harcourt, 10 Oct. 1913, CO 618/2; Memorandum by McClellan, 6 Oct. 1915, incl. Belfield to Law, 29 Oct. 1915, CO 618/12; Kirsopp, "Report," 1926, pp. 7–8. Officials specifically stated that profits were below the interest rate. AR, 1908, p. 80, 1912, p. 52; AgAR, 1911, p. 146.

47. This is clear from data on costs and revenue on Government plantations from 1910 to 1922. AgAR, 1922, p. 103.

48. Such speculative profits could be considerable, for prices varied by as much as 75 percent in a single year. Memorandum of the Chief of Customs, incl. Sinclair to Devonshire, 27 March 1923, CO 618/30.

The clove merchant, the creditor who provided loans to pay labor, and the merchant who supplied household goods on credit was often one and the same. Banks would not lend on agricultural security, forcing planters into a multidimensional dependence on merchant-financiers. Unable to take full advantage of rising clove prices, caught by the frequent dips in the market, and often forced by liens on crops to sell cloves at below-market rates, landowners fell into a form of indebtedness that they could not overcome.[49]

The postwar boom looked as if it would generate sufficient profits to break the creditors' hold. It offered a long-indebted aristocracy a chance to clear the books in one big leap.[50] So more labor and other resources were poured into cloves in the early 1920s. Planting was extended, and the most ambitious bought up clove plantations. Because clove trees were already densely planted in suitable areas, both new land usable for cloves and old plantations shot up in price. Planting was laborious and costly. Planters had to borrow heavily, for a short time they thought, to have a chance to liquidate their long-term debts and amass wealth.[51]

When the boom ended just as the first postwar trees were beginning to bear, plantation owners were trapped. Their means to repay debts were gone, their borrowed capital tied up in clove trees. Land values fell, al-

49. AgAR, 1911, p. 6, 1912, p. 139, 1927, p. 246; AR, Pemba, 1925, p. 65; Sinclair to Harcourt, 10 Oct. 1913, CO 618/2; AgCom p. 11; Kirsopp, "Report," 1926; Extract from Report of Dr. Andrade, incl. Clarke to Grey, 17 May 1910, FO 367/200. The Agriculture Director thought that European banks did not enter plantation financing because they would not get the double profits of the merchant-financier. The Government periodically talked of starting a land bank, but did nothing until the 1930s (Lyne, *Zanzibar in Contemporary Times*, pp. 271–72; Pearce to Harcourt, 11 July 1914, CO 618/7; AgCom, pp. 11–12). In the southern United States, the weakness of banking facilities also helped put a yoke on agriculturalists through the concentration of economic power in the hands of merchant-financiers. Ransom and Sutch, *One Kind of Freedom*, pp. 106–25. Wiener (*Social Origins of the New South*, pp. 79–80) also notes the adjustment of interest rates to fit the harvest, speculation in crops by middlemen, and the flexibility of methods of control over producers.

50. The importance of "gambling" by farmers who hoped to get out of debt has also been emphasized by Gavin Wright and Howard Kunreuther to explain the overplanting of cotton in the postbellum southern United States. Here the circumstances differ. Because Zanzibari planters—unlike Southern tenant farmers—had a great deal to lose and because middlemen siphoned off much of the speculative gains in a good year, gambling was not a year-to-year choice, as it was in the South. In direct contrast to the generally declining price of cotton, the sudden rise in clove prices after World War I induced the gambling. But trees, unlike cotton, are premanent crops, and Zanzibar was stuck with the results of this episode. ("Cotton, Corn and Risk in the Nineteenth Century," *Journal of Economic History*, 35 (1975):526–51). Ransom and Sutch also emphasize the allure of high cotton prices just after the Civil War and the importance of debts to entrenching cotton cultivation. (p. 165).

51. Pearce to Long, 24 March 1918, CO 618/19; AgCom, pp. 11–12; Lofchie, p. 107. In 1924, toward the end of the boom, Arabs were "without capital." Hollis to Coryndon, 2 Aug. 1924, incl. Coryndon to Thomas, 5 Sept. 1924, CO 618/33.

though they were still inflated relative to the price of cloves since so much money was in trees.[52] As the vanillin crisis gave way to the post-1929 depression and clove prices kept falling, the magnitude of indebtedness rose and Arabs lost effective control of as much as a quarter of the islands' clove trees. Many planters lost all their trees; others could no longer maintain a plantation properly. When pressed by their own creditors in the depression, mortgagors began to take over property. Only then, after 1933, did the Government intervene to ban the alienation of clove properties to Indians and to reorganize marketing and credit to preserve the Arab planter class.[53]

Although indebtedness is difficult to measure, one survey in 1934 estimated that nearly 63 percent of all clove trees were encumbered. The average debtor owed Rs 2,277 in Zanzibar, Rs 497 in Pemba, where estates tended to be smaller and—as we shall see—more self-sufficient. A quarter of the debts were in the form of "fictitious sales," conveyances under which the creditor promised (sometimes verbally) to return the property to its original owner if the debt were repaid. Interest rates were high, mostly 10 to 15 percent in Zanzibar, while over half in Pemba were over 15 percent. Short-term loans had equivalent annual interest rates of 25 to 100 percent.[54]

The moneylenders, according to a report in 1931, used plantations as a "milch-cow." The owner might not be displaced, but the sum collected as interest would rise if his sales did and the principal would never be reduced.[55] The control the creditor exercised, therefore, was substantial. He could prevent the selling of cloves through more advantageous marketing channels.[56] He could insure that the planter continued to cultivate cloves by threatening to displace him altogether. The price decline had also reduced the number of clove marketing firms, narrowing the

52. C. F. Strickland, "Report on Cooperation and the Economic Condition of the Agriculturalists in Zanzibar," incl. Strickland to Acheson, 12 June 1931, CO 618/49; Kirkham, Memorandum on the Maintenance of the Clove Industry in Zanzibar, incl. Resident to CO, 11 June 1930, CO 618/48.

53. C. A. Bartlett and J. S. Last, "Report on the Indebtedness of the Agricultural Classes," 1933, p. 7. Sales to Indians in the early period of falling prices, 1926–30, were high in Zanzibar—248 Arab estates worth Rs 1,200,000—but low in Pemba—825 acres. Some of these sales, however, were in reality mortgages, and it is even more likely that Swahili sales to Indians—whose average value was quite small—were mortgages (Strickland, "Report," 1931). See also the fine discussion of the debt crisis in Lofchie, pp. 107–26.

54. Bartlett and Last, "Report," 1933, pp. 4, 6–7. The Debt Commission ("Report," 1935, pp. 22–23) thought these estimates of indebtedness were high.

55. Strickland; AgCom, p. 17; Bartlett and Last, pp. 6–7.

56. Kirsopp, 1926, stresses the importance of monopolistic control of clove marketing, especially in Pemba. The Government felt that Indian merchant-financiers blocked its efforts to encourage the Clove Growers' Association to develop its own marketing system. AgAR, 1927, p. 246.

planters' choice even further.[57] The indebtedness crisis all but precluded innovation or improvement of estates or crop diversification. To improve an estate would merely tempt the creditor to take it over; to change from cloves to another crop or attempt to increase the self-sufficiency of the plantation would threaten the merchant-creditor's role and might also result in foreclosure. The crisis in clove production led to more clove production. When, later in the 1930s, the Government blocked some of the leverage of the Indian creditor—in the face of vigorous opposition from Indians—the dependence of the landlord on his creditor was transferred to the state.[58]

The very nature of the postabolition plantation system enhanced its vulnerability to indebtedness.[59] Because a wage-labor force requires cash for an entire season before the crops come in, money must be obtained when it is least available. Moreover, as the personal dependence of ex-slaves became less, the life style that distinguished the upper class came to be based more on items that were bought than on relationships with subordinates. The rural houses of Zanzibar's planters—no more the center of a socioeconomic unit—were abandoned in favor of the city. The slave plantation's capability, in times of trouble, to turn inward and meet much of its subsistence requirements was lost as planters concentrated their failing labor supply on cloves.[60] The postwar inflation hit the upper class's staple of rice—up 54 percent between 1914 and 1922—as well as luxury goods, while the common man's staples—cassava, millet, fish, and salt—went up much less.[61] Cash was thus becoming all the more necessary for the plantation owners just as laborers were insisting on their share and creditors, as always, were waiting for theirs. Borrowing

57. Pim, 1932, p. 84.

58. On indebtedness and lack of improvement, see Kirkham, Memorandum, incl. Resident to CO, 11 June 1930, CO 618/48. The normal effect of a competitive situation, the elimination of the most inefficient producers, was impeded by the fact that liens on estates formed such a labyrinth that potential purchasers found it difficult to see their way through to a clear title. Clarke to Grey, 12 Jan. 1912, FO 367/298; Minute, 15 Nov. 1921, to Pearce to Batterbee, 11 Nov. 1921, CO 618/28. On the state's role in the 1930s, see Lofchie, pp. 107–26.

59. Indebtedness to outsiders is characteristic of plantation agriculture. It affected most slave plantations, and emancipation either exacerbated the problem or, as frequently happened with sugar, led to the absorption of plantations into vertically integrated corporations. See Beckford, *Persistent Poverty,* and for a case study, Adamson, *Sugar without Slaves.*

60. AgCom, p. 2. A survey in 1948 found that all the large plantation owners in Zanzibar lived in town. In Pemba, planters lived in rural areas. Edward Batson, "The Social Survey of Zanzibar," 1961, vol. 15.

61. AgAR, 1922, p. 102. Much of the borrowing was in fact to meet living expenses (Bartlett and Last, 1933, p. 21). The tendency of plantation owners to consume imported goods is widespread. Beckford, pp. 210–11.

was indispensable for both production and consumption by the planter class, even more so than in an earlier epoch, and it was a trap that left planters no escape from the clove plantation.

Smallholders acquire debts as well, but the incomplete integration of peasant producers into market relationships often gives them a means of resisting subjugation to the creditor. When such subjugation had developed, it has frequently been in situations where smallholders had to purchase seeds, fertilizers, or tools and market a high proportion of their output—as in the cultivation of cotton, which required fertilizer, in the postbellum South—and the pressures leading to inescapable indebtedness must be analyzed in terms of all the mechanisms of class domination that impinge upon them.[62] Zanzibar's smallholders—above all Wapemba, Wahadimu, and Watumbatu—faced a landlord class that did not control village lands and could not contain competition within itself for tenants and laborers. The smallholders produced their own food; they used no fertilizer and only simple tools; and they were only partially caught up in the vagaries of the clove market. Not being an old aristocracy, they did not have to live like one in order to guard their status. They could mobilize family labor: it was adequate for a small clove shamba, called for no Government assistance, and was cheap.

Many smallholders did incur debts to local shopkeepers and had to deliver produce to them. But because only one of their resources—clove trees—were valued by moneylenders, such cultivators could only borrow to a limited extent.[63] The scanty evidence available suggests that their problems lay toward the opposite extreme from those of the planters: too little access to markets and credit. Such problems tended to thwart their efforts to increase production and income but did not threaten their way of life. The debt crisis that followed the clove boom was above all a problem of the planter class.[64]

---

62. On the pressures leading to the entrapment of tenants in the southern United States in the crop-lien system, see Ransom and Sutch. Bauer ("Rural Workers in Spanish America") adds a cautious note on this issue, asking how much "debt bondage" was really bondage and how much borrowing was done at the tenant's initiative and for his gain. The relationship of indebtedness to control by landlords and/or moneylenders must be considered in context.

63. Kirsopp, 1926, p. 11; Strickland, 1931.

64. That much is clear from the political crisis of the 1930s. The evidence on smallholder indebtedness is largely circumstantial, owing to the exclusion of properties with only small debts from the survey of Bartlett and Last. As discussed below, Pemba had a strong smallholder sector, while Zanzibar was dominated by large plantations. Pemba's clove producers, in 1933, owed an average of Rs 497, 55 percent of the value of their estates, while the proprietors of Zanzibar owed an average of Rs 2,277, 83 percent of the value of their estates. These data suggest that smallholders may have borrowed often but did not encumber their assets as heavily as did planters (Bartlett and Last, p. 6). Pim (1932, p. 14)

The "Arab planter class"—in good times and in bad—was receiving the attention of the Administration. Yet the structure of production was not evolving in quite the direction in which the Administration was pushing it. The Arab planter class did not dominate the production of cloves nearly as much as Government rhetoric and policies would suggest. This fact emerges from the evidence on the ownership of clove trees compiled for the Bonus Scheme in 1922 and summarized in Table 4.2.

The situation had apparently changed since the British takeover. As good an observer as W. W. A. Fitzgerald, studying agriculture in Zanzibar and Pemba in 1891, saw little evidence of clove production by Wahadimu, although some Wapemba had small holdings. At the time of abolition, the situation was similar.[65] But afterward, officials noted, Swahili were buying small clove estates. By the 1920s, Wapemba above all had become a major factor in clove production. There were more clove trees on Swahili mashamba (farms, plantations) in Pemba than on the larger plantations owned by Arabs. Wapemba were planting more trees, and the price of small mashamba was rising faster than that of large ones. Given the interspersed nature of Arab and Wapemba settlements and the fact that ridges where cloves flourished were adjacent to valleys suitable for Wapemba ground crops, Wapemba could plant clove trees near their villages or buy small pieces of Arabs' estates. In the village areas, individual Wapemba acquired rights to use or dispose of trees, but the land was subject to a complex group of rights vested in kinship groups and the village as a body.[66] Even in Pemba, production on a plantation scale remained a largely Arab phenomenon—thanks, mainly, to the use of labor imported from Zanzibar and the mainland.

On Zanzibar Island, however, the Arab plantation was dominant and growing. Swahili—Wahadimu and ex-slaves are not distinguished in the 1922 data—owned a much lower proportion of trees, and each owner had fewer of them than owners in Pemba. The contrast of large Arab plantations and extremely small Swahili farms is even clearer in data

argues that large estates and Arabs were more beset by debts than small estates and Swahili. The contrary argument is made by Strickland (1931), but his calculations, based on admittedly scanty data, are undermined by his failing to mention that the large numbers of sales and mortgages by Swahili must be measured against the fact that Swahili estates, although small, were far more numerous than those of Arabs.

65. Fitzgerald, *Travels*, pp. 540–41; Farler to Rogers, 15 Aug. 1904, FOCP 8382, p. 108; Last, Report, 8 Feb. 1903, incl. Cave to Lansdowne, 18 March 1903, FO 2/728. See also Cooper, *Plantation Slavery*, p. 71.

66. Newman, *Banani*, p. 74; AR, Pemba, 1925, pp. 63–64; Hollis to Amery, 15 Jan. 1926, CO 618/39; Kirsopp, 1926. In Pemba, there eventually evolved a "shareplanting" arrangement by which owners let squatters plant trees, tend them until the bearing stage, and then keep half of the trees so planted. This may have evolved rather recently. Charles Meek, *Land Law and Custom in the Colonies* (London, 1949), p. 72.

TABLE 4:2
THE OWNERSHIP OF CLOVE TREES, 1922

Group	No. of Owners	No. of Properties	Bearing Trees	Trees per Owner	% of Trees Owned
Zanzibar					
Swahili	4,840	7,070	236,758	50	22
Arab	1,218	1,869	735,544	604	68
Indians	165	262	52,768	320	5
Other	80	122	49,835	623	5
Total	6,303	9,323	1,074,905	171	100
Pemba					
Swahili	8,717	15,117	896,439	103	47
Arab	2,973	6,819	888,259	299	46
Indian	158	1,038	99,722	631	5
Other	169	182	41,628	246	2
Total	12,017	23,156	1,926,048	160	100
Totals	18,320	32,479	3,000,953	164	

SOURCE: Zanzibar, AgAR, 1922, p. 99.

from 1932, shown in Table 4.3. Arabs were a smaller proportion of the population of Zanzibar than of Pemba—5 percent, compared to 12 percent in Pemba—but their hold over clove growing and the plantation economy was tighter. Moreover, it was in Zanzibar that clove production was being extended more rapidly, although from a smaller base. Zanzibar's output rose 78 percent from 1895 to 1924, compared with 33 percent in Pemba. In absolute terms, Pemba's output rose slightly more than Zanzibar's, and the contribution of peasant production to the overall growth of clove exports was clearly important.[67]

The starting point for the economic power of Omani Arabs in Zanzibar was their nearly exclusive control over clove land, established in the nineteenth century but extended in the twentieth. Unless one accepts that the Wahadimu preferred bad land in southern and eastern Zanzibar to good land in the north and west, the use of force would appear to have been a major component in the establishment of Omani control of land.[68] Because of the clear division on Zanzibar Island between good clove land and coral land in the south and east—compounded by the

67. Kirsopp, 1926, p. 46.
68. Cooper, *Plantation Slavery*, pp. 57–58. See the contrasting views of Middleton, *Land Tenure in Zanzibar*, pp. 11–12, and John Gray, *A History of Zanzibar from the Middle Ages to 1856* (London, 1962), pp. 167–68.

proximity of the center of Omani strength in Zanzibar town to the clove land—the interpenetration of crops and peoples that characterized Pemba did not develop on Zanzibar. Although Wahadimu did plant or acquire clove trees in the fringe areas of the plantation zone, those who purchased land or trees in the central area had to make a break with their villages and became unable to exercise, on a daily basis, the variety of rights in land that community membership conveyed. They could not simply plant trees near their homes. Indeed, many Wahadimu who bought small clove properties also became squatters on Arab land so that they could grow subsistence crops.[69] Because Wahadimu faced more difficulty than Wapemba in integrating clove growing into their village structure, they were less able to avoid wage labor on Arab plantations, including those of Pemba. It is not surprising that the largest surge in Zanzibar Island's exports came in 1905–09, just when the state's recruitment drive hit the Wahadimu.[70] Zanzibar Island's pattern of growth came closer to the image in the official mind than that of Pemba, namely, Arab plantation owners and Swahili workers. It was, of course, a self-realizing image, requiring the continual exercise of state power, which the human geography of Pemba partially thwarted.

Not merely the size of agricultural units and the ethnic origins of their owners, but the character of agricultural society differed somewhat between the two islands. In a 1948 survey, the owners of all large plantations (1,000 or more trees) in Zanzibar Island lived in the city; in Pemba 85 percent of the Arabs and all of the small number of Wapemba owning large plantations lived in rural areas.[71] In Zanzibar Island, the land was more likely to be caught up in the web of commercial transactions. Although specific data on sales and land values are lacking, summary figures for 1915 to 1922 indicate that the value of property sold or conveyed in Zanzibar was three to six times as high as that conveyed in Pemba each year, although Pemba had nearly twice as many clove trees. The disparity in property mortgaged was even greater.[72] Finally, an extremely rough estimate of land under various crops in 1916 suggests that patterns of land use in the two islands were different, as Table 4.4 shows. Zanzibar's population was higher—by 31 percent in 1924—but it had less land in food crops. It also took far more imports, 65 percent of the major items- despite its lesser contribution to exports.[73]

Although neither island was self-sufficient in rice, Pemba's economy

69. Godfrey Dale, *The Peoples of Zanzibar* (London, 1920), p. 14; Middleton, p. 45.

70. In that period, Zanzibar Island's production more than doubled. Kirsopp, 1926, p. 46.

71. Batson, "Social Survey," vol. 15. The trend toward absenteeism was noted earlier in AgCom, 1923, p. 2.

72. AgCom, Minority Report, p. 50.

73. Kirsopp, 1926.

TABLE 4:3
SIZE OF PLANTATIONS IN ZANZIBAR, 1932

	Number of Trees			
Group	Under 100	100–499	500–999	Over 1,000
Arab	1,236	772	169	177
Swahili	5,880	493	28	8

SOURCE: Pim, Report, 1932, p. 83.

NOTE: Comparable figures for Pemba are not available.

was more fully integrated, Zanzibar's closer to the classic plantation model. The polarization between owner and worker, landlord and squatter in Zanzibar Island was to grow.

But one should not assume that Pemba was an island of egalitarian farming. Arabs, with 12 percent of the population, owned 46 percent of the trees; the average Arab plantation was nearly three times the size of the average Swahili plantation. Only the richest Wapemba employed immigrant laborers to clear or weed mashamba. Officials directed labor to Arab plantations and sought it from Wapemba villages, although not as successfully as in Zanzibar. Despite the extension of clove cultivation to Wapemba, the majority of Swahili in Pemba did not own clove trees.[74]

What the strength of the smallholder sector of Pemba does show, however, is how errant were British conceptions of how the clove industry *must* run. A majority of the trees on the more productive of the two islands were not owned by either Arabs or planters or picked by a disciplined wage-labor force. That Swahili smallholders did so well in the face of all the supports lavished on Arab plantations and the drain of labor away from Swahili farms makes one wonder how the economy would have evolved if the Government had supported Swahili agriculture, or—after abolition—just ignored it. The experiences of several African areas that successfully produced export crops through peasant cultivation—cocoa in southern Ghana and western Nigeria, cotton in

74. In the 1924 census, 10 percent of "Swahili," 10 percent of Wapemba, and 28 percent of "Shirazi" were listed as "shamba owners," but both occupational and ethnic classifications are unclear, as discussed below. The Bonus Survey lists 8,717 Swahili clove-tree owners, but its definition of Swahili includes virtually any non-Arab or non-Indian. There were 23,322 adult male non-Arabs in the 1924 census, and females could own clove trees as well (Native Census, 1924, p. 11). On the limited use of mainland labor by Wapemba, see Observations by Lieut. Clark on Capt. Craster's Report on Pemba, 8 May 1912, FOCP 10239, p. 17.

Uganda—all suggest the importance of bringing extra labor into peasant households in order to expand production. One need not espouse the myth of peasant egalitarianism to argue that the lack of sharp differentiation between what workers did and what owners did, combined with low entry costs and the absence of an upper class that dominated access to resources, made it possible for expansion to take place through the entry of new producers, not just investments by a dominant group.[75] But labor is a scarce resource even within small farming units, and the efforts of the Government of Zanzibar to pull it out helped shape the nature of rural society.

But there was another Zanzibar, scarcely mentioned in official reports, a dimension of the local economy which clearly existed but which cannot be fully understood—if it ever will be—until detailed local studies are done. Even in the days of slavery, the plantation economy was not exclusive. Not only did plantations grow a variety of foods for internal consumption—cassava, grains, oranges, mangoes, bananas, and vegetables—but a lively market developed in Zanzibar town, in which slaves participated actively on their free days. Sidney Mintz has stressed the importance of small-scale produce marketing for the slaves of Jamaica, arguing that by the time of abolition the strength of such patterns of exchange equipped slaves with an effective mechanism for the distribution of small quantities of produce throughout the island. Such marketing was never fully independent of the plantation economy—it was fed by the purchasing power of plantation wages—but even the sugar workers could buy food from someone other than a planter. Others could avoid plantation labor altogether, and the economic importance of small-scale farming grew and even extended to the production of modest quantities of export crops.[76] The marketing system became a means of resisting the dominance of the plantation.

The inadequate information on marketing in Zanzibar after abolition hints at the existence of a dual system. Clove buying was centralized and closely linked to the selling of imported goods and the provision of credit. A small number of Indian brokers in town took cloves on com-

---

75. In western Nigeria, working for a cocoa farmer was often a step toward becoming one, and capital and labor were both mobilized through kinship systems, factors which blurred class distinctions in agriculture, particularly in the expansionist phase. But the need for extra labor was acute in this and other cases of smallholder production. Sara Berry, *Cocoa, Custom and Socio-Economic Change in Rural Western Nigeria* (Oxford, 1975); Polly Hill, *Migrant Cocoa Farmers of Southern Ghana* (Cambridge, 1963); A. I. Richards, F. Sturrock, and J. M. Fortt, eds., *Subsistence to Commercial Farming in Present-Day Buganda* (Cambridge, 1973); John H. Cleave, *African Farmers: Labor Use in the Development of Smallholder Agriculture* (New York, 1974).

76. Mintz, *Caribbean Transformations*, pp. 180–224.

TABLE 4:4
CROP ACREAGE IN ZANZIBAR AND PEMBA, 1916

	Zanzibar		Pemba	
	Acres	% of Acres Planted	Acres	% of Acres Planted
Cloves	20,000	20	40,000	25
Coconuts	35,000	35	10,000	6
Native crops	45,000	45	110,000	69
Unplanted coral	300,000		85,000	

SOURCE: Memorandum on the Clove Industry of the Zanzibar Protectorate by McClellan, 1916, incl. McClellan to CO, 25 March 1916, CO 618/16.

mission, got them through customs, and sold them to a small number of European and American clove-buying houses. Near the town, large-scale growers were often able to organize their own packaging and transport, but in Pemba the few Indian firms that controlled shipping to Zanzibar and the distribution of the bags used for packing, plus costly inland transport over poor roads, effectively controlled clove marketing. The monopoly of the large Pemba firms, compounded by the "sharp practices" that officials noted but did not stop, reduced the benefits which producers in Pemba received for cloves, raised the cost of imports, and above all undermined the greater potential Pemba had for integrating clove production into a varied local economy. On both islands, the independent traders—Indian or Omani—or agents of brokers who collected and bulked cloves and coconuts in the villages, also sold cloth, utensils, and simple imported goods. By providing goods on credit to both large and small producers and by financing the labor costs of planters, the traders insured that the people who bought imports had to sell them cloves and coconuts.[77]

Distinct from this network of import-export traders spreading outward from Zanzibar town were local markets in the villages, where fish, eggs, goats, and local crops were exchanged.[78] In Pemba, immigrant workers who did not grow their own food bought it in markets from

77. The best analysis of clove marketing is in Kirsopp, 1926, pp. 16–18. See also H. Lister, Report on Trade in Pemba, incl. Clarke to Grey, 11 Aug. 1909, FO 367/354; O'Sullivan, Report on Pemba, 1896, PP 1896, LIX, 395, p. 44; D&C, Pemba, 1912; Report on Pemba by Capt. Craster, 29 Feb. 1912, FOCP 10239, p. 8; Craster, *Pemba*, pp. 147, 150, 188; Report of Director of Agriculture, Akers' Report, 1907, FOCP 9122, p. 72.

78. As Joel Migdal argues, not only do local and regional marketing systems involve less risk to peasants than international markets do, but they also embody different kinds of social relations. *Peasants, Politics, and Revolution*, p. 55.

local farmers and fishermen. Near Zanzibar town, squatters on Arab lands often sold produce to feed the growing urban population, and only toward the end of the colonial era did landlords begin to exploit that source of income themselves, using wage labor they had hitherto limited to cloves.[79]

Besides the many fruits and other farm products that thrived in the islands, fish were an important part of the village marketing system. Officials estimated there were 4,000 fishermen in Zanzibar and Pemba, including many on the east coast, where other sources of income were meager. In Pemba and to a lesser extent eastern Zanzibar, there was livestock. In addition, Wahadimu cut mangrove poles—used for building—on the inlets of the eastern region and brought them to Zanzibar by boat. Coconut trees, more spread out than cloves, provided fibres for making rope as well as roofing material and firewood. Rope making was an especially important craft, as was the manufacture of bags, mats, and lime. There were Swahili tailors, carpenters, and smiths as well.[80]

But there were limits to the strength of the other Zanzibar, and British policy and plantation development were pressing against it. Food markets in the town were made subject to licensing in 1915, and the "public health" was invoked to justify restricting commerce to licencees, most of whom were Arab and Indian. Such laws defined as illegal an important part of the complex division of labor and exchange relationships among people who operated on a small scale and at a small margin.[81]

More serious was the extent to which imports—purchased with the earnings of the clove industry—narrowed the opportunities for local production. The most important staple import was rice, a crop which could thrive in Pemba and was even ecologically capable of coexisting with clove cultivation.[82] Once a rice-exporting region, Zanzibar and Pemba had begun to import rice after clove plantations developed. In 1902, an official in Pemba thought it was an "economic blunder" that over one-third of Pemba's cloves were devoted to paying the cost of im-

---

79. Pearce, *Zanzibar: The Island Metropolis of Eastern Africa* (London, 1920), pp. 165-66, 246, 324-25; Ingrams, *Zanzibar, Its History and Peoples*, pp. 354, 330-31; Middleton, *Land Tenure in Zanzibar*, pp. 46-47.

80. BB, 1925, p. 124; J. S. Last, "The Economic Fisheries of Zanzibar," 1929, p. 1; Pearce, pp. 152-53, 170; Craster, pp. 99, 103, 185; Dale, p. 14; AR, 1914, pp. 10-11; W. H. Ingrams, "Native Industries and Occupations," in British Empire Exhibition, *Zanzibar*, pp. 82-84.

81. Pearce to Belfield, 26 April 1915, incl. Belfield to Harcourt, 11 May 1915, CO 618/12.

82. Rice grows in valleys, cloves on ridges. There is also some rice cultivation in Zanzibar. Tidbury, p. 17.

ported rice. But nothing was done to encourage the growing of rice, while the programs that supported cloves made the opportunity costs of rice cultivation all the higher. Rice imports rose steadily in value, except during the war. The wartime import shortage revealed that Zanzibaris still had the skills and resources to grow their own rice, but the postwar clove boom was paralleled by a surge in rice imports, up 74 percent by volume, 24 percent by value between 1921 and 1925. The favorable terms of trade of cloves against rice helped undo the self-sufficiency regained in the war.[83]

Expansion of clove plantations may have encroached on land that could be used for fruit trees, coconuts, and maize, but not so much for rice. The real bottleneck was labor. Rice cultivation required not only a great deal of work, but organization and long-term commitment to well-irrigated valleys. The slave plantation—and rice plantations existed even after most planters had turned to cloves—had provided organization, forced people to work, and bound them to a particular place. Later, planters turned their fading control of labor more exclusively to cloves not only because they promised more cash, but because the assistance of the state and financiers was limited to clove cultivation.[84] Had planters permitted their squatters to grow marketable quantities of rice on their own, the rice growers would have had no need to perform plantation labor. Because many of Pemba's rice valleys were on land owned by Arabs but not cultivated, the squatters who used such lands were in a delicate position. They could grow rice as long as they did not grow too much of it.[85] Moreover, ex-slaves and other squatters knew that their bargaining position depended on the possibility of moving, as well as on the interplay of seasonal tasks on their own plots and their landlords' trees. The year-long process of rice cultivation would have bound them in a new way to a particular landlord. Cassava—a far less nutritious food—was more suitable for the social conditions of squatter agriculture.[86]

83. D&C, Pemba, 1901–02, p. 4; BB, 1925, p. 65. Rice imports averaged £122,000 per year in 1894–97, £233,000 in 1921–25 (ibid., and Crofton, "Statistics of the Zanzibar Protectorate," 1892–1920, p. 20). The wartime expansion in local rice production is noted in Armstrong, "Agriculture," p. 33.

84. Similarly, after abolition planters in British Guiana dropped all minor crops and concentrated on sugar. Adamson, p. 28.

85. The effect of planters' control of land and labor on the lack of rice cultivation has been stressed by F. B. Wilson, "Emergency Food Production in Zanzibar," *East African Agricultural Journal* 10 (1944):93. The Administration was quite explicit in asserting that growing crops other than cloves would deplete the labor supply. Cave to Grey, 23 Feb. 1908, FOCP 9331, p. 7. On Arab ownership of rice land, see McClellan, Memorandum on Cocoanut Industry, incl. McClellan to CO, 25 March 1916, CO 618/16.

86. Because cultivating cassava involved no labor peaks, required no fixed capital beside land, and the product could be left in the ground and harvested if a squatter had to

Wapemba did grow rice, but growing it on a large scale for export was more difficult than either planting clove trees or supplementing village agriculture with seasonal forays onto Arab plantations. The Government laid out roads in accordance with the location of clove plantations; marketing facilities and credit for rice farmers were not developed; the Government did nothing to organize irrigation works, and cooperative efforts by local people were discouraged by the uncertainty of land tenure. So the watercourses in many of Pemba's valleys became clogged, and rice-fields degenerated into swamps.[87]

With chillies—once a significant source of cash income for Wahadimu—decline was more clearly a result of other opportunities. When cash could be earned by picking cloves without disrupting village agriculture, burning one's fingers in order to have a cash crop became less appealing.[88] But the combination of opportunity and constraint created by the expansion of clove production in conjunction with the use of state power had a cumulative effect: Swahili became increasingly dependent on the clove tree, in whatever role they could find.

The Zanzibar of varied food crops and local crafts was more a defense against the import-export market than a part of it. Local agriculture and industries were a source of economic protection for ex-slaves, Wahadimu, Wapemba, and Watumbatu, helping to keep wages up and the terms for squatters and seasonal workers relatively favorable. As in many plantation economies, the health of export agriculture and that of local agriculture were at odds. In Zanzibar and Pemba, the two sectors remained in a standoff: planters failed to establish tight control over laborers and tenants, while the plantations hemmed in the other dimensions of the economy.

Again and again, one finds that plantation economies are more fully integrated into world markets than into market networks in their own lands. Comparative advantage is at best a partial explanation for producers' choices about what crops to grow and sell and a poor guide to the effects of such decisions. A "society" did not decide how best to organize its "economy," nor were individuals making profit-maximizing decisions in a social vacuum.[89] They were wrapped up in particular structures, in

---

depart, it was an ideal squatter crop. Wilson, p. 93; Acland, p. 33; McClellan, "Agricultural Resources," p. 426.

87. Last to Cave, 23 May 1908, FOCP 9401, p. 80; "Production and Uses of Rice," *Bulletin of the Imperial Institute* 15 (1917):218; Craster, p. 99.

88. AgCom, pp. 8–9; McClellan, p. 414; AgAR, 1917, p. 4; Armstrong, p. 33. Chillie exports were worth Rs 102,390 in 1894; they oscillated between Rs 15,720 and Rs 75,568 in 1913–22. Fitzgerald, p. 574; AgAR, 1922, p. 98.

89. W. A. Lewis tries to juxtapose a favorable view of monoculture and regional disparities to an attack on the "political evil" of Government favoritism toward particular interests or regions. The two are not autonomous. *Tropical Development*, p. 38.

the cumulative effect of past decisions, and above all in changing relations and conflict between classes.

Stephen Marglin has argued that the factory system in England did not evolve because of the imperatives of technology but as a result of decisions made by a particular class seeking to establish its control over the production process. By atomizing the way goods were produced—reducing the function of an individual to a narrow role—capitalists insured that they would have a necessary role in production. The craftsman who saw his product through from raw material to finished good might not need a boss; a factory hand did. Marglin simplifies the nature of the labor process in industry, but his central question can well be adapted to a situation where neither technological change nor economies of scale were important considerations: what do planters do?[90] Planters in Zanzibar did not earn profits because they performed necessary economic functions; certain functions became necessary because planters made profits.

Cloves could be, and were, grown without planters. However, the atomization of the agricultural process—the development of specialized enterprises for growing cloves, the separation of managing from working, the undermining of self-sufficiency, the duality of marketing systems, and the specialization of particular groups in specific niches of agricultural labor—contributed to the control and profits of the planters.

Atomization was also in the interest of the colonial state. This process took place on a worldwide scale, of which the production of cloves in Zanzibar, of rice in India, and of clove oil in England is but one dimension.[91] For cloves to be grown inZanzibar and rice in India, rather than cloves and rice together in Zanzibar, may or may not be more efficient in some objective and measurable sense. But planters and the state—or classes subject to their power—were deciding what to grow, and to grow rice on Zanzibar would have undermined the planters' control of labor for cloves.

90. Stephen A. Marglin, "What Do Bosses Do? The Origins and Functions of Hierarchy in Capitalist Production," *Review of Radical Political Economics* 6, no. 2 (1974):33–60. The argument is derived from Marx, *Capital*, 1:322–68. Little mechanization in clove production was possible and less was tried. In 1925, only £2,084 worth of agricultural machinery was imported for all purposes in Zanzibar. If anything, better methods were used in the nineteenth century, for the painstaking planting techniques that once were used could not be employed with scarce labor. BB, 1925, p. 95; McClellan, "Agricultural Resources," p. 414; Tidbury, pp. 46, 90. This is a contrast with the sugar industry, where labor-saving machinery was a crucial aspect of the struggle between planters and workers. Mintz, "Rise of Peasantries."

91. The world's largest importers of rice in 1918 were plantation areas—Malaya, Indonesia, and Ceylon—which used it to feed workers who grew something else. Charles C. Stover, "Tropical Exports," in Lewis, *Tropical Development*, pp. 56–57.

Control over production, in British eyes, would be limited to a small aristocracy, and that aristocracy would become increasingly dependent on the state. Peasants in many lands have also been reduced to dependence on the state, on creditors, and on landlords. But as officials repeatedly acknowledged, such control was difficult to establish when "no one could starve in Zanzibar."[92] The plantation system, however, would exclude the actual producers from decisions about production. Planters, as opposed to small-scale cultivators, had a greater need for state assistance in obtaining labor; they required cash at more stages of their operations and thus depended more on credit; specialization implied greater reliance on the continued output of the export crop in order to keep buying food; economic failure in a plantation economy was less cushioned by diversified crops and by the forms of "social insurance" characteristic of peasant communities; for an aristocracy, economic failure could mean social disaster as well; and a society polarized into owners and workers posed a more serious challenge to social order than a less differentiated structure, accentuating once again the planters' dependence on the state. In the nineteenth century, Zanzibari planters had kept the state at arm's length through the strength of their relationship with their followers. After that relationship was broken, the colonial state had little trouble reducing Omani plantation owners to a dependent aristocracy. Even when—decades later—Arabs challenged the British, their aim was more to preserve the role of the state than to change it.

Because of their far greater cash needs, planters were not only more likely than peasants to try to put resources into export crops, but they were less able to get them out. Elsewhere, for example on the coast of Kenya, peasants often frustrated colonial officials by their ability *not* to produce for export, and the more differentiated and flexible a marketing system, the more choice peasants had over what to grow or not to grow. Monoculture, plantation production, and narrow marketing facilities were mutually reinforcing.[93]

The state and the creditors helped to rigidify the process of capital accumulation, making qualitative change more unlikely. The state raked

92. Pearce, pp. 324–25. For other expressions of dismay at the independence of ex-slave and Swahili cultivators, see Hardinge to Salisbury, 10 Jan. 1896, PP 1896, LIX, 395, pp. 24–25; Lyne, Report on Agriculture, 1902, FOCP 8177, p. 66; McClellan, Memorandum on Cocoanut Industry, incl. McClellan to CO, 25 March 1916, CO 618/16; Hollis to Coryndon, 2 Aug. 1924, incl. Coryndon to Thomas, 5 Sept. 1924, CO 618/33.

93. Michael Lipton argues in favor of redistributing large land holdings on the grounds that small producers are more responsive to price changes than large ones. That is one reason why colonial governments opposed land reform. Smallholders had too much choice. "Toward a Theory of Land Reform," in David Lehmann, ed., *Peasants, Landlords, and Governments: Agrarian Reform in the Third World* (New York, 1974), p. 293.

off 25 percent of clove exports, plus a share of imports, and used the revenue both to perpetuate itself and to perpetuate and extend clove production. Much of its surplus revenue was invested in India. Yet the state ended up imprisoned by its own narrow policies, for years of substantial (if irregular) budget surpluses turned into a decade of deficits when clove prices fell in 1925.[94]

The credit system had the same effect. The overlap of moneylenders with clove brokers—and with importers, wholesalers, and rural retailers as well—meant that plantation monoculture was enabling merchant-financiers to take profits in various stages of their operations. Much of these profits went back into perpetuating the system that provided the moneylenders with such a high degree of control. Little of it went to diversification, for it was the specialization of the plantation—as well as the very weakness of marketing systems—which gave power to the merchant-financiers.

The state and the merchant-financiers could channel their shares of the surplus outside of Zanzibar as well as within it. But landowners were tied to their clove trees. Capital, for them, had no independent existence; they could not shift it to other investments or accumulate it in forms other than still more clove trees. The Government's capitalist conception of production thus only partially reflected reality: the capitalists had little control over capital and were thus protected against both improvement and collapse.

The conjuncture of the interests of Arab planters seeking to hold onto property, labor, and status, of a colonial state eager to expand exports and maintain control over producers, and of creditors striving to make the most of the role of intermediary reinforced the plantation system and monoculture. The vulnerability of the plantation economy to problems of labor supply, export prices, and an inadaptable credit system, evident in the nineteenth century, became more pronounced in the twentieth.

The very structures which perpetuated the dominance of an Arab planter class narrowed its options. In Marx's terms, its ability to accumulate relative surplus value—through investments that raised productivity—was blocked; its quest for profits was limited to maximizing absolute surplus value—getting more labor for lower wages.[95] The state itself worked hardest to bind laborers to plantations, to bring in new workers, to discipline labor, and especially in the 1920s, to cut wages and increase tasks. Its failure

94. Akers Report, 1907, FOCP 9122, p. 40. For details of annual revenue and expenditures, see Crofton, "Statistics of the Zanzibar Protectorate," 1892–1932.

95. Marx, *Capital*, 1: 508–19. The importance of particular class structures to shaping the ways capital can and cannot be accumulated is stressed in Leys, "Capital Accumulation, Class Formation and Dependency," p. 245, and Brenner, "The Origins of Capitalist Development," pp. 84–86.

to create an agricultural proletariat eventually gave way to efforts to prevent local food production and exchange from undermining plantation labor. The consequence of this way of extracting surplus value was a daily struggle on the part of resident and migrant workers within the islands to control the amount and timing, as well as the rewards, of labor, to maintain access to land, and to preserve varied economic activities. The pressures and restrictions of the Government were not enough, and even the narrowing of workers' roles to specific components of clove production stopped short of breaking workers' access to the means of production.[96]

But the standoff between planters and the state on the one hand and tenants and workers on the other produced a peculiar brittleness in the clove economy. The paralysis of the planters was all the more severe because their control of labor needed to make any changes was so fragile. Tenants, meanwhile, were prevented from planting trees or growing marketable quantities of rice by the landowners' fear that their property rights would be called into question and that their squatters would become less likely to work.[97] Tenants themselves were afraid to make any permanent improvements on the land because they might tempt owners to evict them. So squatters stuck to the most basic of crops, notably cassava, supplemented by a few crops that could be sold through the Swahili petty trading network. They could defend themselves against demands for labor or rent that they deemed excessive, but they had little scope to alter what they did with their land. Wapemba and Wahadimu had less to fear about the lands they farmed, but for a cash income they had little alternative to cloves. For all these groups, the heart of the defense against dependence on wage labor or bondage to the shopkeeper lay in subsistence cultivation. They had to combat what in other parts of the world has meant subordination: the efforts of landowners, merchants, moneylenders, and the state to interpose themselves between the cultivator and his food.[98]

96. How much it took to constrain African agriculture in South Africa and Rhodesia is explained in Bundy, *Rise and Fall of the South African Peasantry,* and Robin Palmer, *Land and Racial Domination in Rhodesia* (Berkeley, 1977).

97. The British put pressure on Arabs to cut down on squatters' rights and above all to be sure that the squatters did not acquire rights of ownership. However, the rights of tenants to land and their exclusion from growing trees became deeply ingrained. See the memoranda of the Agriculture Director (McClellan), incl. Sinclair to CO, 10 Oct. 1913, CO 618/2, and McClellan to CO, 25 March 1916, CO 618/16; McGeach and Addis, "Review of the System of Land Tenure," 1945; Middleton, *Land Tenure in Zanzibar,* esp. pp. 43–44; "Report on the Economic Development of the Zanzibar Protectorate," 1962, pp. 36–37.

98. Such dangers are emphasized in a variety of contexts by Scott, *The Moral Economy of the Peasant;* Migdal, *Peasants, Politics, and Revolution;* Ransom and Sutch, pp. 149–70. They are ignored by economists who equate differentiation and specialization with development

Economic Roles, Social Identity, and Class Formation

It was important for the state to conceive of economic roles in ethnic terms. Not only did the supposed talents of "the Arab" as a supervisor of "the native" serve as a rationale for the concentration of economic power, but the coincidence of ethnicity and economic function would hopefully reinforce the particularity of each role, strengthening the atomization and interdependence upon which the control of the planters and the state depended. In reality, however, ethnicity and economic role did not coincide so neatly. Yet myths often create their own reality, although not always in the way wheir creators intended. The myth of an Arab upper class was to a large extent a self-fulfilling one, for the conferring of agricultural services, labor recruitment, education, and civil service posts on a small segment of the Omani population helped to shape such a class. Officials persisted in seeing other economic categories in ethnic terms. "Freed slave" became a synonym for a squatter on an Arab clove plantation, especially a lazy one. "Mainland African" or "Nyamwezi" meant someone working for wages on such a plantation. "Wapemba," "Wahadimu," and "Watumbatu" were people who lived outside the plantation system and hence were unproductive except for providing harvest labor. Such associations could mean that different peoples had different opportunities and preferences, or else that officials were defining ethnicity by economic role.

It is the very circularity of this process that is significant, for the ambiguity of ethnic designations made possible the redefinition of social identity in conjunction with economic change. Such changes can be assessed only tentatively, for the published censuses of 1924 and 1931 are virtually the only data that suggest how people identified themselves *at particular times.* Both occupational and ethnic designations in the censuses are extremely imprecise. What differentiates a "shamba owner" from a "cultivator" in the 1924 categories is not clear and may reflect the preconceptions of the census takers.[99] By listing only one occupation per adult male, they underestimated the ownership of land by traders and government servants; and the omission of women is misleading, for each

---

and can only see resistance to domination as intractability. See, for example, Johnston and Kilby, *Agriculture and Structural Transformation;* Fei and Ranis, *Development of the Labor Surplus Economy;* de Wilde, *Experiences with Agricultural Development in Tropical Africa.*

99. The procedures for the censuses are only vaguely described. Because census workers were literate, they may have provided a reference group for claims of identity. Aside from purely instrumental claims—for example, to avoid labor demands—an assertion of group membership that is not accepted serves only to weaken ties within one's own group. This may account for a certain realism in the identifications that comes out in the data. Procedures are discussed briefly in Edward Batson, "Report on Proposals for a Social Survey of Zanzibar," 1946.

female child had a half share in the inheritance of property. Both factors also minimized the proportion of Arabs owning land.

The ethnic categories do pose problems. "Hadimu" is clear enough, but "Shirazi" and "Swahili" are two denominations that are both crucial and elusive. Shirazi—after the Persian city of Shiraz—invokes claims made by the dynasties of early coastal city-states to be of Persian origin. The actual connection is remote, but in ideologies that stress both genealogy and Islam, it makes an important point. Wapemba, Watumbatu, and Wahadimu all have myths of Shirazi origin, but the use of the concept as an ethnic label emerges under specific circumstances.[100] "Swahili" is not originally a local term, except for the language (properly "kiswahili"); it appears in foreign accounts as a catchall for a Swahili-speaking Muslim who identifies himself with coastal culture and society but not with a specific ethnic group. Because of its vagueness, it fit ex-slaves in a changing society, reflecting both their assimilation to coastal culture and their exclusion from equal status in coastal society.[101] Most of the Swahili in the 1924 census were probably ex-slaves. But other ex-slaves apparently were identified by their ethnic group of origin in mainland Africa, for large numbers of Nyasa, Yao, Manyema, and Zaramo also appear in the census—all important sources of slaves but not (except for Zaramo) of migrants. Together, these groups contained 41 percent adult males, while the groups that were predominantly migrants—Nyamwezi and a much smaller number of Kikuyu—were 65 percent adult male, confirming the distinction between residents and migrants. But there was clearly much overlap between the aggregates I have labeled "mainland ex-slave" and "mainland migrant" which would blur distinctions, making all the more striking the differences in occupational roles that emerge in the census statistics.[102] The census classification "Other African" probably includes a mixture of ex-slaves and

100. Neville Chittick has made a large step toward separating the ideological content of Shirazi traditions from historical events, in "The 'Shirazi' Colonization of East Africa," *JAH* 6 (1965): 275–94. See also Gray, *History of Zanzibar*.

101. Pearce, a former Resident, calls the Swahili "a coast man" and concludes that the term is "indefinite" (*Zanzibar*, pp. 236–39). More recently, some scholars have tried too hard to pin down who are and who are not Swahili; the point is that this cannot *be* pinned down. Carol M. Eastman, "Who Are the Waswahili?" *Africa* 41 (1971): 228–35; Richard Arens, "The Waswahili: The Social History of an Ethnic Group," ibid. 45 (1975): 426–38.

102. Not surprisingly, Zaramo fall between in statistical breakdowns, although nearer the ex-slave side. Partial figures on the ethnic identity of slaves freed in 1900–01 confirm the prevalence of Nyasa, Yao, Manyema, and Zaramo. They also include quite a few Nyamwezi, but the extent of postabolition migration overwhelmed them. The "Other African" category probably included peoples like Ngindo, who were numerous in the statistics of freed slaves. Last to Mathews, 10 Jan. 1901, PP 1901, XLVIII, 173, pp. 29–30; Last to Raikes, 5 Feb. 1902, PP 1903, XLV, 955, pp. 8–9.

migrants, but in age-sex composition and occupational distribution, it resembles the four named ex-slave ethnic groups.

Tables 4.5 and 4.6, which show the numbers and percentages of each ethnic category in the most important occupational classifications in the 1924 census, raise important questions. In Zanzibar Island, mainland ex-slaves were ten times more likely to be cultivators than shamba owners. Some had bought land from Arabs but most had not.[103] Given their lack of communal land, this evidence confirms the predominance of squatting as a means of access to land. However, Swahili—also ex-slaves for the most part—were only one and a half times more likely to be cultivators than owners. Perhaps the fact of owning a shamba made it more likely for a person to claim a status that confirmed his place in coastal society. Wahadimu and Watumbatu were no more likely to be shamba owners than were ex-slaves, but for them being a cultivator meant access to land through some form of communal tenure. Shirazis, on the other hand, were more likely to own land than any other non-Arab group. But the difference between a Shirazi and an Mhadimu is one of self-definition and acceptance by the census-taker. Is someone called an Mhadimu because he cultivates but does not own property, or is he called a cultivator because he calls himself Mhadimu?

The census clearly shows the association of being a mainland migrant with working as a weeder; others may have weeded, but they were not called weeders. Outside of plantation work, the job of laborer—mainly comprising port and urban workers—provided employment to over a fifth of the Swahili, mainland ex-slaves, and other Africans, the three categories where ex-slaves were numerous. Such work was an important alternative to them, and they were important to Zanzibar in this role, providing 80 percent of Zanzibar Island's laborers. One final category is curious: general trader. While Arabs (meaning Omanis), Shihiris (the census's term for Arabs from the Hadramaut), and Comorians tended toward this calling, all ethnic groups are well represented. But a trader could be a substantial merchant or a petty hawker in Zanzibar town: this category tells little about what people actually did. For some, it may even be a self-flattering designation for urban poor or unemployed.

In Pemba, Arabs were just as prominent as shamba owners, but there were even more Arab cultivators. Non-Arabs from all groups seem to have had slightly more chance to become shamba owners. Watumbatu were more likely to own land in Pemba than in Zanzibar. Mainland ex-

103. On ex-slaves' purchases of bits of plantations being sold by financially troubled Arabs, particularly before 1905, see Farler, Report on Pemba, 1902, PP 1903, XLV, 955, pp. 12–13; Lyne, *Zanzibar*, p. 271; C. C. Frewer, "Extension Movement in Pemba," *Central Africa* 22 (1904): 86; McGeach and Addis, "Review of the System of Land Tenure," 1945, p. 10.

TABLE 4:5
ETHNICITY AND OCCUPATION IN THE 1924 NATIVE CENSUS, ZANZIBAR

Occupation and % of Each Group (Adult males) in That Occupation

Ethnic Group	Population (Adult male)	Shamba Owners		Cultivators		Weeders		Laborers		Traders	
		No.	%	No.	%	No.	%	No.	%	No.	%
Arab (Omani)	2,502	740	30	182	7	35	1	90	4	512	20
Swahili	6,270	758	12	1,151	18	160	3	1,349	22	464	7
Hadimu	5,404	651	12	2,383	44	123	2	295	5	630	12
Tumbatu	6,647	179	3	3,761	56	485	7	95	1	368	6
Shirazi	4,603	842	18	1,728	38	40	1	227	5	425	9
Pemba	81	3	4	4	5	4	5	26	32	5	19
Mainland ex-slave	7,743	211	3	2,012	26	492	6	1,654	21	745	10
Mainland migrant	3,161	34	1	249	8	2,331	74	183	6	102	3
Other African	7,501	515	7	1,738	23	480	6	1,728	23	717	10
Hadramis and Comorians	2,138	43	2	34	2	30	1	275	13	493	23

SOURCE: Zanzibar, Native Census, 1924, p. 8.

TABLE 4:6

ETHNICITY AND OCCUPATION IN THE 1924 NATIVE CENSUS, PEMBA

Occupation and % of Each Group (Adult males) in That Occupation

Ethnic Group	Population (Adult male)	Shamba Owners		Cultivators		Weeders		Laborers		Traders	
		No.	%	No.	%	No.	%	No.	%	No.	%
Arab (Omani)	3,880	1,159	30	1,281	33	42	1	24	1	388	10
Swahili	5,826	600	10	3,218	55	101	2	105	2	314	5
Hadimu	202	13	6	95	47	7	3	14	7	20	10
Tumbatu	1,771	375	21	1,027	58	17	1	15	1	44	2
Shirazi	4,201	1,157	28	1,738	41	129	3	93	2	157	4
Pemba	4,286	438	10	2,851	67	44	1	48	1	143	3
Mainland ex-slave	4,470	531	12	1,757	39	393	9	227	5	202	5
Mainland migrant	2,934	102	3	314	11	1,728	59	167	6	115	4
Other African	4,403	569	13	1,469	33	317	7	192	4	365	8
Hadrami and Comorian	232	33	14	78	34	3	1	6	1	33	14

SOURCE: Zanzibar, Native Census, 1924. p. 11.

slaves, as well as Swahili, were shamba owners in relatively similar proportion; neither group had the outlet of urban labor or petty trade as in Zanzibar. And the association of Shirazi identity with land ownership was even more striking than in Zanzibar.

It became more so. In 1931 census did not include an ethnic breakdown of occupations, but the changes in ethnic identity are themselves dramatic, as Table 4.7 reveals. The overall rate of population growth is unremarkable; there were no major migrations. The drastic change in the populations of different groups was not a demographic phenomenon but a social one.[104]

The increase in Arabs can only be explained by the fact that members of other groups—probably Wahadimu, Wapemba, Watumbatu, and Shirazi—called themselves Arabs. Given Government policy, this was sensible and may have been intended to deceive no one but officials. Meanwhile, Swahili—a category still used by the enumerators—virtually disappeared. The loss of Swahili is roughly equivalent to the gain of Arabs and Shirazis. But the dramatic increase in Shirazis occurred only in Pemba; they lost numbers in Zanzibar. In Pemba, Wapemba declined in numbers; in Zanzibar, Wahadimu and Watumbatu increased. Mainland ex-slaves decreased more markedly in Pemba than in Zanzibar.[105] These patterns make sense when one considers the relationship of Shirazi identity to land ownership as disclosed in the 1924 census and, above all, the different patterns of ownership of clove trees in the two islands. Wapemba were acquiring substantial holdings throughout the postabolition period; non-Arabs on Zanzibar at best acquired miniscule clove properties. Changes in ethnic boundaries in Pemba paralleled the expansion of clove cultivation beyond the Arab plantations.

This does not explain how people went about asserting a new ethnic identity, how others accepted or rejected such assertions, or how the stark categories of the census were reflected in daily life. But the trends are clear enough to require probing beneath the seemingly implacable image of "primordial loyalties" and racial or ethnic designations.

Shirazi is a different sort of social category than Mpemba. It stresses transcendence of locality and participation in an interconnected part of the world, a network of relationships seen in religious terms. To assert Shirazi identity was not to deny Mpemba identity—for Shirazi origins were part of the mythic past of Wapemba—but to emphasize one side of

104. However, the demographic questions are a thicket through which even the detailed study of R. R. Kuczynski has not cut. *Demographic Survey of the British Colonial Empire* (London, 1949), 2: 650–706.

105. Some mainland ex-slaves undoubtedly made the jump directly to Shirazi, and Swahili became Shirazi as well. But given the significance of the term *Shirazi,* it is likely that various categories of ex-slaves became Wapemba, and then Wapemba became Shirazi.

TABLE 4:7
POPULATION CHANGE, 1924-1931

		Zanzibar Island			Pemba Island	
Group	1924	1931	Change (%)	1924	1931	Change (%)
Swahili	14,806	2,038	−86	19,138	28	−99.9
Shirazi	13,602	8,642	−36	12,828	32,249	+ 151
Hadimu	16,454	27,732	+69	598	779	*
Tumbatu	21,288	27,663	+30	5,094	7,312	+ 44
Pemba	143	480	*	12,496	11,276	− 10
Mainland ex-slave	18,425	16,066	−13	10,751	7,184	− 33
Mainland migrant	4,568	4,061	−11	4,844	2,770	− 43
Other African	15,597	24,365	+56	10,643	11,387	+ 7
Comorian	2,244	2,101	− 6	262	333	*
Total native population	107,127	113,148	+ 6	76,654	73,318	− 4

	Both Islands		
	1924	1931	Change (%)
Arabs	18,884	33,401	+77

SOURCE: Native Census, 1931, pp. 1, 2.

*Number insignificant.

an essential duality: the wider community versus the local community. Just as clove trees were owned and cultivated by an individual Mpemba but on land in which kinsmen and villagers had an interest, so Shirazi identity involved an ideological assertion of independence and transcendence without loss of local involvement.[106] Claiming Arab identity—if it meant more than an effort to avoid Government pressure—would have been a more specific and exclusive assertion of genealogical connections and involved a bigger break with local communities.

It should not be assumed that identifying oneself as Shirazi mechanically followed the acquisition of clove trees. Identification is a social phenomenon, more a question of a certain kind of economic activity becoming part of community life than of individuals buying clove trees. The

106. On the importance of Islamic transcendence to an elite's establishing hegemony within a regional economic and political system that involves interconnections among localities, see Cooper, "Islam and the Slaveholders' Ideology."

meaning of Shirazi identity was in continual flux. In the 1920s, the extension of clove ownership in Pemba went along with a flexibility in ethnic boundaries, epitomized by the growth of the Shirazi category. But later the blockage of the trend toward peasant production of cloves and the continued economic dominance of the Arab planters turned the significance of Shirazi identity from assertiveness to defiance. By the late 1940s, "Shirazi" had become a general term of identification for Wapemba, Wahadimu, and Watumbatu. The acquisition of small holdings of cloves had not ended the basic polarities of a plantation society. The same concepts of religion and genealogy with which Arabs claimed superiority and in terms of which Wapemba had insisted on their inclusion in an Islamic society were then used to protest exclusion and to assert a distinct but equally worthy collective identity.[107] That phase of Shirazi history belongs to another era, but the 1920s revealed the dialectical relationship of economic structure and ethnicity. In Pemba, the extension of clove trees beyond Arab planters resulted in a flexibility in ethnic divisions. In Zanzibar, the dominance of the large, Arab-owned plantation was reflected in a sharper contrast between Arabs as owners and Wahadimu and ex-slaves as cultivators and clove pickers without an expanding segment in between.

For ex-slaves, the question of social identity was equally acute. The process of redefinition was no doubt a long one. In the days of slavery, the social identification of slaves pointed in two directions. On the one hand, slaves learned the tenets of Islam and could use their increasing mastery of it to deny their owners' claims to religious and cultural superiority. On the other hand, slaves could deny the inferiority of the culture of their homelands and see in their common origins in the African hinterland a shared identity that negated the view that they were nothing but inferior members of coastal society.[108] The two tendencies were not mutually exclusive; both sets of values could be mobilized under different circumstances.

In the post abolition situation, the former tendency might have made slaves more likely to assert a "Swahili" identity, associating themselves with Islam and coastal culture.[109] If they could obtain stable access to

107. The Shirazi Association, which was founded in 1939 and began to assert itself after the war, articulated this new sense of political identity (Lofchie, *Zanzibar*, esp. p. 99). The political implications of economic changes are discussed more fully in my Epilogue.

108. Cooper, *Plantation Slavery*, chap. 6.

109. Studies of two towns on the mainland coast (Bagamoyo and Lamu) suggest that in the years after abolition, ex-slaves used a number of Islamic movements to assert their place in coastal religion and society. August H. Nimtz, Jr., "The Role of the Muslim Sufi Order in Political Change: An Overview and Micro-Analysis from Tanzania" (Ph.D. diss., Indiana University, 1973); Abdul Hamid M. El-Zein, *The Sacred Meadows: A Structural Analysis of Religious Symbolism in an East African Town* (Evanston, Ill., 1974).

land and buy or plant some trees—especially in areas where other squatters or smallholders of various origins were moving in and acquiring access to land on a similar basis—they might take the further step of identifying themselves as Wahadimu, Wapemba, or Shirazi, depending on who the other people were and the nature of the interaction. Some officials began calling such people simply "shamba people."[110] On the other hand, rejecting Islam might make ex-slaves identify more closely with homeland ethnic groups.

The 1924 census suggests that both alternatives were chosen. It counted 29,176 Nyasa, Yao, Manyema, and Zaramo, most of whom must have been descended from slaves. In Zanzibar Island, as noted above, Swahili were four times as likely to own a shamba as people from these ex-slave groups, although in Pemba access to ownership was more open. As of 1924, the choice of Swahili identity appears related to the acquisition of land. The census provides no information about ex-slaves' relationships with landlords, but the information we do have suggests that even the ex-slave who did not become a shamba owner was likely to acquire an increasingly secure access to land. After a period of experimentation and readjustment, squatting became a right that most often lasted a lifetime; rent was not charged; and squatters came to have definite rights. These trends toward a more secure stake in land for ex-slaves— limited as they were—may explain the changes between the 1924 and 1931 censuses. The direction of change was away from identification with homelands and toward identification with coastal society. A further step beyond Swahili identity was apparently being made, the claim of being Wahadimu, Watumbatu, or Wapemba, or even Shirazi. The expansion of Wahadimu and Watumbatu in Zanzibar Island is more likely explained by the claims of ex-slaves than by a population explosion among those groups. The acquisition of more substantial economic roots in Zanzibar and Pemba as an established squatter or the owner of a small farm, could manifest itself in efforts to become more deeply rooted socially.[111]

Ex-slave identity did not disappear, however. Observers into the 1920s mention that particular communities consisted of freed slaves.[112] How-

---

110. AgAR, 1898, p. 31, 1911, p. 105. The latter report divided shamba people into three categories: ex-slaves; *Maskini Mungu* ("God's poor"), who were apparently ex-slaves from other plantations; and miscellaneous people who had come seeking access to land. The blending of ex-slaves into Wapemba is noted by Craster, Report on Pemba, 1912, FOCP 10239, p. 8.

111. The wearing of Swahili dress by ex-slaves might make the same point. Pearce, pp. 240-41, 246-47.

112. Dale, p. 16; Ingrams, *Zanzibar Its History and Peoples*, p. 222; Craster, *Pemba*, p. 159. The ambivalent identity of ex-slaves was made clear in a letter from eight Manyema—

ever, the trend was in the opposite direction, and the frequent claim that the freed slave population was declining may only partly reflect a low birthrate but, more importantly, the redefinition of identity, especially among children born after abolition.[113] Such changes were not simply passive reflections of changing economic roles, but an active strategy to foster and cement the stake of the onetime field hand, now squatter or smallholder, in the economy of Zanzibar and Pemba.

The actual patterns of interaction, intermarriage, and cultural change demand further study. That change in social definition paralleled economic change belies any stark dichotomy between ethnicity and class as divisions of society. Neither is a fixed entity; both are relationships that develop over time. The crystallization of a planter class and a lower class in opposition to one another took place slowly. For all the tendencies of the slave economy of the nineteenth century to polarize society into masters and slaves—with Wahadimu and Wapemba more excluded than subordinated—the Omani plantation owners had not coalesced into a class capable of acting as such. They had begun to do so by the 1930s, and the period discussed here was crucial in redefining the basis of power and of struggle.

Change came about not out of the internal contradictions of slave society but as a consequence of the intervention of the colonial state in the production process. Through political domination and the abolition of slavery, the state ended the primacy of planters' ties to their dependents. The peculiar relationship of the planters to the state helped define plan-

---

people from the eastern Belgian Congo—who had been brought to Zanzibar long ago, still identified themselves as Manyema, but resented being put under the jurisdiction of the Belgian Consul, arguing that they were subjects of the Sultan. Petition incl. Pearce to Milner, 13 April 1920, CO 618/23.

113. Differential birth and death rates are of course likely. Although registers kept in Zanzibar are unreliable, a crude index of relative fertility comes from the figures on children under twelve in the 1924 census. At first, they suggest that the mainland ex-slaves had half as many children (as a percentage of group population) as the Swahili, Arabs, Wapemba, Watumbatu, Shirazi, and Wahadimu in Pemba, while in Zanzibar Island the percentage of children among ex-slaves was lower still, although it was lower for Swahili and Arabs too. Mainland migrants had an even lower percentage of children, as one would expect. The mainland ex-slave population consisted of only 17 percent children in Pemba, 8 percent in Zanzibar; Wahadimu in Zanzibar included 28 percent children, Wapemba in Pemba, 30 percent children, Shirazi around 30 percent in both islands. There is, however, a social explanation as well as the possible ones of lower fertility or higher infant mortality. In Zanzibar (as in many Islamic areas), a man could marry beneath his status but a woman could not. The children of ex-slavewomen by men outside their group would therefore augment other groups, but since the men of the lowest status group could not marry outside their own group, there would be no compensatory influx of children. On problems of using demographic data on Zanzibar, see Kuczynski, p. 673. See also Blacker, "Population Growth and Differential Fertility in Zanzibar Protectorate."

ters as a class, set apart from the rest of society by the very nature of that relationship and its importance to the control of labor. The transition from a society of strong planters, each with his own personal followers under a weak state, to a society of dependent planters under a strong state eventually forced planters to act collectively to insure that the state would continue to maintain their control over trees and labor. By supplying labor and other resources to "leading Arabs"—in the face of contrary tendencies in the Zanzibari economy—by directing education toward that same group, and by coopting its members into governmental institutions, the state helped make this small group of planters into a coherent social and political group. The state tried to divide the Arab planter class from a native population that would become a working class, tempered by limited relations of dependence within the plantation and migratory patterns between plantations and marginal lands. It even helped plan one of the first organizations that brought Arab planters together as a class for a political purpose, the Clove Growers' Association, which proved to be the springboard for further political action by planters. One of the major issues faced by the Clove Growers' Association in the late 1920s was lowering wages through common action: the lines of class struggle were being drawn, with the colonial state constantly urging, pressuring, and manipulating.[114]

Despite the ethnic, ideological, and social separation of the state and the planters, and despite the state's inability to mold the actual relationships between planters and workers to its wishes, the planters still owed their economic domination over squatters and smallholders to the actions of the state. Their collective dependence was exacerbated by their lack of control over credit and marketing. As early as 1924, the planter-dominated Arab Association was addressing the indebtedness issue, and the debt crisis facing the plantation system in the 1930s became the primary issue behind the increasing politicization of Arab organizations.[115] The class consciousness of the planters was formed not from the strength of their control over the productive process but from its fragility.

Both the British state and the Indian financiers were ensnared in the class system they had helped create. The financiers had only one real alternative to continued support of the planters—to take over plantations themselves—and it was a choice they had wisely resisted until the

114. The association worked through district committees of leading planters, who were supposed to set local wages; but it came under the thumb of agriculture officers until the debt crisis of the 1930s stimulated planters to act. Strickland, Report, 1931, p. 10; Lofchie, pp. 113–15.

115. Memorandum of the Arab Association, 26 Sept. 1924, to East Africa Commission, incl. Coryndon to Amery, 25 Nov. 1924, CO 618/33; Lofchie, pp. 121–26.

depression made it hard to avoid, and action was then blocked by the state in the interests of social stability. The state had fostered the separation and interdependence of the components of the plantation system in order to enhance its control over production, but the state, too, lost its freedom of action, for it gave itself no alternatives to the extremes of maintaining the status quo or overturning the entire social system.

It was not the owners of clove trees as such who were being defined as a planter class but a segment of them, set apart by the way they used labor. On Zanzibar Island, the Arab planter was dominant: Arabs together owned over 70 percent of all clove trees, and a mere 177 Arabs (and only eight non-Arabs) owned all the big estates. These planters lived in town and adopted a style of life which the British, for all their prejudices, could still identify as that of "gentlemen."[116] Even in Pemba, the big planters who employed regular wage labor were also Arabs, and Arab landowners held on the average three times as many trees as non-Arab clove growers.

To some writers, the development of associations and political solidarity among Omanis as a whole has seemed to show the primacy of ethnicity over class.[117] That is to mistake the mere facts of ownership or occupation for the process of developing class control. The Omani smallholder or petty trader might, in terms of narrowly defined economic interests, have more in common with the Mpemba smallholder or the Swahili trader than with a major planter. Yet upper classes often try to extend their appeal and legitimize their position by invoking religious or social affiliations while retaining control and directing political action in accordance with their own interests. Petty bourgeois elements and the upper crust of the peasantry are the most likely followers to recruit. Omani smallholders were likely to be involved in relationships of clientage with the leading planters, relationships rooted in the political alliances of the nineteenth century, while the immigrant Omani shopkeepers— Wamanga as they were called—were the last stage in the complex network of import-export trade that rural cultivators came to see as exploitative. The Swahili hawker's trade was closely bound to rural smallholder production, an economic tie reinforced by social links; the city was merely a market. The Mmanga's economic base was the port and his social ties were in the city; the countryside was merely a market.[118] The combination of rich planters and poor shopkeepers in Arab associations

---

116. Pearce, pp. 222–24.

117. Leo Kuper, *Race, Class and Power* (London, 1974).

118. Strickland, Report, 1931. Immigrant Hadrami Arabs did not enter this kind of network, for their connections were with the annual dhow trade and with the Hadramaut itself. They were more of a group apart. W. H. Ingrams, "A Report on the Social, Economic, and Political Condition of the Hadramaut," 1936, pp. 157–60.

thus embodied more than simple ethnicity, but one thing it did not embody was any sense of equality among Omanis; at times, this became quite a sore point. Even the bond of religion among Omanis—who practiced the Ibadi creed as opposed to the Sunni Islam of Swahili—reinforced hierarchy, for the leading Ibadi scholars had close family and personal ties with the leading planters: religion was part of defining cultural hegemony.[119]

Who controlled the mobilization of followers and to what end became clear from an early date: a series of Arab newspaper articles from 1913 equated "the Arab" with "the shamba owner" and identified him with the typical issues facing planter classes: export taxes and labor costs. The Arab Association and the Clove Growers' Association both focused on indebtedness and cutting labor costs. In the 1930s, the interests of the planter class became ever more decisive in Arab politics.[120] The ties of religion, ethnicity, and clientage did not supercede the ties of class but were used to maintain the domination of the planter class.

When the planter-controlled political movement later tried to extend its appeal beyond Omanis, the degree of its success reflected the structure of the clove economy that had evolved by the 1920s. Omani leaders appealed to Shirazi as fellow Muslims and clove producers. The appeal worked to a significant extent in Pemba but failed in Zanzibar. In the latter island, the dominance of the plantation structure had polarized society and the invocation of common interests rang false. In Pemba, the greater fluidity of tree ownership and ethnic boundaries was reflected in a greater flexibility of political relationships, but the ambiguity in the class position of the Pemba Shirazi lessened once it became clear that they were being recruited as followers of Omani planters, not as equal partners.[121]

Just as the transformation of the relationship of the state to the plantation system in the years after abolition helped to shape the interests and consciousness of an upper class, so the same process slowly and incompletely helped to shape a lower-class identity. The people this identity came to embrace came from diverse places and varied experiences, practiced different religions, and performed different roles on the planta-

119. Cooper, "Islam and the Slaveholders' Ideology"; B. G. Martin, "Notes on Some Members of the Learned Classes of Zanzibar and East Africa in the Nineteenth Century," *African Historical Studies* 4 (1971): 525-46.

120. See the series of articles translated from "El-Najah," 1913, incl. Sinclair to Long, 11 April 1917, CO 618/17, and Arab Association Memorandum, 1924, incl. Coryndon to Amery, 25 Nov. 1924, CO 618/33. This problem has been ably analyzed by Lofchie, who stresses the efforts of the Arab elite to control and manipulate, even when it recruited followers who were not planters or not Arabs.

121. Lofchie, *Zanzibar*.

tions. But all were defined as workers in relation to the clove economy and the state. Between the workers and peasants of Zanzibar and Pemba differences were muted, for each group did what the other did for part of the year. Nor was there a sharp division between town workers and country workers, for the ex-slaves who dominated urban work in the 1920s had close rural ties, and the mainland immigrants who increasingly undertook urban labor not only shared working conditions with them but slowly developed social connections with those ex-slaves within the fluid structure of the town's African quarter, Ngambo, while mainland weeders became caught up in the relationships of subordination and labor discipline of the plantation.[122] The crucial cleavage was between those who used labor and those who provided it. The wage cuts and speedups of the late 1920s affected all these peoples and presaged increasingly tense relations on the land.

The inability of the state and the planters to undermine completely the agrarian independence of ex-slaves, Wapemba, and Wahadimu made the threat of subordination only less immediate. Alternatives to plantation labor, especially in Zanzibar Island and especially where cash was concerned, were marginal. All rural people were confronted with a marketing system that was both weak and exploitative, and the hostility that eventually took in Indian and Wamanga shopkeepers as well as Omani planters reflected the multiple dimensions of economic power.[123]

Squatters had an ambiguous role in the process of class formation, for their ties with planters were more personal than those of migratory laborers, and the very act of using such ties to enhance security could diminish solidarity among squatters. Yet there is a dialectical relationship of antagonism and affiliation in these bonds of subordination.[124] The rights of ex-slaves and other squatters were both affirmed and limited by evolving customs. Deference—presence at certain ceremonial occasions, acknowledgement of the ex-master as legal guardian—was a way for each side to accept the other's commitments.[125] Deferential culture only went so far: squatters used it to gain as much economic indepen-

122. See my Epilogue for discussion of the evolution of class relationships and rural-urban ties.

123. The important gap between the Arab planter and the Indian merchant-financier did not look so large from below. Lower-class hostility to the structure as a whole came to the fore during the 1948 strike in Zanzibar town, when African women of various origins boycotted Indian shops. Later, boycotts spread to the rural areas, hitting both Indian and Arab traders, while squatters were conspicuously violent against the planter-dominated political party. See Clayton, "General Strike in Zanzibar in 1948," p. 431; Lofchie, p. 188; and Epilogue.

124. For a dialectical view of paternalism, see Genovese, *Roll, Jordan, Roll.*

125. On continued relations of dependence, see Craster, *Pemba,* pp. 80, 215, and Ingrams, *Zanzibar, Its History and Peoples,* p. 205.

dence as possible, avoiding more than minimal work for their patrons. But this culture helped make explicit in daily life a structure of social inequality that was deeply felt by those on the bottom. The suppressed resentment and bitterness that lay beneath the deference of squatters were one day to surface.

With planters guarding their rights in trees, squatters and cultivators their rights in land, the structure of Zanzibari agriculture was brittle. For a squatter or a landlord to plant rice was a problem of class control. To allow or prevent certain categories of people from planting clove trees was a question of defining collective rights.

Class struggles came to a boil at a time beyond this study, above all when the state was about to lose its detached—although hardly neutral—character, but it was in the period between 1890 and 1925 that the power of the state became crucial to class domination and the plantation structure. That conflict developed under cries of "Muslim Unity" ranged against "African Unity" does not mean that ancient antagonisms and loyalties lay behind it. Most Zanzibaris were both Muslim and African; how they chose to identify themselves was a matter of changing perceptions.

The planter class tried to extend its power by invoking a hegemonic ideology—couched in religious language—that it hoped would simultaneously have appeal beyond a single class yet define and legitimize that class's domination. Ex-slaves, in the early part of the century, came increasingly to see themselves as Muslims and as Swahili as their stake in society and in land became more secure. But slowly a sense of lower-class unity came to link ex-slaves and other diverse peoples who shared a subordinate relationship to the plantation system and the state. Political organizing began among the most clearly excluded, mainland migrants—most of whom were not Muslim—but spread to squatters, Wahadimu, Watumbatu, and—despite misgivings and contrary tendencies—Wapemba. The appeal of the evolving organizations was to Africans as subordinated and impoverished people. The way the plantation structure narrowed economic opportunities, the increasing tensions in tenancy and wage labor, and above all the deadly serious stakes that both classes had in the struggle for control of the state made it necessary for Zanzibaris to reconstruct their perceptions of themselves and their relationships with each other in a manner consistent with the increasingly harsh realities of economic and social life.

5 From Planters to Landlords:
Labor, Land, and the Plantation Economy of the Coast of Kenya, 1907–1925

The productivity of the grain fields of the coast of Kenya in the nineteenth century was a consequence of the exercise of power: both force and social and political domination kept slaves at work throughout the entire year, for long hours each day, five days a week, under regular discipline, nearly all for the export economy and the planter's profit. The survival of the plantation economy of Zanzibar and the rise of the settler economy of Highland Kenya also owed less to the efficient use of resources than to pressure on workers, restrictions on economic activities by Africans, and discriminatory allocation of resources, all of which required—in different ways—the intervention of the state. The fate of the grain plantations of coastal Kenya reveals the other side of this process, what happens when power is not exercised on behalf of a planter class.

Behind the thinking of Kenyan officials at the time of abolition was a similar model of economic progress to that of the Zanzibar Government: labor for landowners was the only real alternative to idleness. The modest revival in grain production brought about by ex-slaves and Mijikenda, although evident by 1907, did not in the least affect official assessments of the potential of African agriculture. The differences between Zanzibar and the Kenyan coast thus had little to do with basic assumptions or with the laws promulgated in the two colonies. If anything, the legal apparatus of capitalist agriculture was more fully developed in Kenya. It was intended to benefit whites but on paper provided the same legal protection to any property owner, while labor was freed from the shackles of slavery to enter a labor market open to all. Once powerful Arab and Swahili families retained most of the productive land of the coast. What they lost was the ability to use that land through the control of a labor force. They remained landlords but ceased to be planters.

To some economists, a "liberal" system of land tenure, through which land becomes a commodity that any individual can buy, sell, and possess provides an important basis for economic development. The possibility of ownership provides scope for personal initiative and direction, permits reallocation of resources to the most able, and creates security for the credit necessary for agricultural production. To others, absolute ownership rights in land can easily go too far. Without periodic land redistribution or reform, privately owned land can become concentrated in a few hands and lead to reactionary economic policies, stagnation, and immiseration. Both views place too much weight on the ownership of land per se. Marx, in his discussion of "so-called primitive accumulation," provides a clearer analysis of the relationship of the acquisition of land to capitalist development.[1] It is not the amassing of the means of production that is the essential step in the evolution of capitalism, but the elimination of the actual producers from access to the means of production. Accumulation and dispossession may seem like two sides of the same process, and they often were, but the crucial question was what was done with the commodities that were accumulated. The land titles that Arab and Swahili ex-planters retained would mean little unless the people on those lands were prevented from farming them on their own account, and throwing them off would mean little unless the narrowness of resources gave them no alternative but to return to those lands as workers. The focus must be on the actual relations of production on the land, and the overall structure of opportunities—subsistence production, labor migration, cash crop production, casual labor—in which agrarian relations were nested.[2] There is no neat dichotomy between agricultural worker and independent producer, but a continuum—wage worker to sharecropper to renter to small-scale landowner—shaped by the resources and power that producers and landowners can mobilize. In postabolition Kenya, ex-slaves were able to free themselves altogether from the year-long routine of closely supervised labor and to combine relatively favorable terms as squatters, producing exports as well as food for themselves, with part-time wage labor for landowners or in the towns. They were joined as squatters by a new wave of producers from

1. For an example of the argument for individual tenure, see Andrew W. Kamarck, *The Economics of African Development*, rev. ed. (New York, 1971). Although the World Bank now knows how complicated putting land in private hands can be, it still insists that "all possible steps need to be taken to improve the land market," and it agrees with the Kenya Land Committee of 1905 that land registration is a crucial step. *Kenya: Into the Second Decade* (Baltimore, 1975), p. 475. The reasoning behind these views has been criticized by Irving Gerschenberg, "Customary Land Tenure as a Constraint on Agricultural Development: A Reevaluation," *East African Journal of Rural Development* 4, no. 1 (1971):51–62. Michael Lipton argues against the concentration of individual holdings in "Towards a Theory of Land Reform," pp. 169–315. On primitive accumulation, see Marx, *Capital*, 1:713–74, and Brenner, "Origins of Capitalist Development," pp. 66–67.

2. Stanley Trapido distinguishes between the initial acquisition of land by white settlers in South Africa, which did not mean loss of access for Africans, and the "second alienation" of 1890–1910, which was the crucial process in creating capitalist relations of production. "Landlord and Tenant in a Colonial Economy," p. 56.

the Mijikenda ethnic group, who moved onto the land even as the Arab and Swahili owners were claiming their titles.

But the fact that the producers, ex-slaves and Mijikenda, did not have legally enforceable title to the land they farmed was quite important, and the tension between title holders and squatters helped move the coastal economy into a state of paralysis. Owners lacked the labor, squatters the security, to improve the land, experiment with new crops, and accumulate trees and other productive capital. The state made the situation worse, for it thwarted the very people, who were doing the most to revive regional and export production, namely, the squatters.

That the state should try to thwart squatters and regard ex-slaves generally as at best useless is not surprising; governments rarely look kindly on such people. But why did the British in Kenya fail to assist the Arab and Swahili planters as the British in Zanzibar were doing at the same time? In Zanzibar, the colonial state found quite a lucrative export crop and a plantation system that, while shaken during the 1890s, still functioned. The workers of Zanzibar had to be remade, but in Kenya, officials thought, the entire economy had to be created. The coastal plantation economy, off which the I.B.E.A. company had vainly tried to live, had collapsed by the time of abolition. Not only was the value of the coast's grain and copra exports in 1905-06 only a fourth that of Zanzibar's cloves in 1895, but these products, being local staples as well as export items, could not easily be controlled and exploited by the colonial state. By 1907, the coast and its planters were of minor importance to the Kenyan state. The Administration was concerned that the legal apparatus of a capitalist economy apply to the coast but saw little point in using that system to resurrect an already decrepit planter class, when the Uganda railroad, the embryonic settler community of the Highlands, and even the small and ultimately unimportant European plantations of the coast presented more immediate demands and more hope. Finally, the coastal plantations had less fixed capital in the form of trees and did not dominate the region to the extent of the plantations of Zanzibar. To round up and direct labor—unassisted by the economic narrowness and small size of Zanzibar—would have required great expense and considerable force.[3]

This chapter will examine the simultaneous processes of the ossification of landownership and the loss of power over labor by the former planters of coastal Kenya. The following chapter will turn to a problem that compounded those discussed here, the consequences of the incor-

3. On British attitudes toward the coast and economic development, see G. Mungeam, *British Rule in Kenya, 1895-1912* (Oxford, 1966); M. P. A. Sorrenson, *The Origins of European Settlement in Kenya* (Nairobi, 1968); and Salim, *Swahili-Speaking Peoples.*

poration of the coast into the wider economic structure of the colony of Kenya.

THE END OF SLAVERY

By 1907 British officials—seeing both the experience of Zanzibar and the slow decline of plantation agriculture on the Kenyan coast—no longer looked at slaves as a potential working class that could be properly disciplined and socialized but as a useless and diminishing lot. The abolition of slavery in Kenya was not advanced as a great step in civilizing Africa but as a clean-up operation. The real changes had already occurred. The ordinance of 1907 purified the British flag. It brought policy on the mainland into harmony with that on Zanzibar and prepared the way for a declaration, planned for three to five years hence, that would finally do away with all the claims procedures in both areas and declare slavery ended. The law finally took account of all the dislocation caused by the loss of power over slaves by allowing slaveowners to obtain compensation from the state when a slave departed. Policymakers thought abolition would do more for slaveowners than for slaves.[4] As in Zanzibar ten years earlier, officials thought of the possible social and economic effects of abolition in negative terms—as a disruption—but they now believed such effects would not be severe.[5]

The abolition ordinance that went into effect on 1 October 1907 reflected the unraveling of plantation slavery in the decade since abolition in Zanzibar. Instead of permitting slaves to go to court to claim their freedom, the Kenya ordinance gave slaveowners the right to demand compensation in court for slaves who left or refused to work as a consequence of the law's ceasing to recognize rights over a slave. The courts were instructed to tell slaves that they were "at liberty to remain as before" with their owners or they were "at liberty to go away." As in Zanzibar, they would not be allowed to retain property they had acquired as slaves. The court appearance was not used, as it was in Zanzibar, to pressure slaves into entering contracts—although they could do that too— and slaves were in fact not required to appear before the judge at all. Slaveowners had to prove that the slave was not held illegally under any of the antislave trade decrees. They also had to prove a loss: that the slave

---

4. FO to CO, 20 Dec. 1906, FOCP 9102, pp. 71–73; Sadler, to Elgin, 4 June 1907, FOCP 9133, p. 12. Even the more zealous abolitionists were by then arguing that slavery should be ended because of its stigma, not because of the physical sufferings of the slaves. Brooks to Grey, 1 July 1906, FOCP 8882, pp. 5–6.

5. Memorandum by Sub-Commissioner MacDougall, 25 April 1907, incl. Sadler to Elgin, 4 June 1907, FOCP 9133, p. 15.

had gone away after 1907, not before. Compensation was supposed to average Rs 64 for an "able-bodied shamba slave."[6]

In the first two years, 3,593 cases were heard and compensation of £7,053 was paid. In the end, Rs 450,000 has been paid on 7,683 slaves. Slaveholders had to go through the ruse of claiming that their slaves stopped work as a consequence of the abolition act, but officials seem to have accepted that their rules telescoped a long period of social change.[7] As court proceedings dragged on, ending in 1916, a decree went into effect in 1909 declaring that there were no longer any slaves in British East Africa.

The compensation process, for all its procedural complexity, recognized the interest of the state in maintaining a relationship with an old elite. The most ill-documented claim of all was treated with particular sympathy. Rashid bin Salim Al-Mazrui, the candidate for the Liwaliship of Takaungu whom the British had supported in the "Mazrui Rebellion," claimed to have lost 1,000 slaves worth Rs 40,000 to Rs 50,000. All concerned knew that actual control over most of these slaves had evaporated long ago, but Rashid was able to come up with an extraordinary list of 379 slaves, specifying name, ethnic group of origin, and occupation. The Administration waived the requirement that Rashid appear in court and awarded him Rs 20,000.[8]

Compensation—supposedly based on the age, condition, and skills of the slave—rose from an average of under £3 the first year to about £6 in 1911–12.[9] As in Zanzibar, these amounts were a better reflection of a slave's market value in the 1870s than of more recent slave prices or the cost of labor. The average compensation scarcely covered the wages of a worker for six months. The total money provided slaveowners in the most active years of the emancipation process (1907–13) was only about a third of the money extracted from the province in these years through hut and poll taxes. The Administration spent more on agricultural ser-

6. Ordinance no. 7 of 1907, in EAP, Ordinances and Regulations, vol. 9 (1907), pp. 18-20; Instructions for the Guidance of Slavery Compensation Courts, incl. Sadler to CO, 2 April 1908, CO 533/43. The courts were generally run by district officers, while Kenneth MacDougal was appointed Registrar of Slaves to oversee the procedure.

7. Between 1907 and 1909, the courts were accepting 88 percent of the claims, but by 1913-14 they had become suspicious and more cautious with the dwindling appropriation they had no intention of exceeding, and so rejected most claims (EAP, AR, 1912-13, p. 60, 1913-14, p. 60; Malindi, AR, 1912-13). See also the compensation claims filed by the Administrator General on behalf of the estates of Bakari Marwan, Rashid Ali Mona, and others, in Town Magistrate's files, Mombasa, 1909-11, and Salim, p. 112. The final figures are from Sr. Comr., Coast, to Col. Secr., 20 May , CP 47/1123.

8. Claim for compensation by Rashid bin Salim, CP 62/46; Acting Gov. to CO, 23 Dec. 1908, and CP to Gov., 8 March 1909, CO 533/48.

9. EAP, AR, 1910-11, p. 51; 1911-12, p. 56; Sadler to CO, 18 Jan. 1909, CO 533/57.

vices for white settlers in *each* year than on compensation in the entire period. Compensation might reward certain allies of the state; it was not designed to provide an infusion of capital to help plantation owners create a new economic order.[10]

The number of slaves for whom compensation was paid represented a small fraction of those who had once picked coconuts and harvested grain. The 7,683 total was half the estimate of officials in the planning stages and less than a third of a rough count made in 1897. In the town and fields of Malindi, as many as 10,000 slaves may have once been at work; in the district of Malindi, a larger unit, slightly over 2,000 were involved in the emancipation process.[11]

The modest impact of the act of 1907 reflected the extent to which slaves had left plantations or adjusted patterns of labor in the preceding decades. To officials, the loss of legal control over slaves was one more step toward loosening old bonds and could only bring out the laziness and "improvidence" that was "so deeply rooted in their nature."[12] A senior official looking back on the aftermath of 1907 observed, "their very freedom was the undoing of the ex-slaves, for landless and fatherless, they lacked initiative and dreading the responsibilities of life, took fright and died, while their children drifted to the towns."[13]

The reality was more diverse and more complex. Some slaves stayed with their old masters. Such decisions did not reflect dread of responsibilities as much as the tangible benefits that paternalism provided once its teeth were removed. Those who had the most to gain by staying were the old or infirm. Even among the old slaves, a local officer observed, "there is a growing tendency ... to become more and more independent." Some moved to Crown Land, some to a neighboring plantation.[14]

10. Comparisons were calculated from EAP, AR, 1913-14, p.5. In contrast, compensation in the British West Indies did assist planters in shifting to wage labor and in buying machinery to make sugar production less labor-intensive. Credit and merchandising facilities, however weak, also helped prevent capital starvation at this crucial juncture. In Brazil, the ending of the slave trade freed capital to flow to southern Brazil, where a capitalist form of accumulation was beginning even before abolition. Genovese, *World the Slaveholders Made;* Green, *Slave Emancipation;* Adamson, *Sugar without Slaves.*

11. Malindi, AR, 1907-15.

12. Seyyidie Prov., AR, 1913-14, p. 4. Slaves continued simply to leave even after 1907, and others were freed by their owners under Islamic law. Sadler to CO, 2 April 1908, CO 533/43; 18-20 B of 1911, 611 A of 1908, Reg., Msa.

13. Report on Coast Production and Trade, 1923, by J. Ainsworth Dickson, Acting Sr. Comr., Coast CP 56/1525. See also Malindi, QR, 4th quart., 1911; Memorandum by J. E. Jones, Malindi Planter, Jan. 1910, incl. Girouard to Crewe, 27 Jan. 1910, CO 533/71; Mervyn Beech, "Swahili Life," MS, c. 1915, Fort Jesus Library, Mombasa.

14. An Omani Arab claiming a large shamba north of Mombasa said that "our old slaves" were still there, and three of them, aged fifty to sixty, appeared in court, one observing that in former times he was but "one of many slaves." Testimony of Salim bin

The Government provided little alternative for slaves who could not farm themselves. Although it had feared the burden of destitute ex-slaves, the Administration provided only a handful with the merest pittance—Rs 3 per month.[15] Officials also gazetted a small reserve for ex-slaves, who had to pay Re 1 per year for plots which they had rights to use during their own lifetimes. The bush was thick, the water supply bad, and only some fifty ex-slaves, all old, settled there. Yet the Administration made it explicit that able-bodied ex-slaves had no right to land in a Reserve.[16] The plantation, however oppressive, had been a social and economic unit; a new basis of security had to be found.[17]

Nevertheless, the tendency to remain on old plantations was probably weaker among mainland ex-slaves than among those of Zanzibar. Officials in 1910 estimated that 2,000 slaves "have remained loyally in their masters'" service so that masters would delay as long as possible before putting in a claim for compensation. By that time nearly 6,000 claims had been filed and many more slaves had long since disappeared.[18] Such figures are extremely imprecise, yet it is clear that the mainland offered alternatives which Zanzibar, dominated by the clove tree, did not, and that these alternatives were crucial to the slaveowners' loss of power over labor.

Mombasa provided new possibilities. Even before 1907, slaves from as far away as Lamu were deserting the large, regimented grain plantations of the Lamu mainland for wage labor in the expanding colonial city.[19]

Ali bin Salim Al-Mandri and others in a/c 117 N of 1916. See also Malindi, AR, 1915–16; Testimony of K. MacDougall, NLC, p. 95. The author of a recent study of the Bajun Islands observed, in 1965, the funeral of an aged-slavewoman arranged by the family of her former owners. Janet Bujra, "An Anthropological Study of Political Action in a Bajuni Village, Kenya" (Ph.D. diss., University of London, 1968), pp. 145–48.

15. Only 44 ex-slaves were on the rolls in 1911–12, 112 the next year. The severe famine during World War I exhausted the relief appropriation—£29, EAP, AR, 1909–14; PC to Actg. Chief Secr., 19 Aug. 1918, CP 47/1123.

16. Malindi, HOR, 7 Feb. 1914; MacDougall, to PC, 13 March 1916, CP 16/45; PC to Chief Secr., 7 Aug. 1913, CP 7/55; DC, Malindi, to PC, 4 Jan. 1915, CP 20/128a; Malindi, AR, 1915–16, 1916–17; Takaungu, AR, 1913–14, 1914–15, 1915–16.

17. Freed slaves did help each other out, but their kinship groups had no communal rights in land. While the absence of slave families is a myth, the wide kinship networks that provided ex-slaves in the southern United States with protection and sustenance were less developed in coastal Kenya, for the rise and fall of slavery had taken place in only a couple of generations and rates of manumission and death were both higher than in the Old South. On mutual assistance among ex-slaves, see Malindi, HOR, 7 Feb. 1914, and for comparison, Herbert G. Gutman, *The Slave Family in Slavery and Freedom, 1750–1925* (New York, 1976).

18. MacDougall, Memorandum, 24 Aug. 1910, Judicial/1/147b, KNA; EAP, AR, 1909–10, p. 48.

19. Rogers to Hardinge, 3 Feb. 1898, CP 64/22.

Zathaka, a slave of a Lamu woman, simply got on the Government steamer and left for Mombasa, leaving her mistress to file a compensation claim. Other slaves headed for the more fertile agricultural districts around Malindi, and some slaves on Lamu Island moved to the mainland mashamba, which the island-dwelling planters could no longer effectively control.[20] This was not a sudden dash toward the lights of freedom, but a slow, long-term migratory pattern toward places where alternatives to continued dependence presented themselves. A substantial number of free but poor and heavily indebted Bajuni farmers joined migrating ex-slaves from the Lamu area throughout the colonial era.[21]

Meanwhile, many of Malindi's ex-slaves left for Mombasa, as both European observers and the memories of the descendants of slaveowners and slaves attest. One informant of slave descent asserted—with considerable exaggeration—that half the working people in Mombasa were from Malindi. Actually, one neighborhood of Mombasa, Haliendi, was a center of ex-slaves from Malindi.[22] Omar wa Fundi, son of a skilled slave of one of Malindi's leading Swahili planters, worked for awhile taking people to Mombasa on a bicycle. He also labored as a hamali (port carrier) in Mombasa—where he lived among ex-slaves from all over the coast—and at various times in his life worked in Malindi and Lamu. He managed to get access to a small farm in Malindi.[23]

The opportunities in Mombasa were not necessarily good ones; they were alternatives to rural subservience. Some ex-slaves worked in the port or the railroad yards; others followed the railroad upcountry, working for wages, joining the still ongoing caravans, or engaging in petty trade. The influx of officials, European and Indian merchants, and settlers created jobs for domestics as well as a need for local police and porters. An experienced official thought that 60 percent of the houseboys, policemen, and porters calling themselves Swahili—as most did—were ex-slaves.[24] They were part of an increasingly complex labor market in Mombasa, ranging from the highest paid workers in East Africa, port workers, to a "floating population" drifting into and out of em-

---

20. Slavery Court Comr., Lamu, to DC, Mombasa, 22 July 1908; CP 84/107; Sadler to CO, 2 April 1908, CO 533/43; PRB, Lamu, p. 67, DC/LMU/3/2.

21. Seyyidie/Coast Prov., AR, 1921, 1923; Bujra, "Anthropological Study," pp. 133, 150–51. The migration of Bajuni women to Mombasa also dated at least to the time of World War I. Janet Bujra, "Production, Property, Prostitution. 'Sexual Politics' in Atu," *Cahiers d'Etudes Africaines* 17 (1977):20.

22. MacDougall to DC, Malindi, 7 June 191, in PRB, Kilifi, 1; Mohamed Khamis Muhando; Awade Maktub; Salim Mohamed Al-Kathiri (MAL).

23. Omar wa Fundi (MAL).

24. Beach MS; PC to Chief Secr. 10 Aug. 1917, CP 39/625.

ployment: ex-slaves could find a place in this relatively open and changing environment.

In rural areas, ex-slaves could find work as *tembo* tappers, taking liquid
from the coconut tree that quickly ferments into palm wine. The increasing wealth of the non-Muslim Mijikenda (and, some officials thought,
the increasing decadence of Muslims) was making the tembo trade a
growing business. Fishing was also open to ex-slaves. The transition of
crafts and service occupations from the control of slaveowners to a more
open market gave slaves, including those who had worked in the fields,
increased flexibility.[25] Mohamed Khamis Muhando, born at the end of
the nineteenth century, worked in the District Office, then for a doctor.
After that he went to work for a Baluchi woman who owned a large
plantation, bringing goods from her estate into Malindi town. He also
got a job as a crewman on a sailing vessel (dhow) taking produce to
Mombasa, Lamu, and Somalia. He was paid no wages, but the crew got
half the profits to divide among themselves and traded on their own
account. Muhando also worked as a cook and assisted a leading import-
export broker. His father had left him a shamba, which some of his relations cared for while he was otherwise occupied.[26]

The agricultural realm itself was changing. Once compensation cut
the legal and social ties of slave to master, slaves could move around
within the community as well as leave it, and they could approach any
landowner for work or a place to farm. The constraints on ex-slaves were
no longer those of personal bondage but of landlessness. Those who did
not leave the rural areas slowly became part of a new category of dependent person, the squatter.

Ex-slaves, wrote an official in Malindi in 1909, were either working for
themselves or for the Arabs.[27] The line between the two could be fine.
Ex-slaves were getting permission to stay on Arab and Swahili land and
grow millet, maize, cassava, and beans. What they had to do in return
varies in different accounts and most likely varied with the situation. The
Provincial Commissioner, C. W. Hobley, noted that Arabs and Swahili
owned the best land behind Malindi, but they got little from it: "large
numbers of squatters" lived on their land and some paid rent, while oth-

25. DC, Malindi, to PC, 4 Jan. 1915, CP 20/128a. For an example of the son of a
farm-slave becoming a fisherman, see the testimony of Takut b. Farjalloa, in *Thelatha Taifa*
vs. *Wakf Commission* vs. *Gov. of East Africa*, a/c 15 of 1912 (Three Tribes Case). One informant of slave origin had been a fisherman at Malindi. Juma Rubea (MSA).

26. Mohamed Khamis Muhando (MAL). Swahili hands were paid relatively good
wages to bag maize and load dhows during the prewar expansion of Malindi's grain exports. Malindi, HOR, 7 Feb. 1914.

27. Malindi, HOR, 1909.

ers did not. Hobley feared that the squatters would acquire legal rights
to the land they effectively occupied, for under Kenyan law twelve years
occupation gave a clear title.[28]

Hearings on land titles from 1912 to 1924 provide a wealth of information on such cases. They sometimes reveal that a landowner had lost
virtually all contact with his land, leaving his ex-slaves, other people's
ex-slaves, and anyone who wanted to plant crops to use it. One Arab
estate near Malindi was "occasionally cultivated in temporary crops by
ex-slaves and wandering unattached people," another "by those who
were very poor and who wanted to grow some food. . . . We charge nothing for they were poor." Many years later, in 1953, an Arab petitioned
for title to a large piece of land at Mambrui, owned by his father before
his death in Arabia in 1908 and now cultivated by children of his father's
ex-slaves. But he could not convince the court that these ex-slaves were
"retaining physical possession on behalf of the late father of your
petitioner." The ex-slaves had simply had the land to themselves for two
generations.[29] Where owners abandoned all or part of their land or on
the fringes of the former plantation area, ex-slaves and others could
move in, clear land, and farm, most often unmolested.[30]

Several ex-slaves testified in a complex land case at Mombasa in 1912
that they had cultivated a plot on land claimed by the Three Tribes, a
Swahili confederation, without permission and without paying rent.
Some of these squatters had been slaves of members of the Three
Tribes; others had simply settled on the land. Some had jobs as well: a
stone breaker testified, "when I am tired I cultivate."[31]

In the hinterland of Lamu, some 250 square miles of land was claimed
by planters from Lamu Island, but they admitted that they had not cultivated it since the release of their slaves. Some 2,500 people, mostly ex-
slaves and their families, were farming the land.[32]

Near Takaungu, some freed slaves cleared new homesteads while others squatted on land that their once powerful owners, the Mazrui, could

28. PC, note, 9 Sept. 1915, CP 41/733; PC to Chief Secr., 7 May 1915, CP 20/128a.

29. A/c 43 D, 107 D of 1914; Petition of Sulent b. Said Al-Handwan, 26 March 1953,
incl. a/c 200 of 1962, Mambrui.

30. List of applications for land outside boundary between Crown and Private Land,
1914, CP 32/488; Baratum Line cases, a/c 1–101 D of 1915; DC, Malindi, to PC, 13 April
1915, incl. Bowring to Long, 17 April 1917, CO 533/180.

31. Testimony of numerous ex-slaves in Three Tribes Case, and in *Charlesworth and
Masden* vs. *Ebrahimji Allibhai*, Civil Case 35 of 1913, High Court, Mombasa.

32. DC, Lamu, Memorandum re Claim of Certain Arabs, 24 Nov. 1923, CP 54/1425;
précis of events leading up to the petition of Arab and Swahili of Lamu to the Land En-
quiry Commission, by DC, Lamu, 1932, PRB, LMU/7. Officials noted in 1926 that the
population of the southern part of Lamu District was mainly of ex-slave origin. Kenya, AR,
Coast, 1926, p. 2.

no longer employ. The Government offered to give them secure tenure for a small rental in the ex-slave reserve, but they refused. The freed slaves had acquired an interest in the land on which they lived, and what they wanted was security on that land. Along with Mijikenda who had come to the coast and converted to Islam (known as *mahaji*), the ex-slaves were "the most active members of this part of the population."[33]

Ex-slaves could gain access to land; they did not own it. They could be forced off the land or made to pay rent. A large group of ex-slaves who had been freed before 1907 cleared and farmed some land north of Malindi. After thirteen years, they claimed, one of Malindi's leading landowners, Omar Abud, came by and asked for rent. They told him they had cleared the land themselves. Omar started legal proceedings. He has been given title to the land, and that was that. Omar, officials thought, derived Rs 1,000 per year from his rentals, not a bad sum but still only Re .6 for each acre he owned.[34] Another small group of ex-slaves had lived on a plantation for years without seeing anyone. Then they were cleared off by an Arab official at the insistence of the owner, who had subdivided and sold the land. Even if a slave were left undisturbed, his children might find themselves without land on his death, for the owner could insist that the land had been left to his ex-slave for use only during his lifetime.[35]

Informants from the plantation town of Malindi all agree that ex-slaves had no trouble getting permission to stay on their former owners' land or finding a new place to squat. But they differ on the terms. Some claim that ex-slaves had to pay either money or fixed amounts of grain for the right to farm.[36] Others—among them descendants of slaves—said that ex-slaves had to ask for permission to stay but could do so rent-free. A Giriama complained that ex-slaves could stay rent-free but that Giriama had to pay to get land. Some described a situation similar to that in Zanzibar: ex-slaves did not have to pay rent, but they were expected to work for wages when the landowner needed help. For the shamba owner who retained land but not labor, giving permission to squat created a

33. Takaungu, AR, 1908–09, 1911–12, 1915–16. Ex-slaves also squatted rent-free on Mazrui land at Gazi, south of Mombasa. Testimony on Gazi land case, incl. DC, Kwale, to PC, 27 June 1935, file 30646, Land Office, Nairobi.

34. Testimony incl. DC, Malindi, to PC, 22 Oct. 1915, and Atty. Gen to Chief Secr., 2 Nov. 1915, CP 40/723; Malindi, AR, 1915–16. In comparison, one planter at Mambrui earned Rs 16,000 annually from millet sales in the early 1890s, although his expenses were undoubtedly higher (Cooper, *Plantation Slavery*, p. 86). Other examples of rental charges are mentioned in a/c 122 of 1922, Mambrui, and 139 D of 1914, Malindi.

35. *Uledi Juma* vs. *Omar b. Sheikh,* Civil Appeal 68 of 1908, High Court, Mombasa; Kwale, AR, 1927.

36. Swaleh Mohamed Gagi, Omar wa Fundi, Awade Maktub, Suedi Nasibu (MAL).

social relationship that could be used to give him first crack at his tenants in the labor market. On the other hand, this relationship gave the squatter security and a chance to earn wages. He did not acquire much of either, but he did obtain some of each.[37]

Landlords' ability to control how much land ex-slaves planted appears to have been as weak as their ability to extract rent, and ex-slaves were not forced by tiny holdings to work for food or take risks with high-yield crops or investment in fertilizer, a problem which helped drive sharecroppers in the southern United States into dependence.[38] Instead, a market in the surplus grain of squatters was to emerge.

But the produce of trees proved to be a far more complicated problem than rights to plant annual crops. Unlike Zanzibar's cloves, the tree crops of the Kenyan coast—mainly coconuts, copra, and tembo—were not exclusively export items but were used by squatters themselves and channeled into regional trade. Nor did coastal tree owners have the assistance of an Administration obsessed with selling their produce and willing to recruit and direct labor to them. As a result, coconut-tree owners lacked the leverage to create a wage-labor system around their trees, using squatter and outside labor in the manner of the clove-tree owners of Zanzibar.

But they could benefit from their trees in a different way through squatter labor, and the coconut was a much less demanding tree than the clove. Weeding could be done by a tenant in exchange for a share of the coconuts. Often the squatters would be given rights to cultivate ground crops in exchange for taking care of the coconut trees. On a good-sized shamba (40 to 50 acres) three or four residents, receiving wages in addition to cultivation rights, could keep the trees in good condition. The coconut harvest was more spread out and less intense than the clove harvest. Near Mombasa, tree climbers—often ex-slaves, sometimes Mijikenda—were hired specifically for the harvest and given a share of the nuts. Thanks to these arrangements, members of landowning families explained to me, coconut plantations survived, while grain plantations failed.[39]

37. Nzeze Kwicha noted the more favored terms for ex-slaves. Other Giriama who mentioned paying rent: Gari Kai, Ismail Toya, Kazungu wa Kigande, Bisiria Toya (MAL). Some ex-slave informants themselves stayed on rent-free (Juma Kengewa, Jabu Masoya) or found a new shamba where they could stay without paying rent (Juma Mbaraka). Other informants who claimed that no rent was charged include Kassim Omar, Omari Bwana Mkuu, Isa Said Swelem El-Hasibi (MAL), Wazee of Majengo, Mohamed Muhiddin (MSA). The rather general expectations of wage labor were mentioned by Jabu Masoya, Yahya Said, Omar Dahman, Athman Nabahani (MAL); Wazee of Majengo (MSA).

38. Wright, *Political Economy of the Cotton South*, p. 172.

39. Mohamed Rashid Mazrui, Sheriff Abdalla, Al-Amin Said Al-Mandri, Mohamed Hemed Timami, Salim Mohamed Muhashamy, Mohamed Kamal Khan, Mohamed Muhid-

The major problem facing the owner of coconut trees was how to en-sure that he controlled the division of the produce. Anybody could take a coconut, and the distribution of coconuts between squatters and land-lords was in contention. Officials in Kenya, like their colleagues in Zan-zibar, saw the taking of coconuts—by resident squatters as well as passersby—simply in criminal terms: coconut theft. Their concept was shaped by the view that landowners must be sure of reaping the profits if they were to make investments. The Coconut Commission, studying the entire problem of coconut exports in 1914, saw the prevalence of theft as one of the major obstacles to development along capitalist lines. It rec-ommended measures similar to those tried in Zanzibar to combat it. None worked. The chits that were required to legitimize sellers were too much trouble in a society where economic relations were largely con-ducted on a face-to-face basis, and such measures were ineffectual when applied to products that were consumed or passed along personal net-works as well as sold in recognized markets.[40]

The actual effects of coconut theft were twofold. First, landowners, as in Zanzibar, became all the more eager to have some kind of stable popu-lation on their land in order to keep outsiders from taking all the coconuts, even if they had to share rights to land and produce with the residents. Second, the owners of coconut trees sought to profit from them in ways consistent with their degree of control, above all selling palm wine instead of coconuts. There were market advantages to tembo as compared with copra (chapter 6), but at the same time, tapping dam-aged coconut trees and in the long run undermined the most valuable property landlords had. Tapping was also an affront to Islamic prohi-bitions against the use of alcohol, a point emphasized by Arabs whom I interviewed.[41] For Arab and Swahili landowners, producing tembo was a response to an immediate need for cash and a diminishing ability to get it.

Tapping a palm required attaching a container to the tree for long periods every day; it was therefore readily observable. It was also simple to make an arrangement with tappers to share the produce or provide the tapper with a set fee. Since the income from tembo was immediately realizable, cash payments did not pose the problem they did with annual

---

din (MSA); Suleiman Amur Suleiman Daremki, Alyan Hemed, Mohamed Abubaker Abbas (MAL). Merchants also point to the decline of grain sales from Arab and Swa-hili estates and the continuation of sales of coconuts and mangoes. Abdalla Athaman Al-Amudy, Abdulhussein Adamji Saigar, Tayabali Rajabali (MAL). The arrangements by which squatter labor, supplemented by temporary wage labor in the harvest, was mobilized are described in these interviews and in Asst. DC, Malindi, to PC, 22 Oct. 1918, CP 61/113.

40. PC, Circular, 9 Sept. 1915, CP 71/733; CocCom, 1914; Coconut Preservation Or-dinance, 1915, incl. Bowring to Harcourt, 17 Feb. 1915, CO 533/152; Kenya, "Economic and Finance Commission Report," 1922, p. 32.

41. Sheriff Abdalla, Mohamed Rashid Mazrui, Abdulrehman Abdalla Shatry (MSA).

cultivation. Often the tapper would get all the tembo drawn in the evening tapping (about one-third of the total). A tapper might also be leased the trees, disposing of the tembo himself, or he might receive a certain amount of money per tree, the owner then selling the tembo. Tappers were often ex-slaves, although they were eventually joined by Mijikenda migrants to the coastal area. While Government attempts to regulate tembo tapping were never very successful, officials managed to register 1,600 tappers in Kilifi District in 1930. That so many paid the quite high fee of Shs 20—and a much larger number tapped illegally—suggests the attraction and importance of tembo tapping.[42]

Trees, unlike land for annual crops, remained a form of capital from which landlords could profit, although with difficulty. It was thus with good reason that landowners carefully guarded their rights to trees. But if share arrangements could be made to tend trees and harvest produce, planting new trees provided a more touchy problem, pointing to the opposition of landowners and squatters. As in Zanzibar, landowners were wary of letting squatters plant trees on their own account. Not only did they want to keep for themselves the possibility of making the one investment they could exploit, but they feared that squatters would obtain ownership rights to the trees they had planted that would undermine the planters' land titles.[43] Squatters, on their part, feared that the trees they planted would be expropriated, and what is more, that increasing the value of the land might lead to their expulsion and loss of the right to plant ground crops. Unable to make tenants plant trees on their behalf, too poor to pay wage labor for investments that would only be realized after several years, planters found it extremely difficult to add to their stock of trees. The only solution to the impasse was not to plant trees. When squatters finally did so, under Government pressure and strong economic incentives in the 1930s, the fear of conflict that landowners and squatters alike had felt proved to be fully justified (see Epilogue).

The inability of landlords to extract much of the grain their tenants produced, and the tensions and compromises surrounding tenants' use of trees, point to the instability of a situation in which landowners had lost their means of controlling what people did on their property. They stood little chance of making better bargains unless the threat of throwing squatters off the land was a credible one. Not only would evicting

42. Kilifi, AR, 1930; CocCom, p. 39; DC, Malindi, to PC, 22 Jan. 1913, CP 5/353; Shariff Abdalla, Mohamed Rashid Mazrui, Al-Amin Said Mandri (MSA).

43. Under coastal land law, the person who planted the trees owned them. At the very least, an ex-slave who planted trees after being freed was entitled to compensation for them should he be forced off the land. Memorandum on Mazrui Question by D. C. Watkins, incl. Belfield to CO, 30 May, 1916, COCP 1042, pp. 37–38.

tenants require more help from the state than Arab and Swahili landlords were likely to get,[44] but it would require that landlords figure out
another way to farm their land—that they find and pay wage workers. In
fact, landlords were extremely anxious that their tenants stay and opposed the Government's attempt in 1914 to send Mijikenda squatters
back to their reserve (see below). To understand why landlords could not
rely on wage labor requires an analysis of the alternatives that potential
laborers had, something that will be discussed throughout this and the
following chapters. But the fact that ex-slaves and others could get access
to land shaped the possibilities which landlords had for cultivating the
land they had not let out. They could extract only limited labor from
their squatters.

No longer tied to a particular planter, ex-slaves could bargain for the
wages and working conditions they desired. The most popular form of
labor, according to informants, was *kibarua*—day labor. Kibarua labor
was always short-term, involving no commitment by the laborer or
the employer. For the large number of ex-slave—and, increasingly,
Mijikenda—squatters in the coastal zone, kibarua labor provided a cash
supplement to the cultivation of food crops. Although wage data are
meager, I was told repeatedly that Arabs generally paid well below the
wages of European plantations on the coast. Nevertheless, colonial officials constantly complained that coastal people preferred to work for
Arabs or Swahili. The reason is clear: European plantations kept labor
under contract and severe discipline. One official's description of the
required tasks bears a remarkable similarity to the customary work rules
of Malindi's slaveowners in the nineteenth century.[45]

Kibarua labor could be integrated into the workers' economic life far
more easily than contract labor. The wages, security, and working conditions on European estates were not worth the total commitment of labor
time that was expected for a period of at least several months. Even
tenancy arrangements on European estates were often rejected, largely
because they entailed rigid labor demands.[46]

The bargaining position of ex-slaves and ex-slaveowners varied

44. The need for force to expel squatters is a lesson that the independent Government
of Kenya has learned quite well, for it has used security forces against squatter settlements.
Philip Mbithi and Carolyn Barnes, *The Spontaneous Settlement Problem in Kenya* (Nairobi,
1975), p. 130.

45. Bisiria Toya, Ishmael Toya, Bakari Rarua, Awade Maktub, Swaleh Mohamed Gagi,
Alyan Hemed (MAL); Malindi, AR, 1908–09, 1916–17, 1919–20; MacDougall, testimony,
NLC, p. 95.

46. One European planter required four months of labor per year, for which he paid a
comparatively low wage (Rs 7 per month), in exchange for land. It was not surprising that
he got no squatters. DC, Malindi, Report, incl. PC to Chief Secr., 7 May 1915, CP 20/128a.

greatly with circumstances. As an informant explained, the wealthiest farmers were the ones who could get labor. Coming from a leading Arab family also made British officials more willing to enforce one's property rights. It is no coincidence that Omar Abud, who went to court to force long-time squatters to pay rent, was one of the wealthiest men in Malindi, the owner of over 1,600 acres of land. On the other hand, Feruzi, himself a fomer slave from Zanzibar who had become a planter of some importance, died without heirs. The ex-slave who had been his overseer, father of one of my informants, was able to obtain a shamba, plant trees—something most squatters were not allowed to do—and grow maize unmolested. He passed the shamba on to his son, but unbeknownst to him, the title to Feruzi's land had now been claimed by a powerful Arab. Decades later, after the land had changed hands without any owner interfering with the squatters, it fell into possession of someone eager to make use of the land himself.[47]

Another ex-slave acquired relatively secure tenure as a squatter because his father's owner went on to a greater scale of economic activity in Mombasa. Salim bin Khalfan Al-Busaidi was profiting more from his urban real estate in Mombasa than from his plantations at Malindi, and he was wealthy enough to employ upcountry wage labor—as did Europeans—on the plantations he still cultivated. He was thus in a good position to make a generous gesture: he turned 1,000 acres of fine land into *wakf* (a nonalienable trust) for his ex-slaves. His gesture was important both in terms of the Islamic society in which he had lived and prospered and the British one, in association with which he was profiting still more. And Salim—as Arab and Swahili slaveowners had long appreciated—could reinforce his relations with his dependents by acting as providor and patron.[48]

Such relations of clientage could be used from below as well as from above. The personal connection with Salim bin Khalfan proved a valuable one for Awade bin Maktub. He began with an advantage, for he was an *mtoto wa nyumbani*, a person of slave origin born into and raised within the household of a wealthy Omani woman closely associated with Salim. After his mistress died, around 1904, Awade went to Mombasa, where he was able to stay in the vast household of Salim bin Khalfan. Living in Haliendi Quarter, much of which Salim owned, he was among many slaves from Malindi, including some of Salim's own. Through the powerful Liwali, he got a job as an office boy. Later, he worked as a truck driver and coolie in the port. In World War I he served in an African

47. Jabu Masoya (MAL).
48. Juma Kengewa (MAL) still lived on this shamba in 1972–73. On Salim bin Khalfan's land, see below.

regiment which, Awade stressed, was recruited largely from Nyasaland, from which slaves had long ago been taken to the Kenyan coast. After the war, he was a servant and a cook in Nairobi until he returned to Malindi. There, with the backing of Salim's son and successor as Liwali of the Coast, Awade became a headman in one of the heavily cultivated areas behind Malindi where many ex-slaves were still living. Shortly thereafter, he became chief of Ganda, a Government post in that former plantation zone. Awade had used a relationship of personal dependence to acquire a measure of choice and mobility. Nevertheless, Awade continued to think of himself, with pride, as an Mnyasa—refusing to accept the deprecatory cultural values of his patron—even as he made use of his upbringing as an inferior member of an Omani household.[49]

The continuity of such relationships of dependence went along with a partial continuity of social subordination, as it did in Zanzibar. The slaveowners' eagerness to maintain patriarchal roles and images was manifested above all in the question of marriage. Under Islamic law and coastal custom, slaveowners had been the guardians of slaves, responsible for contracting marriages, even with slaves they had manumitted. Many masters did not accept that the abolition act—devoid of meaning within the matrix of Islamic law—dissolved such relationships. Some ex-masters insisted, as late as the 1920s, that their former slaves consult them about marriage plans and pay a token fee that symbolized recognition of the ex-master's responsibility. Local *kathis* (judges) often enforced this rule, refusing to marry former slaves without the fee and the ritual. Only some twenty years after abolition, as a result of Government displeasure and the increasing irrelevance of such patterns of subordination, did the custom die out.[50] Similarly, the Islamic inheritance rule under which a slaveowner could be heir to his slave's property, in the absence of direct descendants, was observed even when there were no more slaveowners.[51] And some Arab slaveowners came to expect help in street brawls from their ex-slaves when conflict broke out between Arabs

49. Awade Maktub (MAL). In 1941 the DC called Awade one of two chiefs in the district "worthy of the name" (Kilifi, AR, 1941). Other chiefs of slave origin were mentioned to me by Awade or are referred to in district reports as early as 1911.

50. Asst. DC, Lamu, to Judge Hamilton, 30 April 1908, Judicial/1/402, KNA; Memorandum by PC, 21 Feb. 1912, CP 2/84, MacDougall to Chief Secr., 5 March 1912, CP 2/84; DC, Lamu, to PC, 26 March 1928, CP 103/17; Memorandum of Chief Justice Pickering, 11 May 1928, CP 2/354; Al-Amin Said Al-Mandri (MSA). See also Strobel, *Muslim Women in Mombasa, 1895-1975*.

51. An ex-slaveowner's claim to inheritance in preference to the grandchildren of the deceased was upheld by the kathi in 1922 but reversed on appeal (*Ahmed b. Abdalla* vs. *Administrator of Native Estates*, Lamu, Civil Appeal 8 of 1925, Court of Appeals for Eastern Africa, Judicial/1/859, KNA). For examples of estates going to the deceased's former owner, see P & A 115 of 1911, 83, 119 of 1912.

and Swahili in 1928; their ex-slaves, however, proved unwilling to fulfill this new version of their old role.[52]

Such practices were not simply an irrational desire on the part of ex-slaveowners to cling to the symbols of their former prestige or an indication that ex-slaves accepted continuing subordination. For both, these customs emphasized the existence of a personal relationship and a moral climate in which mutual expectations would be fulfilled. Both groups wished that commitments to perform services, even if they could no longer be compelled, or to bestow land, even if the law provided no guarantees, would be long-term.

But the basis of such relationships had changed fundamentally. Once slaves could seek new landlord-patrons within their community or find employment elsewhere, a tied relationship had become negotiable. The weakening of slaveowners' control was compounded by the fact that ex-slaves no longer needed personal protection, and Arab and Swahili landlords could do little to help their clients face the most onerous demands that outsiders were making on them—especially the annual demand for hut taxes and the labor roundups of World War I. Ex-slaves had to face the demands of the colonial economy themselves and make the best of whatever opportunities they could find.[53] As in Zanzibar, landlords had to give ex-slaves and other squatters effective control over parts of their plantations in order to create social ties that would, they hoped, provide them with some labor and some rent, or at least keep the land clean and free of outsiders and thieves.

In Malindi, the change was most pronounced, for land had been abundant and the basis of the planters' wealth was the control over labor. Malindi's planters had no clove trees, no officials eager to direct resources to them, and no monoculture that provided virtually the entire population with its only source of cash. On the once flourishing grain plantations, tenants and owners grew the same crops, harvested them at the same time, had the same access to markets and the same ability to subsist on their export crop. It was difficult to keep grain a plantation crop.

Mombasa, unlike Malindi, had few immense grain plantations. Agricultural exports were, in the 1880s, worth about a third of Malindi's, and much of the produce came from the Mijikenda living behind the coastal plain. Coconuts were the favored crop on Arab and Swahili mashamba, and their cultivation was more compatible with the landown-

---

52. Hyder Kindy, *Life and Politics in Mombasa* (Nairobi, 1972), p. 32.

53. The importance of a colonial government's imposing demands directly on ex-slaves to the breakdown of the master-slave relationship is emphasized by Derman in a West African case (see *Serfs, Peasants, and Socialists*).

er's loss of power over labor than was grain. For ex-slaves, the active casual labor market in Mombasa meant that they could stay on a shamba near the city without sacrificing other options. Estate owners could not compete directly with a port that paid the highest daily wages in Kenya. All they had to offer was security on the land or daily labor with immediate payment, both of which could become part of a varied economic life over which the landlord had relatively little control.

In the years following abolition, ex-slaves continued an earlier trend to increase their independence. The ties of a slave to a particular individual, the essence of slavery, had slowly dissolved, to be replaced by a more general source of economic dependence: ex-slaves owned no land. Despite the dire need landowners had for estate residents and laborers, they imposed rent, threatened tenants with eviction, and insisted on personal deference often enough for the squatters to feel their insecurity and for tension between the landed and the landless to lie just beneath the surface. When pressure increased, the conflict would come to the fore. But even before the 1920s, the meaning of holding land—once an abundant resource in the most productive coastal areas—had changed. Exactly what rights in land would mean was crucial to the landlords, the ex-slaves, and the colonial state.

Land and the Planter Elite

When A. I. Salim contends that the Government's land policy, coming on the heels of the abolition of slavery, "dealt a blow to the other major pillar of the Arab-Swahili economic structure—land," he has failed to reach the heart of the matter.[54] To be sure, the Land Titles Ordinance of 1908 and the bias with which it was administered reflected a desire to facilitate the transfer of land from Arabs and Swahili to European settlers and corporations. But the European plantation sector did not develop as envisioned, and Arabs and Swahili lost much less land through the ordinance than they retained but could not use, while some Arabs and a few Swahili prospered in the same manner as the Europeans and Indians whom Salim considers its principal beneficiaries. The imposition of the British version of land tenure altered the distribution of

54. Salim, p. 114. The quantitative parts of this section are a preliminary analysis of data on land sales and credit at Mombasa being studied by John Zarwan and myself. A fuller explanation of the data sets and methodology will be included in that study. Karim Janmohamed also collected some of the data used here, and his analysis puts more stress on urban development than I have here. "A History of Mombasa, c. 1895–1939: Some Aspects of Economic and Social Life in an East African Port Town during Colonial Rule" (Ph.D. diss., Northwestern University, 1977).

land *among* Arabs and Swahili, and, above all, transformed the conditions under which land was held.[55]

Coastal land tenure had been quite complex. Individuals and social groups had various and overlapping rights in land in certain areas, while in other parts of the coast, where land was relatively abundant, rights in land were defined mainly by having slaves to clear it. The Coast Lands Settlement under the 1908 ordinance transformed these complexities into freehold titles issued to individuls, with a few small communal "Reserves" for groups that were able to negotiate a special arrangement. Larger—but less fertile and more arid—Reserves were set aside for Mijikenda in the coastal hinterland.[56] The process of allocating titles clearly discriminated in favor of people whom officials could accept in the role of landlord. The result was to fortify the ownership of land by individuals and to cut off the legal rights to land of people who could not make—or make stick—claims on such an individualistic basis.

The Government's decision to allocate titles was part of the effort it was making at the time to encourage European settlement, and the coast promised to be a good site for new plantations growing tropical produce, especially rubber. The settler-dominated Land Committee of 1905 argued that the development of the coast by white planters was likely to raise land values, but that the confusion over the legitimacy of land titles made investment extremely risky. Moreover, the growing number of squatters on the coast were likely to acquire permanent possession of their plots unless they were made to prove a title. Because other parts of Kenya had no concept of land ownership, the committee thought, only on the coast was a systematic survey of all properties, adjudication of disputed claims, and issuance of title certificates necessary. After that, it would be safe for settlers or corporations to buy land from Arabs, Swahili, or each other.[57]

55. The changing meaning of land in the colonial era has not been studied with the specificity it deserves, but for a valuable general introduction, see Elizabeth Colson, "The Impact of the Colonial Period on the Definition of Land Rights," in Victor Turner, ed., *Profiles of Change: African Society and Colonial Rule* (Cambridge, 1971), pp. 193–215. On other parts of the East African coast, see Ann Patricia Caplan, *Choice and Constraint in a Swahili Community: Property, Hierarchy, and Cognatic Descent on the East African Coast* (London, 1975), pp. 59–83; and R. E. S. Tanner, "Land Rights on the Tanganyika Coast," *African Studies* 19 (1960): 14–25.

56. In Kilifi District, the Nyika Reserve was 1.3 million acres but was only 31 percent arable, while the coastal zone, 166,000 acres, was 79 percent arable. With a lower population, the coast averaged over 18 arable acres per "native," the Nyika Reserve half that. Kilifi, AR, 1920–21.

57. EAP, "Report of Land Committee," 1905, pp. 19–20, 26. As the Administration moved slowly to implement these recommendations, the Governor warned that lack of title adjudication was hurting land sales. Girouard to Crewe, 6 Aug. 1910, CO 533/76.

Title allocation was not a direct means of grabbing land but an attempt to establish the legal prerequisites of a capitalist economy. Officials clearly assumed that the rules of the game—even if enforced impartially—would favor people with the proper entrepreneurial skills, who, they believed, had white skins. Yet the title law was instituted as a matter of universal principle.[58] The allocation process was a logical—although large—step toward a concept of freehold from beginnings made even before the state had become convinced that white landowners were necessary.[59] From 1891 in Mombasa, Arab officials under British supervision were registering transactions involving land—including sales of houses, urban plots, and agricultural land, as well as loans and mortgages. By 1908, over 1,000 transactions were being registered each year. Once the Government began to encourage white settlement, it added provisions for granting or leasing land which the Government claimed was unused.[60] The 1908 ordinance required the claimant to any plot in the coastal zone to produce documentary or oral evidence that he had obtained the land through purchase, clearing of bush, or inheritance, and that it had not been abandoned.

The application of such an approach to the coast in part reflected a belief that Muslim land law was similar to British. In fact, Islamic law treated land as a commodity that could be bought, sold, or mortgaged by an individual. There were differences in content, but the crucial misconception was in the way Islamic law was used and the manner in which it had become entwined with the "customary law" of the coast.

By the time British officials began to study the complex and varied forms of coastal land tenure, they had already changed the conditions under which it operated.[61] The earliest detailed evidence comes from several court cases after the Land Titles Ordinance had been passed and after the land market in Mombasa had been greatly altered. The Nine

58. EAP, AR, 1909, p. 36; Belfield to Harcourt, 6 May 1914, CP 6/295.

59. Recognition of Islamic titles was part of the agreement made by the British with the Sultan of Zanzibar to uphold Muslim law when the coast was ceded to Great Britain. Provision for freehold titles on the coast was included in the 1897 African Order in Council, which also defined some of the rules for ownership that were followed under the Land Titles Ordinance of 1908. For precedents for the 1908 Ordinance and a history of its implementation, see Memorandum on Kenya Coast Belt Land Titles Problem, incl. Sir Ernest Dowson to CO, 14 Nov. 1938, CO 533/488.

60. When it came to abandoned land, officials chose to ignore or misinterpret Muslim law, which did not deny a claim to land because the property was no longer used. Abandonment for twelve years, under British rules, caused the property to be forfeited, and this land could then be granted by the Crown as it chose. For more on the intricacies and manipulations of land law, see Salim, pp. 114–33; Mungeam; and Sorrenson.

61. Claude Hollis, "Report on the Rights of the Natives of the Coast between the Tana River and Mombasa," 1907, copy in CO 533/32.

Tribes of the Mombasa Swahili claimed—as a group—land on the mainland north of the city; the Three Tribes filed a similar claim to land on
the southern part of the island and on the adjacent mainland. This land,
they argued, was held communally under a complex set of rules. Members of each confederation had a right to land; it might be cleared collectively but the actual farming was done individually. A member who
planted trees received absolute rights to the plot when the trees reached
maturity, while the confederation retained an interest in all land under
annual crops. What got sticky was the issue of alienating land. The elders
in each case testified that a person could sell his plot to an outsider only if
he had the permission of the elders of the confederation and gave them
a gift. British officials argued, however, that there was no evidence that
the confederations existed as landholding bodies, and they believed that
the elders' view of custom was cooked up to serve their current interests:
now that land had a rising monetary value, they wanted to cash in on it.[62]

Official suspicion of the elders' motives was not unjustified, but it too
was self-serving. By casting doubt on communal claims, officials set the
conditions for making large parts of the most valuable land of the coast
into Crown Land. In fact, land involved in the Three Tribes Case—some
10 percent of the area of Mombasa Island—had already been leased by
the Crown to a politically important settler, E. S. Grogan, for fifty years.
One official's vehemence revealed the importance of denying communal
claims to the Government's plans: "The Coast Federations are the most
serious enemy the Government has to meet."[63]

Whatever the misrepresentations of the elders, *some* kind of communal rights in land existed among both the Nine and the Three Tribes
in the precolonial era. Within the area of communal claims were also
plots held by individuals from many social groups—Omanis, Hadramis,

62. See especially the testimony of Abdalla bin Rithwani, filed with a/c 42 N of 1918
(Nine Tribes Case), and Abdalla bin Sheikh Mtangana, Three Tribes Case, for the elders'
view, and Registrar of Documents to PC, 14 April 1913, CP 8/171, vol. 2, and PC to Chief
Secr., 20 Sept. 1915, CP 40/698, for the Government's. In another important case, the
customary rights to sell land of the Jibana, a group living just inland from Mombasa, were
denied. An Arab had bought up some land from Jibana for Rs 307 and sold it to a leading
Indian merchant, Alidina Visram, for Rs 7500. Visram invested more in coconut trees, but
his title was denied on the grounds that the original vendors had no right to sell. However,
when a similar case involving land purchased by two Europeans was questioned by the
Provincial Commissioner, the Acting Governor promised that the Administration would
not contest the title. Civil Case 60 of 1913, High Court Nairobi; PC to Recorder of Titles,
18 Nov. 1915, CO 25/271; PC to Chief Secr., 22 Dec. 1915, and Bowring to CO, 4 Jan.
1916, CP 40/709.

63. Memorandum on Coast Land Difficulties by D. F. Watkins, Asst. DC, 1912, PRB,
MSA/6, vol. 2. The lease to Grogan is in 382 A of 1914, Reg., Msa. The disputed land was
330 acres of the southern part of the island, coveted by Europeans. Map of Mombasa,
1913, MPGG 97, PRO.

Baluchis, other Swahili subgroups, Indians, and ex-slaves. Some such claims were quite old and had been acquired in a variety of ways: for instance, marrying a member of a confederation, clearing vacant land, or paying for permission to cultivate from a Swahili elder. It is not clear exactly what rights such claims entailed. Perhaps before the 1890s the person who received permission to cultivate Swahili land only had rights of use. It is also possible that what confederation members thought of as the conveyance of usage rights was regarded by an Arab—making, in his own interest, a literal interpretation of Islamic law—as a sale. Probably, land rights were left somewhat vague: what a planter could get was largely a question of what he could use and what power and social ties he could mobilize. In any case, Mombasa was not a great farming town: no one was likely to get rich just by planting grain there.[64]

However, the Government cut off this land litigation (in 1913 for the Three Tribes, 1915 for the Nine Tribes) without thoroughly investigating the complex mixture of communal tenure with individual holdings and without directly denying the claims of the Swahili elders. Land in these areas could be claimed by individuals—Swahili or otherwise—through the procedures established under the Land Titles Ordinance; otherwise it was Crown Land. Later, similar communal claims by people in Lamu and adjacent islands were denied.[65]

Meanwhile, the meaning of individual rights was being transformed by the simple practice of treating the acquisition of a piece of land as a transaction in freehold. European settlers and Indian businessmen had no desire to get involved in an intricate web of economic and social ties; they wanted titles. Registration of transactions added the mystique of the written document to the fait accompli. The Government pretended that it was not in fact changing land law, and later chastised the Three Tribes for not having complained earlier, dismissing the rather obvious assertion of an elder that he had been afraid to protest.[66] This process of redefinition created an interest on the part of individuals to sell land and later claim that they had always had the right to do so. But if Swahili

64. The dispersal of land among different ethnic groups and the variety of ways it was acquired is clear in the testimony in Three Tribes and Nine Tribes cases, as well as a/c, Mombasa North. Shiabuddin Chiraghdin, Hyder Kindy, and Al-Amin Said Al-Mandri have also discussed these issues with me. The complex mixture of individual and communal rights in land in other Swahili communities is also evident in Middleton, *Land Tenure in Zanzibar*, and Caplan, *Choice and Constraint*.

65. See the case transcripts and the thorough account of them in Salim, pp. 123–30. The Three Tribes Case was decided in 1913. The Nine Tribes withdrew their case in 1915 and threw themselves on the mercy of the Governor, seeking a tribal reserve such as the one given the Mazrui. The petition was rejected promptly. Chief Secr. to Wazee of the Nine Tribes, 30 Dec. 1915, CP 40/698. The Lamu case is a/c 2WS of 1919.

66. Testimony of Sheikh Abdalla bin Sheikh Mtangana and decision of J. MacLean, Three Tribes Case.

distorted the rules on alienating land, the claims of several powerful
Omanis to land in Nine Tribes areas depended on minimizing communal claims, and the testimony of such individuals was brought out in
litigation to deny that communal rights were customary and to assert
that land had long been held by individuals.[67]

The Government's narrowing of Swahili land rights as it set the terms
for adjudicating claims bore most heavily on Mombasa, where land pressure and incentives to sell were greatest.[68] But elsewhere, the region in
which Arab and Swahili claims would be acknowledged at all was narrowly drawn. In 1896, officials drew lines that included forests containing valuable rubber trees that Swahili and others tapped in areas designated Crown Land. Much land outside the boundaries of private
occupation—and some within it that was declared to be abandoned—was
leased to European settlers or corporations in the years after 1905.[69] In
1908, officials decided to separate privately held Arab-Swahili land behind Malindi from Crown Land that was to be the Giriama Reserve, and
they rode roughshod over a pattern of settlement that ignored such
ethnic cubbyholes. In moving people to their designated side of the line
in 1914, particular injustice was done to ex-slaves who had settled, sensi-
bly enough, in the more remote parts of the coastal belt, for the Arab
leaders consulted by the Administration insisted that slaves could not
have acquired freehold.[70]

The survey of coastal farms and plantations finally began in 1910, and
the hearings of the arbitration boards that would settle conflicting claims
began in 1914 at Malindi and 1915 at Mombasa. By 1922, the Land Office had issued 9,190 titles in Mombasa, Malindi, Mambrui, and
Takaungu. Although all urban areas except Mombasa and other farming areas of the coast had not been dealt with, the scheme fell out of use

67. See in particular the highly influential testimony of Ali bin Salim and his brother
Seif in the Nine Tribes Case. See also Salim, p. 130, and Watkins, Memorandum on the
Concession to the B.E.A. Assoc. as affecting Waste Lands, Mombasa District, 1 Oct. 1908,
CP 32/488.

68. Such issues were less acute at Malindi, for no Swahili confederation had an over-
arching claim to land. Arabs and Swahili alike claimed land on the basis of having cleared
it, and such claims were passed on to their descendants. Although after 1905 European
speculators were buying land, land pressure was not as acute and land values not as high as
near Mombasa. On early landholding patterns at Malindi, see Cooper, *Plantation Slavery*,
chap. 3.

69. McClellan to Piggott, July 1896, CP 75/46; Salim, p. 115. In 1905, 64,000 acres in
the coastal region were granted as leasehold. EAP, AR, 1905–06, p. 24.

70. A/c 52 D of 1915 and other claims beyond this line, a/c 1 to 101 D of 1915. A
scandal followed the forced moves in 1914. See EAP, "Report of the Malindi Commission
of Inquiry," 1916, and evidence incl. Bowring to Long, 17 April 1917, CO 533/180. Some
of the displaced, including 41 ex-slave families, were given two-acre plots which they held
as tenants of the Crown at nominal rent. DC, Malindi, to PC, 13 April 1915, ibid.

until the 1930s.[71] The arbitration board was chaired by a European, but the assistant chairman was none other than Ali bin Salim, who with his father Salim bin Khalfan and his brother Seif bin Salim owned more land than anyone on the coast. Their work in each district relied heavily on local Arab officials.[72] As records of the hearings indicate, the boards paid close attention to written deeds of purchase: writing produced its own validity.[73] Otherwise, having witnesses who could point out boundaries and testify to the long occupation of land was important. This procedure and the composition of the board favored claimants from important families: not only did status lend credence to one's claim, it made it more likely that one might find witnesses who were in some way involved in reciprocal relations with the claimant, notably ex-slaves.[74] To challenge a claim could mean taking on figures of local importance and convincing Ali bin Salim. The smallholder was jeopardized by the process itself: he had to know about the land law and submit a claim, actions which implied an acquaintance with the colonial state that not everyone possessed.[75] There were also fees: a title certificate and survey cost Shs 30 at a time when many parcels of land were scarcely worth that.[76]

71. "Report of the Kenya Land Commission" (Carter Commission), 1933, p. 339; Memorandum by Sir Ernest Dowson, 1938, incl. Dowson to CO, 14 Nov. 1938, CO 533/488. The adjudication process was dropped because it was expensive, and the issue—after the collapse of European plantations—was no longer acute. Work was later resumed, but the coast land titles have still not been fully sorted out.

72. Salim, p. 124. The hearings accepted enormous claims from Ali and his father with virtually no consideration, even when their applications, unlike most others, merely said the land had been "bought" and contained no corroborative details. This is especially true in a/c Malindi.

73. Complaints by members of the Nine Tribes that individuals were selling to Europeans without the elders' permission were ignored on the grounds that the adjudication hearings would settle the issue. But at the hearings, written deeds were considered "the best proof of ownership." Abdalla bin Rithwani to PC, 3 July 1912, Acting PC to Acting Chief Secr., 4 July 1912, CP 92/226; a/c 10 and 11 of 1915; a/c 59 N of 1917; Memorandum by E. B. Lloyd, Registrar of Titles, 27 Feb. 1935, CO 533/488; Registrar of Documents to PC, 14 April 1913, CP 8/171, vol. 2.

74. See the hearing transcripts and annual reports on the Coast Lands Settlement, 1914-15, CP 41/724. On the importance of slave testimony, see also "Memorandum with regard to the Land Law in East Africa particularly the Coastal area before the passing of the Crown Lands Ordinance 1915," by three land lawyers, A. Morrison, R. M. Byron, and P. H. Clarke, in R. I. Guthrie Papers, Rhodes House, Oxford University, MSS Afr S 1554 (3).

75. Applications were initially due in 1910, a year after the rules were made known. Although the Government later extended the deadline, it strictly enforced the cutoff, allowing a late applicant, at best, a temporary occupation license for his land. *Gazette for British East Africa*, 1 March 1909, p. 82; PC to DC, Mombasa, 13 March 1915, and DC, Mombasa, to PC, 4 May 1915, CP 40/714.

76. Some Mombasa lawyers called the fees "preposterously high," designed only "to secure by any means as much land as possible for the Government." "Memorandum with

Tables 5.1 and 5.2 show who got what as a result of the adjudication hearings at Malindi-Mambrui and the Kisauni area, one of the principal agricultural districts of Mombasa. Even though the Administration coveted the Mambrui area and had staked out large areas of Crown Land, the title allocation process in Malindi and Mambrui left intact—and most likely strengthened—the landholding patterns of the old plantation economy.[77] Thirteen landholders, from each of the major Arab and Swahili communal groups, were given title to 40 percent of the privately owned agricultural land. Salim bin Khalfan and his sons alone took 16 percent, nearly as much as all European and Indian landowners combined. But neither smallholders nor Swahili—a few of whom were among the landed elite—were left out by the biases of the adjudication process.

The problem for the planters of the once-rich Malindi region was not land but labor. Although it was in the interests of claimants to argue that they had not ceased to cultivate their land, 40 percent of the successful applicants stated they were not cultivating, although some admitted that their squatters were. About 60 percent of Indian landowners left their land idle.[78] The inability to farm was equally striking at Takaungu, despite a special land settlement of some 44,000 acres arranged for the benefit of the Mazrui. Most of the land was left to squatters, and by 1919, 30,000 acres had been sold off, leaving most Mazrui to survive as small-scale farmers, take up trades they considered respectable, or move to Mombasa.[79]

In Kisauni, the Arab and Swahili smallholder, possessing a number of

---

regard to the Land Law." See also Dist. Clerk, Kipini, to Coast Comr., 31 July 1922, CP 42/805; Malindi, AR, 1923, Registrar of Titles, Memorandum, 27 Feb. 1935, CO 533/488.

77. PC Hobley, in 1913, thought that the Government should resist the claims of Mambrui people to large parts of the then uncultivated plantation area. But the hearings at Mambrui were delayed until 1922, when Hobley and the dream of European development were both gone, and huge tracts of land were awarded to Arabs and Swahili, although they were used, if at all, by squatters. The most important piece of Crown Land near Mambrui was Magarini, a plantation confiscated from a rebellious Arab in 1891 and used with singular lack of success by the I.B.E.A. Co. and a series of European lessees. PC to MacDougall, 7 July 1913, CP 3/288; a/c, Mambrui; Malindi, AR, 1915–16.

78. A/c Malindi and Mambrui. Informants of Indian origin often stated that plantations were held more than developed. Tayabali Rajabali, Jivanji Gulamhussein Jivanji, Mussbhai Taibji Walji (MAL).

79. Hollis, Report on Native Land Rights, 1907; statement of Rashid bin Salim, 30 Nov. 1908, CP 64/62; Map of coastal land usage, 1907, MR 760, PRO; Takaungu, AR, 1911–12, 1912–13, 1913–14; Bowring to Harcourt, 29 Nov. 1912, CO 533/108; PC to Chief Secr., 8 May 1918, and PC to Arbitration Board, 4 July 1919, CP 61/129; EAP, *Gazette*, Supplement 5, 31 May 1916, pp. 19–21; Mazrui Trust Board, Minutes, 20 Sept. 1927, LO 30646, Nairobi; Leonard to Trust Board, 29 April 1936, LO 33866; Ahmed Abdalla (MSA).

TABLE 5:1
LANDOWNERS IN MALINDI AND MAMBRUI

Number of Owners from Each Communal Group

Acres Owned	Omani	Hadrami	Shella	Bajun	Ex-Slave	Indian	European	Other	Total
9 or less	10	9	4	11	70	8	0	20	132
10–49	18	27	16	21	31	6	1	22	142
50–99	12	11	9	7	1	5	0	8	53
100–499	15	8	3	8	2	6	7	12	61
500 or more	5	5	2	1	0	1	3	0	17
Total owners	60	60	34	48	104	26	11	62	405
Total acres	14,478	8,178	4,603	3,628	1,352	2,723	4,728	3,738	43,428
Average acres per owner	241	136	136	76	13	105	430	60	107

SOURCE: a/c Malindi and Mambrui.

TABLE 5:2
LANDOWNERS IN KISAUNI

Number of Owners from Each Communal Group

Acres Owned	Omani	Hadrami	3 Tribes	9 Tribes	Arab-Suahili	Ex-Slave	Indian	European	C.M.S.	Other	Total
9 or less	37	12	29	46	181	73	21	4	0	74	477
10–49	16	6	5	15	25	2	15	7	0	7	98
50–99	5	0	0	0	0	0	3	2	0	1	11
100–499	2	0	0	0	1	0	1	3	0	0	7
500 or more	0	0	0	0	0	0	1	1	1	0	3
Total owners	60	18	34	61	207	75	41	17	1	82	596
Total acres	1,227	153	184	412	1,276	247	1,636	1,695	618	452	7,900
Average acres per owner	20	8.5	5.4	6.8	6.1	3.3	40	100	618	5.5	13.3

SOURCE: a/c, Mombasa North.

coconut trees, had long been a factor of importance and continued to be so. But over two decades of making land into a commodity in the Mombasa area had shaken up the patterns of landholding. The Nine Tribes had once held sway in this area, and the disallowance of their communal claims left a surprisingly small number of individuals from this confederation with land. Much injustice was undoubtedly done to those who did not own trees or plant a particular patch every year, as few did in a case where land rotation was important. The buyers of land, not the descendants of long-time users, were obtaining most of the land. About 52 percent of all plots, containing 70 percent of total acreage, had been obtained by purchase, and two-thirds of the purchased plots had been obtained since 1906. Members of the Nine Tribes, however, claimed most of the little land they had on the basis of inheritance.[80]

The traditional landholders had been losing their farmland. The new investors—Indians and Europeans, along with the Church Missionary Society—together had acquired half the private land of Kisauni. Once the hearings made titles secure, Indian interest spurted. Of plots sold after adjudication—records were kept through the early 1920s—41 percent were bought by Indians, although Indians had obtained only 10 percent of the plots at the hearings. Most often, the new owner paid far more than the previous, less secure purchaser.[81] But the reshuffling of property did not leave out a small number of Omanis. Six of the eight Arabs and Swahili who owned over 50 acres were Omani, and all but two of them had obtained all or part of their holdings by purchase. Two leading Omani subgroups—Mandri and Shikeli—along with Salim bin Khalfan accounted for over 1,000 acres, a third of the Arab-Swahili share. Land concentration in the hands of a small number of Europeans, Indians, and Omanis was the other side of the disfranchisement of the Nine Tribes.

People who claimed land on a communal basis were not the only ones who suffered in the land adjudication process.[82] People whose access to land was mediated through another person lost most decisively, and this

80. Over 2.5 times as many Nine Tribes plots had been inherited as bought. But for all other landowners at Kisauni, nearly twice as many plots were bought as inherited. In Malindi, 38 percent of both number of plots and total acres were obtained by purchase. A/c Kisauni, Malindi.

81. Europeans made 8 percent of the posthearing purchases, compared with 3 percent of the adjudicated mashamba. Preliminary results of regression analysis being done by John Zarwan and myself on Kisauni mashamba confirm the importance of the adjudication hearings as a determinant of price.

82. The Mazrui case is the exception that proves the rule. Land was awarded to individuals but also to a communal group, represented by the Mazrui Trust Board chaired by Rashid bin Salim, long a British protégé. The difference between the Mazrui and the Swahili groups whose claims were denied was not that the former were a more authentic

applied with particular force to ex-slaves. By remaining on a plantation after abolition, ex-slaves were trying to preserve, in a new, more flexible context, the occupation rights to small plots of land they had had as slaves. But the land title given the ex-slaveowner did not recognize any subsidiary rights. The landowner could evict ex-slave or impose rent or—more likely—sell the land, thus dissolving the personal relationships and tacit agreements with squatters.

Making land into a readily marketable commodity was the major impetus behind deed registration and title allocation, and it was the most serious threat to squatters. When, for example, an Indian bought a shamba on Nine Tribes land, he paid Rs 320 to the vendors, plus Rs 240 to the elders to get their consent. The people who were actually farming the land were evicted and given—through the generosity of the buyer—Rs 50.[83] When Rashid bin Salim, of the Mazrui at Takaungu, sold an immense property to an Englishman for a sisal plantation, compensation went to "Arabs and natives" for trees and huts. But most of the many squatters who had populated Mazrui land for over a decade grew only annual crops; for those they received nothing.[84]

It was possible for ex-slaves to purchase land, especially where it was relatively cheap. A few—very few—ex-slaves even obtained large pieces of land. In the Malindi-Mambrui area slaves had once far outnumbered freemen; but only a quarter of the landowners, as of the Settlement, were ex-slaves, and they owned a mere 3 percent of the total acreage. In Kisauni, 13 percent of the landholders were ex-slaves, and they had 3 percent of the land. Ex-slaves needed especially clear proof to obtain title, and claims on the basis of having cleared and cultivated land that were accepted from others were often rejected in the case of ex-slaves.[85]

---

communal group but that they were held in higher esteem. Under Rashid's leadership the Trust Board did what Rashid and other Mazrui were doing with their own land—selling it. The Mazrui settlement had the same effect as British support of claims by leading Arab individuals, coopting an elite while fostering the commercialization of land. Supporting the communal claims of Swahili smallholders would have done neither.

83. Testimony in 59 N of 1917, Mombasa. For another case of land being sold over the heads of longtime ex-slave residents, see the testimony of Ibrahim wa Kanyaga, 15 Oct. 1915, incl. Asst. DC, Mombasa, to PC, 17 Oct. 1913, CP 9/309a. It was to provide a safety valve to people like this (if they were not able-bodied), and to avoid having to supply relief, that the Government designated a poor reserve for ex-slaves and a somewhat better one for Mijikenda Muslims. Malindi, AR, 1920–21.

84. Registrar of Slaves to Secr. to Administration, 31 Oct. 1910, CP 64/62.

85. Two people of slave descent became wealthy slaveowners at Malindi in the late nineteenth century. The slave of one of these slaves sold a 187-acre shamba in 1908 for Rs 300. Another large shamba went to the son of a slave, although another of his claims was rejected (A/c 69 D of 1912, 54, 59, 126 D of 1914). However, only twelve plots at Malindi and Mambrui were awarded to ex-slaves on the basis of their having cleared the land, although this is undoubtedly the way most ex-slaves got their plots, especially in fringe areas.

The small mashamba slaves obtained had been acquired over many years, but the registers of transactions do not indicate any trend toward accumulation of property by ex-slaves, as they clearly show, for example, in the case of Indians. In the 20 percent sample of land transactions from Mombasa, ex-slaves bought slightly more mashamba than they sold (21 to 16) in the period before 1906, but sold more than they bought (43 to 30) during the period 1907–19.[86] But the form of property that these people were most likely to have had before abolition was houses—often built by themselves on rented or borrowed land—and particularly in Mombasa, ex-slaves were slowly selling off the houses: 119 sales versus 69 purchases in the Mombasa sample.

Why ex-slaves, despite their apparent success as tenant farmers, were not accumulating property may itself reflect the rigidities of the British land tenure system. For a financially strapped landlord to subdivide and sell off his plantation to smallholders would require high survey and registration fees.[87] Then, too, the comforting clarity of titles was encouraging speculation, stimulated further by the flurry of European interest in plantation land between 1905 and 1912 and the possibilities of nonagricultural uses of land near Mombasa (see below). For the Arab or Swahili landlord, it was far better to sell to an Indian who was trying to put together parcels for eventual resale than to an ex-slave who wanted his small plot to farm. Finally, while tenant farming was keeping ex-slaves alive and reducing their dependence on landlords, the cash surplus it produced was modest, and moneylenders were advancing relatively little credit to agriculturalists, and virtually none to ex-slaves.[88] Squatting would remain the most important means by which ex-slaves obtained access to land.

What saved ex-slaves from disaster and provided opportunities to a new wave of squatters was the failure of coastal agriculture to develop along the capitalist lines envisioned by the Land Committee of 1905. The excitement over coastal land turned out to be an episode in speculation rather than a sustained effort at development. The possibility of a world rubber boom sent European planters scurrying for land on which to plant rubber, and the declining plantations of Malindi were inviting. Crown Land was leased to quickly organized companies, and between 1906 and 1911 Europeans bought up sixty-four plantations from Arabs

86. At Malindi, 19 purchases and 14 sales of mashamba by ex-slaves are recorded since 1906. It is possible that slaves became less identifiable by name as time went on. Forms of names by which I identified ex-slaves, such as Uledi wa Hamid bin Rashid, may have gone out of style.

87. Malindi, AR, 1923; Kenya, AR, Coast, 1926, p. 23.

88. The Malindi transaction registers (complete) record only four loans against mashamba made to ex-slaves from 1903 to 1920, while the Mombasa sample has 12 such loans between 1891 and 1919.

and Swahili, two more from Indians. But although the Malindi planters spent Rs 17,440 buying up land, they spent Rs 68,620 selling it back and forth to each other. P. H. Clark, for example, bought four mashamba in 1911 from Arabs for Rs 800 and sold them in 1912 to Anglo-East African Rubber Plantations for Rs 8,750.[89] One thing the Malindi planters did relatively little of was plant: at the peak of the plantation period, they had only 4,370 of the 15,515 acres leased or bought under crops, mostly rubber.[90]

For labor, the plantations depended on migrants from central Kenya, above all Kikuyu: about six hundred of them were working in 1912. The supply was ample in the crucial planting years, but the laborers were so decimated by coastal diseases and appalling conditions on the estates that the Administration cut off recruitment to all but a few plantations in 1912.[91] But by then even the favored rubber plantations were facing a crisis in the world price of rubber, caused by expanded production in Malaya. The Malindi plantations were not well-developed enough to streamline operations and rationalize their labor force as did the Malayan rubber estates. By 1913 they were failing, and before the end of World War I almost all of them had been sold to Indians or abandoned to squatters, like the lands of Arabs and Swahili. They had never produced much rubber.[92] Provincial Commissioner Hobley, who had tried to remake Malindi District to suit plantation development, did not take long to dismiss the entire episode as a "small land boom" that had briefly sent the value of land to "fictitious" levels. The District Commissioner admitted unhappily in 1916 that "the future of this part of the coast must depend to a great extent on the development of Arab lands."[93]

89. A/c Malindi-Mambrui; 54 A of 1911 and 1 A of 1912, Reg., Mal.

90. Attempts to establish coconut plantations were never pushed, and the efforts of the British East Africa Company to develop cotton depended on African cultivators. The company would supply seeds and do the ginning. Even that was badly managed and came to little. Malindi, AR, 1908–09 through 1912–13; Seyyidie, AR, 1912–13.

91. Malindi, AR, 1908–09; Belfield to CO, 29 Nov. 1912 (telegram), CO 533/108; Testimony of J. E. Jones, NLC, p. 276; Labour Inspection Reports, Malindi Dist., CP 7/128; Takaungu, AR, 1914–15; PC to Chief Secr., 24 Nov. 1915, incl. Belfield to Law, 20 Nov. 1915, CO 533/157. Medical Officer, Inspection Report on Malindi Estates, 11 Aug. 1911, MD/28/479, KNA.

92. Their annual output only exceeded exports of wild rubber—which Mijikenda and Swahili had collected for years—in 1915, when the collectors were quicker than the planters to abandon rubber. Figures from EAP, Blue Books, compiled in David Miller, "The Failure of European Plantations on the Coast of Kenya to 1914: A Case of Competing Economic Systems," unpublished paper. On wild rubber, see Asst. DC, Takaungu, to PC, 10 Jan. 1914, CP 7/132. For comparison, see James C. Jackson, Planters and Speculators: Malaya, 1786–1921 (Kuala Lumpur, 1968), pp. 226–67.

93. PC to Chief Secr., 14 Jan. 1915, CP 32/488; Malindi, AR, 1915–16. For accounts of the demise of the plantations, see Malindi, AR, 1912–13 to 1918–19, and EAP, AgAR, 1913–14, pp. 21–22.

Near Mombasa, the possibility of a new wave of plantation development also led to speculation on undercultivated coastal lands as well as on Mijikenda land. For example, an Indian named Gulamhussein Essaji bought up plots from 24 people—ex-slaves, Swahili, and Arabs—mostly for Rs 200 or less. He put together 414 acres and sold the package to a European syndicate in 1914 for Rs 16,848. Two Europeans picked up 36 plots near Changamwe from Swahili vendors for Rs 5,479 in 1906 and 1907 and unloaded the bundle to Miritini Rubber Estates Limited for Rs 90,000 in 1910. By 1913, the land boom was over, and when it came to production, especially of rubber, the Mombasa estates did little better than the Malindi ones.[94] Near Lamu to the north and Gazi to the south the story was similar. The biggest embarassment of all was the concession of 260,000 acres of land south of Mombasa made by the Government to East African Estates in 1908. By 1922, less than 3,000 acres were under sisal and coconuts, and even that was badly managed. Much of the land was used by squatters.[95]

The most important exception to the rapid demise of European plantations on the coast was in sisal production, hardly surprising, for sisal is the one coastal crop (and along with tea the only Kenyan crop) where capital requirements give advantages to large-scale production. The big sisal estate founded by Powys Cobb near Takaungu, for example, was built with upcountry labor and continued, after the war, with a mixture of upcountry and Mijikenda workers.[96]

The brief episode of intense speculation and lackadaisical planting was one more step toward widening the gap between land ownership and land use. The period before World War I was a time of expanding smallholder cultivation, mainly by squatters, on coastal land. The bidding up of land prices by speculation bore no relation to the actual costs or conditions of production by such producers and not even much relation to realistic considerations of plantation cultivation.[97] Indian purchases of agricultural land were less clearly linked to rubber and took place over a longer period, but such land—except for some coconut plantations—was

---

94. Another piece of land at Kisauni was acquired by a European from an Arab for Rs 900 in 1907, passed through various hands, and was bought by a European planter in 1911 for Rs 25,000. A/c 208 N of 1916, 25 N of 1918; PC to Chief Secr., 22 Dec. 1915, CP 40/709.

95. In 1912, East African Estates were employing 250 Africans, mostly from western Kenya. Testimony of Manager, NLC, p. 107. See also Handing Over Report, Coast Comr., 5 Oct. 1922, incl. in Coryndon Papers, box 5, Rhodes House. See also Tanaland, AR, 1915–16; Seyyidie, AR, 1913–14; EAP, AR, 1913–14, p. 58; Mombasa, AR, 1920.

96. Malindi, AR, 1918–19; Kilifi, AR, 1921.

97. The average value of a shamba sold at Malindi followed the rise and fall of plantation speculation, rising after 1906, peaking in 1909–11, and collapsing after 1914.

rarely developed.[98] The liveliness of the coastal land market thus made it less likely that the actual producers could buy land or that land would provide a reasonable basis for the supply of credit for agricultural production (see below). The rapid turnover in agricultural land was based more on a chimera—the rubber boom—than on the conditions of coastal production. When the rubber crisis hit, planters and officials briefly thought of switching to coconuts as Arabs and Swahili were doing, but little came of it, for coconuts, which demanded relatively small inputs but produced small profits and provided no returns to scale, were much more the crop of a declining aristocracy with an uneasy grip on squatters than of boom-minded planters who had just overinvested in land.[99] But the speculative period before World War I had given a new meaning to the ownership of agricultural land: the land title itself could be a source of money regardless of what was done with the land.

Urban land, above all, enabled a portion of the old Arab and Swahili elite to live off land titles and avoid being reduced to the lot of the ordinary agriculturalist. Salim bin Khalfan epitomizes the changing basis of wealth for those who could master the transition to a colonial economy. His fortune had its origin in the grain fields of nineteenth-century Malindi. When he died in 1920, the value of his urban property had overwhelmed the value of his agricultural assets, as Table 5.3 suggests. Even while accumulating these vast holdings, he cashed in on the appreciation of land values on Mombasa Island by selling land to the Government, including one hundred-acre plot for £7,000, and by renting property to Europeans and Indians, such as a plot leased to E. S. Grogan for Rs 5,157 per year. In 1920, the rentals on stone houses were bringing him Shs 180,000 per year, while mud huts rented to Mombasa's poor brought in Shs 22,296 annually. He owned one of the principal markets in Mombasa and collected rents from the stalls. And Salim was probably the leading private moneylender in Mombasa, with over Shs 300,000 out on loan in 1920 to clients ranging from ex-slaves to leading Arabs and Indian merchants.[100]

98. Evidence by PC Hobley to EAP, Economic Commission, 1919, p. 71; Committee Report on Coast Production and Trade, 1923, CP 56/1525. For examples of undeveloped land being held, see 110 D of 1915 (a/c, Malindi), 59 N of 1917 (Mombasa), and PC to Land Office, 30 April 1936, LO 33866, Nairobi. Shariff Jaffer cultivated his holdings but still employed only 25 to 30 Africans on them (testimony to NLC, p. 105). The most notable exception was Alidina Visram, who used copra from his plantations to supply oil and soap factories in Mombasa. Janmohamed, "History of Mombasa," p. 212.

99. Seyyidie, AR, 1913–14; Tanaland, AR, 1915–16; EAP, AR, 1913–14; Malindi, AR, 1915–16.

100. P & A 114 of 1920; PC to Chief Secr., 2 June 1913, incl. Bowring to Harcourt, 10 June 1913, CO 533/119. His son Ali was also accumulating urban property and leasing or selling it at high prices. See, for example, 794 A of 1906 and 196 A of 1912, Reg., Msa.

TABLE 5:3
PROPERTY OF SALIM BIN KHALFAN AL-BUSAIDI, 1920

	Value—Shs
Stone houses, Mombasa Island	1,800,000
Huts, Mombasa Island	222,960
Land, Mombasa Island	782,680
Land, Mombasa mainland	549,412
Land, Malindi and Mambrui	87,358
Total	3,442,410

SOURCE: P&A 114 of 1920.

Salim bin Khalfan—Liwali under the new and old regimes—was by far the most successful Omani under both. But others realized capital gains on urban property that made land values in the late nineteenth century appear puny. Rashid bin Sud Al-Shikeli sold land near the new harbor in Mombasa to a European for Rs 25,000 in 1912. He died in 1940 still owning twenty houses on Mombasa Island, 200 acres of mashamba on the adjacent mainland, and other assets worth a total of Shs 587,000.[101] Two members of the Mandri family, among the oldest Omani residents of Mombasa, leased houses to a British firm for Rs 2,160. Other Mandris were buying up small mashamba—often from Swahili vendors with dubious claims—and reselling them at a large mark-up. Three other Arabs sold plots on the island to the Government for a total of Rs 58,000.[102]

A look at probate files suggests how much property leading families retained. Salim bin Khamis Muhashamy, trader and landowner, died in 1910, leaving three plots with stone houses in Mombasa, valued at Rs 13,095, and four mashamba worth Rs 9,170. Kassim bin Rashid bin Abdalla Al-Mandri, who had been buying and selling land since at least the 1890s, died in 1932 leaving 168 acres of land on the mainland worth Shs 19,800 and less than an acre in town, with houses, worth Shs 15,800.[103]

101. 781 A of 1912, 75 A of 1905, Reg., Msa; P & A 27 of 1940, cited in Janmohamed, "History of Mombasa," pp. 220–21.

102. 25 A of 1898, 436–38, 441–42 A of 1914, Reg., Msa. For a look at Mandri speculation in mashamba, see the Jibana Land Case, Civil Case 60 of 1913, High Court, Mombasa; but the principal in that case, Ali bin Salim bin Ali Al-Mandri, was also buying and selling land at Junda (north of Mombasa) and Malindi. 122 A of 1905, 620 A of 1907, Reg., Msa; a/c 117 N of 1916 (Mombasa North); 31, 51, 54 A of 1911, Reg., Mal.

103. P & A 92 of 1910; P & A 4 of 1932. Said bin Ali bin Khamis Al-Mandri died in 1919, leaving mashamba, houses, and debts due him amounting to Rs 58,131. P & A 201 of 1919.

Still, there are far more cases like Khamis bin Mahufu of the Three Tribes, who left only a shamba worth Rs 250, or Mwana Aisha binti Mwinyi Haji of the Nine Tribes, whose entire estate consisted of a shamba worth Rs 38. Many Omanis died poor; few ex-slaves, as far as probate records tell, died anything but poor. A shamba worth Rs 300, a house worth Rs 50, offset by equally modest debts, were typical ex-slave estates.[104] What characterized coastal people after abolition was not overall impoverishment, but a contrast of landed wealth with lack of property.

Salim bin Khalfan and others were not only profiting from the commercial development of Mombasa, but also from the influx of African workers. As early as 1898, Salim was subdividing his vast holdings in undeveloped quarters of the island and renting small plots, for Rs 12 per year, to a mixture of coastal people—slaves, freed slaves, and freemen—who were establishing an urban population independent of the large households of the elite. Others, including Swahili, took advantage of this market, as more and more of the island was turned over to housing.[105] The business became highly speculative as African workers flocked in from upcountry and as employers took little initiative to provide housing. A landowner—often an Arab, Indian, or European—would rent or sell land to someone—frequently a Swahili—who would in turn build a house; the house would then be rented to workers, many of whom were jammed into a single one. Housing the poor had become a big business.[106]

For someone like Salim bin Khalfan or Kassim bin Rashid bin Abdalla Al-Mandri, real estate was an enterprise. As Table 5.4 suggests, Omanis were buying houses, houses with land, and mashamba more often than

104. Swahili examples cited are P & A 55 and 87 of 1912. See also P & A 53, 55, 56, 57, 58, 62, 69 of 1912. One ex-slavewoman left an estate worth Shs 14,720, but that was rare (P & A 17 of 1924, plus many others, 1911–12). For some ex-slave estates at Malindi, see Register of Estates, Kathi's Court, Malindi, 1937–49.

105. See the list of rentals by Salim bin Khalfan for 1898 and 1899 in volumes AS 1 and 2, Land Office, Mombasa. In transactions involving houses, the owner of the land on which the house was built is identified in 280 cases in the Mombasa sample. In 94 of them, the landowner was Salim bin Khalfan. He appears more often than all Indians combined. In such transactions, a Swahili landowner is mentioned 63 times, and the children of a member of the Three Tribes, Abdalla bin Shimbwa Al-Tangana, appear to have been the most important Swahili owners of land for houses. Bi Shafi binti Matano, also of the Three Tribes, is also remembered as an important owner of such property, and one quarter where workers lived was named after her. Juma Rubai (MSA).

106. PC to Chief Secr., 2 June 1913, incl. Bowring to Harcourt, 10 June 1913, CO 533/119; PC, Memorandum on Settlement in Native Locations, 17 Sept. 1913, incl. Bowring to Harcourt, 3 Oct. 1913, CO 533/123; NAD, AR, 1923, pp. 16–17; Kenya, "Report of the Commission of Inquiry Appointed to Examine the Labour Conditions in Mombasa," (Willan Commission), 1939, esp. p. 61; Richard Stren, *Housing the Urban Poor in Africa: Policy, Politics, and Bureaucracy in Mombasa* (Berkeley, 1978).

they were selling them, although they were selling off urban land. Yet the figures are deceptive, for two Omani subgroups, Busaidi and Mandri, account for 54 percent of all Omani purchases. Indeed, Salim bin Khalfan and his sons were doing most of the accumulating. For others, selling property that had become valuable was a means of economic survival. It was, of course, a self-liquidating means of surviving; only the holder of extensive property could take advantage of the appreciation of real estate and slowly sell off plots.[107] The figures show a marked net outflow of all types of property to Indians and Europeans from Arabs and Swahili over the period 1891 to 1919.

In Malindi (Table 5.5) a similar pattern held, but to a lesser extent. In both areas, Swahili sold off land more rapidly than did Omanis. With the Twelve Tribes of Mombasa, the alienation of long-held land—already cut into by the title rules—is particularly clear. In Kilindini, once the part of the island the Three Tribes dominated and now the modern port and railway terminus, the Three Tribes members in the sample sold 18 properties and only bought three. In Old Town, parts of which were once the center of Nine Tribes residence, Nine Tribes members sold 34 properties and bought 18. But with the Twelve Tribes—more so than with Arabs—the tendency was to sell off farmland, undermining the potential for agriculture and self-sufficiency of these groups. While Omanis sold twice as many urban properties as mashamba, the Twelve Tribes sold 50 percent more mashamba than urban properties. Farms were being sold from the traditional farming areas of these groups: members of the Three Tribes sold 136 plots and only bought 50 in their customary farming center of Changamwe, while members of the Nine Tribes sold 25 farms, against 7 purchases, in Kisauni.[108] The timing of these sales is also revealing, for the big expansion in shamba sales occurred in 1906–10, just when abolition put more pressure on landowners and when the prospect of European plantation development brought about a flurry of speculation by both Indians and Europeans.[109]

107. Of all the money Omanis made selling urban land, Salim bin Khalfan made 71 percent. Overall, he bought 92 properties and sold 25 in the sample, while all other Omanis bought 190 and sold 289. Mandris bought 60 properties and sold 63. Examples of people slowly selling off property can be found in Reg., Msa: there are 22 sales by Jerada binti Masudi Al-Mazrui over nineteen years in the 20 percent sample.

108. In both island and mainland areas, members of each of the two confederations obtained plots in the other's bailiwick, through marriage or purchase, but the extent of alienation of land in the other's territory was much less than in each one's own.

109. The number of shamba sales on the northern mainland doubled from the previous five-year period. On the western mainland, a farming area of the Three Tribes, sales tripled. After 1911, sales fell. Closer analysis indicates that it was indeed the Twelve Tribes and the Arab-Swahili (names that could not be further classified) who were responsible for the increase in sales, while Indian purchases rose fivefold. European purchases rose to 27, from one in the previous five years. Omani sales and purchases both rose after 1906.

TABLE 5:4
PROPERTY SALES, MOMBASA, 1891–1919

Sales of Houses in 20 Percent Sample, by Ethnic Group (Values in Rs)

	Sold		Bought		Change		
Group	No.	Total Value	No.	Total Value	No.		Total Value
Omani	40	20,379	52	29,625	+12	+	9,246
Hadrami	22	3,418	39	8,586	+17	+	5,168
Nine Tribes	23	6,979	19	3,272	− 4	−	3,707
Three Tribes	40	12,535	21	2,683	−19	−	9,852
Non-Mombasa Swahili	44	6,477	38	2,946	− 6	−	3,531
Arab-Swahili	85	15,527	79	15,787	− 6	+	260
Ex-slave	119	16,145	69	6,526	−50	−	9,619
Indian	32	48,961	79	68,835	+47	+	19,874
Baluchi	10	7,507	17	4,622	+ 7	−	2,885
European & govt.	10	10,258	7	6,129	− 3	−	4,129
Other	39	6,594	41	5,378	+ 2	−	1,216
Total	464	154,780	461	154,389			

Sales of Urban Land in 20 Percent Sample, by Ethnic Group (Values in Rs)

	Sold		Bought		Change	
Group	No.	Total Value	No.	Total Value	No.	Total Value
Omani	134	192,901	63	27,072	−71	−165,829
Hadrami	22	5,966	34	8,952	+12	+ 2,986
Nine Tribes	56	22,320	22	3,753	−34	− 18,567
Three Tribes	74	28,173	39	6,213	−35	− 21,960
Non-Mombasa Swahili	21	6,987	7	1,003	−14	− 5,984
Arab-Swahili	86	46,870	69	17,156	−17	− 29,714
Ex-slave	10	8,625	29	2,691	+19	− 5,934
Indian	159	424,575	241	483,132	+82	+ 58,557
Baluchi	9	4,074	29	6,151	+20	+ 2,077
European & govt.	28	28,921	66	243,837	+38	+214,916
Other	10	7,256	5	3,530	− 5	− 3,726
Total	609	776,668	604	803,490		

Sales of Houses with Land in 20 Percent Sample, by Ethnic Group (Value in Rs)

Group	Sold No.	Sold Total Value	Bought No.	Bought Total Value	Change No.	Change Total Value
Omani	28	39,986	31	42,210	+ 3	+ 2,224
Hadrami	10	10,028	10	9,695	—	− 333
Nine Tribes	16	8,847	8	7,970	− 8	− 877
Three Tribes	26	34,008	12	6,435	−14	− 27,573
Non-Mombasa Swahili	8	4,160	8	3,022	—	− 1,138
Arab-Swahili	35	53,989	22	15,223	−13	− 38,766
Ex-slave	7	3,746	8	3,124	+ 1	− 622
Indian	44	243,706	79	394,469	+35	⊢150,763
Baluchi	13	46,376	10	18,163	− 3	− 28,213
European & govt.	6	88,070	3	26,400	− 3	− 61,670
Other	1	1,095	1	2,000	—	+ 905
Total	194	534,011	192	528,711		

Sales of Mashamba in 20 Percent Sample, by Ethnic Group (Value in Rs)

Group	Sold No.	Sold Total Value	Bought No.	Bought Total Value	Change No.	Change Total Value
Omani	112	85,846	137	83,291	+ 25	− 2,555
Hadrami	31	18,293	38	14,106	+ 7	− 4,187
Nine Tribes	118	29,663	35	7,768	− 83	− 21,895
Three Tribes	240	62,899	96	19,871	−144	− 43,028
Non-Mombasa Swahili	37	18,842	21	3,540	− 16	− 15,302
Arab-Swahili	167	43,549	97	25,348	− 70	− 18,201
Ex-slave	59	11,173	51	6,393	− 8	− 4,780
Indian	53	43,601	273	137,534	+220	+ 93,933
Baluchi	22	13,952	42	19,861	+ 20	+ 5,909
European & govt.	24	31,780	70	57,269	+ 46	+ 25,489
Other	30	19,898	32	3,280	+ 2	− 16,618
Total	893	379,496	892	378,261		

SOURCE: Calculated from Reg., Msa.

NOTES: Discrepancies between totals under Sold and Bought columns result from the omission of unknowns.

These tables distinguish houses and urban land, sold separately, and houses with land, sold together—all of which are in the city—and mashamba, most of which are outside the city proper.

The "Arab-Swahili" group are people whose names indicate that they are either Arabs or Swahili but who cannot be classified into one of the more specific categories used above.

TABLE 5:5

SHAMBA SALES, MALINDI, 1903–1920

	Sold		Bought		Change	
Group	No.	Total Value	No.	Total Value	No.	Total Value
Omani	50	11,373	59	15,580	+ 9	+ 4,207
Hadrami	36	5,229	29	3,394	− 7	− 1,835
Shella	12	1,148	4	1,165	− 8	+ 17
Bajuni	22	2,447	5	384	−17	− 2,063
Arab-Swahili	131	22,494	38	3,138	−93	−19,356
Ex-slave	19	2,552	19	1,654	—	− 898
Baluchi	4	775	2	282	− 2	− 493
Indian	11	2,193	73	9,058	+62	+ 6,865
European	8	68,620	69	86,060	+61	+17,440
Totals	293	116,831	298	120,715		

SOURCE: Reg., Mal, all recorded transactions.

By 1914, even the elders who served on the Native Councils of Changamwe and Jomvu (Three Tribes areas) were poor in land: of 13 councilors at Changamwe, two were considered wealthy, five had small mashamba, and the rest had no property; 10 of the 13 councilors at Jomvu had no shamba.[110]

The leading buyers were Indians and Europeans. Their interest was above all in urban land. Unlike agricultural land, urban land was being developed into residential and commercial premises, not just bought.[111] Indians spent seven times as much buying urban property as buying mashamba, although they bought many mashamba at low prices.[112] Indian investment was concentrated in the harbor area of Kilindini in the period when the railroad was being built and switched to Commercial Street and Ndia Kuu after 1910, as the commercial hub of the city expanded.

Although coconut trees remained valuable around Mombasa, any kind of land acquired a much higher market value if it had potential nonagricultural uses. Although mashamba on the island had not been very important for agriculture, the average sale value of island mashamba was twice that of a shamba on the more fertile mainland. The mainland near Mombasa was still more valuable than the far better farm-

110. "Native Councils at Changamwe and Jomvu Kwa Shehe," by M. W. H. Beech, 30 July 1914, PRB, MSA/173.
111. On urban development, see Janmohamed, "History of Mombasa," esp. pp. 204–07.
112. Europeans spent four times as much on urban property as on rural.

land near Malindi. Although no figures link price with acreage in the Malindi data, the average shamba there, according to title hearings, was nine times the size of the average shamba at Kisauni, while the average shamba near Mombasa sold for over twice as much as the average shamba at Malindi, a gap that widened with time.[113] Both rural and urban property at Mombasa went up in value at the time of adjudication hearings, but the land market at Malindi fell apart after the failure of plantation agriculture around 1912–13. Between 1921 and 1924, Arabs and Swahili at Malindi sold only ten pieces of land—eight of them in town—to Indians, none to Europeans.[114] At this very time, evidence points to an expansion of smallholder cultivation at Malindi, while near Mombasa, the most important agricultural developments were among Mijikenda, whose land was not for sale. That land could be sold and that it had a potential for urban development seemed to shape the nature of the land market more than the possibilities for agriculture.

Urban development also conditioned the flow of credit. While Indians and Europeans (including banks and Government) were the largest suppliers of mortgage money at Mombasa, Indians and Europeans were also the major users, and 78 percent of all money lent out against property went into the city. Most of the money lent against farmland also went to Europeans and Indians, so that in the 20 percent Mombasa sample, over all 28 years, only Rs 120,000 was lent to Arabs and Swahili against mashamba. Omanis supplied 56 percent of these funds, Indians 22 percent. Nearly 80 percent of the loans made by Omanis were provided by the Busaidi and the Mandri, the same groups that were the leading rentiers and real estate dealers.[115] A tiny group thus dominated the access to credit on farmland for Arabs and Swahili, although there was not much credit to be had at all. In Malindi there was even less—a total of 38 loans to Arabs and Swahili between 1903 and 1920, for a total

113. Calculated from a/c Malindi-Mambrui and Mombasa North, and Reg., Msa, Mal. According to the U.S. consul, land within five to ten miles of Mombasa was worth over ten times as much as land farther away. *USCR* 107 (1917):503.

114. The mean value of a shamba sale at Malindi was Rs 144 in 1906–08, Rs 1,117 in 1909–11, Rs 648 in 1912–14, and Rs 106 in 1915–17. Even if one excludes sales from one European to another, the fall is substantial, from Rs 215 in 1909–11 to Rs 106 in 1915–17. Officals commented that it was not worth paying title fees at Malindi. Seif bin Salim, cited in Sr. Comr., Coast, to Chief Native Comr., 10 Nov. 1921, CP 40/714; Acting DC, "Malindi D.—Sales of Lands," 22 Sept. 1924, CP 56/1525. In 1921–24, no Arab-Swahili land on the southern coast was alienated, and in Lamu District 56 plots were sold, mostly on the island, However, in Mombasa District, there were 126 sales by Arabs or Swahili to Indians or Europeans, and most of them were in the city. Sr. Comr., Coast, to Chief Native Comr., 28 Jan. 1925, CP 56/1525.

115. Even Omanis put most of their money—64 percent of all loans—into the city. The entire sample includes 742 loans.

of Rs 24,000. Only two of these loans were made after 1914. Even in Malindi, an agricultural outpost, mashamba accounted for only a third of loan money.[116]

Only rarely were mortgage deeds linked with a purchase. In most cases a long-owned property was mortgaged to raise cash.[117] It is possible that money was loaned against crops without registered collateral; merchants certainly advanced goods to smallholders against crops. Yet one of the main arguments for the economic utility of private ownership of land is that the land, in itself, will provide security to raise the credit that agriculturalists usually need. In Zanzibar, clove plantations did in fact serve such a purpose, for all the weaknesses of the credit system. But on the coast of Kenya, money flowed where it would reproduce itself, and that meant urban real estate and to a lesser extent the largely speculative rural investments of Indians and Europeans. The value of a land title bore little relation to agriculture.

Behind British land policy on the coast of Kenya lay the confident assumption that making land titles clear and marketable would bring about a transfer of land to the most efficient producers. It did nothing of the sort. Once the possibility of a bonanza had passed, European planters proved as unable or as unwilling as Arabs and Swahili to face the difficulties of producing the old crops of the coast or new ones. By the time of World War I, British land policy, while grievously hurting Swahili smallholders and anyone whose access to land came through another person or membership in a community, had had the unintended effect of preserving a portion of a precapitalist elite, not as a productive element in coastal agriculture, but as the possessors of titles. For some, ownership provided a new way of making profits, especially through urban real estate transactions, while for others titles were a safety valve, warding off—temporarily—the consequences of declining control over labor.

The changes were most dramatic at Mombasa, where all groups became enmeshed in a volatile market in land and houses. The title allocation process, officials had predicted, would itself foster sales and push prices upward, and indeed it did, especially on the island, where the average plot sold for £600 per acre in 1919.[118] The Swahili, ex-slaves,

116. This may be a slight underestimate, since in some cases the mortgage deed does not specify the type of property involved.

117. That a sale and mortgage are sometimes recorded together makes the rarity of such transactions significant. Many mortgage deeds also mention when the property was acquired. See for example, 211 and 212A of 1908, Reg., Msa.

118. PC to Chief Secr., 2 June 1913, incl. Bowring to Harcourt, 10 June 1913, CO 533/119; "Report of the Mombasa Municipality Commission," 1919, p. 3. Average transaction values on the island, from sales in the Mombasa sample, rose 2.7 times after 1916, while prices of mashamba off the island went up 1.8 times.

and other squatters who had farmed unmolested in the Kilindini area were soon dispossessed by the development of the port. Half the land at Kisauni was alienated by the time of the adjudication hearings, and the expansion of suburbs, transport complexes, and eventually industry, slowly forced agriculturalists off land around the city.[119] At Malindi, a small Arab and Swahili elite remained in possession of most of the agricultural land, and the land that had been bought or leased by Europeans and Indians soon lay as open to squatters as the land of Arabs and Swahili. Only decades later would the theoretical authority of the landowner to displace people on his land be exercised on a large scale. At Takaungu, a large sisal plantation grew up on Mazrui land, but on other lands, either retained by Mazrui or sold to speculators, squatters were moving in. On the mainland opposite Lamu, the Government's rejection of communal claims by the Swahili of Lamu and the nearby islands ended the hope of regaining land that had once been profitable but was now effectively lost to squatters.[120]

Abolition and land policy were two sides of the same coin, part of the long and complex process of the extension of capitalism into Africa. The Government had no desire for slaves to be, in the broadest sense of the word, "free"; it wanted slaves, lacking access to the means of production, to become workers. But if slaves owed their legal freedom to ideologies and policies that had their roots in the development of capitalism, they owed the increasing economic independence that they were acquiring in the early twentieth century to the failure of the coastal economy to develop along capitalist lines. The imposition of a rigid concept of ownership had created a division among coastal people, sharper than it had ever been, between the landed and the landless, but—in itself—ownership could not determine the relationship between the two.

THE LANDLESS: THE MIJIKENDA IN THE COASTAL ECONOMY

As land titles became more rigid and labor control less firm, the origins of squatters' social and political dependence on a landlord became less crucial to defining their economic position and the terms of their access to land more essential. Ex-slaves, while redefining their position, were joined on coastal lands by a new wave of settlers, who had been largely excluded from the fertile soil of the coast and ready access to grain markets by the dominance of the plantation system in the nineteenth century. The migration of Mijikenda from the coastal hinterland—from

119. Janmohamed analyzes the expansion of the city.
120. The large amount of vacant land—land being used by squatters meant vacant land to officials—is emphasized in the Report of the Committee on Coast Production and Trade, 1923, CP 56/1525.

Vanga to Malindi—to the declining plantations made the fundamental divisions of coastal society less clearly those of ex-slave and ex-master, Swahili and Wanyasa, and more strikingly those of landlord and squatter.

The Mijikenda did not figure in the plans of the colonial Adminstration except as potential laborers. In fact, they turned out to be the most dynamic element of a troubled economy. But because Mijikenda preferred to work for themselves instead of for others, officials perceived them to be lazy and intractable. The narrowness of official vision led the Provincial Administration to stand in the way of the market-induced changes that colonial rule, we are told, was supposed to facilitate.[121] By seeking to impose a particular form of order and work on the Giriama subgroup of the Mijikenda, the Government provoked a violent confrontation and an economic disaster. Then, by failing to follow up its repression of Giriama resistance, the Administration was able to watch grain production revive.

Mijikenda expansion onto coastal land was a continuation of an older process—the extension of settlement, led by "new men," beyond the defensive villages of each of the nine Mijikenda subgroups. As intermediaries in the ivory trade and as suppliers of grain to coastal ports like Mombasa and Mtanganiko, Mijikenda had played an important role in the economy of the nineteenth century. The northern part of the Kenyan coast, toward Malindi, provided the best opportunities for seeking new and better land, and the Giriama were the northernmost Mijikenda subgroup. This section will dwell on them—not because they were typical, for all Mijikenda responded in various ways to local situations with little regard for subgroup boundaries—but because the northern area presents the most striking instance of economic change. In 1890, missionaries noted, Giriama were crossing the Sabaki River behind Malindi. They were settling an arable area, although one not nearly as fertile as the coastal plain itself, peopled by scattered Oromo and Sanye as well as by runaway slaves living in fortified villages.[122]

Expansion toward the coast was checked by the military strength of Arabs and Swahili and by their control over land. In the nineteenth century, raids and skirmishes, as well as active trade and occasional military cooperation, were part of the relationship of coastal and Mijikenda peoples. Not even the Mazrui could subordinate the Mijikenda of their

121. This is the view of the role of colonial governments in West Africa advanced by Hopkins, *Economic History of West Africa.*
122. The migrations were noted by Binns to Lang, 28 Jan., 19 Feb., and 26 March, 1890, CMS G3/A5/0/1890/33, 49, 157, and Alexandre LeRoy, "Au Zanguebar anglais," *Missions Catholiques* 22 (1890):607. For two fine studies of Mijikenda history, see Spear, *The Kaya Complex,* and Cynthia Brantley, *The Giriama and British Colonialism in Kenya: A Study in Resiliency and Rebellion, 1800–1920,* forthcoming.

hinterland, although a bad famine in 1884 weakened the Mijikenda, forced some of them to pawn dependents in order to survive, and gave coastal potentates a somewhat better chance to stage raids and capture badly needed laborers.[123] All this changed with the erosion of Arab and Swahili power and plantation production in the 1890s.

With their own production of grain declining, coastal people became increasingly eager to tap—via trade—the productivity of the new Mijikenda settlements behind Malindi. That region supplied the maize which kept Malindi alive as a grain-exporting port after abolition: 33,000 cwt, valued at over Rs 84,000 in 1909–10, more the following year. Mijikenda took grain to coastal ports, and traders began to roam the hinterland purchasing maize. The town-dwellers of Malindi and Mambrui were themselves living off Mijikenda grain, as well as imported rice. Behind Mombasa, Mijikenda was also sending out grain: 445,000 lbs. from Rabai District in 1910–11.[124]

On the hills behind Mombasa where coconut palms grew, Mijikenda sold nuts to Swahili and other traders, who took them to Mombasa to be made into copra. Rabai (a Mijikenda subgroup) also began to make copra themselves. Other palms were tapped for palm wine, tembo. Because some districts had palms and others did not, although the coconut zone was being pushed northward, trade in palm wine became important. In parts of Rabai, grain was exchanged for tembo; elsewhere, tembo was sold to Giriama in exchange for grain. Coastal people also exchanged tembo—tapped by ex-slaves or Mijikenda—for Mijikenda grain.[125] Some of these transactions were apparently barter; others were for cash via middlemen. In either case, the perishability of tembo required an efficient organization of distribution: a tree owner had to rely on people he could trust to take tembo at the proper time, rush it to consumers, and return with the proceeds.[126] Together, palm wine and maize contributed to the development of a network of exchange within the coast and its immediate hinterland.

Tembo, at this time, was a more important palm product than copra. In the minds of officials living in the legacy of Victorian England, such alcoholic drinks were intimately associated with idleness and disorder,

123. The raids and pawning left a legacy of bitterness evident in interviews: Chimwenga s/o Ndoro (MSA), Alfred Yongo, Kazungu wa Kigande, Bisiria Toya (MAL). See also Spear, *Kaya Complex,* and Koffsky, "History of Takaungu."

124. Nyika Dist., AR, 1914–15, in CP 16/49; DO, Malindi, to Acting Secr., Mombasa, 19 Sept. 1906, CP 85/115; PC to Chief Secr., 5 July 1913, CP 9/295; Takaungu, QR, 1st quart., 1912, Takaungu, AR, 1914–15; Asst. DC, Jilore, to DC, Malindi, 9 Aug. 1915, and Asst. DC, Mangea to PC, 22 March 1914, CP 11/105; Rabai, AR, 1910–11.

125. Rabai, AR, 1910–11, 1911–12, 1912–13; Rabai, QR, 4th Quart., 1911.

126. David J. Parkin, *Palms, Wine, and Witnesses* (London, 1972), pp. 10–12.

the antithesis of the work ethic they hoped to develop among Mijikenda. Tapping also reduced the production of copra, which could be exported and taxed. Nevertheless, several investigations, reports, licensing rules, and other efforts to suppress tembo traffic failed.[127] The increasing strength of the internal market system in tembo and grain did little more than convince officials that the Mijikenda, socially and economically, were not fulfilling their assigned roles.

There were severe limits to the opportunities which the homeland of the Mijikenda offered for agricultural expansion. The hinterland zone was subject to uncertain rainfall. Disastrous famines had struck in 1884 and 1898–99; drought returned repeatedly in the decade 1910–20. But even in good years, the cost of transport to coastal ports discouraged grain production. To cross the land which Arabs and Swahili owned behind Malindi was at least a ten-mile hike; women laboriously carried much of the grain to the port. Officials noted that good roads or a rail link were needed to create outlets at Malindi and Mombasa for different parts of the Mijikenda region. But such forms of assistance were largely reserved for white farmers.[128]

The transport bottleneck gave opportunities to merchants, mainly Indian but including some Arabs and Swahili, with the capital and connections to obtain trading licenses, set up interior trading posts, and organize expensive human and donkey transport. They were in a good position to operate together, fix prices, and keep a large portion of the export price to themselves. Like many agriculturalists, some Mijikenda became indebted to these merchants, and the periodic droughts forced them to purchase grain on credit in a bad year, making the problem all the more severe.[129]

The increasing pace of coastward migration was a response to these problems, bringing Mijikenda onto better land with more reliable rainfall as well as decreasing the distance to export centers. By the early twentieth century, moreover, the social and political importance of the hinterland villages had diminished; the Mazrui and the Maasai would raid no more.[130]

127. Officials' obsession with the "drunken idleness" of Mijikenda is evident in Asst. DC, Rabai, to PC, 19 March 1919, CP 38/607; Report of Sr. Agricultural Supervisor, Coast, Nov. 1925, CP 52/1311; Kenya, AR, Coast, 1926, p. 14. These concerns parallel the Zanzibar Government's concern in suppressing drinking and dancing as well as interests at home (Harrison, *Drink and the Victorians*). For the antitembo campaign, see CocCom, 1914, and EAP, "Report of the Agriculture Commission," 1929.

128. PC to Chief Secr., 5 July 1913, CP 9/295; Asst. DC, Mangea, to PC, 22 March 1914, CP 11/105.

129. Asst. DC, Mangea, to PC, 22 March 1914, CP 11/105; Sr. Comr., Coast, to Chief Native Comr., 12 May 1923, CP 56/1525; Malindi, AR, 1918–19.

130. Takaungu, AR, 1908–09, 1912–13; Malindi, AR, 1912–13.

From the time of abolition through 1914, reports of the migration to the coast are continual in the area north of Mombasa. Sometimes Mijikenda took up land which owners no longer effectively controlled. "I took my jembe [hoe] and cultivated," testified a Giriama about how he acquired a farm in an area once dominated by Mombasa Swahili. In the Takaungu hinterland, many settled in or near old Swahili villages, like Mtanganiko, Konjoro, and Roka, apparently coexisting peacefully with coastal inhabitants.[131] The Provincial Commissioner was afraid that these Mijikenda, like ex-slaves, would establish effective ownership of the mashamba, contrary to his belief that "bona fide" coastal people were the real owners of the land.[132] On land claims at Malindi, some owners recorded that their plot was "cultivated by Wanyika [a somewhat pejorative term for Mijikenda]." Others asserted that they rented plots to Mijikenda. A few Giriama informants, now middle-aged, described what must have been a common pattern: their grandfathers moved from the old Giriama center northward, still in the hinterland. Their fathers, however, moved to the coastal strip, squatting and working. My informants were born on the coast and remained there. The area of these interviews, once the heart of Arab-Swahili plantation land, is also mentioned in reports from before World War I as centers of Giriama settlement. There, Giriama received permission to settle on Arab or Swahili estates. On the edges of the plantation zone—Goshi, Kikuyuni, Myomboni, and Tezo—Giriama hamlets were arising.[133]

The most dramatic movement was the northward migration of Giriama. More and more crossed the Sabaki, settling along its banks, where the river protected them from drought, or going beyond. Although little is known of the villages in the Sabaki area, it is likely that Giriama assimilated the runaway slaves who had once dominated the hinterland. The area became—as it had once been under plantation cultivation—a "rich grain producing area."[134]

The trans-Sabaki area, behind Mambrui, had been the site of the Malindi region's newest, largest, and most labor-hungry slave plantations. The decline of these plantations was particularly decisive. Inland and

131. Hollis, Report on Native Rights, 1907, CO 533/32; PC to DC, Malindi, 15 Sept. 1915, CP 19/88; Takaungu, AR, 1912–13, 1914–15; Malindi, QR, 1st quart. 1912; Testimony of Hamis b. Haji MGiriama, Three Tribes Case.

132. PC to DC, Malindi, 4 Feb. 1913, 1 Sept. 1915, in PRB, Kilifi.

133. A/c 53, 70, 135D of 1914; Arthur Champion, Report on the Present Condition of the Administration of the Wagiriama and Kindred Wanyika Tribes, 28 Oct. 1913, in PRB, Kilifi; Acting DC, Malindi, to PC, 10 Oct. 1916, CP 18/67; Alfred Yongo, Gari Kai, Nzeze Kwicha, Kazungu Wa Kigande (MAL).

134. EAP, AR, 1897–98, p. 3; Takaungu, AR, 1908–09; PC, Inspection Report, 4 July 1913, CP 64/261; Timothy Ngoma, Alfred Yongo, Ishmael Toya (MAL).

along the Sabaki River, Giriama set up their own villages, often on un-
claimed land. But most settled on land that had been claimed by Arabs
and Swahili but was not adjudicated until 1922–24. They were staying
with the owners' permission, tacit or explicit, and the owners were not in
a strong bargaining position. So dependent had the inhabitants of Mambrui become on grain grown by the immigrant farmers that they pro-
tested strongly against the subsequent decision of the Administration to
move out the trans-Sabaki Giriama. "We have stopped growing grain,"
said their petition, and would be deprived of food without the
Giriama.[135] All in all, just under 5,000 men, with around 10,000 women
and children, had made their homes across the Sabaki at the time of a
rough count in 1913–14.[136]

The District Officer in Malindi in 1912 was close enough to the situation to realize that the Giriama were an "agricultural tribe par excel-
lence." But officials in Mombasa were more concerned with their absence from the labor market. A few local officials frankly admitted that
the problem with squatter agriculture was not that it was unproductive,
but that its very productivity gave Giriama an alternative to wage
labor.[137] But most did not treat the question of Giriama labor in so forth-
right a manner, and the unwillingness of Giriama to work for Europeans
became an integral part of the aura of drunkenness, laziness, and disorder that surrounded their activities in the tembo trade. As reports rose in
the colonial hierarchy, the myth developed that, in the words of Governor Belfield, the Giriama led a "useless and degenerate existence."[138]

The confrontation of British and Giriama was no mere cultural mis-
understanding. Nor was it simply a direct and immediate attempt to
round up labor and clear off land for European occupation. Officials
were trying to make the map of the coastal region and the activities of its
people conform to their concept of order, "closer administration" as they

135. PC to MacDougall, 7 July 1913, CP 9/288; DC, Malindi, to PC, 13 April 1915, and
Acting DC, Memorandum, 29 Sept. 1916, incl. Bowring to Long, 17 April 1917, CO 533/
180; DC, Malindi, to PC, 16 May 1914, CP 5/336. There were also pockets of settlement by
two other Mijikenda subgroups, Kauma and Kambe, who had leapfrogged north. Champion, Report, 1913, PRB, Kilifi.

136. PC to Malindi Commission, 11 Dec. 1916, incl. Bowring to Long, 17 April 1917,
CO 533/180.

137. Malindi, QR, 1st quart., 1912; Champion, Report, 1913, PRB, Kilifi. Officials expressed annoyance with Indians for buying Mijikenda grain and therefore keeping them
out of the labor market. Another official did not like Mijikenda scattering over Arab estates. If they stayed in a Reserve that provided only some of their subsistence requirements, they would work more. Takaungu, QR, 1st quart., 1912; Malindi, AR, 1915–16.

138. Belfield to Harcourt, 4 May 1914, CO 533/136. Belfield, in this despatch, noted
that Giriama grew grain but that did not affect his opinion of them in the least. See also
Brantley.

called it. But it was a very particular kind of order they sought to create, the precondition for a regional economy based on African labor coming from reserves to privately owned and (in official minds although not in law) European-run plantations on the more fertile land of the coast.[139] What began in 1913 as an attempt by the Administration to put pressure on Giriama chiefs to recruit labor, remove Giriama to the Native Reserve they were seeking to leave, and collect taxes more efficiently soon ended up with an obsession with boundaries and control that left the underlying objectives forgotten and led to violent resistance, economic disorganization, and failure. Even as the state began to return Giriama to the Reserve, European planters had largely lost interest in coastal lands, while Arab and Swahili planters had all along sought squatters and opposed their removal.

Behind Malindi, a line separated the privately owned land of the "bona fide" coastal people from the Native Reserve of the Giriama. In forcing people to move to the side of the line corresponding to their ethnic group, the Administration burned huts and destroyed household possessions of ex-slaves and Giriama alike. Grain growers were moved to lands which, as one local official later admitted, were "too far from the markets of Malindi" for them to sell grain.[140]

This pattern was repeated in the removal of the trans-Sabaki Giriama in 1914. People were moved by armed patrols and their huts were burned; they were made to rebuild in inadequately planned settlements vastly inferior to the ones they had left. Again, ex-slaves and former runaways were disrupted and dispossessed along with Giriama.[141]

In the central plantation area of Malindi in 1916, local officials began to implement what amounted to a general assault on squatting. Only "wage earning labourers on private lands" would have the right to plant crops, and other Giriama would be expelled. Arabs would not be allowed to rent land to Giriama, only to hire them for wages and then allow them to settle. Hobley approved this action but later claimed that he had meant only for "vagrant" Giriama to be expelled from coastal districts. But by the time ninety people had been arrested and sent to the Reserve, Giriama policy had become a scandal, and the Governor stopped the move.[142]

What the Government did behind Malindi mirrored state actions in the mining and settler economies of southern Africa: attempts to bring

---

139. EAP, "Report of the Malindi Commission of Inquiry," 1917. For a sensitive discussion of the meaning of closer administration, see N. Leys, *Kenya*, pp. 146–47.

140. DC, Malindi, to PC, 13 April 1915, incl. Bowring to Long, 17 April 1917, CO 533/180; Malindi Commission, p. 3.

141. Malindi Commission, pp. 2–3.

142. Ibid., p. 4; Malindi, AR, 1915–16.

into line people whose innate conservatism was supposedly blocking progress most severely affected the most progressive members of the community.[143] All Giriama were affected by "closer administration," but those who were migrating to the east and north experienced the sudden reversal of a trend toward improved access to land and markets of nearly two decades' duration.

The way in which grievances and disruption were perceived by Giriama and translated into rebellion has been analyzed by Cynthia Brantley, as has the repression of the rebellion of 1914.[144] Officials created the kind of disorder—and expense—that home offices always hate, and the removal of some 15,000 people from good land to unprepared, less fertile land set them up for just the condition the migrant farmers had sought to avoid, a drought.[145] The Government had little choice but to counteract the famine by bringing grain to this formerly grain-producing area. All this took place in the midst of World War I and so annoyed the Colonial Office that an investigatory commission and a committee on food production went off to Malindi. The committees, the new Governor, and the Colonial Office—without questioning the economic ideology that underlay the bureaucracy's actions—criticized the insensitive manner in which people had been shuffled about.[146]

But the investigations had the fortunate effect of paralyzing local administration.[147] Although the Giriama had lost their rebellion, the Government policies that had brought it about foundered. Hobley, the Provincial Commissioner who had pushed European plantations, wage labor, and "closer administration," now pointed to the "risk" that is "ever present" in actively recruiting labor when administrative control is not strong enough. The pressures used to recruit labor elsewhere in Kenya

143. Arrighi, "Labor Supplies"; Bundy, *Rise and Fall of the South African Peasantry.*

144. Brantley. In the rebellion, 250 Giriama were killed, 70 percent of all Giriama huts were burned, and 6,000 goats were captured. A fine of 33,000 goats was levied, and the Giriama were made to supply porters. Nyika Dist., AR, 1914–15.

145. Malindi Commission, pp. 3–4; de Lacy to CO, 11 Aug. 1917, CO 533/191; Bowring to Long, 3 Jan. 1918, CO 533/193; Northey to Milner, 22 Feb. 1919, CO 533/207. In addition to the Malindi area, the hinterland of Mtanganiko was so badly disturbed that grain production was disrupted. Takaungu, AR, 1915–16.

146. Malindi Commission. A new Governor concluded that the PC, Hobley, had made "very grave mistakes." Northey to Milner, 11 Sept. 1919, CO 533/213. See also East Africa Commission, Report, 1925, p. 159.

147. One local official felt that he and his colleagues were being harshy criticized, while the top Administration hid behind the "astute phraseology" of the policies the men in the field thought they were implementing. This sense of having been let down added to the caution of local officials. DC, Malindi, to PC, 5 Nov. 1917, CP 38/603.

in this period could not be applied.[148] Even more important, the disorder and famine caused by putting the Giriama into their Reserve raised the cost of keeping them there.

So, shortly after having been moved south of the Sabaki, Giriama began to move north again. By 1917–18, officials thought 5,000 people had gone north, and the Food Production Mission was now encouraging such moves. Giriama were returning to Arab- and Swahili-owned mashamba, where the rains—as always—were better.[149]

The result was a new flourishing of agriculture: "The north bank of the Sabaki is rapidly becoming, under Giriama settlement, a great grain producing area." In the Malindi and Kilifi areas as well, Mijikenda moved toward the coast and were welcomed by Arab and Swahili landowners.[150] The renewed prosperity of Giriama, officials believed, was again hurting the labor supply.[151]

The reversal of British efforts to apply to the Giriama labor and land policies already used elsewhere in Kenya was a result of the rebellion, but it was a failure the Government could afford. The labor system of Kenya was already so ramified that the inability to bring some potential laborers into it could be compensated by the pressures successfully brought to bear on others. But the implications for the people of the coast and its immediate hinterland were important: policies that did much in certain upcountry districts to restrict the rights of squatters and force Africans into agricultural labor were applied to the coast slowly and halfheartedly. The Resident Natives Act of 1918 was designed to prevent just the form of squatting that was evolving on the coast. Only tenants who worked 180 days or more for the landowner each year could remain on the property, while tenants' cultivation and grazing rights were restricted. This act assisted the quest for labor by the more capitalist of the white farmers against the competition of landowners, like the Arabs and Swahili of the coast as well as many whites in the Highlands, who wanted tenants who would pay them some form of rent.

148. PC to Chief Secr., 20 Nov. 1917, CP 38/607.

149. Acting DC, Malindi, to PC, 10 Oct. 1916, CP 18/67; PC to Acting Chief Secr., 15 Nov. 1917, PRB, Kilifi; Malindi, AR, 1917–18; Nyika Dist., AR, 1919–20.

150. PC to Ainsworth, 3 Oct. 1917, CP 61/113; Kilifi-Rabai, AR, 1920–21; NAD, AR, 1920–21, p. 35; Malindi, AR, 1925. Some officials complained of the loss of population in the Nyika Reserve, although there was a back migration when rains in the Reserve were good (Kilifi, Native AR, 1920–21, CP 52/1289; Kilifi, AR, 1923). In retrospect, the Governor admitted, his predecessors' views of the useless existence of Giriama were "incorrect and misleading." Notes on Administration in Malindi District, incl. Northey to Milner, 11 Sept. 1919, CO 533/213.

151. Acting DC, Malindi, to Sr. Comr., 16 Feb. 1925, CP 56/1525.

It was hard enough to enforce this act against unwilling whites in the Highlands; on the coast, in the aftermath of the Giriama rebellion, officials were too frightened to try.[152] Occasionally, officials considered expelling all Giriama who were not working for wages on private land, but they had learned enough not to do so.[153]

Official caution eventually went beyond nonenforcement of the Resident Natives Act. The Government, on a number of occasions during the 1920s and 1930s, blocked land claims and concession agreements which it feared would lead to "resentment" among squatters that would reawaken fresh memories of conflict. It even stopped a bank which had acquired land from the Mazrui from charging rent to squatters who lived on that land.[154] Such actions were a reversal of Government efforts to make land more readily saleable and more profitable to landowners. Squatter agriculture on the coast had become a reality that the Kenyan Government could not negate.

Government timidity left squatters to make a variety of arrangements after the rebellion, as they had done before it. Some found land to which they could help themselves, either Crown Land or plantations whose owners had given up agriculture altogether. Squatters on such land did not have to contend with landlords but only with the Government, which feared that such people would be under no one's control, would be lost to the labor market, and would eventually acquire a claim to the land. They were vulnerable to the crackdowns of the Giriama moves and to recruitment for the Carriers Corps during the war. But the threat of expulsion was often in the background before 1914, and after the crisis, officials came to understand the costs that disruption of Mijikenda ag-

152. For the worried reaction of Hobley to the 1918 act, see PC to Ainsworth, 17 Sept. 1918, CP 61/113. As early as 1915, local officials were taking a more tolerant view of squatting, and Ali bin Salim made it clear to Hobley that Arabs were thinking more in terms of regularizing tenancy and collecting rents than of obtaining labor. Asst. DC, Mombasa, to PC, 17 Sept. 1915, and DC, Malindi, to PC, 12 Sept. 1915, CP 41/733; PC to Chief Secr., 10 Aug. 1917, CP 39/625.

153. Reports indicate that specific decisions were taken not to expel squatters (Kilifi, AR, 1925, 1926, 1930). Another Government device for extracting labor, the Native Authority Ordinance, which made all Africans who had not met a work quota for a private employer subject to forced labor for the Government, had the reverse of its intended effect on the coast. Instead of encouraging labor to come forth, it induced Mijikenda to register a bogus contract with a Swahili landowner, thereby evading forced labor while in practice incurring few labor obligations to the landowner. Suggestions by Mr. Fazan, Acting DC, Malindi, incl. Chief Native Comr. to PC, 2 Aug. 1919, CP 38/607.

154. Sr. Comr., Coast, to Chief Native Comr., 13 Nov. 1924, CP 58/1607; DO, Kilifi, memorandum, 23 Jan. 1935, CO 533/488; Kenya, "Report of the Judicial Inquiry into Arab Claims to Land on Wasin Peninsula," 1932. By 1921, officials thought it might be time to organize native councils for Mijikenda in the coastal strip. Kilifi-Rabai, AR, 1920–21.

riculture might entail. Many were living unmolested on vacant Crown Land in the 1920s, while the Administration still thought about getting rid of them.[155]

Most squatters came to terms with an Arab or Swahili landowner. Unlike ex-slaves, the Mijikenda had no preexisting relationship of dependence to restructure. That may well be why, according to Giriama informants, Giriama had to pay rent while ex-slaves generally did not. Yet the realities of the labor situation were such that landowners could not insist on terms that were significantly different. As the Provincial Commissioner observed, the squatters on "nearly every Arab and Swahili property of any size" would "remunerate the owner in various ways, some in cash, some in kind, some in labour, some by a division of the proceeds of the tembo tapped by the squatter from the owner's coconuts."[156] But landlords were unable to impose any "obligation to work for definite periods" on their tenants, and collecting rents was a delicate task. The shamba owners of Malindi were so wary of exercising what the British regarded as the natural prerogatives of the landowner that the Administration called a meeting to exhort them to raise their rents. All agreed that Rs 4 per year for a modest plot would be a good figure, but the District Commissioner privately admitted that this was double what Arabs expected to get, and probably could not be collected.[157]

Testimony at land hearings confirms that rent was in fact collected, although irregularly and in modest amounts, from Mijikenda squatters. "In some years," rent was paid in produce, read one land application. When squatters were being moved in 1914, Arab and Swahili landowners at Malindi petitioned that Mijikenda be allowed to stay, for many paid a small rent or cleared the shamba of bush in return for access to land.[158]

Giriama squatters shared with ex-slaves the same insecurity of tenure and the same need the landlords had for their presence. Both grew annual crops—cassava and maize—on their own account, and both helped keep coconut plantations clean for their landlord's benefit. The same

155. DC, Malindi, to PC, 13 April 1917, incl. Bowring to Long, 17 April 1917, CO 533/180; Malindi Commission, p. 3; Asst. DC, Malindi, to PC, 22 Oct. 1918, CP 61/113; DC, Lamu, to Sr. Comr., Coast, 5 March 1925, CP 61/113; Kilifi, AR, 1926.

156. PC to Ainsworth, 17 Sept. 1918, CP 61/113.

157. DC, Malindi, to PC, 13 April 1917, incl. Bowring to Long, 17 April 1917, CO 533/180; DC, Malindi, to PC, 31 Aug. 1915, CP 41/733.

158. A/c 105 D of 1915 (Malindi). See also 53 D of 1914 and others, as well as Asst. DC, Malindi, to PC, 22 Oct. 1918, CP 61/113. A squatter might be allowed to clear and plant as much land as he could cultivate on the promise of payment of one load of maize at the harvest. Malindi, AR, 1917-18.

prohibition against planting trees applied: Mijikenda squatters were not allowed to plant coconut or other trees on their own behalf.[159] Both peoples could obtain work from their landlords, and they generally sought wage labor on the same terms—kibarua work. During the post-removal famine, Giriama often came to an Arab shamba, worked three or four days for 25 to 30 cents per day, bought food for their families, went back to the Reserve, and returned later when the food was exhausted. In better times, both squatters and Mijikenda still living in the hinterland worked on a daily basis.[160] However, landowners—growing the same crops as Mijikenda—faced their peak labor demands at the same time as did their potential laborers. As the District Commissioner of Malindi observed, only land shortage would provide landowners with a labor supply from squatters.[161]

As with ex-slaves, the labor that landowners could extract from Mijikenda depended on the overall structure of opportunities. Short-term, high-paying labor in Mombasa offered an alternative to local landowners that many Mijikenda, especially in the 1920s, began to use (chapter 6). European-owned plantations, although nearer to home than Mombasa and offering better wages than Arab and Swahili estates, were not attractive, for they demanded long-term, full-time commitments from their workers.[162] Mijikenda could intergrate wage labor for Arabs and Swahili or casual labor in Mombasa into their lives, diversifying their options. Squatting and kibarua labor could be mutually enforcing activities in ways that wage labor on long contracts was not.[163]

The ability of Mijikenda to work their way into coastal agriculture

159. DC, Malindi, to PC, 30 Nov. 1914, CP 3/207; Nzeze Kwicha, Ishmael Toya, Kazungu wa Kigande (MAL); PC, circular, 9 Sept. 1915, CP 71/733. The exception to the prohibition of planting trees appears to have been the trans-Sabaki region, probably because planters had lost control altogether of their land and because the premigration stock of trees was small. By 1914, an estimated 4,300 coconut trees had been planted and were mainly used for tembo. Belfield to Harcourt, 4 May 1914, CO 533/136. But elsewhere the reluctance to plant trees continued. Kilifi, AR, 1937; Agriculture Officer, Coast, to Agriculture Deputy Director, 28 Aug. 1935; PC Coast, T & C 4/18, no. 38; DO, Kilifi, Memorandum, 23 Jan. 1935, CO 533/488.

160. Another official said a Giriama could earn half a pishi of maize in a five-hour day, working for an Arab or Swahili, with no supervision and no commitments. DC, Kakoneni, to PC, 8 March 1919, CP 38/607; Malindi, AR, 1917–18; DO, Malindi, to PC, 13 Aug. 1917, CP 39/625; Gari Kai, Awade Maktub, Alyan Hemed, Omar Dahman, Mselem Khalfan Jaafiri (MAL).

161. DC, Malindi, to PC, 13 Sept. 1915, CP 41/733.

162. Arthur Champion, Memorandum on Labour Supply and the Giriama, 1914, PRB, Kilifi; DC, Malindi, to PC, 28 Dec. 1915, incl. Bowring to Law, 11 Jan. 1916, CO 533/166.

163. The importance of the interplay of different economic activities is stressed by Sara Berry, "Risk Aversion and Rural Class Formation in West Africa," colloquium paper, University of California, Los Angeles, June 1978.

owed much to the earlier efforts of slaves and ex-slaves to bring plantation labor to an end. Ex-slaves had suffered along with Giriama from the drive against squatters in 1914, and they had benefited from the Administration's caution afterward. The ways in which ex-slaves and Mijikenda who had migrated to the coastal belt obtained land, farmed, and sought wage labor came to be quite similar. However, Mijikenda brought with them a different set of experiences. They shared with ex-slaves memories of conflict with slaveowners, but not the legacy of relationships that, while tense and exploitative, were also intimate. The history of life together with their slaves provided ex-slaveowners with an ideology that could be used to rationalize the basis of continuing dependent relationships with ex-slaves, even though the power and most of the profit of those relationships had slipped away; and it gave ex-slaves a foothold based in the landlords' cultural and religious norms to assert their own rights to land and patronage.[164]

Some Giriama voluntarily developed this religious idiom of dependence by converting to Islam. Converts, known as *mahaji,* were closely associated with the individual who converted them. In the late nineteenth century conversion was linked to clientage. The tumultuous politics of the regions behind Gazi and Takaungu had induced many Mijikenda to seek powerful patrons among the Mazrui, while Mazrui had been eager to build an economically and politically useful clientele. Famine could induce a similar process: in the harsh years at the turn of the century, many Mijikenda became clients and converts of Arabs on the coast, accepting food and access to land. But by the time of abolition, land could be obtained without establishing such a personal relationship and without accepting so much of the provider's religion and culture.[165] On the contrary, the patrons' loss of political power and the new rigidity of property rights often jeopardized the economic security of mahaji. If land were sold, mahaji had no rights whatsoever. Some Mijikenda still converted to Islam, but the significance of that act was altered.[166]

The relationship of Mijikenda squatters and Arab-Swahili landowners was thus not heavily invested with personal submission and ritual. It was

164. The two versions of this ideology run through almost all interviews with descendants of landowners and squatters in the Malindi area. They are also clear in testimony in the Gazi land case, incl. DC, Kwale, to PC, 27 June 1935, LO 30646, Nairobi.

165. Bakari Rarua, Awade Maktub, Nzeze Kwicha, Khamis Mohamed Muhando, Mohamed Omari Toya, Mohamedi wa Mweni (MAL).

166. That was why some mahaji entered Government-designated Reserves (Takaungu, AR, 1916–17). In 1910, there were reportedly 1,355 mahaji squatters in Takaungu District. MacDougall to Secr. to Adminstr., 17 June 1910, CP 64/62. On the changing significance of conversion, see David Parkin, "The Politics of Ritual Syncretism: Islam among the Non-Muslim Giriama of Kenya," *Africa* 40 (1970):217–33.

a flexible and practical one, involving rents, services, and access to land. But to a limited extent—as in references in land applications to allowing "poor people" to stay on the land—tenancy was seen by landowners in patriarchal terms.[167] Giriama, unlike ex-slaves, could maintain relations with kinsmen in the hinterland that gave them an option to return, but the advantages of coastal lands for the Giriama behind Malindi (although not so clearly farther south) meant that the economic relationships Giriama established within the coastal belt were at least as important to them.[168]

Ex-slaves were evolving toward similar pragmatic relationships with landlords, but from a different point of departure. They too had alternatives, and the memory of ties of dependence was important in so far as it was used to strengthen one of these options. Such ties were becoming less useful, as ex-slaves moved about, went to new plantations or new cities, and as more of the people upon whom landowners relied for labor or rent came to be Mijikenda. By the 1920s, the fact that the grain growers of the coast were squatters was more important than their origins.

As the nature of the relationships of Mijikenda and ex-slaves with Arab and Swahili landowners converged, their relations with each other became closer. The interior portions of the Malindi hinterland had, by 1913, become a region of interspersed settlements. Two villages in that area, Shauri Moyo and Goshi, contained 474 families, one-third ex-slaves, two-thirds Giriama. The immense shamba that Salim bin Khalfan turned over to his ex-slaves soon became a settlement of Giriama, mahaji, and other immigrants as well.[169] Near Mombasa, shamba areas like Kisauni attracted extremely diverse populations: Giriama, Digo, other Mijikenda, ex-slaves, and migrants from other parts of the coast.[170]

Despite religious differences, intermarriage between Mijikenda and ex-slaves took place. Mijikenda society also provided mechanisms by which both men and women could be absorbed into Mijikenda kinship

167. A/c 107 D of 1914 (Malindi).

168. A mark of the importance of the relationships developed in the coastal area, in a more recent period, was that Arab landowners in Mambrui loaned bridewealth to Giriama clients. This would have been done by close kinsmen in hinterland communities. G. E. T. Wijeyewardene, "Some Aspects of Village Solidarity in Ki-Swahili Speaking Communities of Kenya and Tanganyika" (Ph.D. diss., Cambridge University, 1961), p. 191.

169. Hollis, Native Rights, 1907; map. incl. DC, Malindi, to PC, 13 April 1915, incl. Bowring to Long, 17 April 1917, CO 533/180; DC, Malindi, to PC, 1 July 1913, CP 7/55; PC to Chief Secr., 7 May 1915, CP 20/128a; Juma Kengewa (MAL). Watoro and Giriama mixed as well. Timothy Nguma, Bisiria Toya (MAL).

170. A/c, Mombasa North; Wazee of Kisauni, Ibrahim Shaib, Mchangamwe Umar (MSA).

institutions.[171] As a result, ex-slaves were acquiring options in their social self-definition, as they were in Zanzibar. If absorption into the groups that were beginning to provide the largest number of squatters was a possibility, Swahili culture provided another option. While participation in coastal institutions might involve reminders of continued low status, the control of people of high status was weakening. In Mombasa, as Margaret Strobel has shown, ex-slavewomen were eventually able to take a fuller part in the ritual and social life of the Swahili community, and also to retain cultural practices of their own. Even in the 1970s, it is possible to find people of slave descent who have actively participated in the Islamic culture of the coast, often without denying their own hinterland origins.[172]

This is not to deny the importance of origins or status to social interaction, but only to assert that social identity itself could change along with economic and political power. A much more detailed study of social interaction in particular environments would be extremely valuable.[173] At the very least, it becomes impossible to accept at face value the persistent reports of British officials that ex-slaves were dying out, failing to reproduce, or losing economic vigor.[174] British prejudices against masterless men were too strong for officials to separate the decline of ex-slaves as a category from their decline as people. In fact, the availability of land through the ex-slaveholding, Swahili-speaking community defined a social field, in which the spectrum of responses is a better indication of social structure than are group boundaries. The children of ex-slaves could choose between adopting and manipulating the Islamic, Swahili-based idiom of the landowners or becoming more closely involved with the Giriama-speaking, predominantly non-Muslim culture of the new wave of tenants. In the Malindi area, unlike Zanzibar, the latter option seems to have been the stronger: the landed did not have much to offer through a personal bond. In Mombasa, at the other extreme, the continued wealth and social predominance of a number of Arab and Swahili

171. Timothy Nguma, Alfred Yongo, Nzeze Kwicha, Bisiria Toya, Juma Kengewa, Jabu Masoya, Awade Maktub. See also PC to Chief Native Comr., 15 Feb. 1928, CP 42/784. Morton shows how ex-slaves were absorbed by the Rabai subgroup of the Mijikenda: blood brotherhood would be established between an ex-slave and a Rabai, bringing partial membership in a Rabai clan. Then children of a marriage between such a person and a Rabai woman would acquire full Rabai status. "Slaves, Fugitives, and Freemen," pp. 326–29.

172. Strobel, *Muslim Woman;* Awade Maktub; Khamis Mohamed Muhando (MAL).

173. Caplan and Bujra have studied relatively small, isolated, and poor communities, and Wijeyewardene has made a comparative study of three Swahili villages. More prosperous and economically active communities should also be examined, preferably with the historical depth of Strobel's work on women in Mombasa.

174. These reports are accepted far too uncritically by Morton, pp. 380–84, 388.

families, plus the growing viability of an urban, Swahili-speaking under-life, made different segments of the Swahili milieu more attractive. Ex-slaves and Mijikenda did not become a single, undifferentiated people. Each group looked two ways: Mijikenda to their hinterland brethren as well as their coastal neighbors; ex-slaves to the Islamic community of which they had been a subordinate part, as well as to the new migrants who had come to share their economic life.

Conclusions

By the 1920s, ex-slave and Mijikenda squatters were growing grain on their own time and for their own profit. Landowners could still enjoy the produce of coconut trees, but only by making share arrangements, pay-ing daily wages, and granting rights in land. Grain plantations had ceased to exist, and coconut plantations were less tightly controlled. By the time of World War I, Arab and Swahili landowners had virtually ceased trying to preserve their control of a labor force but had come instead to depend on the squatter system. The colonial state had initially tried to smash squatter agriculture on the coast. It failed, and by the 1920s officials had grudgingly admitted that Mijikenda, like ex-slaves, were not going to be made into a working class.

The squatters had not entrenched themselves in the coastal economy without a struggle. Refusal to accept plantation discipline, settling with-out permission on vacant land, breaking of seemingly ingrown patterns of personal deference and submission in order to find new patrons or new ways of life, and the assertion of rights to coconuts and other pro-duce were all parts of a pattern of action by slaves and ex-slaves that forced ex-slaveowners to accept new forms of agrarian relations. Mijikenda, deserting the security of their homelands, were equally asser-tive. The "internal siege" of plantation land by the ex-slaves and the "external siege" of the Mijikenda were mutually reinforcing, whittling down the power of the landlords and improving access to the means of production.[175] It was out of such struggles that the squatter economy was built, and it was the fear of more conflict and more disruption that made officials unwilling to attack it further after World War I.

Yet squatter agriculture was not the "peasant" or "African" economy that is often contrasted starkly with plantation or settler economies. By creating the shell of a capitalist economy without its substance, the state helped to bring into existence a class of owners who could not produce and a class of producers who did not own. The former remained depen-dent on the state's willingness to enforce its land titles and the conditions

175. The phrases are from Kay, "Development of the Chilean *Hacienda* System," p. 105.

that shaped land values; the latter remained vulnerable to the state's willingness to coerce labor or evict squatters and to the conditions that shaped production. Squatters, after the state's onslaught against Giriama migrants, knew the potential for state action; they had experienced the threats of the imposition of rent or sale to another landlord who would dispossess them. While the failure of plantation development on the coast shielded squatters from too many events like these, the urban development near Mombasa—stimulated by the allocation of titles—had rapidly removed squatters from lands to which they had gained access over the previous decades.

Caught between the commercialization of land and the resistance of ex-slaves and Mijikenda to the commercialization of labor, the coastal economy inhibited investment and change. Landlords lacked the labor to cultivate intensively or make improvements on their land. Squatters could neither innovate nor develop the most important form of productive capital on the coast—coconut trees—for fear of expropriation and eviction. Neither landlords nor tenants could accumulate capital.

Yet the demarcation of land and the judicial enforcement of titles are not the only means through which agricultural capital can be accumulated. The extensive planting of cocoa bushes in West Africa was done by migrant farmers who, like Mijikenda, moved onto undercultivated land. However, they came to terms—outside of any state-run system of titles and contracts—with local landholders who were willing to allow tenants to plant trees as long as their own claims to land were recognized and compensated. Capital and labor were mobilized through kinship systems, and working for a tree owner was often a step toward becoming an owner oneself. The fact that the value of land came only through its agricultural uses, its flexibility of access, and the mobilization of social ties was crucial to the extraordinary growth of cocoa production.[176] Nearer to the Swahili coast, Giriama "accumulators" living within the palm belt but outside the zone of title allocation assured possession of their coconut trees, not by registering titles, but by relying on the testimony of witnesses to establish their rights over particular trees. This required the careful cultivation of ties of clientage and community but did not prevent the emergence of a number of active, productive agriculturalists with growing capital in trees. Neither the cocoa-growing nor the coconut-growing communities were egalitarian or without tension, but the principal threat to the maintenance of reciprocal relations and the

176. Berry, *Cocoa, Custom, and Socio-Economic Change;* Hill, *Migrant Cocoa Farmers of Southern Ghana;* Jean Pierre Chauveau and Jacques Richard, "Une 'Péripherie recentrée': à propos d'un système local d'économie de plantation en Côte d'Ivoire," *Cahiers d'Etudes Africaines* 17 (1977): 485–523.

delicate accumulative mechanisms was posed when guarantees of ownership and means of mobilizing resources came from *outside* the community. That is exactly what the state did for landlords in the coastal strip of Kenya, thereby polarizing society into the landed and the landless.[177]

The coastal region of Kenya offered enormous opportunities for tree crops and a rich and varied agriculture. Officials frequently discussed nurturing such enterprises without confronting the real reasons why nothing was done.[178] So the producers were left with ground crops, more suitable for the insecurities and antagonisms of squatter agriculture, and the landlords were left to extract their uncertain surplus out of rents, the existing stock of coconut trees, and the nonagricultural uses of land. Seeking to develop structures that would enable accumulation to take place along capitalist lines but unwilling and unable to exercise the necessary force, the state only impeded the accumulation of capital within an emerging peasant economy. Just like their colleagues in Zanzibar, Kenyan officials then harked back to their old view of Africa to explain their failure: stagnation on the coast stemmed from the laziness of the workers and the managerial incompetence of the landlords.[179]

---

177. Parkin, *Palms, Wine, and Witnesses.* This study focuses on Kaloleni, an area west of Takaungu, in a recent period, when copra was in demand. Nearer to Mombasa, the principal copra market, such tendencies were probably felt earlier. Polarizing tendencies fostered by the Kenyan state since independence have led to increased conflict within Giriama communities. Accumulators were likely to use institutions created by the state or a national political party to forge an alliance independent of the witnesses they had depended on within their community. Many turned to Islam to justify increasing nonobservance of Giriama norms. In turn, the "losers" in the competition for resources were likely to stress the internal solidarity of the community and what they regarded as traditional norms. Accusations of witchcraft made against accumulators by losers opposed the invocation of outside forces by the former. In addition to *Palms,* see Parkin's "Politics of Ritual Syncretism" and "Medicines and Men of Influence," *Man* 3 (1968):424–39. A similar opposition is discussed in P. M. van Hekken and H. U. E. Thoden van Velzen, *Land Scarcity and Rural Inequality in Tanzania* (The Hague, 1972), and the general issue of the difference between internal and external support mechanisms is stressed by Migdal, *Peasants, Politics, and Revolution.*

178. Rabai District—a Mijikenda area—turned out to have the highest number of coconut trees in the coastal region. CocCom.

179. Such was the conclusion of the PC during the most important years of development of the squatter economy. C. W. Hobley, "Native Problems in Eastern Africa," *Journal of the Africa Society* 22 (1923):191, 196. See also EAP, Economic Commission Report, 1919, pt. 1, p. 15; NAD, AR, 1927, pp. 9–10.

6   The Coast in the Colonial Economy of Kenya, 1907–1925

From the weakening plantation system on the Kenyan coast in the years before World War I a peasantry was slowly emerging. Tenants of ex-slave and Mijikenda origin led a modest revival of grain production for local use and export. Yet to point to the shift in the locus of production from the slave plantation to the peasant household is only to begin to analyze the economic lives of peasants and their relationship to wider economic structures.

As we have already seen, the state, especially before 1914, harassed squatters and undermined capital accumulation by peasants. The Provincial Commissioner at this time, C. W. Hobley, thought no better of productive peasants than of idle ones and ordered his subordinates in 1915 to keep a "sharp look-out" for richer peasants who tried to keep their sons on their farms instead of in the labor force. A homogeneous and propertyless African working class was his ideal, and although he backed away from pushing it after the Giriama rising, he unrepentently stuck to his belief that, left to themselves, Africans were hopelessly lazy, primitive, and unproductive.[1] His successors regarded the renewed trend toward squatter agriculture more with grudging acceptance of an economic and social structure they could not bring down than with enthusiasm for the exports the trend produced or the hardships it avoided.

Only the crisis of 1920–21 in the export markets for the major settler crops made Kenyan officials realize what they had not learned from nearly two decades in which most expenditures went to whites and most revenues came from Africans: that Africans, far from being productive only under supervision, required less fussing over than Europeans, once they were incorporated into an import-export marketing system. The "Dual Policy" of 1922–29, however, was not a retreat from earlier approaches but an attempt to have things both ways—to stimulate both settler and African agriculture. The policy was rendered largely ineffectual by the insistence of settlers that African agriculture not be allowed to hurt their labor supply—which it was quite likely to do—the settlers' ability to influence the implementation of London's policies, and the

---

1. PC, circular to DCs, 1915, CP 20/103; Hobley, "Native Problems in Eastern Africa," pp. 191, 194.

parsimony of the Administration.[2] What coastal people could do with the lands they farmed would still be strongly influenced by the demands for their labor.

The Colonial Office and local officials, in periodic moods of handwringing in the 1920s, admitted that they had done little to promote agriculture on the coast.[3] In fact, they had done much to damage it. Excessive taxation not only made difficult the accumulation of capital by peasants struggling to establish themselves, but it forced them to sell grain too quickly to get a good price and in too great quantities to avoid having to buy grain back later and, often, go into debt to shopkeepers. The state not only failed to build an adequate transportation system for the coast—comparable to the subsidized railroad that served upcountry farms—but grievously damaged the old Indian Ocean dhow trade that was still taking out grain. The state discouraged competition in marketing—particularly by the small-scale, small-margin traders who have often met the needs of small-scale producers—and thus weakened the bargaining position of the cultivators. These policies not only diminished the incomes of peasants but also discouraged them from devoting more labor or land to marketable crops, investing in trees or better implements, or improving techniques. The state's marketing, taxation, and agricultural policies thus reinforced the tendency of the coastal land tenure system to push peasants into a defensive approach to farming. Anything that might tempt a landlord to evict squatters, that would make it difficult to move to another piece of land, or that would make peasants dependent on merchants for essential supplies—especially food—had to be avoided. Factors such as these, not any cultural orientation toward "subsistence agriculture," made insecure cultivators give highest priority to crops that were both annual (requiring no permanent capital) and consumable.

The stunted evolution of the coastal economy was also shaped by the consequences of the new spatial system into which the coast had been thrust.[4] Plantations all along the coast had been linked to a trading system extending along the shores of the Indian Ocean and indirectly con-

2. Spencer, "Development of Production and Trade"; Brett, *Colonialism and Underdevelopment.*

3. East Africa Commission, Report, 1925, p. 159; Kenya, Report of the Agriculture Commission, 1929, pp. 23–24.

4. It would be misleading, however, to consider these problems as attributes of geography per se rather than of the exercise of power over space. The idea that there is a normal pattern of spatial systems, deviations from which must be explained, mars P. A. Memon and Esmond B. Martin, "The Kenya Coast: An Anomaly in the Development of an 'Ideal Type' Colonial Spatial System," *Kenya Historical Review* 4 (1976):187–206.

nected to Europe. The creation of British colonies and the building of the Uganda Railroad gave the coast an enormous and dynamic hinterland linked to international trade and the coastal region at one point—Mombasa.

Behind development policies which promote investment in the most favored agricultural regions, which encourage the expansion of modern ports, commercial centers, railroads, and services about those favored regions, and which encourage the activities of "entrepreneurs" within agricultural and commercial centers lies an assertion that the expansion of poles of development will create opportunities for work and sale of goods in other areas, so that the benefits will trickle down. But the history of Mombasa suggests that such centers could act less as poles of development than as drains.

Mombasa attracted resources—above all labor—that might otherwise have promoted agriculture in the coastal region, but the benefits of Mombasa's presence did not necessarily go to its neighbors. Not only was there competition from upcountry to supply both the labor and the produce that Mombasa demanded, but the competition was stacked by the policies of the state. The ability of ex-slaves and Mijikenda to play off against each other the options of growing subsistence crops, selling produce, and working for wages protected them from the dominance of landowners but provided little basis for improving the level or techniques of production. In the absence of such developments, coastal people became vulnerable to changes in the demand for their labor or their produce in an increasingly narrow, Mombasa-centered economic system. Through Mombasa, coastal people were subject to the competition of producers from more dynamic and more heavily subsidized regions and to the competition of the laborers that land expropriation and economic differentiation upcountry pressured into the labor market. By the 1920s, the opportunities which ex-slaves and Mijikenda had used to undermine the plantation economy had become the constraints of the colonial economy.

THE COAST IN THE COLONIAL LABOR SYSTEM

Landlords and tenants did not work out their relations among themselves. Even by 1907, the coast of Kenya was tied into a regional labor system. It was not simply a colony-wide labor "market," for labor did not flow along the network in response to market conditions alone: pressure and coercion were integral parts of the system, affecting not only the people who were pressured or coerced, but the opportunities and working conditions of all who sought work. For the coast, Mombasa was the crucial link with the wider system, generating large labor demand, pulling in labor from upcountry and along the coast, and distributing labor to specific niches of the coastal economy.

The evolution of the Government's efforts to shape the Kenyan labor system has been studied at length, although the ways in which these policies affected Africans have only been sketched in.[5] On paper, the techniques used to bring forth labor paralleled measures taken in Zanzibar. But the group for whose benefit labor was being pressured was not the same, and the interdependence of different facets of the Kenyan economy—in contrast to the simpler tension between tree-owner and land-tiller in Zanzibar—meant that similar policies had very different results.

The early empire builders failed to find in Kenya an entrenched landed elite as in Zanzibar or a powerful kingdom as in Uganda, and they looked upon their colony as sparsely populated, disorderly, and poor.[6] Having built a railroad to economically and strategically valuable parts of Uganda and the Victoria Basin, officials were faced with what seemed to them a void between the declining coast and the useful deep interior. Reasoning quite similar to that which led them to despair of the ability of Zanzibar's ex-slaves to do anything other than work on plantations led the Administration to think of Kenya's Africans mainly as potential laborers. By 1902, the decision to use white settlers to develop the lands of Kenya, to provide export crops, and to make the railroad pay had been made. Although the settler economy remained a minor source of exports and revenue until the first world war, and can only be termed a success for a brief period after the second, its voracious demands for labor were a constant preoccupation of the state.[7]

5. The most detailed account is Clayton and Savage, *Government and Labour in Kenya 1895–1963*, and the following pages draw heavily on it. There is already an important tradition of Marxist scholarship on labor in Kenya, but it has not quite made it to ground level yet. Wolff, *Economics of Colonialism;* Roger van Zwanenberg, *Colonial Capitalism and Labour in Kenya, 1919–1939* (Nairobi, 1975); Sharon Stichter, "The Formation of a Working Class in Kenya," in Richard Sandbrook and Robin Cohen, eds., *The Development of an African Working Class: Studies in Class Formation and Action* (London, 1975), pp. 21–48. Studies of particular parts of Kenya that shed light on how and why people sought wage labor include Tignor, *Colonial Transformation of Kenya,* and J. Forbes Munro, *Colonial Rule and the Kamba: Social Change in the Kenya Highlands 1889–1939* (Oxford, 1975).

6. Such attitudes are particularly clear in High Commissioner Eliot's Annual Report, 1900–01, in FOCP 7867, p. 10, and Report on Native Tribes of East Africa, incl. Eliot to Lansdowne, 9 April 1902, FO 2/570. See also Mungeam, *British Rule in Kenya,* and G. N. Uzoigwe, "The Mombasa-Victoria Railway, 1890–1902: Imperial Necessity, Humanitarian Venture, or Economic Imperialism?" *Kenya Historical Review* 4 (1976): pp. 13–14.

7. Uzoigwe, pp. 11–34; Mungeam; Clayton and Savage; Sorrenson, *Origins of European Settlement.*

Encouraging labor required the usual arsenal of techniques. A hut tax, frankly intended to make life expensive for Africans, was imposed in 1901 and rose from Re 1 to Rs 8 by 1920. Contracts and legal sanctions were used, more forcefully than in Zanzibar, to define new notions of idleness and useful labor and to bind Africans to particular employers. From vagrancy laws to harsh penal sanctions against Africans who broke contracts—enforceable after 1920 by pass laws that made the tracing of deserters relatively easy—enactment after enactment insisted that employers and the state should determine the frequency, duration, and rhythm of work.

At the center of labor recruitment, in the murky realm between forced and free labor, were the district officer and African chiefs and headmen. Cut off from the diverse sources of wealth and power they had once possessed or owing their appointments to the Administration, chiefs in many parts of Kenya had little choice but to respond to official pressure to cajole or force their subjects to work for public and private employers. As one coastal official put it, getting labor for white settlers from a chief "depended on how far he could be induced to exceed his instructions."[8]

The importance of pressure was clear from the early days of settlement, but World War I brought about a full appreciation of its importance to both Africans and officials. The demands of the Carriers Corps for porters added to the usual complaints of labor shortage, creating a crisis solved mainly by force. On the coast, recruitment among Swahili and Mijikenda was extensive. To some, the passage of officials and chiefs through villages searching for able-bodied men must have resembled a slave raid: in remote areas behind the coast entire villages sometimes fled into the bush and lost their crops. Others took jobs with the Government or Europeans to gain exemption from recruitment.[9]

The end of the war brought expanded agricultural activity, despite a setback in 1921, a new labor shortage, and new efforts at pressure of which the controversy over "encouragement" was a small part. The Government insisted that squatting take the form of labor tenancy, with 180 days of work required each year. A stricter Masters and Servants Ordinance increased punishments and regulated the number of days that contract workers had to put in each month. Labor registration laws restricted mobility, and a new Native Authority Ordinance made Africans

8. Asst. DC, Kilifi, to PC, 18 Oct. 1918, CP 38/582.
9. Tanaland, AR, 1915–16, 1916–17; Malindi, AR, 1915–16; Takaungu, AR, 1915–16; PC to Chief Secr., 11 July 1917, CP 61/113. Women coming to Malindi were sometimes seized and released only when their menfolk enlisted (DC, Kakoneni, to PC, 18 July 1917, CP 49/1195). On the importance of this period to the development of a labor force, see Clayton and Savage, pp. 81–107.

who had not worked for three months out of any year liable to compulsory labor for state purposes.[10]

The land situation upcountry enhanced the effectiveness of all the other measures and by the mid-1920s resulted in a better supply for settlers, deteriorating conditions for squatters, and—very gradually—the continued availability of labor without all the direct compulsion of the earlier period. There were prosperous Kikuyu, Luo, and Luhya farmers growing maize and other crops, but for many others, especially young men, the extension of white farms into the best agricultural areas, prohibitions against Africans competing with settlers in producing the most profitable export crops, increased needs for cash for taxes and consumption, and the very differentiation within African communities made it imperative to work at least part of the year.[11] Population growth and erosion of the overstretched land slowly made the situation worse. But different groups faced pressures at different times and in different ways. In 1925, 55 percent of adult male Kikuyu were at work at one time, compared to 42 percent of Luo and Luhya—called "Kavirondo" by the British—and 15 percent of the Kamba. Kikuyu most often became workers or squatters on European farms in the Highlands and Rift Valley or else relatively short-term workers near their homes in central Kenya. "Kavirondo," far away from places of employment, were more prominent as long-term contract workers, leaving their farms to the women, and came to be the most important suppliers of urban labor to Mombasa, on the other side of the colony from their homes. Kamba were initially able to hold out for certain kinds of jobs, as skilled workers or policemen, but eventually many joined the ranks of squatters and agricultural laborers.[12] The integration of the coastal people into the labor system was slower still, and took its own direction.

On the coast of Kenya and its immediate hinterland, it was quite clear for whose benefit labor policies were intended. The section on labor in

10. The intent of the Administration to step up pressure was made clear by top officials at a meeting in Nairobi, and the word was passed to District Commissioners. PC, circular to DCs, 26 Feb. 1917, CP 39/622. See also Clayton and Savage, pp. 108–39.

11. Lonsdale and Berman ("Coping with the Contradictions") stress that young and propertyless men frequently sought wage labor in order to acquire resources needed to enter commodity production, as well as to meet the inflation and increased monetization of communal obligations. The position of colonial chiefs both in exerting pressure on men to enter wage labor and in expanding their own cultivation intensified labor migration as a means of either meeting the demands of the chief or getting away from him.

12. Figures from Red Book, 1925–26, p. 124. On differential entry into the labor force, see Tignor, Munro, and Frank Furedi, "The Kikuyu Squatters in the Rift Valley, 1918–1929," in B. A. Ogot, ed., Hadith 5, pp. 177–94. Even in sugar-dominated Cuba, only some provinces had a population consisting primarily of cane workers; others were dominated by peasants or tenant farmers. Rebecca Scott, cited in Mintz, "Rise of Peasantries."

each quarterly or annual district report invariably describes the European employers of the district, their demands for labor, and how they are being met. Arab or Swahili employers are scarcely mentioned, in contrast to British reports on Zanzibar. During the period of wartime recruitment for the Carriers Corps, officials made clear that Arab plantations were dispensable while European ones were not: "In this Province we have carefully combed out men from the Arab plantations where they are not adequately employed, but have not interfered with any registered labourers on European estates."[13]

But if the Administration did little *for* Arab or Swahili planters, it did less *to* their former slaves than it did to other Africans. Only in the war was labor recruitment within the coastal strip pursued with any vigor.[14] In part, officials were inhibited by their own prejudices: ex-slaves were a feckless and diminishing people and were hardly worth seeking. They were also constrained by the economic rules they had created: the coastal strip was not a Reserve but an area largely subdivided into private holdings, on which the landlord, as well as the Government, had a say over people living on estates.[15]

When the Government thought about labor from Coast Province, it thought above all about the Mijikenda. The desire to create the conditions to foster control and labor recruitment had led to a rebellion, and the disorder, famine, expenses, and criticism from London that resulted led to an easing of pressures through chiefs and the various ordinances.[16] Mijikenda were still made to work, above all in their own dis-

13. A list of employers in Malindi District in 1919 included Europeans, Indians, Salim bin Khalfan and his son Ali, two Liwalis, and only four other Arabs or Swahili—this at a time when the European plantation sector had already failed and hundreds of Arab and Swahili landowners were employing squatters and workers. Asst. DC, Malindi, to PC, 18 Sept. 1919, CP 38/582; PC to Chief Secr., 11 July 1917, CP 61/113.

14. Outside of the war years, there are no references like the above, or the PC's claim to have "swept clean" the coast of unemployed Swahili. PC to Chief Secr., 24 Nov. 1915, incl. Belfield to Law, 30 Nov. 1915, CO 533/157. See also Malindi, AR, 1915–16, and Takaungu, AR, 1916–17.

15. When ex-slave and other Swahili laborers were obtained, officials complained that they were a "lazy and degenerate lot." Takaungu, AR, 1915–16; Malindi, QR, 4th quart., 1911. In 1930, when squatter agriculture had long been established, officials complained of their lack of control of ex-slave, mahaji, and Mijikenda squatters on Arab land: no native courts or similar institutions had jurisdiction. Kilifi, AR, 1930.

16. Hobley's earlier bluster that the Carriers Corps would "break in these somewhat reluctant workers and accustom them to the idea of regular work," making the Mijikenda into a "reservoir for labour" soon gave way to fears of the "risk" of recruitment. PC, despatch, 23 May 1916, CP 38/581; PC to Chief Secr., 20 Nov. 1917, CP 38/607. See also suggestions by Mr. Fazan, Acting DC, Malindi, incl. Chief Native Comr. to PC, 2 Aug. 1919, ibid,; DC, Mombasa, to PC, 5 Nov. 1917, CP 38/603; Asst. DC, Rabai, to DC, Mombasa, 5 Oct. 1918, CP 38/582; Kilifi, AR, 1925.

trict, and many more came to work in Mombasa and elsewhere, but with their options of staying in the hinterland or squatting on Arab-Swahili land they had considerable choice about the conditions under which they would seek wage labor.[17]

Given the relative lack of administrative powers, the broader attempts of officials to reform society and create a stable, hard-working and sober labor force through contracts and the criminal law never even got as far as they did in Zanzibar. In 1898, a vagrancy regulation was issued for Mombasa (and was later extended to other parts of the coast) that reflected fears of rootless slaves, casual labor, a "floating population," and urban society that ran deep in Victorian attitudes. The decree was aimed "at checking, not only the influx into the town of Mombasa of idle and criminal runaway slaves, but also of disreputable free people of all sorts, who come to get an "odd job" on the railway, then throw up their work when tired of it, or are discharged, and take to drink and rioting, thus augmenting to an undesirable extent the disorderly floating population of Mombasa."[18] But unlike in the case of Zanzibar, such fears and notions of labor were not part of a coordinated effort to organize plantation labor. In the years after abolition in Malindi—when idleness, by Zanzibar standards, was rampant—there were no convictions for vagrancy.[19] Nor were officials especially worried about the myriad crimes that ex-slaves, cut loose from their masters, supposedly committed in rural areas: they seemed satisfied that the rural districts of the coast suffered little from violence. Outside of Mombasa, there were few prosecutions for violating contracts or registration laws. The one exception was coconut theft, which officials believed was widespread and largely perpetrated by ex-slaves. But they scarcely prosecuted anyone for it.[20] The idea of a work-oriented rural social order failed in Zanzibar; it was not tried in coastal Kenya.

Within Mombasa, the situation was different and very much a consequence of the casual labor system which the colonial economy itself did much to create. Most coastal crime was urban crime. In the early 1920s,

17. Labour returns, incl. Ainsworth to PC, 29 Dec. 1919, CP 38/582; Acting PC to Chief Native Comr., 10 Feb. 1920, ibid. Provincial officials also did not have to worry about a vocal settler contingent after the decline of European plantations.

18. Hardinge to Salisbury, 16 Jan. 1898, FOCP 7024, p. 122.

19. Malindi, AR, 1911–12; Reports of DCs, 1920–23, CP 53/1371.

20. The rarity of crime—including that under the Masters and Servants Ordinance, even at the height of the plantation boom—is evident in Malindi, ARs. The Coconut Commission claimed that 20 to 70 percent of all coconuts were stolen, depending on the district, and that freed slaves were the main culprits, along with Africans from outside the coast and "loafers." But there were only three or four convictions annually in each coastal district. CocCom; correspondence related to the Coconut Industry Ordinance of 1923, 1916–1927, CP 36/547.

the labor laws were enforced vigorously in the city: there was an average of 142 cases brought under the Masters and Servants Ordinance each year between 1921 and 1924, plus 407 under the Native Registration Act. These were crimes associated with failing to work steadily, and the number seems high for a work force of 8,000 to 10,000, especially considering the low incidence of crimes against persons and property. The Native Authority Ordinance—putting to work people who had not already worked sufficiently—was also used much more frequently in Mombasa: in 1923-24, 425 to 622 people were doing Native Authority labor each month in Mombasa District, compared with 16 to 41 in all the other coastal districts.[21] The "floating population" that officials had feared in 1898 had grown. There was a large demand for labor and a large potential supply. The Government was putting pressure on those who were not working and seeking to control those who were. But with the kind of casual labor system found in most ports, periodic idleness— dangerous as it was in governmental eyes—was as much as part of the work situation of Mombasa as actual labor. The Government continued to arrest people; it did little to change the basic structure of urban labor.

Mombasa's evolving labor force was drawn in different ways—and worked on different bases—from upcountry and the coastal region. The origins of the urban labor force go back to a population of slaves, exslaves, Muslim converts from the interior, immigrants from the Hadramaut, and others who performed jobs for hire. While slaves in the nineteenth century had to remit about half their wages to their owners, they often lived and sought work on their own. They worked on the docks or carried goods around town or went inland as porters. Kibarua (day) labor came to be an accepted way of organizing work, and heterogeneity a characteristic of the workers.

Railroad construction and the bustle of a new colonial headquarters stimulated migration to Mombasa in the 1890s, including that of slaves. The work-or-leave approach implied in the vagrancy act of 1898 was not easy to enforce, and the so-called vagrants created a pool from which casual labor could be drawn, following the comings and goings of vessels and caravans. Intense caravan traffic to Uganda increased the demand for porters until the completion of the railroad after 1901 knocked it out, but increasing commerce was expanding the demand for casual workers.[22]

21. Mombasa, AR, 1922, 1924. This accounts for most of the crime in Coast Province reported in NAD, AR, 1924, p. 35. On registration violations, see Chief Registrar of Natives, circular, 17 July 1924, CP 39/636. There were 7,500 registered workers in Mombasa in 1925, plus casuals. NAD, AR, 1925, p. 81.

22. Porters readily found work with the railroad and elsewhere. Eliot to Lansdowne, 25 Jan. 1904, FO 2/834.

At the heart of urban labor was the port, and the tonnage of steamers passing through it doubled between 1903 and 1913, fell during the war, and regained its position by 1923. With goods from Uganda, the Victoria Basin, northern Tanganyika, and parts of Kenya coming down the railroad and more goods going up, commercial enterprises in the city also needed more workers. But the most important characteristic of such work was its irregularity. As much as Europeans complained about the unwillingness of Swahili and Mijikenda to work for long periods, the casual labor system suited the demands of the port. And officials' displeasure that Mombasa was a "native town" which they did not control as tightly as they did the colonial town of Nairobi was offset by the fact that neither employers nor the Government had to take responsibility for housing or feeding workers.[23]

Port labor required strength, experience, and skill within a flexible organization of work. The old floating population was augmented by more ex-slaves, Nyamwezi immigrants from Tanganyika, and Arabs newly arrived from the Hadramaut. In 1911–12, they could earn Rs 1/25 per day for loading and unloading ships or porterage. They could earn in less than ten days as much as unskilled contract workers could get in a month. In 1915, officials thought port workers put in an average of 15 days each month; a day ran from 7 A.M. to 5 P.M. with a one-hour break. Although the war reduced civilian port traffic, it made other demands on labor, so that wages shot up. By its end, hamalis (port carriers) were making Rs 2/55 per day.[24] But efforts at registering workers revealed that of the 2,000 registered dock workers, an average of under 200 were at work each day. This is below the actual number of workers, for many avoided the official labor bureau, but dockers clearly could not work every day even if they wanted to. The shipping lines estimated they needed 4,840 man-days of labor per month, an average of 186 per day; but on some days they needed 500, plus as many as 200 colliers, pier handlers, and others.[25] By the 1920s, the casual labor pool had grown.

The core of these port workers, and of general labor in the city, were landless Swahili and coastal migrants: even if they did not have to work every day, they had no choice but to work for wages. Their numbers

23. Figures on port traffic are in Red Book, 1925–26, p. 184. The continuing interest of employers in the casual labor system is stressed in Willan Commission, 1939, and Janmohamed, "History of Mombasa," pp. 437–44. These issues are taken up in my current study of railwaymen and dockworkers in twentieth-century Kenya.

24. Seyidie Province, AR, 1911–12; PC to Col. Shepard, GSO, 27 Nov. 1915, CP 38/603; NAD, AR, 1918–19, p. 23; PC to Atty. Gen., 9 Jan. 1919, CP 38/611.

25. NAD, AR, 1918–19, p. 23; Monthly returns on registered port labor in CP 38/611 and 39/629; PC to Shepard, 27 Nov. 1915, CP 38/603.

grew as people from the poorest areas of the coast, such as Lamu, moved to the city.[26] But the casual labor pool of Mombasa included many people who lived nearby and farmed. Some came to work during the day and returned to their mashamba in the evening. Even those from farther away often left urban employment during the harvest season, causing a seasonal shortage of labor and a slight rise in wages.[27] As more Mijikenda sought wage labor, they preferred to come to Mombasa to work on a kibarua basis in the port or elsewhere, though not losing touch with their own communities or land. Such preferences left Swahili— including many ex-slaves—with little competition for a number of other kinds of jobs, above all domestic service, interpreter, and safari head-man.[28]

In contrast, upcountry workers were the key to contract work—for periods of several months or more—from an early date. There were many jobs in railroad shops, municipal service, and the port that con-stantly needed doing. Kikuyu walked 300 miles to the coast for such work. "Kavirondos" were coming to Mombasa as well, as were a smaller number of Kamba. Teita were also important in the early phase, a reflec-tion not so much of land shortage and pressure as of the fact that a major source of cash income, the Kilimanjaro trade route, had been eliminated by the colonial frontier and new pathways.[29]

That Mombasa, as well as European plantations on the coast, had to draw from relatively remote areas meant that local wage rates had to be higher than upcountry. In 1903, the monthly wage in Mombasa was around Rs 10–15 plus rations, compared to Rs 4–5 in the Highlands and Rs 7–8 in Nyanza. Coastal wages did not rise very much, but the dif-ferential remained. Even in 1924, when more of Kenya's peoples had been brought into the work force, average wages were Shs 10 in the Highlands and Shs 16 on the coast.[30] Coastal employers often paid

26. Dickson, Report on Coast Production and Trade, 28 Aug. 1923, CP 56/1525.

27. Mombasa, QR, 4th quart., 1911; W. J. Simpson, "Report on Sanitary Matters in the EAP, Uganda and Zanzibar," 1914, in COCP 1025, p. 40. In 1925, medical officials vacci-nated 7,113 people by waiting at the ferries for people going into and out of Mombasa Island. Janmohamed, "History of Mombasa," p. 172.

28. Suggestions by Mr. Fazan, incl. Chief Native Comr. to PC, 2 Aug. 1919, CP 38/607; Kilifi, AR, 1929; EAP, AR, 1900–01; Beech, MS on Swahili Life; Maalim Mzagu, Mzee Juma (MSA); K. K. Janmohamed, "African Labourers in Mombasa, c. 1895–1940," in Ogot, ed., Hadith 5, p. 158. Servants received Rs 10–30 per month, laborers Rs 10–15. EAP, AR, 1906–07, p. 39.

29. Girouard to Crew, 6 Aug. 1910, CO 533/76; Seyidie, AR, 1911–12; Mombasa, QR, 4th quart., 1911, and 1st quart., 1912; Mombasa, AR, 1915–16; Teita, AR, 1911–12.

30. Monson, Report on Labour, 1903, PP 1903, XLV, 745, p. 7; Bowring to Milner, 21 April 1920, CO 533/232; Red Book, 1925–26, p. 122.

workers from upcountry less than their coastal employees, although it is not clear whether this meant that the smaller number of local people were used in special roles, such as headman.[31]   *1924*

The Mombasa labor market thus depended on a combination of coastal people who could go in and out of urban jobs with relative ease and upcountry laborers who had to work for longer periods. Colonial development upcountry was primarily agricultural, competing (with state aid) with African agriculture and in a variety of ways forcing Africans to seek wage labor. Urban development in Mombasa created some new opportunities for its rural neighbors. Grain and coconuts were sent to the city and tembo was sold to upcountry workers. Within the city, Arabs and members of the Twelve Tribes rented land and houses to workers, officials, and merchants. Others provided services.[32] Nairobi, too, created such demands, but settlers—controlling much land both in and around the city—seized many of the opportunities for themselves. When, in the 1920s, wage labor in Mombasa became less favorable to coastal people, the change was as much the result of increased pressures on people in the Highlands and Nyanza to migrate in search of work as it was of changes on the coast itself.

Early attempts to recruit Mijikenda, the main potential source of labor on the coast, failed miserably: their opportunities in agriculture were improving. From the northernmost of the Mijikenda subgroups (the Giriama) to the southernmost (the Digo), men continued to stay at home, evade the encouragement of chiefs and district officers, and desert if they were recruited.[33]

But when times were bad or when they could control the conditions of their labor, Mijikenda were willing to work for wages. A famine hit the hinterland in 1912–13, and Giriama came to work in Mombasa. Despite the hardships, they still avoided working on European plantations because there they would be bound by contracts. Between 1914 and 1919 there was a series of bad harvests compounded by the forced move into the Reserve. Again, Mijikenda sought work in forms that would not be too disruptive of their lives. In Malindi District they would work for an

31. The Kikuyu influx is all the more remarkable because they, coming from a highland area, were devastated by coastal diseases (Malindi, AR, 1908–09; EAP, AR, 1910–11, p. 92). According to the latter, Swahili received Rs 12 per month, Kikuyu, Rs 8.

32. Near Kampala, according to Walter Elkan, opportunities for growing cash crops did not stop local people from seeking wage labor in the city, but it did give them more choice over the kind of jobs they took. *Migrants and Proletarians: Urban Labour in the Economic Development of Uganda* (London, 1960), pp. 33–47.

33. MacDougall to Secr., 10 Sept. 1907, incl. Sadler to Elgin, 18 Sept. 1907, CO 533/31; Champion, Memorandum on Labour Supply and the Giriama, 1914, PRB, Kilifi; Kwale, AR, 1915–16; PC to DC, Nyika Dist., 18 March 1915, CP 38/580.

Arab or Swahili for a few days to buy food, returning as needed. If they wished to stay on, Arab landowners would let them bring their families; Europeans would not. Gradually, working became squatting once again, although periodic difficulties in the hinterland brought more laborers onto Arab and Swahili farms. In the mainland farm areas near Mombasa, Giriama also worked for Arabs, Swahili, and Indians during hard years.[34]

In order to turn Giriama misfortune into European profit, officials and employers had to give in to the preference for short periods of labor: the district administration at Takaungu decided to reduce the period of contractual service on European estates to one month, on condition that another batch from a list of able-bodied men would replace them, letting the first group go home for three months. But having to make such concessions indicated that the Administration had little power over laborers. Later, the manager of a sisal plantation tried withholding a worker's final pay until he brought in a replacement for himself, but this simply discouraged Mijikenda from coming at all, and the Government made the manager drop his plan.[35]

Mombasa, however, fit better into Mijikenda preferences: kibarua labor was available and daily wages were relatively high. Mijikenda seeking work thus generally took one of two options: high wages for short periods in an alien urban environment or low wages in a relatively adaptable work situation nearer to home.[36] The postwar revival of Giriama cultivation cut down on the labor they had supplied during the crisis years, and only later—as population expanded, land filled up, and changes took place within coastal agriculture—did Giriama begin to lose control over the kind of work they would accept.

Mijikenda living nearer to Mombasa could not find new land so readily, but there was a ready market for coconuts, copra, and tembo from the hills behind the city. Moreover, the proximity of Mombasa

34. Fazan, Suggestions, incl. Chief Native Comr. to PC, 2 Aug. 1919, CP 38/607; DC, Kakoneni to PC, 8 March 1919, ibid.; Malindi, AR, 1912–13, 1917–18; Ishmael Toya (MAL).

35. Takaungu, AR, 1914–15; Acting DC, Malindi, to PC, 17 May 1916, CP 38/580. Another Official's attempt to get Giriama labor for a sisal estate in the midst of a famine brought forth few workers, and those who came deserted. Asst. DC, Giriama, to PC, 22 Jan. 1917, CP 38/581.

36. Fazan, suggestions, incl. Chief Native Comr., to PC, 2 Aug. 1919, CP 38/607; Acting DC, Malindi, to PC, 18 July 1919, CP 38/582; Champion, Labour Report, PRB, Kilifi; DC, Malindi, to PC, 9 Jan. 1918, CP 49/1195; Sr. Comr., Coast, to Chief Secr., 24 Feb. 1925, CP 56/1525; Malindi, AR, 1917–18, 1924; Takaungu, AR, 1914–15; Kilifi, AR, 1925; Maalim Mzangu, Mzee Juma (MSA); Nzeze Kwicha, Alfred Yongo (MAL). Only 482 people from "coastal tribes" were at work on long contracts in a 1924 labor survey. NAD, AR, 1924, p. 57.

meant that it was relatively easy to adjust to daily labor. The earliest indications from official sources that certain Mijikenda were becoming dependent on wage labor refer to the Chonyi and Kauma behind Takaungu. Perhaps they fell between the Malindi area, with its plentiful land, and the outskirts of Mombasa, with its ready access to urban daily labor. Nevertheless, most of the potential laborers in Takaungu District—2,000 Mijikenda and Swahili in 1915—had their own mashamba, some kind of squatting arrangement, or another job like fishing. Thus European plantations, which needed 500 workers, could only get 100 from the district, and even the tightening situation of the next decade did not end the plantations' need for upcountry labor.[37] At the other extreme, in Lamu, wage labor meant a long journey and often permanent dislocation. As one official at Lamu noted, the region's agriculture was caught in a "vicious circle" of "more migration, less development; less development, more migration."[38]

Coastal people were using their ready access to the relatively favorable labor market of Mombasa not simply to maximize wage earnings, but to improve the total structure of opportunities, adapting the casual labor demands of the city to their needs to supplement farming. For this period it is impossible to calculate annual earnings that could be expected from farming, urban labor, or a combination of the two, and in any case annual earnings were not the only consideration. Becoming committed to wage labor could be an irreversible move, and neither the utter lack of security of employment nor the poor housing and expensive food of the city encouraged Mijikenda or ex-slaves to make a break with agriculture as long as they had a choice.[39]

That money could be earned in Mombasa affected the agricultural economy of the rest of the coast. Arab and Swahili landlords could not pay wages that were competitive with the town, or even with European

37. Asst. DC, Takaungu, to PC, 21 Dec. 1916, CP 39/622; Takaungu, AR, 1914–15, 1915–16; Labour Inspection Reports, 1922, CP 38/581; Sr. Comr., Coast, to Chief Native Comr., 13 Nov. 1924, CP 58/1607.

38. Dickson, Report on Coast Production and Trade, 28 Aug. 1923, CP 56/1525. Relatively short periods of labor by Malindi people in Mombasa were probably made easier by a substantial community of Malindi people in the city. Omar wa Fundi, Awade Maktub (MAL), Juma Rubai (MSA).

39. On the crowded and expensive housing of Mombasa, see PC, Memorandum on Terms of Settlement in Native Locations and Proposed Native Town, incl. Bowring to Harcourt, 3 Oct. 1913, CO 533/123; PC to Gen. Manager, Railroad, 14 Feb. 1913; CP 7/60; Native Annual Report, Mombasa, 1919, CP 52/1289; NAD, AR, 1923, pp. 16–17; Report on Native Affairs, Mombasa, 1930, DC/MSA/3/3. Decisions like these will hopefully be studied in terms of family groups and life cycles, but it is doubtful that such data could be pushed back to the period of this study.

plantations.[40] They could, however, compete on the conditions of work; tenancy and kibarua labor offered benefits which regular wage labor did not. A Giriama daily worker on a farm in Malindi might get 30¢, compared to 50–75¢ for a trolley boy or Rs 2 for a dockworker, but he was only one or two miles from home. Alternatively, he could make the Arab's farm his home and grow his own food.[41] The presence of Mombasa made it more difficult for the former planters to maintain grain production on a plantation basis and also made it particularly important for landowners to make tenancy attractive.

If Mombasa pulled in workers, affecting the labor situation along the coast, it also distributed workers to other coastal districts. But that role was played in regard to European employers only, above all to the short-lived plantation sector. As early as 1908–09, Kikuyu coming through Mombasa were spreading out to European plantations all along the coast. Even in Tanaland, far to the north, the bulk of the workers on the major European estate were Kikuyu. In this period, Kikuyu—and to a lesser extent Nyamwezi—were plentiful, and in 1909–10 the Tanaland estate was therefore able to reduce its wages.[42] But planters were vulnerable to colony-wide trends, and the 1912 labor crisis elicited pained cries from Europeans. Still, from Vanga to Tanaland, Kikuyu, people from Nyanza, and to a lesser extent Kamba remained the backbone of plantation labor. During the war, when Mijikenda were suffering from famine and having a European employer at least offered protection from the Carriers Corps, more Mijikenda came forth, yet most preferred Arab-Swahili employers.[43] By the 1920s, the plantation sector was employing

40. On the effects of competition with Mombasa for labor, see the Report on Economic Progress made in the Coast Province during 1924 by Sr. Comr., CP 56/1525. Monthly wages were often 50 percent higher in town than on the mainland. DC, Mombasa, to PC, 28 Oct. 1918, CP 38/582.

41. DC, Malindi, to PC, 9 Jan. 1918, CP 49/1195; Champion, Memorandum on Labour, 1914, PRB, Kilifi; Malindi, AR, 1917–18.

42. Malindi, AR, 1908–09; Malindi, HOR, 1909; Lamu, AR, 1909–10; Acting Gov. to CO, 9 Dec. 1908, CO 533/48. The Tanaland plantation employed 700 workers, mostly Kikuyu plus some Kamba (Tanaland, AR, 1909–10). Like Zanzibar, Mombasa and the Malindi plantations were on the extraordinary Nyamwezi migration network, and they had a small community of their own at Mombasa. They were lost during the war but returned in smaller numbers later. EAP, AR, 1905–06, p. 90; Medical Officer, report, 11 Aug. 1911, MD/28/479, KNA; Sr. Comr., Coast, to Chief Native Comr., 18 Jan. 1922, CP 61/113; EAP, Economic Commission, Evidence, 1919, p. 206; Kilifi, AR, 1924.

43. Testimony from Malindi Planters in NLC, 1912–13; Vanga, QR, 1st quart., 1912; EAP, AR, 1911–12, p. 53; Takaungu, AR, 1914–15, 1916–17, 1920–21; Malindi, AR,

between 1,000 and 2,000 workers—most of them in sisal—and a modest increase in the availability of Mijikenda did little to ease the estates' dependence on Kikuyu and "Kavirondo."[44]

European and Arab-Swahili landholdings thus existed side by side but drew labor from separate channels and on different terms. Ali bin Salim and his father hired workers for their plantations on the same basis as Europeans: they were Kikuyu, Kamba, and Nyamwezi contract laborers. But other Arabs and Swahili had little access to upcountry labor. They could not offer competitive wages and lacked influence over District Officers or contacts with professional recruiters. Nor did the terms they could offer Mijikenda or ex-slaves appeal to Kikuyu, Luo, or Luhya: these people lived far away and would be isolated on the coast.[45]

Coastal farms and European plantations also interacted directly: Swahili coconut planters supplied tembo to workers on the European estates. Swahili fishermen supplied fish. While European plantations— which had more land than could be kept under export crops—often devoted some labor time to producing food, they often did not bother or else fell short. This opened up a market for maize to local farmers.[46] Mijikenda and ex-slaves could sell goods to plantations instead of working for them.

Mombasa's demand for labor and the coast's market for grain gave ex-slaves and Mijikenda alternatives to working for Arabs, Swahili, or Europeans, and thus helped to establish squatter agriculture. Meanwhile, the effectiveness of Mombasa as a labor distribution center reduced the pressure on the Administration to continue the very difficult task of breaking the squatters.

Yet urban labor—especially for ex-slaves and others who had migrated to Mombasa—was so important to the overall structure of oppor-

---

1915–16, 1916–17; Kwale, AR, 1915–16. The overwhelming dominance of upcountry laborers is clear in figures on each plantation in Medical Officer, Report, 11 Aug. 1911, MD/28/479, KNA; Labour Inspection Reports, 1915–18, CP 38/586.

44. In 1927, officials remarked on the fact that Kilifi Plantations was employing 300 Giriama (Kilifi Station Diary, Nov. 1927, CP 57/1564D). But for the continuity of upcountry labor, see Malindi, AR, 1923, Sr. Comr., Coast, to Chief Native Comr., 13 Nov. 1924, CP 58/1607; East Africa Commission, Report, 1925, p. 159; Kilifi, AR, 1924, 1925. The 2,000 workers employed in the average month on European land on the coast in 1920 constituted only 4 percent of the agricultural work force of Kenya. Kenya, Agriculture Dept., *Agricultural Census*, 1920, table 18.

45. NLC, p. 92. Aside from Ali, the written and oral evidence on squatters makes no mention of Kikuyu or other upcountry Africans.

46. PC, Inspection Report, Malindi, 17 July 1915, CP 17/61; Inspection Report of Labour Camp at Sokoke Estate, 20 March 1915, CP 38/601; Kilifi, AR, 1925. Similarly, Bonde in Tanganyika largely escaped labor on nearby sisal estates because they could sell food. Iliffe, *Modern History of Tanganyika*, pp. 152, 163.

tunities that coastal people were vulnerable to the fluctuations of labor policy and the labor supply in Kenya as a whole. During the war, the Government attempted to step into the casual labor market of the port, seeking to reduce the workers' flexibility, keep down their rising wages, and enhance the reliability of port labor. Because of wartime labor shortages, employers were competing with each other and with employers outside the port, and workers, now receiving higher daily wages, were refusing to work every day or under conditions—for example at night—which they did not like. In 1916 port workers were made to register: shippers were only allowed to employ registered workers at preset wages. Workers who did not put in a sufficient number of days were supposed to lose their registration. Later, the District Commissioner was empowered to order any unemployed African to work.[47]

This attempt at direct labor control ran up against a long-established pattern of labor organization, and it failed. The port workers were registered but could not be made to work when they did not want to. Much of the labor was obtained through subcontractors, who withheld their labor gangs to get more out of employers and gave their laborers advances in order to create indebtedness and thus obtain a hold over them. Figures under the registration scheme suggested that port workers were only putting in five or six days per month, although the decentralized nature of hiring meant that they were in fact working more. Wages could not be stabilized, and sometimes surpassed Rs 3 per day, ending up around Rs 2/55, double the prewar rate.[48]

These measures were discontinued soon after the war, although stronger colony-wide labor legislation soon came into force. But the most important effects of the postwar labor situation came to Mombasa along the railroad. Migrants from Nyanza came in ever larger numbers to the coast, and by 1921 or so, labor shortages were no longer a problem. In 1925, "Kavirondo" and Kikuyu each outnumbered coastal people—both Swahili and Mijikenda—among the 7,555 registered laborers in Mombasa. Only 17 percent of the city's registered work force were from the coast.[49] In the port, Luo and Luhya were competing with Swahili and Hadrami Arabs. Upcountry people were moving into domestic service, once the province of ex-slaves. Upcountry workers, as District officials soon realized, had two advantages to employers: they accepted lower wages and—having invested in a long journey—they worked longer and more regularly. By 1922, officials were no longer referring to the pref-

47. Government actions are summarized in Clayton and Savage, pp. 97–98.

48. PC to Chief Secr., 9 Feb. 1917, 1 Aug. 1917; PC to Atty. Gen., 9 Jan. 1919; DC, Mombasa, to PC, 12 Dec. 1917, 1 July 1918, all in CP 38/611; DC to PC, 9 Aug. 1918, and PC to Acting Chief Secr., 12 Aug. 1918, CP 39/629; NAD, AR, 1918–19, p. 23.

49. Seyidie, AR, 1920–21; NAD, AR, 1925, p. 81.

erance of Mombasans to drift in and out of work at their own choice but were worrying about "unemployment."[50] Competition for port jobs increased in the 1920s and 1930s, leading to a corrupt system whereby headmen gathered groups of clients whose access to work depended on their intervention. While daily wages remained higher than in other parts of Kenya, they fell in the early 1920s to about half their wartime peak and remained at that level until they were cut further during the Depression. More important, casual laborers often could work so few days that they could barely get enough money to support themselves and their families. In the Depression "daily" workers could frequently work only one day out of five.[51]

For both workers and employers, casual labor represented a delicate balance that worked well, for one or the other, only under particular conditions. Casual labor offered Africans important advantages when it could be combined with other sources of food or cash in a situation where wage labor itself provided no security and poor living conditions. Even the landless could have more choice about when to work than the full-time laborer. Employers could adjust their payrolls to meet daily needs and avoid all responsibilities toward the social costs of labor.[52] However, employers needed a large labor pool in order to be sure that the number of workers required on the busiest days would be forthcoming, and when that failed to happen during World War I, the state intervened, albeit ineffectually, to make casuals work more often. When, on the other hand, upcountry workers came in greater numbers to Mombasa in the 1920s, the position of coastal workers was threatened by the same menace of underemployment that has made the lot of casual

50. NAD, AR, 1920–21, p. 35, 1923, p. 16; Mombasa, AR, 1922; Janmohamed, "African Labourers," p. 163.

51. Port wages were Shs 2 to Shs 2/50 per day in the 1920s, equivalent to Re 1 to Rs 1/25 at the official conversion rate, compared to Rs 2/55 during the war. The wage cuts in the early 1920s were colony-wide, and port wages would still have compared favorably with those paid on settler farms—Shs 16–24 for 30 working days—if port workers had been able to work steadily. Changes in currency and taxes make comparison of wage rates a complex question that is unraveled in Clayton and Savage (pp. 139–46), although as yet no price index is available with which to calculate real wages. Reports after the war do mention high prices. For data on wages and living conditions, see Mombasa, AR, 1919, 1923; NAD, AR, 1923, pp. 16–17, 1924, p. 56; Report on Native Affairs in Mombasa, 1930, PRB, DC/MSA/3/3; Willan Committee, 1939, p. 22; Clayton and Savage, pp. 219–20; and for an overview of changes up to 1939, see Janmohamed, "History of Mombasa."

52. Port employers insisted that casual labor was necessary in any port even when the Government, extremely anxious after the 1939 and 1947 strikes, began to argue that the casual labor system was a threat to order. See the voluminous correspondence on these issues in the Labour Department files, LAB/9/1835 and LAB/9/1838, in KNA; and for another study of the contradictions of cheap labor and public order, see Stedman Jones, Outcast London.

and seasonal workers in much of the Caribbean and Latin America particularly miserable and degrading.

For squatters on coastal lands, the deteriorating labor situation in Mombasa meant that sources of cash outside the rural economy were less sure, and that jobs which had previously been considered disruptive of agriculture and home life now had to be accepted more often. By 1926, Mijikenda were taking jobs on sisal estates, and such workers were soon staying an average of three months.[53] But the viability of maize and coconut farming shielded them from the urban squeeze, so that their economic independence did not decline as sharply as that of other Kenyan peoples in the 1920s. But decline it did, gradually and unevenly, in the ensuing decades.

The situations of people who did not have access to land—including the ex-slaves who had been drawn to Mombasa when its casual labor market offered both good wages and independence—was potentially more grave. They were stuck with the consequences of their earlier commitment to wage labor and had to face the competition of upcountry migrants for jobs as servants or contract laborers or struggle with a tightening casual labor market. The District Officer wrote in 1923 that the local population was "being driven from the labour market and forced to eke out a precarious existence in some cases by petty trading but in most cases by 'living on their wits.'" The riots that erupted between upcountry and coastal workers in that year were probably less a matter of primordial loyalties than of increased competition.[54]

Exactly how hard the propertyless people of Mombasa were hit by the tightening job market is impossible to tell. Casual labor did not dry up, and the informal sector—offering low-cost services to workers and other city people outside of a regularized wage-labor system—provided some cushion against destitution, although little more than that.[55] Both the

53. Kilifi, AR, 1926, 1927, 1930. In 1930, 4,000 Mijikenda worked for three months for Shs 10 per month, while some worked for longer periods for Shs 20 per month. Short-term labor in Mombasa was still eagerly sought if it could be found. Ibid., 1929.

54. Mombasa, AR, 1923. On the continued tension in Mombasa, see Clayton and Savage, pp. 220–21; Janmohamed, "History of Mombasa," and Willan Report, 1939.

55. Janmohamed, "History of Mombasa," pp. 170–79. The fact that employment in the informal sector has enabled many more people to survive in cities than could be supported by wages paid by officially recognized employers has recently received a good deal of attention. But scholars have lately stressed that such employment—since it provides services to workers in the formal sector at very low cost and therefore makes it possible to keep down formal sector wages—is actually a severe form of exploitation and offers little possibility of further transformation (C. Leys, *Underdevelopment in Kenya*, pp. 266–99, and Sara S. Berry, "Custom, Class, and the 'Informal Sector': Or Why Marginality Is Not Likely to Pay... ," Working Papers, n.s. no. 1, African Studies Center, Boston University, 1977). Fear of an urban underclass is an important theme of Carla Glassman's current research on Nairobi and my own on Mombasa.

urban poor and casual laborers from nearby farm areas were at the center of the strikes and disturbances that hit Mombasa between 1939 and 1947, a period when the growing necessity for a cash income and extreme inflation in Mombasa brought all workers into the struggle for better urban wages. The ex-slaves and other landless people in Mombasa were the beginnings of an urban underclass, moving back and forth between wage labor, activities in the informal sector, and no work at all. They were people whom the colonial regime understood little and feared greatly, and they have since become a much larger—and still little understood and much feared—part of African cities.

Although the success that coastal people had when they sought jobs in Mombasa was strongly affected by trends upcountry, their position vis-à-vis other Kenyans in the labor force showed considerable continuity. Even in the 1940s and 1950s, the percentage of adult males in the labor force was lowest in all of Kenya for "coastal tribes" and well below the colony-wide average for Mijikenda. While the desire of upcountry migrants to keep jobs for long periods and the increasing interest of employers in stabilization had narrowed the opportunities for casual laborers in Mombasa, most casuals remaining in the 1950s still came from the coast or its nearby hinterland.[56]

The interplay of urban casual labor with agriculture was thus crucial in helping ex-slaves free themselves of the economic power of the planters. For both ex-slaves and Mijikenda, the urban alternative was a buffer against crises in agriculture and a bargaining tool to be used against rural landlords, and from it they obtained not so much better wages as more advantageous conditions of tenancy and more flexible terms of daily labor on Arab and Swahili farms. The personal relationship of landlord and squatter came to be more favorable to the squatter and more secure. The development of the modern, commercially active, wage-labor center of Mombasa helped strengthen the precapitalist character of the relations of production in coastal agriculture.

The urban alternative—which was weak in Zanzibar and nearly absent

56. In a 1942 survey, 40.3 percent of able-bodied adult males in Kenya as a whole were in civil employment, compared to 9.25 percent of "coastal tribes," 19.1 percent of Giriama, and 27.8 percent of Digo and Duruma (Report of Labour Committee, Jan. 1942, appendix B, copy in Ministry of African Affairs, file MAA/8/123, KNA). Data from a scheme to register all casual laborers in Mombasa port reveal that in 1954 nearly three-quarters of registered casuals were from Coast Province. The largest single ethnic group among port casuals was Giriama: 24 percent (Labour Department, Memorandum on Casual Labour Scheme, Mombasa, appendix 11, LAB/9/217, KNA). At the same time, employment records of the Kenya Landing and Shipping Co. from the 1950s (found in a storage shed of the Kenya Cargo Handling Co.) indicate that the large majority of employees on monthly contracts were Luo, Luhya, Kamba, and Teita.

in Pemba—made the transformation of slave plantations into wage-labor plantations all the more unlikely, but it also made it more difficult and expensive for peasants to mobilize the labor which they, too, needed. Especially given the tensions associated with squatter agriculture and the discouragement given smallholders by the state, combining periods of wage labor with farming was often a more promising—and usually safer—alternative to planting new cash crops (see below). Wage labor in Mombasa provided a safety valve in case of drought, money to pay taxes, bridewealth, and other expenses, as well as a way of refusing onerous demands by landlords. But wage labor was a slow and painful way for rural people to accumulate capital to plant coconuts in the hinterland or buy the plots where they lived as tenants on the coast. Wages were higher than in other parts of Kenya, but they were still not enough—and work was not sufficiently steady—to supply more than a few rupees each month, especially for those who did not live close enough to the city to avoid the high cost of urban life. Most important, the crucial period after World War I, when the harassment of squatters finally abated and squatter production expanded, was a time of declining wages.[57]

Mombasa's expansion increased its demands for produce to feed workers as well as labor, preventing coastal people from becoming overly dependent on urban labor. Yet the very cause of Mombasa's growing demands, its connection with the hinterland and with export markets, also brought in laborers and produce from upcountry. Because upcountry laborers were subject to strong pressures to work more, the hinterland connection eventually undermined the favorable conditions under which coastal people entered wage labor in Mombasa, while the services and subsidies given settler agriculture—and the neglect and harassment given coastal farming—reduced the advantages of proximity that coastal produce-sellers had.

Being able to balance rural and urban sources of income was vitally necessary to people who were landless and vulnerable, but the alternatives were decidedly limited, and the very act of balancing them made the strengthening of coastal agriculture all the more difficult. Proximity to the most active port of East Africa helped break down an economic system that had once been oppressive, but the city siphoned off the most vital resources needed to develop a new and more viable economic structure, whether based on a modified form of plantation agriculture or peasant production.

57. Agricultural officials in the 1920s made the connection between the withdrawal of labor and agricultural decline on the coast. In Kilifi District in 1930, very rough estimates of Giriama earnings suggested that wages brought in less than half what the state took out in hut taxes. Copra and tembo sales accounted for over half of Giriama income, wages for 28 percent. Kenya, Agriculture Commission, 1929, p. 37; Kilifi, AR, 1930.

THE MAKING OF A BACKWARD REGION

Recent studies of the coast of Kenya have accepted too readily the views of colonial officials that the abolition of slavery led directly to the collapse of coastal agriculture, the impoverishment of the Arab and Swahili slaveholders, and the decrepitude of the former slaves.[58] While the Zanzibar Government used its dim view of ex-slaves and ex-slaveowners to justify its efforts to control the plantation economy, the Kenya Government found the apparent uselessness of both groups to be a good reason to ignore them. Above all, seeing the very real problems of coastal agriculture in terms of the inherent inability of particular social groups to function outside of an archaic and immoral social system saved officials from having to question how the structure of the colonial economy inhibited production, investment, and innovation.

When a group of coastal Arabs complained to a Government commission in 1930 that abolition resulted "in the levelling *down* of the Arab rather than in the levelling *up* of the freed slave," they disingenuously ignored what slave labor had been like and what ex-slaves—whatever the intent of their liberators—had done with their freedom.[59] The plantation economy of the coast, unlike that of Zanzibar, had indeed collapsed, exports had shrunk, and many Arabs and more Swahili planters had suffered, but smallholder production and regional marketing were expanding, and grain exports—except when the Government disrupted them—revived after abolition, while copra held steady.

It is very difficult to analyze changes in production because so little is known about where the produce mentioned in export statistics came from, let alone what was consumed in a city like Mombasa. Marketing mechanisms are also little understood. What follows is tentative and incomplete.

Malindi had once been the granary of the coast. Its exports had fallen badly by 1900, but they slowly revived even as the plantation system eroded and squatters became the primary producers (see tables 6.1 and 2.1). Nevertheless, grain exports, both by weight and by value, only rose to a third of what they had been in the late 1880s, not even counting the

---

58. The view that Arabs' "traditionalism" in the wake of abolition was the cause of their decline may be found in Esmond Bradley Martin, *The History of Malindi: A Geographical Analysis of an East African Coastal Town from the Portuguese Period to the Present* (Nairobi, 1973), pp. 276–77. See also Salim, *Swahili-Speaking Peoples*, p. 100, and Morton, "Slaves, Fugitives, and Freedmen," pp. 380–84.

59. Memorandum by Sheikh Hemed Mohamed bin Isa and Mbarak Ali Hinawi, PP 1930–31, VII, 1, vol. 3, pp. 67–68. This statement is mentioned approvingly by Salim, *Swahili-Speaking Peoples*, p. 114.

TABLE 6:1
GRAIN EXPORTS FROM MALINDI, 1910–1925

Year	Maize		Millet		Sesame	
	1000 cwt.	£	1000 cwt.	£	1000 cwt.	£
1910–11	49	9,031	6	1,293	3	1,702
1911–12	76	18,507	5	1,205	3	1,698
1912–13	17	5,202	2	670	3	2,053
1913–14	33	6,640	.4	119	3	1,940
1914–15	19	4,492	.4	123	1	567
1915–16	.01	5	.1	21	1	350
1916–17	—	0	—	0	—	0
1917–18	—	0	—	0	1	410
1918–19	15	6,989	2	1,172	1	—
1919–20	18	6,553	5	2,725	3	1,998
1920–21	10	4,810	7	3,136	4	2,228
1921 (9 mos.)	35	11,168	5	2,357	3	2,712
1922	31	10,014	7	3,058	2	1,186
1923	18	5,314	9	3,076	—	3,292
1924	42	13,515	2	856	—	—
1925	57	22,367	5	2,316	6	4,319

SOURCE: Malindi, ARs.

heavy exports of sesame and other produce that had since declined.[60] But these figures give a somewhat deceptive picture of the state of agriculture. Producers were no longer being made to produce three or four harvests of grain, sesame, and beans each year. Production was not being controlled by export-minded planters but by thousands of smallholders whose first concern was their own consumption. The size of regional markets is unknown, but the existence of exchange mechanisms within the coast is clear. And exports, especially in the early 1920s, showed considerable buoyancy.

60. Cooper, *Plantation Slavery*, p. 85. Millet had been the most important plantation-grown grain in the nineteenth century, although Mijikenda grew more maize. A switch from millet to maize on coastal lands seems to have accompanied the end of plantations, although neither the timing of the change nor the reasons for it are clear. Many Africans made such a change, but over a very long period, and the choice made by ex-slaves, once they could choose, may have something to do with the greater need for organization and common work in millet cultivation as well as the food preferences of ex-slaves. For background, see Marvin Miracle, *Maize in Tropical Africa* (Madison, Wis., 1966).

The port of Kilifi also tapped a substantial and productive area where smallholders—Giriama in the hinterland, mahaji, ex-slave and Mijikenda squatters on the coast—grew grain. It exported over £8,000 worth of maize in 1922. Lamu, once a center of grain production, still exported a little, but it now imported rice. A small amount of maize was exported from the south coast, grown by Digo and Swahili, and more entered the lively produce trade that developed within this complex region, but this area, too, had begun to import rice, a crop it had once exported.[61] The sale of surplus food crops was nothing new for ex-slaves—any more than it had been in the West Indies or Zanzibar—and for the recently freed, taking advantage of whatever opportunities they had, represented a chance to achieve independence as well as profit.[62]

Nevertheless, the Indian Ocean commercial system that had made the coast into a grain-producing area was being eclipsed by ever wider shipping patterns. While Malindi had once fed markets in Arabia and Zanzibar, it now sent most of its maize by dhow to the Benadir coast.[63] The entire coastal zone, however, was being pushed to the side of a direct linkage between upcountry Kenya and a worldwide economic system.

Mombasa's grain exports had been less than half of Malindi's in the 1880s and dwindled to almost nothing by the time of abolition. Grain grown by Luo, Luhya, and Europeans upcountry was consumed locally; it was part of the cumbersome support system for the settler economy. Then the Government introduced subsidized railway rates to make maize competitive overseas. Mombasa's maize exports—although it was the smallholders of Nyanza, rather than white settlers, who grew an embarassingly large proportion of it—rose rapidly, from Rs 107,000 in 1910-11 to Rs 668,000 in 1912-13, finally pushing upcountry maize ahead of Malindi's.[64] The dislocations of World War I virtually stopped maize exports, but in the 1920s, upcountry maize production was stimulated anew by the state's decision to institute a low flat railroad rate and a reduction of shipping costs of Mombasa. Exports of maize via Mombasa

---

61. Takaungu, AR, 1908-09; Malindi, AR, 1918-19; Asst. DC, Kilifi, to DC, Malindi, 27 June 1923, CP 56/1525; Tanaland, AR, 1911-12, 1912-13, 1915-16, 1916-17; Shimoni, QR, 4th quart., 1911, AR, 1911-12; PC to Chief Secr., 10 Aug. 1917, CP 39/625.

62. West Indian peasants after emancipation pioneered new crops and introduced diversity in crops for export and local use into what had been a monoculture. Woodville K. Marshall, "Notes on Peasant Development in the West Indies since 1838," *Social and Economic Studies* 17 (1968):252-63.

63. Malindi, AR, 1910-11, 1923, 1925.

64. EAP, AgAR, 1912-13, p. 19; Malindi, AR, 1912-13. The supports demanded by settler agriculture are stressed by both Brett and Wolff.

65. Maize acreage on European farms expanded greatly in these years (EAP, AR, Trade, 1915-16, p. 29, 1916-17, p. 55; Kenya, AgAR, 1920-21, p. 23, 1922, p. 18, 1924,

spurted from £114,000 in 1920 to £381,000 in 1924.[65] Upcountry production now utterly dominated Kenya's maize exports.

At first, upcountry maize competed in the same markets that the coast had once dominated: over half the maize exports in 1911–12 went to Italian Somaliland. But the postwar subsidies were designed to push Kenyan maize into European markets, and the result was to swamp the older markets in much larger new ones. In the period 1923–25, Europe's share of Kenya's maize exports varied between 75 and over 90 percent.[66] How the state treated the now minor markets is discussed below.

The other mainstay of coastal agriculture, coconuts, faced no upcountry competition, although the main form in which coconuts were exported, dried into copra to be pressed into oil in Europe, competed with a variety of oil-rich crops from all over the tropical world. If the world price of copra never got high enough to stimulate new breakthroughs in production until after World War II, the export market held its own through a number of wobbles, as table 6.2 suggests. In 1922, a local soap industry began to add a small but steady demand for copra not reflected in the export statistics.[67]

Like cloves and unlike grain, coconuts on the coastal belt were more of an owner's crop than a squatter's crop but, unlike cloves, they were fully integrated into the local economy. An estimated six million nuts were used for food in coastal districts each year, and the trees also provided roofing, fibres, and fuel. But the most important alternative to copra was palm wine, and it was consumed by tree owners—especially Mijikenda—and sold to Mijikenda who lacked trees as well as to workers in Mombasa and on European plantations. Stimulated by this regional market, Mijikenda greatly extended the palm belt in the hills behind and north of Mombasa.[68]

Despite repeated official attempts to bury the tembo trade in a mass of regulations, the trade continued to flourish. It worked through efficient networks based on face-to-face relationships that were largely immune

---

pp. 6, 9). That the introduction of railroads could lead to land expropriation and labor exploitation near the line, and the decay of agriculture away from it, is emphasized in different cases by John Coatsworth, "Railroads, Landholding, and Agrarian Protest in the Early *Porfiriato,*" *Hispanic American Historical Review* 54 (1974):48–71, and Ian Phimister, "Peasant Production and Underdevelopment in Southern Rhodesia, 1890–1914, with Particular Reference to Victoria District," in Palmer and Parsons, *Roots of Rural Poverty,* pp. 262–63.

66. EAP, AgAR, 1911–12; Kenya, AR, Trade, 1924, p. 93, 1925, p. 14.

67. Kenya, AgAR, 1926, p. 14; Petition of Ismailji Jivanjee and three other soap manufacturers to Government, 10 Oct. 1929, PC's Archives, Mombasa, T & C 4/4/2.

68. CocCom, p. 103; EAP, Agriculture Dept. Leaflet no. 7 of 1905, p. 81; PC to Supt. of Police, 19 Nov. 1912, CP 5/353; Acting DC, Malindi, to PC, 24 March 1914, CP 7/115; Parkin, *Palms, Wine, and Witnesses.*

TABLE 6:2
COPRA EXPORTS FROM KENYA, 1907–1925

	Cwt.	£
1907	37,068	24,164
1908	32,099	22,554
1909	27,653	14,989
1910	33,209	16,154
1911	36,879	30,608
1912	31,717	28,055
1913	31,283	31,956
1914	31,725	35,587
1915	27,722	24,371
1916	9,774	8,433
1917	28,748	28,784
1918	19,285	18,599
1919	22,124	17,104
1920	33,219	39,004
1921	9,343	22,803
1922	22,220	21,688
1923	13,460	13,521
1924	39,280	46,473
1925	31,298	35,915

SOURCES: Kenya, AR, 1918–19, Trade, p. 38, 1920–21, p. 51, 1923, p. 24, 1926, p. 32.

from bureaucratic pressures.[69] This regional market not only offered producers higher returns per tree than copra, but the nature of tapping made it possible for tree owners on the coastal belt to realize their profits more easily by hiring tappers or making share agreements, thus avoiding the problem of coconut theft. In 1930, licensed tappers in Kilifi District produced an estimated £20,000 worth of tembo, while illicit tapping added perhaps £10,000 more—a business on the order of copra exports for the entire coast.[70]

Near Malindi, where the many Giriama who lived beyond the palm belt provided a large market for tembo produced on the coast, virtually no copra was marketed.[71] In Lamu, however, which had few non-

69. Selling licenses for tembo were cut by as much as 90 percent in 1912, but selling was not cut by a like amount. Malindi, AR, 1912–13, Mombasa, AR, 1912–13. See also Child, *Coconuts*, p. 23.

70. Kilifi, AR, 1926, 1930; Report of the Special Committee on the Coconut Industry, 1923, CP 36/547.

71. Seyidie, AR, 1913–14; Malindi, AR, 1916–17, 1920–21; Testimony of Arab and Indian delegations, Malindi, CocCom, pp. 37–39. Because of the large number of squatters in the Malindi area, coconuts were especially likely to disappear and tapping was all the more desirable. Ibid., p. 37.

Muslim customers, copra was second only to mangrove poles in the export figures. Trees grew mainly on the islands of the Lamu Archipelago, where the island-dwelling owners could retain their trees even though they had abandoned their mainland grain fields to ex-slaves.[72] South of Mombasa, copra exports were also kept up. There, mashamba were smaller than the coastal average—47 trees each, compared to 122 coastwide, in a rough tree census in 1914—and they were therefore more easily watched. Nor did the relatively Islamized Digo of the south coast provide a good market for tembo.[73]

The coastal plain and the hills surrounding Mombasa were much involved in tembo exchange, but Mombasa also offered the most favorable market for copra, since it alone had direct steamer connections to Europe. Nearly 60 percent of the trees enumerated in the 1914 census were in the Mombasa area. However, most of those trees were not in the old Swahili agricultural zones but in the hills inhabited by Mijikenda and a smaller number of ex-slaves: two-thirds of the Mombasa area trees were in Rabai and Ribe. Indian and Swahili traders bought coconuts in those areas, and the Rabai eventually started drying the nuts themselves.[74]

The survival of the coconut industry and its development among Mijikenda does not mean that all was well. Tapping damaged trees, and tappers did not have a long-run interest in keeping plantations clean. Beetles came to be an increasingly dangerous pest.[75] On the coast, improvement or expansion was largely blocked. Although maintaining trees was not expensive, planting coconuts was.[76] The most impressive advances occurred among Mijikenda.

Despite the vitality of squatter grain production, Mijikenda tembo tapping, and regional exchange, the rather flaccid export statistics—in

72. Lamu's copra exports were £5,711 in 1911, rose to £8,643 in 1914, fell during the war, and went back to over £8,000 in 1922 ("Economics—Lamu," prepared for the East Africa Commission, 1924, CP 58/1609). There were also coconut mashamba along the Tana River, and a European even installed a coconut-drying plant on Lamu Island. Tanaland, AR, 1915–16; EAP, AgAR, 1912–13, p. 63.

73. Census data in CocCom, p. 109. Vanga and other southern ports exported almost Rs 40,000 worth of copra in 1911–12, almost half their total exports. AR, Shimoni, 1911–12.

74. Mombasa provided 75 percent of the colony's total copra exports between 1907 and 1913 (EAP, AgAR, 1912–13, p. 3; CocCom, p. 109; Rabai, QR, 4th quart., 1911, AR, 1911–12, 1914–15). Chonyi also sold coconuts to Swahili traders who took them to Mombasa. Asst. DC, Takaungu, to PC, 10 Jan. 1914, CP 7/132.

75. EAP, AgAR, 1907–08, p. 9; CocCom, p. 36; Kenya, AgAR, 1922, p. 21.

76. It takes six years for a coconut tree to produce, during which time it must be kept free from bush. Coconuts, like most tree products, are a crop for people who have something to invest. EAP, Agriculture Dept. Leaflet no. 7, 1905, p. 4; Whyte, Report on the Coast, PP 1903, XLV, 759, p. 7.

an economy that increasingly made cash a necessity—do point to problems that the smallholders of the coast would have to confront one day. If the economic structure of which they had become a part inhibited the development of a variety of crops—shielding them from fluctuations in any one—prevented accumulation of trees and other productive resources, discouraged both the extra effort and new techniques that would expand production, and in general discouraged squatters from producing much beyond subsistence requirements, any increase in population or shrinkage in nonagricultural opportunities was likely to make smallholders more desperate for cash and vulnerable to demands for labor by landowners and pressures from the state.

In fact, the variety of marketable crops being grown on the coast diminished during the early colonial years. The cultivation of rice—the staple and export crop of the south coast and an important crop in river valleys—did not survive abolition, and the coast took to importing rice from Burma.[77] Sesame had ranked with millet as the leading export of Malindi and the Lamu mainland. Although Africans in Nyanza were growing sesame as an export crop in these years, coastal people were then exporting only a trickle.[78] And while Africans in other parts of Kenya took to new crops, coastal Africans resisted the one new crop that officials and European firms were pushing—cotton.[79] New crops only caught on after the Depression had made squatters dangerously short of cash, and under those circumstances they in fact jeopardized the position of squatters.

The incentives that existed for coastal peasants to produce larger quantities of more crops with greater efficiency were dampened both by state policy and by the market dominance—itself partly a product of Government coddling—of other parts of the colony. Even when the state's efforts to control production by suppressing squatting had eased, the Government took such a rigid approach to controlling peasants through commercial and financial mechanisms that conditions remained stifling.

Upcountry farmers had the advantage of a railroad, feeder roads, an increasingly modern port at Mombasa, and steamships that were far faster and more efficient than the dhows that served other coastal ports, as well as Government subsidies and services. The Administration talked

77. PC to Chief Secr., 10 Aug. 1917, CP 39/625; Dickson, Report on Coast Production and Trade, 28 Aug. 1923, CP 56/1525; Acting Sr. Comr. to Director of Agriculture, 27 Jan. 1923, ibid.; Tanaland and Shimoni, ARs.

78. Table 6.1 and Malindi and Lamu, ARs.

79. Malindi, AR, 1908–09; Memorandum by J. E. Jones, Malindi Planter, on Native Cotton and Native Cultivation, incl. Girouard to Crewe, 27 Jan. 1910, CO 533/71; Kenya, AR, Coast 1926, p. 59.

of the need for building more roads on the coast but did little.[80] Hardly any served the Mijikenda hinterland. The area north of the Sabaki River was cut off by the absence of a bridge and the ending of sea transport directly to Mambrui, and the surplus maize of the rich Sabaki valley itself could only be brought out by porters. One official concluded that in this area the peasant's production was "limited by his porterage capacity more than by any other factor."[81] The coasting steamers that served ports like Malindi were unreliable and expensive. When Malindi's grain exports expanded in the 1920s, they were almost entirely sent off by dhow.[82]

It was not just neglect that made the competitive position of the coast so difficult. It also appears that the Government sought to keep the coastal maize-producing zones in their old niche. In British settler colonies, maize grading was often a device for protecting white settlers against Africans, whose production costs and income expectations were lower. Whatever its actual quality, "native maize" and "inferior maize" tended to become synonyms in the colonial vocabulary. At the same time that the Government first subsidized Highland maize transport, it forbade the export *by steamer* of wet or weevily maize. That gave authorities the power to confine the benefits of efficient transport to maize of which it approved. But systematic grading of maize only began with the 1920s maize boom in the Highlands, when a grading station was set up at Kilindini Harbor.[83] Maize from coastal regions could have been sent by dhow, road, or coastal steamer to Kilindini to be graded and bulked, and perhaps some of it was, but export firms and officials did not like the idea and invoked the quality control ideology to justify their position: the low quality of coastal maize risked depressing the price of Highland maize. Nor did local traders like separating grades of maize, so that

80. The most grandiose scheme for improving coastal transport predates the rise of the settler economy and came from a private businessman. He proposed building a railroad from Mombasa to Malindi. Nothing came of it (Anderson to Eliot 18, 29 July 1903, and Eliot to Lansdowne, 31 July 1903, FOCP 8192, pp. 140-42). For continued official awareness of the need for roads, see PC to Chief Secr., 5 July 1913, CP 9/295; Asst. DC, Mangea, to PC, 22 March 1914, CP 11/105.

81. Deputy Director of Agriculture to Director, 10 Sept. 1925, CP 52/1311; DC, Malindi, to Salkeld, 9 March 1923, CP 56/1525; Committee Report on Coast Production and Trade, 1923, ibid.; PC, Inspection Report, 4 July 1913, CP 64/261; Kenya, AR, 1926, Coast, p. 46; Spencer, p. 308.

82. Malindi, QR, 4th quart., 1911, 1st quart., 1912; AR, 1923, 1924; DC, Malindi, to Trade Comr., Mombasa, 17 April 1923, CP 55/1487; Red Book, 1925-26, pp. 184-85.

83. EAP, AgAR, 1909-10, p. 12; Kenya, AgAR, 1924, p. 9; Kenya, Fifth Maize Conference, 1928, pp. 9-10. On the political uses of maize grading in Rhodesia, see Palmer, *Land and Racial Domination*, p. 212.

African-grown maize was most often classed as inferior, given a lower price, and concentrated on the internal or regional market.[84]

But Government policy did not encourage the trade in maize even within the confines to which its transport and grading policies tended to push it. It would not allow the dhow trade to the Somali coast and elsewhere to operate in its accustomed manner. Just as Malindi's exports were reviving, the Government decided to revamp the currency system and in 1921 suddenly declared that Indian rupees were no longer acceptable in Kenya. This was the currency of the coastal dhow trade, and commerce was severely curtailed until the Government—leisurely—set up exchange posts in the ports. Even then, new and higher duties on the goods which dhows brought from the north sent the foreign dhows scurrying to Tanganyika and Zanzibar. The export of mangrove poles, a central element of the dhow trade, collapsed, and the post-1917 revival of agriculture at Malindi was not nearly as strong as it might have been.[85] Observers were impressed by the reviving cultivation but noted how difficult it was to sell the maize that was grown.[86]

A second limitation that peasant producers faced was in the nature of the marketing system itself, a problem fostered by the anticompetitive policies of the Government. Small-scale, itinerant traders, like those of Jamaica, were not only able to collect and distribute the very small surpluses that smallholders produced, but provided a means for families to combine trade with production. This way of doing business was anathema to the British, who thought such people "could be more profitably employed cultivating their shambas," and sought to stop itinerant trading. The Administration tried to limit the selling of grain and the purchasing of commodities to "trading centers" where licensed traders would do business.[87] This concept of commercial order dampened competition and gave the traders a fine opportunity to fix prices in the centers. Producers were sometimes forced to take credit for merchan-

84. Sr. Comr., Coast, to DC, Malindi, 3 April 1923, CP 55/1487; Spencer, p. 241; Memon, "Mercantile Intermediaries," p. 247.

85. Foreign dhow tonnage passing through Kenya fell by 76 percent between 1918 and 1923 (Red Book, 1925–26, pp. 184–85, 213). See also DC, Kilifi, to Sr. Comr., Coast, 26 Oct. 1922, CP 55/1487; Asst. DC, Kilifi, to DC, Malindi, 27 June 1923, CP 56/1525; Malindi, AR, 1923; Clayton and Savage, pp. 139–46. Mangrove pole exports fell from over £15,000 before the currency change to £5,000 afterwards. Kenya, AR, Trade, 1920–21.

86. Sr. Comr., Coast, HOR, 5 Oct. 1922, copy in Coryndon Papers, Rhodes House, Oxford University, Box 5; Sr. Comr., Report on Coast Production and Trade, 1923, CP 56/1525.

87. DC, Digo Dist., to Acting Sr. Comr., 14 May 1926, CP 52/1314; PC, circular to DCs, CP 20/103. An anti-hawker policy was in effect in Mombasa (Janmohamed, "History of Mombasa," p. 176).

dise instead of cash. The problem was most acute in the Mijikenda Reserves and was exacerbated by poor transportation.[88]

British policy made worse a structural characteristic of colonial commerce. Rural merchants had to do business with people who had little to sell and could only buy in small quantities. Only by combining the small profits of produce buying and retail selling could they survive. The merchants depended on close relationships with the wholesalers in Mombasa, who controlled the narrow range of imports—above all cotton cloth—that were the staples of commerce, and they needed to get those goods on credit. These problems were met—quite successfully—by networks based on kinship and communal ties and centered on a small number of Indian firms in Mombasa.[89] Not only did this structure of trade—combined with British fees and regulations—make it very difficult for peasants to break into trade, but the narrowness of commercial pathways gave producers less choice in how they disposed of grain. It was in the interests of traders that as much of the grain as possible be exported while as much of the goods they sold be imported, a situation which sometimes led to dislocations in the grain market that forced peasants to sell grain and later buy it back, a problem compounded by the taxation system.[90]

Indebtedness to traders would close the circle, forcing producers to sell all their grain and buy all their supplies from a single merchant. Periodic shortages of rainfall in the hinterland and heavy taxes throughout the coast in the postwar period often forced Mijikenda to borrow food on security of their next crop, and they frequently had to pay back at least double what they borrowed.[91] The inability of coastal squatters to

88. Officials looked at such practices as Indian unscrupulousness rather than as consequences of state policy. DC, Shimoni, to Sr. Comr., Coast, 5 July 1923, DC, Lamu, to Acting Sr. Comr., Coast, 24 Nov. 1922; Acting Sr. Comr., Coast, to Chief Native Comr., 11 May 1923; and Memorandum on Coastal Trade, 11 May 1923, all in CP 56/1525. A "ring of Indian merchants in Malindi" fixed prices on grain brought there. Asst. DC, Mangea, to PC, 22 March 1917, CP 11/105.

89. Zarwan, "Indian Businessmen in Kenya"; Memon, "Mercantile Intermediaries," pp. 134-44, 190-95. On the importance of firms in Mombasa to the rural trading networks, the relationship of these firms to the European import houses, and the importance of credit supplied from Mombasa, see Janmohamed, "History of Mombasa," pp. 125-27, 143-47.

90. Merchants sent grain directly to the customs houses at Malindi, Mombasa, and elsewhere, bypassing local markets and leading to grain shortages and high prices in grain-producing areas. Rabai, AR, 1914-15; Kwale, AR, 1917-18; Takaungu, AR, 1916-17; Malindi, AR, 1925; DC, Malindi, to Acting Sr. Comr., 11 May 1926, CP 52/1314.

91. DC, Kilifi, to Acting PC, 17 June 1920, DC, Lamu, to Sr. Comr., Coast, 8 March 1921; Resident Comr., Mombasa, to Sr. Comr., Coast, 3 Dec. 1924, CP 52/1277; Acting DC, Malindi, to Sr. Comr., Coast, 4 Sept. 1924, CP 27/332. In the Tana River valley, the

use land as security made them vulnerable to usurious mortgages on their crops if they had to borrow. The marketing system thus cut down on what peasants received for their produce and made the purchase of commodities fraught with the danger of debt bondage to the supplier-buyer-creditor. What the effects of indebtedness would be depended partly on whether debts could in fact be collected and defaulters pursued, thus forcing peasants into a desired pattern of cash crop production. But creditors in coastal Kenya did not have the muscle to gain more than partial control and collect more than a portion of the high interest they nominally charged; farmers often refused to pay or left the district. Especially in the poorer districts, the threat of indebtedness was a good reason to avoid becoming dependent on the market for too many commodities, above all food and tools, while interest rates that varied with the debtor's circumstances only encouraged people who incurred debts to produce less.[92]

The extent to which Mijikenda and ex-slaves were able to bypass the official trading centers and develop exchange systems of their own is, for obvious reasons, largely unknown. Tembo marketing, however, clearly did embody a network of relationships that spread outward from producers rather than from Mombasa.[93]

Nor is much known about the supply of produce to Mombasa during this period, although it would appear that Mombasa's role as an export-import center reduced its stimulating effect on local agriculture. The city clearly was a fine market for both tembo and copra. Maize and a variety of produce were also brought to town from trading centers just up the rail line in Mijikenda areas, and by road and boat from adjacent shamba areas.[94] However, the diet of the city's wealthiest residents relied heavily on imports—rice for Indians and Arabs, wheat and a great variety of food for Europeans.[95] Maize to feed African laborers came from all

riverain marketing system was particularly narrow and the indebtedness of Pokomo farmers especially severe. David Miller, "Agricultural Change on the Lower Tana: Lower Pokomoni, c. 1870–1939," Department of History, University of Nairobi, Staff Seminar Paper no. 4, 1977, pp. 10–13.

92. District officals at Malindi considered the system of cash advances against crops "one of the most formidable obstacles to progress," and it was even worse in Lamu and the Tana valley. Malindi, AR, 1925, Kwale, AR, 1920; Asst. DC, Kilifi, to Sr. Comr., Coast, 27 Sept. 1924, CP 27/332; Miller, pp. 10–13; Walter Deshler, "Land Use by the Bajun People of the Northern Kenya Coast," typescript, 1954, KNA.

93. Parkin, Palms, Wine, and Witnesses, pp. 10–12. This marketing system might be compared with that of Zanzibar, discussed in chapter 4.

94. Produce was sent from the southern Kilifi region into Mombasa but apparently not from Malindi (Malindi, AR, 1924, Kilifi, AR, 1925). Shipments from west and south of the city are mentioned in Rabai, AR, 1911–12, and Kwale, AR, 1917–18.

95. Acting Sr. Comr., Coast, Memorandum on Coastal Trade, 11 May 1923; CP 56/ 1525; Collector, Mombasa, to Acting Sub-Comr., 24 Sept. 1906, CP 94/166.

along the railroad, not just coastal districts, and the practice of some large employers of providing rations to workers diminished the importance of local markets. Surprisingly little mention is made of the Mombasa produce market in coastal district reports. The reports do mention that local producers supplied grain, as well as tembo, to European plantations, which were probably too far away from the railway terminus.[96] But because Mombasa's closest ties were upcountry and overseas, its stimulating effects on local agriculture appear to have been muted. Transport was better from the Highlands than from Malindi. Nearer to the city, labor costs were particularly high and land prices inflated by urbanization and speculation. In the neighborhood of this large, active, and land-hungry city, as a study of land usage in 1907 found, as reports from the early 1920s mentioned, and as a visitor can still see today, that is a considerable amount of fertile wasteland.[97] Tenant farmers near Mombasa could still choose between selling their labor or their produce to the city, but the balance between the two was set at a relatively low level. In the 1920s, as more workers and more maize came from upcountry, it got worse.

A third damper on peasant production was supposed to have been a prod. More effective tax collection had helped stimulate the Giriama rebellion of 1914, and increasing revenue was the one success the Administration had, adding a burden of over Rs 40,000 to defeat and famine. After World War I, hut and poll taxes were raised sharply, from Rs 3 to Rs 5 in 1920, to Rs 8 (equal to, officially, Shs 16) in 1921. The rise—which accompanied wage reductions and inflation—caused hardship and unrest in many parts of Kenya. On the coast its impact was compounded by the Administration's decision to collect it—in cash— right after the harvest. This forced peasants to sell their crops when the market was glutted and prices low; quite often they had to sell so much grain to pay the tax bill that they then later had to buy back grain on credit, falling progressively into debt. In 1922, the hut and poll tax collected at Malindi was nearly a third of the value of the maize sent from that port; in 1923 a smaller harvest increased the proportion nearer to half.[98] Maize sent from the port, of course, is not a total measure of peasant income; on the other hand, Malindi was a particularly well-

96. Labour Inspection Reports, 20 March 1915, CP 38/601; PC, Inspection Report, Malindi, 17 July 1915, CP 17/61; Kilifi, AR, 1925.

97. Hollis, Report on Native Rights, 1907, CO 533/32; map of land usage and holdings on the coast, 1907, MR 760, PRO Mombasa, AR, 1921. Medical Officer to Principal Medical Officer, 30 April 1922, MD/37/390, KNA.

98. Report on Coast Production and Trade by Select Committee of the Chamber of Commerce of Mombasa, 1923, CP 56/1525; DC, Shimoni, to Sr. Comr., Coast, 5 July 1923, ibid.; DC, Lamu, to Sr. Comr., Coast, 11 Sept. 1924, CP 27/332. Hut-tax figures are from Acting DC, Malindi, to Sr. Comr., Coast, 8 July 1924, CP 61/132.

endowed district. Taxation was making it difficult for Africans to purchase imports, let alone accumulate capital and make investments in agriculture. In the most marginal areas, it was hardly worthwhile selling anything, better to be punished for nonpayment of the tax. It soon became clear to officials that this overbearing approach to taxation was having the reverse of its intended effect, and their thinking was aided by severe disturbances in Nairobi. The rate was reduced to Shs 12 in 1923, still double the prewar rate. In 1930, according to rough estimates of the income and expenses of Giriama in Kilifi District, 59 percent of total income went to pay hut taxes—a tax bracket few Americans face. Import taxes—designed to hit the cheap goods that Africans bought more heavily than goods sought by settlers—also stayed high.[99]

Finally, both peasants and landlords were hurt by the diminishing of income-earning opportunities that supplemented agriculture. Hunting and the ivory trade had once been quite important in parts of the coast, but they were quickly choked off, except for Europeans. Collecting rubber or gum copal had also been a good business, especially in times of agricultural crises, and forests, at the very least, provided fuel and other items that would otherwise have to be bought. The most lucrative of such enterprises was cutting mangrove bark and poles (called boritis) from the swamps along the coast. Boriti cutting remained the staple of the dhow trade. In the early twentieth century, mangrove poles were the most valuable export from Lamu, and they were important at Vanga and at certain spots north of Malindi. However, British attitudes toward such bounties of nature echoed the period of the rise of capitalism, when landowners slowly cut off the access to the resources of forests and untilled commonage that had cut down the expenses and increased the incomes of tenants, making their livelihood more marginal and driving many into wage labor.[100] Early on, the Administration granted huge concessions to European companies for rights to exploit the forests, and tenders were extended for several years at a time to European and Indian firms to cut mangrove poles and bark.[101] Because of high fees and

99. Seyidie, AR, 1921; Kenya, Economic and Financial Commission, First Interim Report, 1922, p. 2; Hobley, "Native Problems, " p. 200; Kilifi, AR, 1930. On taxation in Kenya generally, see Brett, pp. 188-195, and Clayton and Savage, pp. 143-46.

100. Salim, pp. 105-06. For English comparisons, see Hay et al., *Albion's Fatal Tree*, and Thompson, *Whigs and Hunters*. The effects of similar exclusions, particularly to hunting, on African people are stressed in Vail, "Ecology and History: The Example of Eastern Zambia," and John Tosh, "Lango Agriculture during the Early Colonial Period: Land and Labour in a Cash-Crop Economy," *JAH* 19 (1978): 415-39.

101. See the concessions marked on Map MR 760, 1907, PRO. Not much came of the forest concessions. An example of a mangrove bark concession is the grant to British East African Trading and Development Syndicate of rights at Kilifi Creek for two years, for Rs 300 per year plus 10 percent *ad velorum* royalties. This company also had a 21-year timber

requirements that royalties be paid in advance of sale, most Arabs and Swahili lacked capital to obtain tenders, and could only cut poles as laborers or subcontractors. By the time the Administration relaxed the monopolistic concession policy in 1924—issuing permits for small quantities of poles—its currency and duty policies had already grievously damaged the entire dhow trade.[102]

In the early 1920s, officials filled file after file with reports on the backwardness of coastal agriculture, and they were well aware of the problems discussed here. Their thinking, however, had only gone far enough to notice bad results, not to ponder underlying causes. Yet there is logic in their obtuseness, a line of reasoning followed in varying ways by other colonial powers as well in the first decades of the century, and in some cases later than that. The difficulty they faced was that economic decisions were far too important to be left to the peasant or the petty trader. At times, peasants produced bountiful export crops and presented colonial regimes with a fait accompli, but at other times they resisted the introduction of cash crops or abandoned export crops they had once embraced. Peasants and petty traders could be too responsive to price changes, too able to survive on the fringes of an export economy. To Kenyan officials, Africans could not be allowed to have "unrestricted choice in the matter of whether they shall lead useful or useless lives," and a life was not useful unless it helped to "add to the wealth of the country as a whole."[103] In such terms, the small-scale marketing mechanisms that were closely linked to peasant production and peasant social networks were anarchic and useless, but the anticompetitive trading center represented commercial order.[104] Every householder had to

concession for 100 square miles of forest near Takaungu, for Rs 1,500 per year. See a number of such concessions in Reg., Mal, 67 A of 1904, 9 and 10 A of 1905, 33-35, 45 A of 1906. On rubber regulations, see Salim, p. 108. Rubber tapping by Africans died a more or less natural death after 1913, when prices fell.

102. Inspection Report, Malindi, June 7-9, 1913, PRB, Kilifi, KFI/11; Acting Sr. Comr., Coast, to Coconut Committee, 11 Jan. 1924; CP 56/1525; Col. Secr. to Conservator of Forests, 1 April 1924, ibid.

103. Asst. DC, Rabai, to PC, 19 March 1919, CP 38/607; Hobley, circular to DCs, 1915, CP 20/103. The need of the state and commercial interests to make peasants' decisions for them has also been stressed in studies of India, and moneylenders and landlords were instrumental in making sure that crop choices would lean toward export or marketable items. Neil Charlesworth, "Rich Peasants and Poor Peasants in Late Nineteenth Century Maharashtra," and Colin Fisher "Planters and Peasants: The Ecological Context of Agrarian Unrest on the Indigo Plantations of North Bohar, 1820-1920," in Clive Dewey and A. G. Hopkins, eds., The Imperial Impact: Studies in the Economic History of Africa and India (London, 1978), pp. 97-131.

104. The British preference for "orderly marketing" conducted by "reputable" traders is stressed by Cyril Ehrlich, "Building and Caretaking: Economic Policy in British Tropical Africa," Economic History Review 26 (1973): 649-67. The benefits of small-scale traders to small-scale producers are discussed by Mintz, Caribbean Transformations, pp. 180-224.

make some contribution to the country's wealth, not for personal gain but out of the compulsion of taxation policies. That coastal peasants often produced more than they had to, owed little to the wisdom of the state, which created so many disincentives to production and so many obstacles to peasants' capital accumulation.

The restrictive commercial policies of the Kenyan Government were similar to the efforts of the state in Zanzibar to restrict the development of a varied and interconnected local economy, directing resources toward clove production. The Zanzibar Government preserved and reshaped a landlord class and a merchant class whose status and income depended on the continual export of large quantities of cloves. The Government of Kenya—having failed to subdue squatters or find a suitable planter class—sought to make the constraints on peasant production and marketing nearly as tight as those it had wished to impose on labor.

These policies were actually less direct than some attempts to control the production of marketable goods. The Belgians, the French, the Germans, and the Portuguese tried—often after the failure of other kinds of schemes—to make cultivation of specific crops compulsory, with prices and production quotas fixed by the state.[105] British policy in Kenya relied on a minimum contribution—albeit a substantial minimum—to the cash economy, plus the restriction of access to certain resources and to markets to state-sanctioned, narrowly defined channels.

Compulsory cultivation generally worked poorly, largely because it was expensive to carry control into the fields, and changes lasted no longer than the official presence. Restrictive marketing met with the resistance of peasants who were only partially dependent on markets. That is why the attempt to link the colonial state to a landowning

---

105. In Katanga, the Belgians tried to foster capitalist agriculture, first with European planters then with Africans, before reverting to compulsory cultivation. In the Ivory Coast, the refusal of Baule to collect rubber when prices were low helped lead the way to compulsory cash cropping. In Mozambique, a British-owned sugar company—anxious that government demands for cotton not give men in the region an alternative to wage labor—devised a scheme of government-business cooperation which foisted compulsory cotton growing onto women. In parts of West Africa, cash crop production preceded colonization, and trading firms had a vested interest in the status quo; but the effects of monopolies, licensing regulations, and produce boards on shaping the ability of producers to make decisions remain controversial. Bogumil Jewsiewicki, "Unequal Development: Capitalism and the Katanga Economy, 1919–40," in Palmer and Parsons, The Roots of Rural Poverty, pp. 317–45; Weiskel, "Labor in the Emergent Periphery," p. 218; Jane Guyer, "The Food Economy and French Colonial Rule in Central Cameroun," JAH 19 (1978): 577–97; Leroy Vail and Landeg White, "'Tawani, Machambero!': Forced Cotton and Rice Growing on the Zambezi," ibid., pp. 239–63; Iliffe, Modern History of Tanganyika, pp. 168–69; Hopkins, An Economic History of West Africa; Bernstein, "African Peasantries."

class—whether European, Arab, or African—whose status and wealth depended on export production was so logical, and why the failure to maintain control over plantation labor in Kenya looms so large.[106] Landowners could not grow the copra and the cotton officials wanted them to; peasants would not. In turn, the restrictiveness of British policy lost its logic, for it only undermined alternatives to a commercial structure that was itself weak. The state, trying to push people into an export economy, encouraged them to avoid it.

The economic history of colonial African can be only partly understood in terms of the response of individuals to global opportunities and trends or in terms of the role of the state in opening markets, liberalizing the exchange of land, and removing restrictions on the movement of labor. The partial success of the Zanzibari economy was a success in the exercise of state power and class domination, a success in controlling a labor force. The weakness of export agriculture on the Kenyan coast was a failure of power, discipline, and repression, as well as a failure to see economic change in altogether different terms.

All the constraints of transportation, marketing, licensing, and taxation compounded problems intrinsic to the system of squatter agriculture, which was itself the product of the state's rigidifying landownership without maintaining control over labor. The caution with which squatters approached new crops or improvement of their land lay not in the supposedly conservative nature of the peasant, but in the supposedly modernizing structure around him. The insecurity of squatters' access to land compounded every other risk and constraint and made improvement as dangerous as failure. Squatters would not plant trees for fear of losing not only the trees but the land. They would not plant rice because it only grew in specific places that others owned and could always try to control and because rice cultivation required a degree of social organization that they, faced with the insecurities and conflicts of squatter agriculture, could not develop.[107]

---

106. Uganda is sometimes cited as an example of pro-peasant British policy, but in its early phases the policy can more accurately be described as pro-landlord—only the prospective landlords were African. In actuality, land policy—as in Kenya—was not enough to foster capitalist relations of production, and British policy moved toward controlling marketing and the licensing of cotton gins. As in Kenya, this policy often had the reverse of its intended effect, encouraging peasant resistance. The Lango, for example, only took to cotton cultivation after a lengthy period of reluctance, when the market became more competitive, prices rose, and alternative sources of income—less closely linked to the colonial state—dried up. Brett; Tosh, "Lango Agriculture."

107. Rebecca Scott (personal communication) found that the tensions of tenancy in postemancipation Cuba caused owners and tenants of similar-sized farms to make different crop choices. Owners of small farms were more likely to plant trees and grow cash crops; tenants were more likely to stick to subsistence crops. Rice tenancy in Southeast Asia

Squatters did grow maize, and their choice of it as both a subsistence and export crop can be explained in terms of William Allan's concept of the "normal surplus" in a situation of considerable insecurity. Farmers devoted more labor and more land to growing subsistence crops then their needs and average expected yields would dictate, so that they would survive in a below-average year and have a surplus in a normal one. Concentrating on producing a normal surplus did not imply any lack of responsiveness to economic incentives but a need to worry about risks—social as well as ecological—and this pattern of production must be considered part of a spectrum of adaptations by farmers.[108] By selling the excess of a crop he ate, the smallholder could obtain cash while making his subsistence more secure, avoiding reliance for essentials on a marketing system that was rigged against him. The expansions in maize exports before the war and in the 1920s reflect the normal surplus of Mijikenda squatters who had just moved to land where the surplus was larger and more normal. But the nature of squatter agriculture made experiments with new crops all the more risky. The failure of cotton—a crop whose peak labor demands coincide with those of grain—in the years after abolition resulted partly from the uncertainties of tenant-landlord relations at that time; and people who did plant cotton were in fact forced to buy at least some of their food at high prices in the market. In the late 1920s, squatter-landlord relations were more stable and Mijikenda squatters had learned that, thanks to more reliable rainfall on the coastal strip, their prudent overplanting of maize could be reduced. But only when the price of maize fell drastically during the Depression and the normal surplus brought in little cash did cotton planting actually take off.[109] Sesame, once an important coastal crop, declined for similar reasons: it was not a staple. Both crops were, at this very period, being

developed under vastly different ecological and demographic conditions and in situations where landlords had far more control. J. C. Scott, *Moral Economy of the Peasant;* Clifford Geertz, *Agricultural Involution: The Processes of Ecological Change in Indonesia* (Berkeley, 1963).

108. William Allan, *The African Husbandman* (Edinburgh, 1965), pp. 38–48. A rather literal example of Allan's concept can be found among maize farmers in the Sabaki valley. They planted both on high ground and in the flood plain. If the river flooded owing to excess rain during the growing season, the high ground crops kept the farmers alive; but if the river did not flood, they had a large surplus. Deputy Director of Agriculture to Director, 10 Sept. 1925, CP 52/1311. Iliffe (p. 313) emphasizes the place of the normal surplus concept within a range of behavior.

109. The disgust of Africans who substituted cotton for maize in 1908 is noted in EAP, AgAR, 1908–09, p. 17. Overplanting of maize as a response to the threat of drought and its consequences for cotton cultivation are discussed in Malindi, AR, 1928. Iliffe (p. 267) argues that the introduction of cotton to Sukumaland, in Tanganyika, was hindered by the need that it be planted at the same time as grain, while labor for cash crops was most readily available when the staple was bananas. Tosh also mentions the importance of competing demands on labor in choosing between cotton and grain. Both the particularities of crops and of social structures must be taken into account.

grown by peasants elsewhere in East Africa. Because squatters (and Mijikenda in the hinterland as well) were in a tenuous economic situation compounded by a restrictive economic structure, they had to put subsistence production first in order to avoid too much dependence on markets and the dangers of debt bondage.[110] And because of the nature of land tenure, squatters had to avoid being tied to any one piece of land or any one landlord. In short, they had to grow a subsistence crop and an annual crop before they could think of anything else. Similarly, when coastal people sought wage labor, their choices revealed a desire to diversify options, minimize dependence on any one employer or cash-earning activity, and avoid jeopardizing access to land or subsistence production.

The economics of survival dominated peasant production, above all in the case of squatters. Landlords, too, were struggling to survive, but the life they were trying to preserve was far different from that of a peasant. The landowners who did best were those who did not produce at all but owned urban real estate in Mombasa. The most productive grain planters of the 1880s, those of Mambrui, fell into poverty, left the area, or cultivated alongside the squatters who were now growing most of the grain. The town fell into "utter decay," and the traders—not even able to tap squatter grain because of bad transport—went elsewhere. In nearby Malindi, nearly half the mashamba were not being cultivated by their owners, yet at the same time a District Officer wrote that his district was "from an agricultural point of view . . . one of the most prosperous in the Protectorate." Squatters were responsible for the cultivation; landlords collected a little rent and sold tembo. Some Arabs could not even afford to pay the non-native poll tax.[111]

Not every Arab or Swahili had been a large-scale planter relying on slave labor. In the aftermath of abolition, many small Arab and Swahili farms remained in cultivation, tended by family labor. Officials in Takaungu noted a burst of cultivation following the division of land among the Mazrui, apparently a consequence of individuals' acquiring security of tenure in a world that had gone topsy-turvy. One informant of Mazrui origin told me that in this rural area, in contrast to the more

110. What coastal squatters feared actually happened to sharecroppers in the southern United States. By keeping plots small, landlords made sure that fertilizer would have to be bought, while concentration of land also meant the rents were high. These, and other factors, insured that croppers would have to borrow, and once they borrowed they had to grow more cotton—which they could sell—and less corn—which they ate. In turn, they had to buy more food and became quickly entrapped in debt bondage which gave landowners and merchants direct power over the choices of crop made by the sharecroppers. See Wright and Kunreuther, "Cotton, Corn, and Risk in the Nineteenth Century," *Journal of Economic History* 35 (1975): 526–51. and Ransom and Sutch, esp. pp. 149–70.

111. Malindi, AR, 1911–12, 1915–16, 1920–21, 1923; PC, Inspection Report, June 1913, PRB, Kilifi; Kenya, AR, 1926, Coast, p. 7.

status-conscious urban centers, Mazrui women shared in the farming when they were needed.[112] Nevertheless, without slaves much less land could be cultivated, and much Mazrui property was sold, allowed to go to bush, or left to squatters. For many Arab and Swahili agriculturalists, it was possible to survive as smallholders, but not as planters.

The failure of the planters of coastal Kenya had little to do with their inability to adjust to wage labor and much to do with the unwilling-ness of the state to organize on their behalf a complex structure that would pressure and channel labor and direct resources to them and away from others. Yet by strengthening the land rights of a portion of the old aristocracy, the state insured that the people who actually grew the grain would lose some of their surplus—albeit a modest amount— would live in danger of losing their access to land, and would have to develop social relations with a group that regarded itself as religiously, socially, and culturally superior. The more commercialized the land situation, as in Mombasa, the more immediate was the threat of expro-priation and the greater the paralysis of agriculture. But even in Malindi the fears, tensions, and antagonisms inherent in the squatter system lay just beneath the surface. Meanwhile, British policy and the structural unevenness of the colonial economy rendered the squatters' position all the more unsure. Out of the struggles between landlords and squatters over what crops would be grown, in what manner, and for whose profit—a struggle shaped by periodic interventions of the state— emerged an economic structure with little potential for change.

The much-lamented "backwardness" of coastal agriculture in the 1920s lay not in the dire poverty of its people, for most were probably better off materially than slaves had been, and they certainly had more control over how they worked.[113] In fact, coastal people had more con-trol over when and on what basis they entered the labor force than many Kenyans. Backwardness—vis-à-vis other parts of Kenya and other parts of the world which are themselves often termed "backward"—consisted of an economic structure that stifled increased productivity, investment, innovation, and capital formation, and a social structure that made eco-nomic stagnation a necessity for social stability. When innovation did take place—the extension of cotton planting and the beginning of cashew tree cultivation in the 1930s—it was the result of increasing pov-erty and the cause of increasing conflict.

112. Seyidie, AR, 1912–13; Takaungu, AR, 1908–09; Ahmed Abdalla Mazrui (MSA). On the other hand, women in the Lamu area would not work in the fields.

113. Similarly, the incomes of blacks in the southern United States rose after abolition, and the hated gang-labor system disappeared, but a system of class domination which prolonged social oppression and stifled economic growth was maintained. For different views of these developments, see Ransom and Sutch, and Wiener, *Social Origins of the New South*.

7   Epilogue
Cloves, Cashews, and Conflict

This has been a study of the penetration of capitalism into a part of Africa. It has focused on an explicit attempt—pushed by liberal opinion in England and implemented by the colonial state—to transform the relations of production in an African society. The state was less interested in bringing Africans into world markets—a process that had already gone quite far—than in enforcing the rights of landowners and facilitating the commercialization of land, creating a rural working class committed to full-time wage labor, and ensuring that the state could predict and substantially control the production process. The transformation that took place was indeed profound, but not in the way that either the antislavery ideologues or the colonial state had intended.

The implications of the social and economic changes that took place between 1890 and 1925 can be only partially understood by taking a snapshot in the year 1925. The best measure of the importance of the structures that were shaped during that period is the way they established the parameters within which different groups responded to the enormous changes of the ensuing decades. The planter class of Zanzibar reacted both to the Depression of the 1930s and the boom of the 1950s in much the same way—by cultivating clove trees more intensely. The standoff between landlords and tenants on the Kenyan coast inhibited the planting of trees or the introduction of new crops, and when such developments did take place they led to the kind of conflict that both sides had feared. The crucial role that the state had come to play in maintaining economic structures and class power emerged most clearly when the decline of the colonial state in the 1950s called all those structures into question. Finally, the lines along which classes began to form first emerged in the period after abolition with the development of a complex interplay among squatters, migrants from near and far, peasants, and urban workers set against the evolving connection of the state and the planters; and in the period after that, the new kinds of economic relationships increasingly gave rise to new forms of political consciousness and collective action.[1] A brief and selective look at economic change

---

1. As E. P. Thompson has written, "If we stop history at a given point, then there are no classes but simply a multitude of individuals with a multitude of experiences. But if we watch these men over an adequate period of social change, we observe patterns in their relationships, their ideas, and their institutions." *Making of the English Working Class*, p. 11.

and class conflict in the years after 1925 will help to explain the significance of what went on before.

What would have happened had the state more relentlessly blocked
the squatters' access to land and pressured them into working for landlords? Or if it had not tried to make slaves into a working class and left
landlords to develop forms of tenancy and personal dependence on
their own? Or if it had permitted peasants to respond to market incentives in their own way, without the threat of exactions and control by
landlords or the heavy-handed efforts of the state to narrow the decisions that cultivators were allowed to make?[2] One of these policies might
have polarized society more than it in fact was; another might have
polarized it less. But any one of them could very well have resulted in
more crops being produced and sold, at least for a time, than the policies
that were actually followed. Robert Brenner, however, is firm in asserting which approach lay behind the continual quest for improved productivity and the ability to make qualitative changes in economic structures that developed in capitalist Western Europe: the exclusion of
cultivators from access to land and the consequent creation of a working
class. When labor as well as its products were exclusively commodities,
the pressure to compete became something the landowner could not
avoid, whereas the peasant, the feudal lord, or the slaveowner could
compete aggressively or not.[3]

Brenner, perhaps, has too static a view of peasantries and underesti-
mates the possibilities for accumulation and change through peasant
production.[4] There is, as Barrington Moore, Jr., has emphasized, more
than one road toward capitalist development, roads which lead to particular kinds of contradictions and conflicts as well as particular forms of
material progress.[5] But the British, at the time of abolition in East Africa,

2. Such alternatives are not entirely hypothetical but reflect some of the variations in
responses by governments and landowning classes within, for example, Latin America.
The differences should not be seen in voluntaristic terms, however, for they reflect the
actual opportunities and power that landlords and states had in different regions. For one
analysis of variations in how landlords tried to increase their exploitation of land and
workers, see Katz, "Labor Conditions on Haciendas in Porfirian Mexico."

3. Brenner, "Origins of Capitalist Development," and "Agrarian Class Structure and
Economic Development in Pre-Industrial Europe," *Past and Present* 70 (1976):30–75.

4. On the possibilities for change in peasant economies in Europe, see E. Le Roy
Ladurie, "Symposium: Agrarian Class Structure and Economic Development in Pre-
Industrial Europe," *Past and Present* 79 (1978):59; in the West Indies, Marshall, "Notes on
Peasant Development"; and in Africa, Ranger, "Growing from the Roots," and Lionel
Cliffe, "Labour Migration and Peasant Differentiation: Zambian Experiences," *Journal of
Peasant Studies* 5 (1978):326–46.

5. Barrington Moore, Jr., *Social Origins of Dictatorship and Democracy: Lord and Peasant in
the Making of the Modern World* (Boston, 1966). In the southern United States after the Civil

chose to follow one road: to foster the division of society into landowners and landless workers.[6] More specifically, they chose to follow a variant of what Moore calls the Prussian Road, based on the alliance of a landowning class and the state which expands production by strengthening authoritarian social relations and engaging in repressive action to tie down a labor force. In a colonial context, the state may be the dominant partner, using a planter class to solve problems of supervision and control of a labor force and committing the entire economic structure to producing a narrow range of commodities for an imperial economic system. In Zanzibar, the state tried both to insure the dependence of the planter class on it and the dominance of that class over the labor force. In Kenya, the rules of landownership—backed up by restrictive but ineffectively used labor laws—were intended to create a new planter class with greater potential than the old. But in different ways, both attempts to travel the Prussian Road ended in a washout. The planters of Zanzibar survived as a class but failed to establish firm control over when and how laborers worked, did not move down any road at all in the direction of economic development, and later proved unable to control the state themselves. In Kenya, neither old nor new landowners got even that far. These failures force us to focus on what the real bases of capitalist development—in its distinct variants—are, to examine how a planter class and the state control access to land, recruit and discipline labor, and limit the choices of workers and peasants, and to see how rural people resist these actions.

Once the state had failed to keep ex-slaves and others off the land and make them work regularly and steadily, its more cautious efforts to impose its conception of labor and commerce had the reverse of their intended effect: the state ended up by encouraging the preservation of precapitalist relations of production and discouraging participation in the market. Not only did the unresolved struggle over land and labor

---

War, the way in which planters exploited labor led to a pattern of development distinct from that of the North and also shaped different patterns of ideology and politics. The Prussian Road did not bypass industrialization but implied that the landowning class shaped the way it took place, avoiding conflicts with its demand for agricultural labor and extending its authoritarian approach into industry. Such an analysis is quite germane to the evolution of South Africa as well. Wiener, *Social Origins of the New South;* Billings, *Planters and the Making of a 'New South';* Stanley Trapido, "South Africa in a Comparative Study of Industrialization," *Journal of Development Studies* 7 (1971): 309-20.

6. This was not a road the British followed everywhere, and many students of African history distinguish between their "West African model"—peasant production of cash crops—and the "South African model"—white settler ownership and African labor. Yet more stress should be given to the process of production than to the race of the planters. The question remains: did peasant production necessarily represent a British success, or the failure of the colonial state to develop a class of African producers and businessmen who would act like good capitalists?

thwart the ambitions of the state, but the stagnation which the conflict helped to induce prevented peasants from adapting to new stresses or increasing their own productivity. Hence, changes from without, such as market fluctuations or competition from more dynamic regions, or from within, such as population growth, threatened to undermine the partial autonomy of peasants and make them more vulnerable to demands for their labor.

In the nineteenth century, the incorporation of the coast of East Africa into world markets had led to a slave-labor system and a landed aristocracy. The colonial state, a half-century or so after the development of plantations, imposed the central features of capitalism on that aristocracy: wage labor and freehold land titles. But the Zanzibar Administration's belief that such an aristocracy was needed to preserve order and direct a labor force, combined with its reluctance to take a step that was vital to the creation of a rural proletariat—forceful eviction of people with no title to land—led instead to the restructuring and reinforcement of relations of dependence on plantations. The favorable conditions of the world market in cloves, the control by a small planter class of a large proportion of all clove trees, the narrowness of opportunities for cultivators to earn cash, the state's determined efforts to direct labor to clove plantations, and the interests of merchant-creditors in preserving the plantation system froze that aristocracy in a position of economic domination and hindered the emergence of more varied agriculture or a more effective commercial system.[7] In coastal Kenya, the state helped an old aristocracy to profit from the ownership of land more than from its productive use and denied the actual cultivators full and secure access to resources and markets. In both areas, landlords needed a steady cash income more than ever and relied on these dependent relationships in order to get it. But while the landlords' need for dependents remained great, their political and social importance—and hence their control—was eroded: no longer were they either tyrants or protectors. The complex social ties of client to patron increasingly came to revolve around a single resource—land.[8] Landowners were not, as in sugar production, providing any capital beyond land or trees or bringing

7. The failure of a commercial revolution in agriculture, Moore argues (p. 477), left peasant institutions intact and subject to the stresses and strains that led to peasant revolutions.

8. Moore contends that both the outside observer and the peasant himself can tell whether the lord is giving something in return for his privileges, and hence that "exploitation is in principle an objective notion" (ibid., p. 471). The importance of the lord's ceasing to perform his old functions for his dependents is stressed by Migdal, *Peasants, Politics, and Revolution*, p. 104; Scott, *Moral Economy of the Peasant*, p. 51; and Manfred Hildermeier, "Agrarian Social Protest, Populism and Economic Development: Some Problems and Results from Recent Studies," *Social History* 4 (1979): 323-24.

in important technology; they did nothing the peasants could not also do, and in fact did. Landowners had become both weak and parasitic.

That is a dangerous combination. Stunted agrarian capitalism has been particularly conductive to upheaval. It subjected workers and peasants to the demands of expanding markets, which landlords could only meet by stepping up their exactions and repression; it stripped away the veneer of paternalism that had once tempered social relations between landlords and tenants; and it rendered ineffective the protection of community and kinship, forcing peasants and workers to develop new patterns of association and self-protection that reflected the nature of economic and social domination; yet it frequently failed to make landlords rich and powerful enough to contain new challenges.[9]

But in 1925, Zanzibar and coastal Kenya seemed remote from the tensions that had already appeared in some agrarian societies and were soon to spread. In part, the apparent tranquility reflected the fact that the problems of the present at least represented a marked improvement over the oppression of the past, rather than the undermining of hitherto relatively independent cultivators. Even for Mijikenda and Wahadimu, the price of independence in the nineteenth century had been exclusion from the best land and from the most lucrative markets, so that access to plantation areas offered advantages as long as the cultivators still had the choice of *not* pursuing these options. Ex-slaves and others took far more effective advantage of the weakness of landlords, the indecisiveness of the state, and opportunities in markets than the British thought they were capable of doing.

Yet the stability of the social structures of both colonies depended on the failure of development along capitalist lines. Such stability was fragile. Misfortune threatened to throw owners and workers alike into penury and make the former all the more eager, although not necessarily able, to appropriate more of the remaining surplus. Prosperity threatened to make land into a scarcer resource, encouraging landlords to calculate carefully how much they could extract from tenants in rent and from workers in labor, and giving them greater power to do so. The alternation of boom and bust was even more likely to undermine the delicate relations of rural society, exposing landlords and tenants more fully to the vagaries of world markets and weakening the mechanisms by which both groups protected themselves. These were brittle

9. Mintz argues that it is not landlessness per se which leads to the formation of a rural working class, but "landlessness in the context of rapidly expanding capitalist enterprise," which engenders an actual transformation in relations of production ("The Rural Proletariat and the Problem of the Rural Proletarian Consciousness," p. 309. See also Hildermeier, pp. 319–32). There are a growing number of case studies that discuss the relationship of capitalism to agrarian revolt, including Scott and Eric Wolf, *Peasant Wars in the Twentieth Century* (New York, 1969).

economies. The smallest question—whether to plant a clove or cashew nut tree—became questions not just of marginal utility but of class power.

How such contradictions within agrarian societies led to the development of rural political movements and conflict has been an intriguing and elusive question. Were landless workers on capitalist estates, relatively independent "middle peasants," or tenants of backward and oppressive landlords the most likely to unite to overthrow a system that impoverished or threatened them? The problem with many answers to such questions is that they attempt to explain the dynamics of political movements by reference to static economic categories. In particular, an analysis of the shaping of classes and the emergence of class conflict in rural areas requires going beyond the concept of the peasant as a social type and the peasant movement as a political type.[10]

There was no simple transition in Zanzibar and coastal Kenya from communal cultivator to peasant or worker, nor any neat division between categories of agriculturalists. Mijikenda from the coastal hinterland, ex-slave squatters on Arab land, and Wapemba who had acquired a few clove trees entered peasant production from different directions and lived and worked under different conditions, sharing above all a carefully guarded partial autonomy in the way they used land. Then, too, wage labor was an essential part of the economic lives of many of these people, and it was becoming more so. In that aspect of their economic lives, people from the coast and its nearby hinterland were joined by Nyamwezi in Zanzibar or upcountry Kenyans in Mombasa.

This was not a homogeneous mass of people who shared community life and a traditional concept of economic justice that was now being challenged or a class of people who were defined by a common work situation. Who was really a peasant, who a worker, who a farmer are much less interesting questions than that of how participation of different people in different ways in a single complex and variegated economic structure came to define new social bonds, new goals, and new kinds of struggle throughout a wider social field.[11]

To explain how agrarian unrest became revolution requires taking the analysis to the level of the state. Theda Skocpol makes the simple but frequently ignored point that although peasants may often have good

10. One of the most ambitious, stimulating, but ultimately ahistorical and mechanical efforts along these lines is Jeffery M. Paige, *Agrarian Revolution: Social Movements and Export Agriculture in the Underdeveloped World* (New York, 1975). Eric Wolf and Sidney Mintz are more historical, subtle, and penetrating in their studies, but sometimes lapse into static, predictive generalizations about who is likely to do what. Wolf, *Peasant Wars;* Eric Wolf and Sidney Mintz, "Haciendas and Plantations in Middle America and the Antilles," *Social and Economic Studies* 6 (1957):386–412.

11. Berry ("Risk Aversion and Rural Class Formation") argues that the attempts of peasants and workers to diversify the way they obtain money and food can lead to the

reason to rebel, only rarely do they have a chance of doing so success-fully.[12] The crisis of the state that buffeted most of Africa in the 1960s—a part of the worldwide process of decolonization—was thus cru-cial, for it exposed the vulnerability of the state at exactly the time when the stakes involved in controlling it were mounting. In an increasingly tense economic and social situation, landowners needed the intervention of police forces and courts to preserve their principal asset, and in Zan-zibar planters needed the help of the state to obtain labor. A government that regarded Arab and Swahili land titles as illegitimate would mean the undoing of the landlords, and their creditors as well. But a state that would vigorously intervene on behalf of the planters could bring disaster to squatters, as the governments in southern Africa in fact did.

But the relationship of agrarian conflicts to the state differed in Zan-zibar and coastal Kenya. In Zanzibar, the clove economy was virtually coterminous with the nation, and the question of who would control the state became vital in the 1950s, while in Kenya both coastal landlords and squatters had been peripheral to the state and were likely to remain so. Agrarian conflict was still endemic to coastal Kenya, but in Zanzibar, escalating disorder culminated in the overthrow of the newly indepen-dent state in 1964 and the destruction of the plantation system. It was a small-scale revolution compared to some, too easily won for the revo-lutionary movement to become internally strong or to clarify its ideology and plans, but the patterns of social and political action leading up to it still reveal the long and complex process of the coming together of a class.

ZANZIBAR

In 1962, the outgoing colonial Government of Zanzibar—now fully im-bued with the idea that its mission was to develop a backward

---

shaping of an "underclass consciousness" across a wide social field. This movement be-tween wage labor and peasant agriculture is not necessarily transitional but represents a distinct economic and cultural type, with important implications for the nature of class formation. Sidney Mintz, "The Plantation as a Socio-cultural Type," in Pan-American Union, *Plantation Systems*, p. 43. See also Richard Frucht, "A Caribbean Social Type: Neither 'Peasant' nor 'Proletarian,'" *Social and Economic Studies* 13 (1967): 295–300; Dun-can and Rutledge, *Land and Labour in Latin America*, p. 5. Such arguments offer a fuller understanding of rural movements than interpretations that stress the homogeneity of rural masses or the universal acceptance of a "moral economy." Paige, p. 34; Scott.

12. Currently, crises of the postcolonial states most often enable long-simmering agra-rian conflicts to shatter state structures in ways that parallel the revolutions that toppled anciens regimes. Theda Skocpol argues that such crises give scope both to peasant action and to marginal political elites who can use them to consolidate mass support, turning unrest into decisive action at the national level. *States and Social Revolutions* (Cambridge, 1979).

economy—commissioned a study of goals and possibilities for economic change. It is hard to read this document without a sense of déjà vu: neither the problems of the economy nor the terms in which officials saw them had changed very much since the 1920s.[13] Zanzibar was still deriving virtually all of its export earnings from cloves and coconuts, mostly from the "highly vulnerable" clove markets of Indonesia and India. The planters were still living off their old trees and had little capital to invest in anything new. The local market was small, and marketing systems had only been developed to accommodate cloves and coconuts. Since Indians—to whom the planters were still indebted—had been largely forbidden from acquiring land, there was inadequate security for loans. Once again the possibility of a land bank was suggested. That these problems stemmed from the plantation system was disregarded; indeed, the authors discussed with apparent regret the peculiar inheritance customs of Islam that had broken up large holdings in Pemba. The report noted that relations between landlords and squatters had grown tense; its solution was to define more clearly the role of each.[14]

In fact, the clove economy had become more involuted since the great boom of the early 1920s.[15] The loss of European markets and then the world Depression forced producers to pick and sell more cloves in order to maintain their income, which in turn—since Zanzibar held most of the world market—accelerated the fall of prices. But the worldwide boom in tropical products after World War II had a similar effect: more cloves than ever were produced. In 1950, reports of imminent "prosperity" echoed those of 1925. This offered planters another chance for a great leap out of indebtedness into an income range appropriate to an aristoc-

13. The old assumptions of the British government also find their way into an excellent study of local land tenure in Zanzibar and Pemba which it commissioned from the anthropologist John Middleton: ex-slaves had gone adrift, commercial agriculture using wage labor was probably more efficent than squatter agriculture, the concentration of land in a few hands could not seriously be questioned. After a long and rather apologetic argument that Arabs used only a little force to acquire land, Middleton insists that this "occurred a long time ago and outright ownership must be accepted." Once that is taken for granted, his recognition that economic efficency, as he conceives it, and social stability were contradictory imperatives does him little good; the problem can only be glossed over, not solved. *Land Tenure*, esp. pp. 77–78.

14. P. Selwyn and T. Y. Watson, "Report on the Economic Development of the Zanzibar Protectorate," 1962, pp. 1–4, 35, 37. See also Zanzibar, "Report and recommendations on the present position and future prospects of agriculture in the Zanzibar Protectorate," 1959.

15. I am not using the concept of involution in as specific a sense as does Clifford Geertz, who refers to the increasing and almost limitless application of more labor to wet-rice cultivation by peasants, but in the more general sense of available resources being concentrated more and more on an old, inadequate system as its inadequacy becomes more and more damaging. See Geertz's excellent study, *Agricultural Involution*.

racy, and so "everything [was] subordinated to the pursuit of cloves."[16] Once again, the cycle of rising prices, expanding production, and declining prices repeated itself. In the early 1950s, Zanzibar was getting over £5 million from a good clove crop; by the early 1960s, harvests brought in £2.1 to 3.5 million.[17] But with each cycle, from the 1840s onward, Zanzibar was left with more clove trees. Estimates from the postwar period ran over four million, up a fourth from the early 1920s. Coconuts, the second crop, had done very well during the war, but were doing very poorly by the early 1960s.[18]

Meanwhile, the planters had to keep pace with retail prices that had risen 80 percent during the war and were not going down afterward.[19] Each cycle was thus having a cumulative effect: clove production was responsive to price increases, but producers could not contract.[20]

The small-scale producers in the fringe areas of Zanzibar and to a lesser extent Pemba, the squatters on both islands, and the mainland migrants who worked on plantations and in town all lost income in times of depression and lost security and independence in times of prosperity. Wages for weeding and picking were stabilized or driven down in the late 1920s. Urban wages gained only slightly during the 1930s and fell relative to mainland Tanganyika. Wages in general rose during the war and went up unevenly thereafter; picking wages rose in the big harvests of the early 1950s and fell in small harvests. How much wages rose in real terms is another question. It is clear, however, that workers—like planters—needed more and more cash.[21]

The upward swings of clove cycles brought people into fuller involvement in the clove economy as squatters and laborers and gave them less choice to get out on the downward swing. Wahadimu became increasingly committed—by patterns of work and consumption established under relatively favorable conditions—to seasonal clove picking by the 1920s. By the 1950s, more Wahadimu had become squatters on Arab

16. Zanzibar, AR, 1949–50, p. 3, 1957–58, p. 16.

17. Zanzibar, ARs; *Plantation Crops* 13 (1970):121, 130. Although the Government and the Clove Growers' Association had stabilized clove marketing since the 1930s, helping out in bad years with savings from good ones, overproduction and declining prices became so severe that the floor price of cloves had to be dropped. AR, 1959–60, p. 4.

18. Zanzibar, AR, 1959–60, p. 18; AgAR, 1961–62; Biennial Report on District Administration, 1962, p. 30.

19. Zanzibar, AR, 1947, p. 8; Clayton, "1948 General Strike," p. 423.

20. A similar phenomenon appeared in cocoa production in western Nigeria during the depression. Berry, *Cocoa, Custom and Socio-Economic Change*, pp. 84–85.

21. Clayton, "1948 General Strike," pp. 421–23. Picking wages were 15–45¢ per pishi in 1946 and went up to 50¢ to Shs 2 per pishi in 1951–52 and again in the big harvest of 1957–58. In the poor harvest of 1959–60, they were only 25–50¢.Wages were less predictable than needs. Zanzibar, ARs.

farms and more had moved to town. In 1960, for the first time, indige-nous Zanzibaris began to take employment as weeders, a job previously left to mainland migrants.[22] This trend was not painful when clove prices and wages were high. But the subsequent decline caused unem-ployment and "very much reduced" workers' purchasing power.[23]

Wahadimu had a village and kinship structure that gave them defined rights in land, albeit in relatively marginal areas; ex-slaves were wholly dependent on the roots they established in plantation areas and in town. But the difference was diminishing, as the Wahadimu village provided less and less of the needs of Wahadimu. They became more involved in relationships with Arab landlords and were faced with the necessity of developing ties with other squatters. Meanwhile, ex-slaves were increas-ingly calling themselves Wahadimu or Wapemba. The trend away from identification with mainland ethnic groups from which slaves had come, noted in the 1931 census, had become stronger in the 1948 census.[24]

A degree of continuity in landlord-squatter relations masked rising uncertainty and tension. Squatters could still obtain land, and they were unlikely to be thrown off it unless they were "trouble makers"—a term which took on new relevance once conflict developed. They were still not charged rent but were expected to work for wages. They could grow, and even sell, food crops, but usually not fruit trees and almost never (in Zanzibar Island at least) cloves.[25] These tacit understandings were sub-ject to strain. When the Government encouraged more food produc-tion to meet shortages during the second World War, as it had in the first, squatters and smallholders were able to earn more cash by growing food, although they quickly ran up against the fact that "partically all the best land" had been covered with clove and coconut trees.[26] But in the 1950s, as more people became dependent on wage labor, landowners

22. Zanzibar, Annual Labour Report, 1960-61, p. 9. On Wahadimu in clove areas, see John Middleton and Jane Campbell, *Zanzibar: Its Society and Its Politics* (London, 1965), pp. 29, 52. Even so, Zanzibaris would cut short their time as clove pickers if wages were too low or their own farms needed immediate attention. Labour Report, 1947, p. 7, 1959, p. 9.

23. Cases of stealing doubled between 1955 and 1959, and the theft of farm produce rose. Zanzibar, ARs, 1955-60; Biennial Report on Agriculture, 1961-62, p. 1.

24. Nyasa and Yao declined about 35 percent in both Zanzibar and Pemba between 1931 and 1948. Manyema and "Other Africans" also declined, while Zaramo (who were migrants as well as ex-slaves) held steady. The principal migrant group, Nyamwezi, grew in Zanzibar and held steady in Pemba. Comparisons in numbers of Shirazi become impossible because enumerators were asked to demand more precise identification from people call-ing themselves Shirazi. Native Census, 1931, p. 2; Census, 1948, pp. 10, 12; Middleton and Campbell, pp. 36, 52.

25. McGeach and Addis "A Review of the System of Land Tenure," pp. 10-11; Meek, *Land Law and Custom,* p. 72; Selwyn and Watson, pp. 36-37; Middleton, pp. 42-45; Middle-ton and Campbell, pp. 33-34.

26. Wilson, "Emergency Food Production," pp. 93-96; Zanzibar, AR, 1946, p. 4, 1949-50, p. 17; "Program of Social and Economic Development in the Zanzibar Protectorate for

began to hire workers in the hope of taking this market for themselves and they even began to replace squatters or resident mainlanders as weeders.[27] These encroachments on squatters' nearly exclusive control of the cultivation of ground crops were not yet made on a large scale—and hardly at all in Pemba—but they posed a threat that had been avoided since abolition: landowners might begin to act like capitalists, denying squatters access to land and creating a class of landless laborers. The undermining of the division between owners' trees and squatters' land was to upset the tenuous stability of the class structure. The slogan of the antiplanter Afro-Shirazi Party, "The trees are yours; the land is ours," was a defensive cry.[28]

Patterns of social unrest suggest how deeply the connections between workers and peasants, Wahadimu, ex-slaves, and migrants, city and countryside, were interwoven for the lower class of Zanzibar Island. The urban poor, who had no access to the means of subsistence, had the least margin in their dealings with landlords, and the attempts of landlords in the African quarter of Zanzibar town to raise rents in 1927 led to the first disturbances. The threat to civic order was sufficiently strong for the Government to block arbitrary rent increases, but it also arrested and deported the alleged leaders of the disturbances.[29]

Since abolition, ex-slaves had been moving to town, where they could find a place in the fluid social structure of the African quarter, Ngambo, and in the casual labor market of the city and port. In 1924, 80 percent of laborers came from groups that were largely ex-slaves, both those who retained mainland ethnic labels and Swahili. Mainland migrants came to play an increasingly important role in the port in the 1930s and 1940s. The ambiguous position of mainland migrants—in the island but not of the island—overlapped with the ambiguous position of ex-slaves. The lines of social action in the city slowly came to be drawn in terms of the structure of the islands, not in terms of origins.[30]

---

the Ten-Year Period, 1946 to 1955," Sessional Paper no. 1 of 1946, Legislative Council, p. 4.

27. Middleton, pp. 46–47.

28. Cited in ibid., p. 77. Scott argues that the crucial impetus behind peasant rebellions in Southeast Asia was not so much the absolute level of a landlord's exactions, but the fear that they might push a peasant below subsistence level in a bad year, expelling him irreversibly into the ranks of the landless. Capitalist penetration and the colonial state made it increasingly likely that the central tenet of the peasants' "moral economy"—the right to minimal subsistence under even the worst circumstances—would be violated. Peasant uprisings were "defensive efforts to protect sources of subsistence." Scott, p. 187. Whether this is complete explanation is questioned by Hildermeier, p. 329.

29. Zanzibar, AR, Zanzibar District, 1927, pp. 89–90.

30. In 1948, 53 percent of the so-called mainland Africans in Zanzibar city were born on the islands. In rural areas, the percentage was even higher, suggesting that many "mainlanders" were in fact of ex-slave origin. This aspect of the situation is neglected by Clayton.

This came out in the 1948 general strike in Zanzibar city. By the 1940s, a longer period of work was needed before a migrant could return home, while a casual laborer was faced with the need for a higher cash income and greater competition. The growing urban population was becoming increasingly caught up in the work situation and demanding higher wages. The strike of 1948 was stimulated by migrants bringing the news of the massive and partly successful strikes in Dar es Salaam and Mombasa. The one known leader was a Muslim from Tanganyika, very much a part of the Swahili-speaking network that connected islands and coast. The strike spread rapidly from port workers to Government employees and domestic servants, and it embraced all segments of the city's ex-slave, migrant, and indigenous Zanzibari population. Women boycotted Arab and Indian shops as the men stopped work. The Government's attempt to recruit Watumbatu in their homeland and bring them in as strikebreakers failed when the Watumbatu left without working. The rapid spread of the strike testifies both to the shared interests of the ethnically mixed working population of the city, and to the formation of an effective social network capable of passing information and pressing people into action in the residential community of Ngambo.[31] Colonial authorities had long feared the fluidity of such urban communities. They had much to fear.

In 1958 disorder spread to rural areas. Landlords began to evict squatters—a direct violation of established custom—and squatters damaged property and engaged in "sporadic outbreaks of violence." Some landlords insisted, as they had once demanded of their slaves, that their dependents follow their political lead, this time by supporting the planter-dominated Zanzibar Nationalist Party (ZNP). Some were evicted for refusing. ZNP backers also tried to install clients in waterfront jobs. This attempt to use coercion and ties of dependence to prevent tenants and workers from engaging in independent politics was typical of "paternalistic" plantation societies. It was countered, however, by squatters refusing to fulfill their weeding obligations and planting crops that damaged nearby clove trees, by African organizations developing settlement schemes for evicted squatters, by vigorous competition in waterfront organizing, by boycotts of Arab stores, and by a political challenge to the very legitimacy of Arab landownership.[32]

31. For a longer version of Clayton's account of the 1948 strike, see *The 1948 Zanzibar General Strike*, Scandinavian Institute of African Studies, Research Report no. 32 (Uppsala, 1976). The importance of the social network of Ngambo, mentioned by Clayton, needs further study. For comparison, see John Iliffe, "The Creation of Group Consciousness: A History of the Dockworkers of Dar es Salaam," in Sandbrook and Cohen, *Development of an African Working Class*, pp. 49–72.

32. Zanzibar, AR, 1957–58, p. 42; Police Report, 1958, p. 5; Zanzibar, "Report of a Commission of Inquiry into Disturbances in Zanzibar during June 1961," 1961, p. 14;

The developing pattern of lower-class action emerged again in the violence that began in an election riot in town in 1961 and spread the next day to rural Zanzibar, engulfing the plantation areas for several days and leaving 68 dead and 381 injured. Arabs and Africans attacked each other at polling places, and Ngambo and rural areas were soon involved. Gangs went around the town "composed of Africans of many tribes from the squatter labour on the surrounding farms." Groups "consisting mainly of indigenous Africans" looted and assaulted Arabs. "Villagers and squatters" roamed the rural areas, "paying off old scores against landlords and shop-keepers." Even after the riots, rural tension continued and urban labor disputes erupted.[33]

These urban and rural disturbances took place in the context of increasingly acrimonious party politics. The arena of electoral politics had been built by the British, but the Zanzibar contestants jumped into it eagerly, for a great deal was at stake.[34] The Arab Association—as much a planters' organization as an ethnic one—dates to the 1920s and spawned the ZNP, which tried to invoke Muslim unity, anti-British feeling, and the ethnic splits among non-Arabs to extend its appeal once the need to win elections loomed. The African Association, which had a mainland membership, denounced the impoverishment of Africans and the domination of Arabs in alliance with the colonial state. But on the eve of the 1957 elections, it was barely able to form an alliance with the indigenous membership of the Shirazi Association. The African-Shirazi Union—later Afro-Shirazi Party (ASP)—was formed without the participation of Wapemba, although Wahadimu supported it. Wapemba formed their own political party, led by a landowner and a former school principal. Shirazi, above all in Pemba, were a people caught between, politically as well as economically.

But the meaning of Shirazi identity had changed since the 1920s, when it was associated with a more fluid economic structure in Pemba. The trend toward smallholder production never did end the unequal distribution of land and trees in Pemba, and it never shook the domination of Arab planters in Zanzibar Island. Shirazi identity eventually lost its connection with owning trees and came to embrace all Wahadimu, Wapemba, and Watumbatu, while the more Islamic and coastal-oriented

---

Lofchie, *Zanzibar*, pp. 185–88; Middleton and Campbell, p. 52. For comparison, see Paige, pp. 5, 21, and Wolf and Mintz, "Haciendas and Plantations."

33. "Inquiry into Disturbances," pp. 2–14; Zanzibar, Police Report, 1961, pp. 10–12; "Biennial Report on District Administration," 1962, p. 22. Indian merchant-financiers played a distinct role in class struggles, for they—unlike the plantation owners—had their economic power rooted in an international commercial system rather than the soil of Zanzibar.

34. Officials remarked on the high level of political excitement among Zanzibaris. AR, 1959–60, pp. 2–3.

ex-slaves eventually claimed to be Shirazi as well.[35] Shirazi identity became a challenge to Arab hegemony. If earlier trends in ethnic labeling paralleled a blurring of economic roles between ethnic groups in Pemba, the later tendency reflected the fact that the boundaries still remained all too clear.[36]

African-Shirazi cooperation in Zanzibar Island was based on shared interests and interconnected social networks—an emerging class consciousness. In Pemba, gradations in economic power were more continuous, the mainland community half the size of Zanzibar's and more likely to be perceived as strangers, and ex-slaves more fully assimilated into Shirazi society, albeit on Shirazi terms. But the limited role of Wapemba in the Arab-dominated coalition that formed the Government of Zanzibar before independence made it clear that Shirazi were to be kept in a subordinate role. By 1963, the majority of non-Arab voters in Pemba had at last come into the Afro-Shirazi fold. The ambiguous identity of the Pemba Shirazi faced with the realities of the efforts of Arab planters at domination, was finally shifting to the African side. The ASP won a majority in the two islands, but flagrant gerrymandering gave the Arab-dominated coalition the victory when Zanzibar became independent in 1963. The aristocracy had lost the support of the "upper crust of the peasantry," its most likely allies.[37]

The Zanzibar Revolution reflected not only the blockage of the aspirations of all but the Arab planters, but the increasingly vulnerability of people who were becoming more dependent on wages and subject to the exercise of power by plantation owners. The grievances were made acute by the fear that the state would soon become an instrument of the planter class in a way that the colonial state had been too detached to become. As the opposition broadened, a more radical segment of it— making an explicitly revolutionary appeal—rapidly gained strength. But the actual revolution came about, as Skocpol's comparative analysis would suggest, through a crisis of the state. In this case, the end of colo-

35. In Pemba, ex-slaves were especially able to be assimilated (Middleton and Campbell, p. 36). On the politics of the Shirazi, see ibid., pp. 51–66, and the excellent account of the entire postwar period in Lofchie.

36. Lofchie notes that the "sole motive for cooperation [between mainland Africans and Shirazi] was resentment and fear of the Arab community." Originally, Shirazi identity was defined, to a large extent, against Africans; eventually it came to be defined against Arabs. Lofchie, pp. 169–70; Clayton, Research Report, p. 13.

37. For a narrative of events, see Lofchie. On the danger of losing the top level of the peasantry, see Moore, p. 474. Here, it is essential to see how hard the ZNP fought to maintain the support of the better-off peasants, playing down its own ethnic particularism, seeking to find themes that would unite all Muslims, broadening its economic appeal. Yet the nature of its interests as a party of planters prevented it from giving substance to its gestures.

nial rule left such a feeble state structure that it was overthrown by a group of recently laid-off policemen of mainland origin after brief fighting.

Yet their action was a catalyst within a situation of polarization and tension. The Sultan and many Omani Arabs had to flee Zanzibar; Wamanga in rural areas were murdered. Out of an ethnically diverse opposition and a confused revolution, a revolutionary government was formed, run by men who considered themselves African and radical, and most of whom called themselves by the Islamic honorific, Sheikh. Planters and merchants were expropriated and most often exiled, but what the new government—itself circumscribed by the predominance of the clove tree and the shallowness of its own educational and revolutionary experience—could do to replace a plantation economy and society still remains in question.[38]

The racial hostility that lay behind the violence was certainly deep, and it transcended narrowly economic issues. Yet it is too simple to attribute such conflict to ancient racial antagonisms—ingrained hostility to people of different color or bad memories of slavery—for such prejudices, however important, had not polarized society in the early twentieth century and had not made some people fear that they would lose their privileges and others, their livelihood. In fact, officials in the 1920s, and even later, thought Zanzibar was remarkably free from ethnic conflict.[39] The tensions that existed at the time of abolition were more acute in the leading clove-growing area of Pemba than in Zanzibar. When conflict emerged in the 1950s, it was sharper where the dominance of the planter class and the state was stronger and more threatening, on Zanzibar Island.[40]

Of the various ways in which ethnic boundaries and alliances could be drawn, the one that emerged by the 1950s followed the increasingly sharp line between the planter class—linked to merchants and

38. Lofchie, pp. 257–81. One problem in assessing the role of the mainland ex-policemen is that the most detailed account of the fighting comes from a rather strange man obsessed with his own importance in the revolution (see "Field Marshall" John Okello, *Revolution in Zanzibar*, Nairobi, 1967). Leo Kuper's attempt to use the Zanzibar revolution as an example of racial conflict—as opposed to class conflict—is a model of how *not* to analyze race and class. Both are seen as rigid, ahistorical categories. Kuper's desire to see the revolution as a conflict between mainland Africans (with Wahadimu tagging along) and Arabs leads him to study a few hours of the revolution instead of the entire process. *Race, Class and Power*, esp. chap. 7.

39. Pearce, *Zanzibar*, p. 158; "Inquiry into Disturbances," p. 2.

40. Lofchie's attempt to find a clue to why relations between Omanis and Shirazi in Pemba were better than in Zanzibar by looking to the distant past is unpersuasive, for the evidence from the early twentieth century suggests that relations were then worse in Pemba. O'Sullivan-Beare, Report on Pemba, 1903, FOCP 8356, p. 90; AgAR, 1911, p. 145, Lofchie, p. 244.

financiers—and workers and peasants. The complex and multidimensional ties among people who shared an ethnic identity were mobilized in a struggle for control of a state that all feared would either entrench or undo the power of a planter class.[41] The "Africans" who came to struggle with "Arabs" were not born into such a neat category; they made themselves into Africans. In an uneven and incomplete fashion, people who were ethnically diverse, who fulfilled different roles in the economy, who had different incomes and ways of living, found common ground in their struggle against an economic structure—based on the interconnections of planters, merchant-creditors, and the state—which had exploited them and narrowed their opportunities and which now threatened to dominate them all.

THE COAST OF KENYA

Like Zanzibar, the coast of Kenya seemed to be doing well in 1925. Like Zanzibar, its structure had become rigid and offered little chance of coping with the strains and conflicts that were to come. The tense equilibrium between landlords and squatters—unsettled by both Depression and the postwar boom—began to crumble once the role of the state in defining control over land came into question. But the implications of agrarian unrest were not as far-reaching as in Zanzibar and did not lead to polarization on the national level, on which political action in Kenya was increasingly focused. The coast's planters were isolated and stood no chance of making the state into their instrument. Instead, Arab and Swahili elites—fearing submergence within an independent state that might be less sympathetic to their interest than the British—began a movement for regional autonomy. Their failure to elicit support from Mijikenda and Swahili workers and squatters made it clear that divisions within coastal society were more important than regionalism.[42]

The linkages of workers and peasants from the coast and from outside were not nearly as close as they were in Zanzibar. To be sure, the general strike of 1947 in Mombasa, like the strike of 1948 in Zanzibar, brought together coastal and upcountry workers. But in Zanzibar rural and urban conflict both focused on a single pattern of domination. Upcountry workers in Mombasa sometimes faced forms of agrarian conflict in their homelands that resembled those of the coast, but not against the

41. Hamza Alavi emphasizes that "primordial loyalties" were used in an early stage of mobilizing class solidarity among peasants. Landowners, on the other hand, saw such loyalties as a resource to be exploited in attracting followers. In either case, the question is how such loyalties are used and, in the process, transformed. "Peasant Classes and Primordial Loyalties," *Journal of Peasant Studies* 1 (1973):58–59.

42. For background, see Salim, *Swahili-Speaking Peoples.*

same people or the same economic structure.[43] Because the state in Kenya embraced a much more varied and complex set of structures and conflicts, the mounting tension between landowners and tenants within the coast did not concentrate on the struggle over state institutions which were likely to make or break either group.

In 1925, landlords had little control over squatters and little command over labor, but the structure of the colonial economy left cultivators and workers in a low-level equilibrium between selling crops and selling labor in a system that had strong disincentives against doing either. After that, the position of squatters slowly worsened.

The increasing vulnerability of squatters can be seen in the case of Malindi District (or, as it sometimes was, Sub-District). The Depression drastically reduced the price of maize and threatened the main source of cash that tenant farmers had. Cash was so short that the tax burden became enormous. Crops had to be sold quickly with no provision for food storage. Wage labor was an increasingly necessary and undesirable alternative, for the entire export economy was in dire trouble and wages were falling throughout Kenya. Even after the Depression, wage labor remained essential to a larger proportion of coastal people, as it did in Zanzibar.[44]

The best protection Giriama and ex-slave squatters had against the fluctuations of the cash economy, in so far as the tax collector gave them any leeway, was subsistence cultivation. With more and more people seeking access to the more reliable coastal belt after a series of droughts in the 1930s, the Mijikenda population of the coast was growing, while ex-slaves staying on ex-masters' land and "migrating wazalia" (people of slave descent) looking for new places to squat remained important parts of the coastal economy.[45] The inability of squatters to make permanent investments or improvements in their land and the way the state, the marketing system, and the nature of squatter agriculture itself discouraged improving productivity began to hurt.

The weakness of squatters—especially their need for cash—helped landowners get more wage labor. In Malindi this trend boosted a crop that officials had been pushing for decades—cotton. Production jumped

43. The situation of squatters on European farms in the Rift Valley has some parallels with squatter agriculture on the coast, but the heavy impact of capitalist agriculture during the postwar boom upcountry had a softer echo on the coast. Coastal people played no significant part in the rebellion which convulsed central Kenya in the 1950s.

44. Malindi, AR, 1932, 1933, 1935; Kilifi, AR, 1947, 1950.

45. The DO of Kilifi noted the influx and the eagerness of Arab and Swahili landowners to have new tenants, but he observed that the situation could not continue (Memorandum, 23 Jan. 1935, CO 533/488). See also Kilifi, AR, 1937, 1939; Kenya Land Commission, 1933, p. 342.

from 170,000 pounds in 1928 to 1,840,513 pounds in 1935, although it fell when cotton prices, like those of maize, dropped. However, cotton, along with cashews, was to become the leading cash crop of the District, replacing maize.[46] The use of wage labor to produce cotton was aided by the old Giriama preference for working on Arab and Swahili farms as opposed to European plantations. But soon, Giriama began to grow cotton themselves—it was a fine smallholder crop—and the labor supply once again became problematical.[47]

Slowly, tree crops—mangoes and coconuts—became increasingly profitable. The opening and improvement of motor roads to Mombasa in the 1920s and 1930s helped. The postwar export boom helped even more. Tree crops in the coastal belt were owners' crops. The new, more commercial direction in agriculture was favoring owners over squatters, but the balance of power was only slowly changing.

More than anything else, the commercial cultivation of the cashew nut tree threw awry the relations of squatter and landlord. Cashew trees had long grown on the coast but were of minor importance. But in the early 1930s, an Englishman opened up a cashew-packaging factory at Kilifi, employing—to a large extent—women and children. He used his own trees, distributed seedlings, set up buying stations, and paid—by Depression standards—good prices.[48] But he ran up against the fears and rigidities of the squatter system. Arab and Swahili landowners still lacked the cash and economic power to plant, cultivate, and harvest cashew nuts on a plantation basis. Squatters still feared that the labor they exerted to plant trees would only result in the owners' seizing the trees, and probably their land.[49] The anti-improvement bias of squatter agriculture, despite good prices and bad times, was only overcome by state intervention. Forced planting was instituted in 1937, and the Government convened a meeting of landowners and squatters from which emerged, for the first time, official acknowledgment that squatters might have subsidiary rights in a planter's land. The agreement guaranteed to squatters who planted cashew trees rights to those trees, although they had to pay either a share of the crop or rent. But the agreement left ambiguous the

46. Malindi, AR, 1924, 1925; Kilifi, AR, 1934; Martin, *History of Malindi*, p. 97; I. D. Talbott, "The Development of Lamu Cotton Production prior to Kenya's Independence," *East African Journal of Rural Development* 1-2 (1973):22-26.

47. Malindi, AR, 1932, 1935, 1936; Kilifi, AR, 1937.

48. Memorandum on the Cashew Nut Industry by Messrs. Gibbons & Co., Secretaries to Lillywhite, incl. Agriculture Director to CO, 12 Aug. 1936, PC's Archives, Mombasa, T & C 4/8, no. 43.

49. At least one official commented that these fears were well founded. Agricultural Officer, Coast, to Acting Deputy Director of Agriculture, 28 Aug. 1935, PC's Archives, Mombasa, T & C, 4/8, no. 38.

most crucial elements in a situation where personal relationships were deteriorating: did a squatter plant particular trees as a tenant, in which case he had rights to them, or as a laborer, in which case his employer possessed all rights to the trees? The question remained temporarily in abeyance as cashew planting spread and the packing factory's business grew.[50]

By the 1950s, relations between landowners and the greatly increased number of squatters had become more impersonal, commercialized, and tense. Rent was now regularly charged, and it was often high.[51] The power of the landowner to evict became more of an immediate threat, and squatters were sometimes thrown out or threatened with eviction for refusing to work for the landowner. Land was being sold more often, to Indians and Europeans as well as to Arabs and Swahili, and the new landlord often had new ideas of how to use the land: a modern mango plantation might rely on tractors to clear weeds between the trees and dispense with squatters. On the surviving European plantations, local labor had become more plentiful than in the days when squatters were flourishing, and labor relations were becoming tense.[52] As early as 1950, an official noted, "With the increasing development of alienated land on the coast, the squatter problem has become more acute."[53]

In 1952, the Malindi landowners denounced the cashew agreement of 1937, insisting that tenants would have no claims at all to trees planted after that date unless the landlord specifically agreed to it.[54] Landowners were becoming increasingly reluctant to have tenants on their property, realizing that their power as landowners depended on the ability and willingness of the state to eject tenants and doubting, given the political climate during the Mau Mau Emergency, that they could be sure of the state. Meanwhile, the Administration was eager for more cashews to be planted and saw the need to "clear land of squatters who are unwilling to work" as a concomitant of development.[55]

The tension over the eviction of squatters which officials noted in 1955 became a "political drama" by 1959. Gangs of Giriama went around tak-

50. Kilifi, AR, 1937, 1960; Report on Cashew Nut Industry by Agricultural Liason Officer, Coast, 10 Sept. 1947, PC's Archives, T & C, 4/8, no. 15; Erastus Tsuma, Bisiria Toya, Alfred Yongo (MAL).

51. Rents ranged from Shs 17 to over Shs 100 per year. Malindi, AR, 1958; Bakari Rarua (MAL). There were an estimated 27,000 Mijikenda squatters on the coastal strip of Kilifi District in 1960, plus 75,000 Swahili, many of whom were squatters. Kilifi, AR, 1960.

52. Kilifi, AR, 1947, 1950, 1953, 1954. I have visited modern mango plantations near Malindi.

53. Kilifi, AR, 1950.

54. Ibid., 1960.

55. Ibid., 1953.

ing cashews from Arab estates, and a brief strike of hotel servants and a bus boycott were organized at Malindi. The cashew nut question became the leading issue in politics in Malindi District, and Ronald Ngala, the Giriama leader, drove home the squatters' claims to the trees in meetings and organization drives. The land and tree issue, in one form or another, affected other coastal districts as well, and gave much impetus to the efforts of the Kenya African Democratic Union to organize the Mijikenda and other Africans on the coast, as well as to oppose the movement for regional autonomy led by landowning Arabs and Swahili.[56]

The British Administration tried to head off trouble by arbitrating the disputes over the ownership of cashew nut trees. But the state was an umpire who made his own rules, and "general recognition of security of tenure" was the primary rule it had long been trying to establish. Almost all the arbitrator's decisions were in favor of landowners.[57]

The controversy did not end with Independence, for the Kenyan Government has been equally anxious to preserve the sanctity of property. Officials have favored various resettlement schemes that put squatters on land that belonged to the Government or was purchased in large blocks from people who were letting it stand idle, thus preserving the principle of private landownership and establishing Goverment control over squatters. The state thus remains an outside force, sufficiently caught up in the contradictory values of order and property, insufficiently tied to either landlords or squatters, to act decisively in either's favor. Like the colonial state, the independent state recognized property rights but did little to convert them into power over labor.[58] What looked like a developing revolt of the dispossessed, escalating as it had in Zanzibar, has turned into an uneasy standoff. So landowners still need squatters and still must share cashew nut trees with them in a variety of ways, but the threat of capitalist development continues to loom over the squatters.

Before 1937, squatters had not been primitive or foolish in their reluc-

56. Kilifi and Malindi, ARs, 1955–61; Erastus Tsuma, Awade Maktub, Ishmael Toya (MAL); "The Kenya Coastal Strip: Report of the Commissioner," 1961, pp. 12–13. There were tensions over tenancy in other coastal districts. Kwale, AR, 1955, 1957; Stren, *Housing the Urban Poor*, pp. 159–75. See also Salim.

57. Kilifi, AR, 1961; Coastal Strip Report, p. 8; M. M. Shambi, "The Problem of Land Ownership and Cashewnut Claims in Malindi Coastal Belt," paper prepared for District Records, 1972, pp. 13–18. Such views of land tenure are still current among development planners. See World Bank, *Kenya: into the Second Decade*, p. 475.

58. When the Kenyan Government wanted to intervene against squatters in other areas, raids by the police, hut burning, and forced resettlement were necessary. The process often had to be repeated. Mbithi and Barnes, *The Spontaneous Settlement Problem in Kenya*.

tance to plant trees. Their fears were proven correct. In the abstract, some kind of arrangement, such as sharecropping, could have been devised to apportion risks and rewards in cashew cultivation. But the problem was that the landowner played no essential role in turning a seedling into a cashew nut: the rewards that capital would gain depended on what it could extract. The possibility of an effective arrangement foundered on a past of tension and antagonism, a present in which neither side could exercise decisive power over the other, and a future in which either side could lose everything it had.[59]

For squatters, stagnation was the price of independence. One generation's partial success in tearing down slavery and fending off the advance of capitalism left another generation to fight the same battles against the same antagonists with the same means, only each period of adjustment or confrontation endangered the position of the squatters a little more. Since Malindi District became a major exporter of cotton and cashews, the position of Mijikenda and the descendants of slaves has become less independent, less secure, and more exposed to the vagaries of markets and politics than it was when they grew and exported maize. Food shortages have become chronic not just in the hinterland, where they have long been a problem, but also on the coastal plain. Wage labor is more often a necessity, and a job something that cannot be jeopardized by frequent returns to a farm. Even now, squatters often continue to devote first priority to crops they can eat and grow less of the more lucrative cash crops than the land would allow.[60] They realize that it is better to face a low price for surplus maize in a good year than to fall short in a bad one, for their relative self-sufficiency is their best defense against what they regard as predatory landlords, predatory merchants and moneylenders, and a predatory state.

Giriama and the descendants of slaves both express a deep bitterness against the grabbing of land and the exploitation of labor by Arabs. This bitterness embodies an acute sensitivity to history, to the slave labor that the ancestors of some experienced, to the slave raids that the ancestors of others endured, and to the control of the rich coastal land by Arabs and Swahili that has forced all to enter into relationships of subordination in order to farm and to eat. One Giriama squatter referred to squatters as "watumwa wa siri," secret slaves.[61] That slavery should be the image invoked by someone whose ancestors were not themselves enslaved

59. On continued problems, see ibid., pp. 77, 86; Shambi, "Problem of Land Ownership," pp. 20-24; and interview with Erastus Tsuma, chief of Malindi.

60. The more secure peasants feel, according to Migdal (p. 52), the more willing they are to participate in production for the market.

61. For obvious reasons, the identity of people who discussed these subjects with me must be kept anonymous.

suggests a melding of the historical consciousness of ex-slaves and Giriama through generations of common experience on land they did not own. And this sense of history, the autonomy of the squatters' traditions and beliefs from the ideologies of either the Western state or the Islamic milieu of the landlords, provides a clue to understanding the gradual emergence of political consciousness among the squatters.

However much new crops and new techniques might improve the productivity of the soil or the exports of Kenya, squatters have no desire that "the economy" develop at their expense. They remember a form of economic development that once made Malindi into one of the most productive plantation regions of Africa, and they have been struggling, even before the state emancipated them, to free themselves from such forms of progress.

Appendix
The Abolition Decree, Zanzibar, 1897

TRANSLATION OF DECREE DATED 1ST OF ZILKADA, 1314 A.H.

From Seyyid Hamoud-bin-Mahomed-bin-Said to all his subjects:

Whereas by a Treaty concluded in 1290 between Her Majesty the Queen of England and His Highness the late Seyyid Barghash, &c., the importation of slaves into the islands of Zanzibar and Pemba was forbidden and declared to be illegal.

And whereas, owing to the lapse of years and other causes, the number of slaves legally imported and held in these islands has greatly decreased, so that many estates have gone out of cultivation.

And whereas the present system of slavery deters free labourers from coming to Our islands to take the place of those who have, from death or other causes, disappeared, to the detriment of agriculture and of Our subjects, who are thus driven to borrow money at high interest against the Law of Islam and their own welfare, both of which are the objects of Our deepest solicitude.

And whereas the Apostle Mahomed (may God grant him blessings and peace!) has set before us as most praiseworthy the liberation of slaves, and We are Ourselves desirous of following his precepts, and of encouraging the introduction of free labour.

And whereas Our late predecessor, Seyyid Ali, in the Decree in which he forbade for the future the sale of slaves or their transmission except by direct inheritance, declared that, subject to the conditions stated in that Decree, all slaves lawfully possessed on that date by his subjects should remain with their owners, and that their status should be unchanged, so that it would not be equitable to deprive them of any rights enjoyed under that Decree without awarding compensation to their present possessors.

We, therefore, having considered this question most carefully in all its aspects, and having in view the benefiting of all classes of Our faithful subjects, have decided, with the advice of Our First Minister, to promulgate, and We do hereby promulgate the following Decree:

Article 1. From and after this 1st day of Zilkada, all claims of whatever description made before any Court or public authority in respect of the alleged relations of master and slave shall be referred to the District

Court (Mehkemet-el-Wilaya) within those jurisdiction they may arise, and shall be cognizable by that Court alone.

Art. 2. From and after this 1st day of Zilkada, the District Court shall decline to enforce any alleged rights over the body, service, or property of any person on the ground that such person is a slave, but wherever any person shall claim that he was lawfully possessed of such rights, in accordance with the Decrees of Our predecessors, before the publication of the present Decree, and has now by the application of said Decree been deprived of them, and has suffered loss by such deprivation, then the Court, unless satisfied that the claim is unfounded, shall report to Our First Minister that it deems the claimant entitled, in consideration of the loss of such rights and damage resulting therefrom, to such pecuniary compensation as may be a just and reasonable equivalent for their value, and Our First Minister shall then award to him such sum.

Art. 3. The compensation money thus awarded shall not be liable to be claimed in respect of any debt for which the person of the slave for whom it was granted could not previously by law be seized.

Art. 4. Any person whose right to freedom shall have been formally recognized under the 2nd Article shall be liable to any tax, abatement, corvée, or payment in lieu of corvée, which Our Government may at any time hereafter see fit to impose on the general body of its subjects, and shall be bound, on pain of being declared a vagrant, to show that he possesses a regular domicile and means of subsistence, and where such domicile is situated on land owned by any other person, to pay the owner of such land such rent (which may take the form of an equivalent in labour or produce) as may be agreed upon between them before the District Court.

Art. 5. Concubines shall be regarded as inmates of the Harem in the same sense as wives, and shall remain in their present relations unless they should demand their dissolution on the ground of cruelty, in which case the District Court shall grant it if the alleged cruelty has been proved to its satisfaction. A concubine not having borne children may be redeemed with the sanction of the Court.

Art. 6. Any person making any claim under any of the provisions of this Decree shall have the right to appeal from the decision of the District Court to Ourselves, or to such Judge or other public authority as We may from time to time see fit to delegate for the purpose.

Written by his order by his slave, Salim-bin-Mahomed.

(signed) Hamoud-bin-Mahomed-bin-Said

(from PP 1897, LXII, 707, pp. 4-5)

People Interviewed

MALINDI (1972–73)

Mohamed Maawia. An Mshella, now working for the Land Office in Mombasa and intimately acquainted with the intricacies of land tenure as well as the history of Malindi.

Gulamhussein Tayabji. Very old Indian of the Bohora community. Son of the first Indian to settle in Mambrui.

Said Khalid Abdalla. Of mixed Shella-Omani origin.

Nassor Said Nassor Al-Busaidi. From a minor branch of the politically dominant Omani communal group.

Swaleh Mohamed Gagi. A Baluchi descended from one of the original soldiers sent to Malindi and knowledgeable about many aspects of Malindi social history.

Mohamed Hemed. Baluchi. Former dhow captain.

Erastus Tsuma. Giriama. Chief of Malindi. Very involved in the recent ramifications of the cashew nut controversy.

Tayabali Rajabali Mulla Bhaiji. Son of an Indian trader in Malindi in the 1880s. Well informed about his community, commerce, and agriculture.

Ali Salim Salim. Mshella farmer.

Jivanji Gulamhussein Jivanji. Grandson of the most important Indian import-export merchant in Malindi, who was accumulating land at the time of abolition, most of which the family has since lost.

Abdulla Athman Al-Amudy. Hadrami trader who came to Malindi in the earth twentieth century.

Mohamed Lali. Bajuni.

Salim Alyan Hemed Nahwy. Son of one of my best Omani informants, now active in agricultural affairs.

The Reverend Kalume. Giriama political leader.

Abdalla Omar Nabhani. From a Lamu group that migrated to Malindi.

Bakari Rarua. A Giriama Muslim and an elder. Very knowledgeable about Giriama relations with Arabs and ex-slaves.

Abdalla Seif. One of the oldest surviving Washella, with personal experience of the period discussed in this book.

Alyan Hemed Nahwy. The oldest Omani, in his eighties. Very knowledgeable about agricultural and social relations.

Omar Dahman Al-Amudy. A leader of the Hadrami community, an important merchant, and owner of a large plantation.

Omar Ali. Very old Mshella.

bin Omari. Expert on Malindi's mosques.

Mohamed Said Nassor Al-Busaidi. Knowledgeable about Omanis in Malindi.

Abbas Abdulhussein Adamji Saigar. Indian trader.

Omar wa Fundi. An Mzalia, son of a skilled slave owned by a leading Mshella and a superb source—through personal experiences—on the lives of ex-slaves.

Said Abdalla Mohamed Saiban. Hadrami trader.

Khalifa wa Lali Hadaa. Descendant of a leading Bajuni planter.

Mohamed Abubakar Abbas. An old Mshella well versed in his community's history.

Yahya Said Hemed Al-Busaidi. Son of the Liwali of Mambrui in the early days of British rule, and knowledgeable about the experiences of Omanis before and after abolition.

Omar Ahmed Barium. Hadrami.

Awade Maktub. Born in the household of a leading Omani slaveowning family. He eventually became chief of Ganda after a varied career that illustrates the kinds of things ex-slaves did to earn a living. Also knowledgeable about ex-slave–Giriama relations, landlord-tenant conflict, and other aspects of economic and social history. In his eighties.

Suede Nasibu. Mzalia, son of the slave of a Bajuni.

Mselem Khalfan Jaafari. Omani. His grandfather was an overseer for Salim bin Khalfan.

Salim Sabiki. Bajuni sailor and fisherman.

Juma Kengewa. Lived on the plantation that Salim bin Khalfan made *wakf* (trust) for his ex-slaves. Described conditions on this shamba and the interaction of ex-slaves and Giriama.

Jabu Masoya. Son of a slave who was an overseer. He was caught up in a bitter, but typical, land dispute that revealed the vulnerability of squatters.

Sheriff Mohamed Said Al-Beith. Islamic teacher in Mambrui.

Omar Salim Batheiff. Hadrami. Descendant of old settlers in Mambrui.

Juma Mbaraka. Son of slaves of an Omani and a squatter living north of Malindi.

Ahmed Salim Bawazir. Hadrami trader and landowner.

Salim Mohamed Islam Al-Kathiri. Grandson of an important Hadrami landowner at Mambrui.

Ali Athman. Bajuni of Mambrui.

Mussbhai Tayabji Walliji. Brother of Gulamhussein Tayabji and personally acquainted with decline of trade at Mambrui.

Mahfudh Mohamed Ali Basharahil. Grandson of a leading Hadrami farmer and trader in Mambrui whose fortunes reflect the undermining of the wealth of the most important Mambrui landowners.

Dewel Said Badwill. Nearly one hundred years old, he experienced some of the changes of the early period of British rule and is knowledgeable about most aspects of the history of Mambrui.

Athman Mohamed Nabhani, Maalim Abud Abdalla Bajuni, and Mohamed Abubaker Yusuf (from Lamu). Joint interview that yielded good information on the Mambrui area, especially about runaway slaves just before abolition.

Kassim Umar. Bajuni. Lived in an area north of Mambrui largely inhabited by Bajuni and provided information on cultivation, ex-slaves, mangrove-cutting, and trade in that area.

Ahmed Mbarak Handwan. Descendant of one of the wealthiest Hadrami landowners of the early twentieth century.

The Reverend Timothy Ngoma. Pastor of the church at Jilore, the first mission station near Malindi and a refuge for runaway slaves just before abolition. Provided an account of the interaction of runaways, slaves, and Giriama in this region.

Alfred Yongo. Giriama elder, who himself had worked on Arab mashamba and provided useful data on kibarua labor.

Dola Bakari. Bajuni of Mambrui.

Mzee Jabu. Son of a slave at Mambrui, born just before abolition and who farmed all his life.

Omar Bwana Mkuu. Bajuni from north of Mambrui, who gave a picture of smallholder farming in this area.

Maalim Mohamed. Bajuni from north of Mambrui. Former dhow captain, well informed on the dhow trade.

Gari Kai. Giriama elder, living at Kijiwetanga, in the old heart of a plantation area that has since become a squatter area. Provided important information on Giriama squatters and kibarua workers.

Nzeze Kwicha. Also a Giriama of Kijewetanga and knowledgeable about land problems, squatting, labor, and relations with ex-slaves.

Suleiman Amur Suleiman Daremki. From a leading Omani family that has since fallen on hard times. Along with other informants of similar background, he provided a landowner's perspective on the decline of grain plantations, the continuity of coconut plantations, and changes in labor.

The Reverend Ishmael Toya. Giriama from the mission station at Jilore. Very old Giriama Christian, extremely knowledgeable about the Malindi hinterland, Giriama affairs, and interaction with ex-slaves.

Hassan Said El-Homar. Hadrami living in Mambrui hinterland.

Isa Said Al-Hasibi. From an important Omani family.

Suleman Ali Mselem Al-Khalasi. Son of a former kathi of Malindi.

Mohamed Khamis Muhando. Mzalia of Zigua origin, who had lived a varied life—working in many ways—during the colonial era and who knew much about the economic and cultural life of people of slave

origin and the relationship of Malindi and Mombasa, from the point
of view of workers who had connections between the two.

Kazungu wa Kigande. Giriama elder, born in the 1890s and living at
Maweni. Knew from experience the changing situation of squatters.

Mohamed Omari Toya. Giriama Muslim living in Kakuyuni, on edge of
an old plantation area.

Mohamed wa Mweni. Giriama Muslim from Kakuyuni.

Bisiria Toya. Giriama elder interviewed at Ganda, once a plantation
area, now a squatter settlement. Well informed on Giriama-Arab relations, squatting, labor, relations with ex-slaves, and the cashew nut
controversy.

Mohamed Omar Al-Amudy. Interviewed in Shella Lamu about Shella
people who went to Malindi.

Abdulla Kadara. Mshella, interviewed at Lamu.

MOMBASA (1972–73)

Lance Jones Bengo. Grandson of William Jones, who was taken from a
slave dhow by the British and became an important missionary.

James Juma Mbotela. Son of a slave taken off a dhow and brought up at
Freretown. Age eighty-four at time of interview, he knew the history
of the northern Mombasa area and mission people intimately.

Mohamed Rashid Al-Mazrui. In his sixties, and the leading Mazrui historian in Mombasa. Knew much about farming after abolition and the
reactions and problems of Arab landowners.

Ahmed Abdalla Al-Mazrui. A young well-educated relative of Mohamed
Rashid, who had learned much from his elders and had considerable
insight into coastal society.

William George Kombo. Son of slaves of Giriama, born 1896 and raised
at Jomvu mission. Told me about experiences of ex-slave workers
from the Mombasa hinterland in urban labor.

Gibson Koboko. Living at Rabai, his own origins reflect the intermixture
of people there.

Newland Gibson Ngome. Born 1895 and lived at Rabai. Well informed
on mission life and role of educated mission people in the early colonial era.

Mzee Benjamin Chimwenga, son of Ndoro. Ribe elder. Excellent on the
interaction of Arabs, Mijikenda, and runaways in the coastal hinterland.

Shiabuddin Shiraghdin. Swahili scholar, extremely knowledgeable about
Swahili traditions and customs in Mombasa. One interview was con-
ducted jointly with Hyder Mohamed Kindy, a Swahili political
spokesman.

Samuel Levi. From Freretown church and knowledgeable about the experiences of the mixed people who lived north of Mombasa, including questions of land, farming, and labor.

Mohamed Ali Mirza. From a leading Baluchi family of Mombasa and well informed about life and business in the city.

Salim Mohamed Muhashamy. Former Liwali of the coast and a member of a leading Omani landholding family. Provided important information about the operations of a sizeable coconut shamba in Kisauni after abolition.

Sheriff Abdalla Salim. Former Arab member of the Legislative Council and an estate agent in Mombasa. Very knowledgeable about land, coconuts, and commerce in the early part of the century.

Al-Amin Said Al-Mandri. Former Liwali of Mombasa and leading member of an old and important Omani family of that town. He taught me much about Islamic law and coastal customs, as well as about the lives of several members of his family, who were among the leading landholders of the Mombasa area. His perspective on the workings of coconut mashamba, commerce, and land transactions—as well as social relations between ex-masters and ex-slaves, Arabs and Africans—was vital to my understanding of these subjects.

Said Mohamed Al-Mandri. Expert in the history of Mandris in Mombasa.

Shariff Mohamed Abdalla Shatry. Member of an important Hadrami trading family.

Shariff Abdulrehman Abdalla Shatry. Brother of the above and port manager at Kilindini Harbor. Well informed on trade and shipping throughout the century.

Mohamedali Bhaiji. Indian trader, born around 1890 and active in the copra trade.

Ali Jemedar Amir. Of mixed Baluchi-Swahili descent and well versed in the history of Mombasa.

Famy Mbarak Hinawy. From a leading Omani family, brought up in a household that included people of slave descent who had stayed on after abolition.

Abdalla Saleh Al-Farsy. The leading Islamic scholar of the coast who explained many aspects of Islamic law and practice to me, and also told me much about the history of Zanzibar, where he lived most of his life.

Yahya Ali Omar. Swahili scholar.

Mohamed Hemed Timami. From a Suri family with long ties to Mombasa. Former Liwali, with much to say about land and labor in Mombasa.

Said Karama. Swahili poet.

Mohamed Khammal Khan. Baluchi teacher with a broad knowledge of local history.

Mohamed Kassim Al-Mazrui. Former chief kathi of Kenya and a leading Islamic scholar.

Mohamed Ahmed Al-Mandri. Grandson of a leading Omani landowner and speculator.

Muhiddin Mohamed Al-Changamwe. From an important and wealthy Swahili family of Mombasa, very knowledgeable about Swahili problems with agricultural and urban land.

Wazee of Majengo. Joint interview with four elders from this working-class district of Mombasa, arranged by the chief of Majengo. Important information on economic and social position of ex-slaves in Mombasa was discussed.

Mohamed Said Al-Busaidi. Administrator of the remaining portion of the estate of Salim bin Khalfan.

Ibrahim Shaib. Aged Bajuni living north of Mombasa, who explained the agricultural situation at Kisauni and the problems of squatters.

Mchangamwe Umar. Digo born at Kisauni. Explained the nature of the very mixed population at Kisauni, and the land situation.

Wazee of Kisauni. Joint interview with eight elders of various origins, arranged by the chief of Kisauni. They stressed the importance of Mijikenda in the origins of Kisauni and the tension between them and Arab landlords.

Said Salim Ruwehi. From a leading Omani family of Zanzibar.

Said Mohamed Baghozi. From an important Hadrami family of Mombasa.

Ahmed Said Riami. From an important Omani family of Zanzibar.

Juma Rubai. His father was an ex-slave in Malindi. As a child he came to Mombasa with his mother and later worked in both Malindi and Mombasa. Provided valuable information about life in the mixed population of working-class districts and about the variety of activities in which he and other wazalia engaged.

Maalim Mzagu and Mzee Juma. Joint interview with two old dockworkers, both Mijikenda Muslims. Provided an account of the varied work force, including ex-slaves, and of the nature of port work.

CAMBRIDGE, ENGLAND (1977)

F. B. Wilson. Former Director of Agriculture in Zanzibar, who had been in charge of the food production program during World War II. Has considerable respect for and knowledge of African agriculture in Zanzibar.

Bibliography

Archives

Public Record Office, London
  CO 533, Kenya
  CO 618, Zanzibar
  FO 2, Africa
  FO 107, Zanzibar
  FO 367, Africa
  Colonial Office Confidential Prints
  Foreign Office Confidential Prints, Africa and Numerical Series
  Map Room, early maps of Kenya

Rhodes House, Oxford University
  British and Foreign Anti-Slavery Society Papers
  Robert Coryndon Papers
  R. I. Guthrie Papers
  A. C. Hollis, Autobiography
  Frederick Lugard Papers

Friends' Library, London
  MS Narrative of visit of Theodore Burtt and Henry S. Newman to Zanzibar,
      Pemba, and the East Africa Protectorate, 1897
  Correspondence, Pemba

Other Mission Archives, London
  Church Missionary Society, Correspondence, East Africa
  Universities' Mission to Central Africa, Correspondence, Zanzibar

Kenya National Archives, Nairobi
  Provincial and District Records, including Annual and Quarterly Reports,
      Political Record Books, and Handing Over Reports
  Coast Deposit, 1 and 2
  Records of the African Affairs, Judicial, Labour, and Medical Departments

High Court of Kenya, Nairobi
  Probate and Administration files
  Records of cases heard by the High Court Mombasa, plus scattered files from
      Town Magistrate's and Resident Magistrate's Court, Mombasa

Land Office, Nairobi
  Files 30646 and 33866, on Mazrui land

Land Office, Mombasa
Adjudication causes pursuant to the Coast Land Settlement: Malindi, 1912–
15, Mombasa, 1916–18, Mambrui, 1922–24
Register of Deeds, Malindi, 1903–20
Registers of Deeds, Mombasa:
 A-series (land), 1891–1919
 B-series (miscellaneous), 1892–1912
 AS 1 and AS 2 (rentals), 1899

Provincial Commissioner's Archives, Mombasa
Trade and Commerce files

Other Papers and Unpublished Documents
Edward Batson, "The Social Survey of Zanzibar," 1961, copy in Foreign and
Commonwealth Office, London
Mervyn Beech, "Swahili Life," n.d. [ca. 1915], Fort Jesus, Mombasa
William Mackinnon, Papers, School of Oriental and African Studies, Univer-
sity of London
"Mombasa Social Survey," 1958, copies in University of Nairobi Library, and
Rhodes House, Oxford University

Official Documents

Great Britain
Parliamentary Papers
Foreign Office, Diplomatic and Consular Reports, Annual Series, Zanzibar
and Pemba
G. D. Kirsopp and C. A. Barlett, "Report of a mission appointed to investigate
the clove trade in India and Burma, Ceylon, British Malaya and the Dutch
East Indies," 1933
Pim, Sir Alan, "Report of the Commissioner appointed by the Secretary of
State for the Colonies to consider and report on the Financial Position and
Policy of the Zanzibar Government in relation to its Economic Resources,"
1932
"Report of the East Africa Commission," 1925
"Report of the Kenya Land Commission," 1933

Zanzibar
Annual Reports
Annual Reports of the Agriculture Department, Labour Department, and
Police
Official Gazette and Blue Books
C. A. Bartlett and J. S. Last, "Report on the Indebtedness of the Agricultural
Classes," 1933
Edward Batson, "Report on Proposals for a Social Survey of Zanzibar," 1948
Biennial Reports on District Administration, 1961–62

B. H. Binder, "Report on the Zanzibar Clove Industry," 1936

Census Reports, 1921 (Non-Native), 1924 (Native), 1931, 1948

R. H. Crofton, "Statistics of the Zanzibar Protectorate," 1921, 1933

Sir Ernest M. Dowson, "A Note on Agricultural Indebtedness in the Zanzibar Protectorate," 1936

J. M. Gray, "Report on the Inquiry into Claims to Certain Land at or near Ngezi, Vitongoji, in the Mudiria of Chake Chake in the District of Pemba," 1956

W. H. Ingrams, "Memorandum on Native Organization and Administration in Zanzibar," 1926

G. D. Kirsopp, "Memorandum on Certain Aspects of the Zanzibar Clove Industry," 1926

Law Reports, 1868–1918

Legislative Council, "Program of Social and Economic Development in the Zanzibar Protectorate for the Ten-Year Period, 1946 to 1955," Sessional Paper no. 1 of 1946

W. R. McGeach and William Addis, "A Review of the System of Land Tenure in the Islands of Zanzibar and Pemba," 1945 (written in 1934)

R. H. W. Pakenham, "Land Tenure amongst the Wahadimu of Chwaka, Zanzibar Island," 1947

"Report and Recommendations on the Present Position and Future Prospects of Agriculture in the Zanzibar Protectorate," 1959

"Report of a Commission of Inquiry into Disturbances in Zanzibar during June 1961," 1961

"Report of the Commission on Agricultural Indebtedness," 1935

"Report of the Commission on Agriculture," 1923

"Report of the Retrenchment Committee," 1927

"Report of the Zanzibar Clove Mission to India, Jan. 6–20th 1958," 1958

P. Selwyn and T. Y. Watson, "Report on the Economic Development of the Zanzibar Protectorate," 1962

Staff List, 1924

C. F. Strickland, "Report on Co-Operation and Certain Aspects of the Economic Condition of Agriculture in Zanzibar," 1932 (unpublished sections may be found in typescript in CO 618/49)

R. S. Troup, "Report on Clove Cultivation in the Zanzibar Protectorate," 1931

East Africa Protectorate and Government of Kenya

Annual Reports

Native Affairs and Agriculture Departments, Annual Reports

Official Gazette and Blue Books

Censuses, 1911, 1921

Department of Agriculture, Agricultural Census, 1920

———, "Coconuts," Leaflet no. 7, 1905

Walter Deshler, "Land Use by the Bajun People of the Northern Kenya Coast," 1954

Economic and Financial Committee, Report of Proceedings during 1922

A. C. Hollis, "Report on the Rights of the Natives of the Coast between the Tana River and Mombasa," 1907, copy in CO 533/32

"The Kenya Coastal Strip: Report of the Commissioner," 1961

Law Reports, 1897–1921

Native Labour Commission, 1912–13, Evidence and Report

"Report of the Agricultural Commission," 1929

"Report of the Coconut Commission," 1914

"Report of the Commission of Inquiry Appointed to Examine the Labour Conditions in Mombasa," 1939 (Willan Commission)

"Report of the Economic Commission," 1919

"Report of the Judicial Inquiry into Arab Claims to Land on Wasin Peninsula," 1932

"Report of the Land Committee," 1905

"Report of the Malindi Commission of Inquiry," 1917

"Report of the Mombasa Municipality Commission," 1919

"Report of the Proceedings of the Fifth Maize Conference," 1928

M. M. Shambi, "The Problem of Land Ownership and Cashewnut Claims in Malindi Coastal Belt," 1972

W. J. Simpson, "Report on Sanitary Matters in the East Africa Protectorate, Uganda, and Zanzibar," 1914

Miscellaneous

Documents relatifs à la repression de la traite des esclaves, Brussells, 1892–
United States House of Representatives, Reports upon the Commercial Relations of the United States with Foreign Countries

Published Works, Dissertations, and Conference Papers

Acland, J. D. East African Crops. London: Longman, 1971.

Adamson, Alan. Sugar Without Slaves: The Political Economy of British Guiana, 1838–1904. New Haven: Yale University Press, 1972.

Allan, William. The African Husbandman. Edinburgh: Oliver & Bond, 1965.

Anstey, Roger. The Atlantic Slave Trade and British Abolition. Atlantic Highlands, N.J.: Humanities, 1975.

Armstrong, R. "Agriculture." In Zanzibar: An Account of Its People, Industries and History. Zanzibar: Local Committee of the British Empire Exhibition, 1924.

Arrighi, Giovanni. "Labor Supplies in Historical Perspective: A Study of the Proletarianization of the African Peasantry in Rhodesia." In Essays on the Political Economy of Africa, edited by Giovanni Arrighi and John Saul. New York: Monthly Review, 1973.

Bauer, Arnold J. "Rural Workers in Spanish America: Problems of Peonage and Oppression." Hispanic American Historical Review 59 (1979): 34–63.

Beckford, George L. Persistent Poverty: Under-Development in Plantation Economies of the Third World. New York: Oxford University Press, 1972.

Beech, Mervyn W. H. "Slavery on the East Coast of Africa." Journal of the Africa Society 5 (1916): 145–49.

Bennett, Norman R. "The Church Missionary Society in Mombasa, 1873–1894." *Boston University Papers in African History.* Vol. 1, edited by Jeffrey Butler. Boston: Boston University Press, 1964.

————. *A History of the Arab State of Zanzibar.* London: Methuen, 1978.

Berg, Elliot J. "The Development of a Labor Force in Sub-Saharan Africa." *Economic Development and Cultural Change* 13 (1965): 394–412.

Bernstein, Henry. "African Peasantries: A Theoretical Framework." *Journal of Peasant Studies* 6 (1979): 421–43.

Berry, Sara. *Cocoa, Custom and Socio-Economic Change in Rural Western Nigeria.* Oxford: Clarendon, 1975.

————. "Risk Aversion and Rural Class Formation in West Africa." Colloquim paper, University of California, Los Angeles, 1978.

Billings, Dwight B., Jr. *Planters and the Making of a "New South": Class, Politics, and Development in North Carolina, 1865–1900.* Chapel Hill: University of North Carolina Press, 1979.

Binns, Harry K. "Slavery in British East Africa." *Church Missionary Intelligencer,* n.s. 23 (1897): 462.

Blacker, J. G. C. "Population Growth and Differential Fertility in Zanzibar Protectorate." *Population Studies* 5 (1962): 258–66.

Blais, J. "Les Anciens Esclaves à Zanzibar." *Anthropos* 10–11 (1915–16): 504–11.

Bolt, Christine. *The Anti-Slavery Movement and Reconstruction: A Study in Anglo-American Co-operation 1833–77.* London: Oxford University Press, 1969.

————. *Victorian Attitudes to Race.* London: Routledge Kegan Paul, 1971.

Brantley, Cynthia. *The Giriama and British Colonialism in Kenya: A Study in Resiliency and Rebellion, 1800–1920.* Forthcoming.

Brenner, Robert. "The Origins of Capitalist Development: A Critique of Neo-Smithian Marxism." *New Left Review* 104 (1977): 25–92.

Brett, E. A. *Colonialism and Underdevelopment in East Africa: The Politics of Economic Change 1919–1939.* New York: NOK, 1973.

Brode, H. *British and German East Africa: Their Economic and Commercial Relations.* London: Arnold, 1911.

Bujra, Janet. "An Anthropological Study of Political Action in a Bajuni Village, Kenya." Ph.D. dissertation, University of London, 1968.

————. "Production, Property, Prostitution. 'Sexual Politics' in Atu." *Cahiers d'Etudes Africaines* 17 (1977): 13–39.

Bundy, Colin. *The Rise and Fall of the South African Peasantry.* Berkeley: University of California Press, 1979.

Caplan, Ann Patricia. *Choice and Constraint in a Swahili Community: Property, Hierarchy, and Cognatic Descent on the East African Coast.* London: Oxford University Press, 1975.

Cashmore, T. H. R. "Studies in District Administration in the East Africa Protectorate, 1895–1918." Ph.D. dissertation, Cambridge University, 1966.

Cell, John W., ed. *By Kenya Possessed: The Correspondence of Norman Leys and J. H. Oldham 1918–1926.* Chicago: University of Chicago Press, 1976.

Champion, Arthur M. *The Agiryama of Kenya.* London: Royal Anthropological Institute Occasional Paper No. 25, 1967.

Child, Reginald. *Coconuts.* London: Longman, 1964.

Clarence-Smith, W. G. *Slaves, Peasants and Capitalists in Southern Angola, 1840–1926*. Cambridge: Cambridge University Press, 1979

Clayton, Anthony. "The General Strike in Zanzibar in 1948." *Journal of African History* 17 (1976): 417–34.

————. *The 1948 Zanzibar General Strike*. Research Report No. 32. Uppsala: Scandinavian Institute of African Studies, 1976.

————, and Donald Savage. *Government and Labour in Kenya, 1895–1963*. London: Cass, 1974.

Colson, Elizabeth. "The Impact of the Colonial Period on the Definition of Land Rights." In *Profiles of Change: African Society and Colonial Rule*, edited by Victor Turner. Cambridge: Cambridge University Press, 1971.

Cooper, Frederick. "Islam and the Slaveholders' Ideology on the East Coast of Africa." Paper for Conference on "Islamic Africa: Slavery and Related Institutions," Princeton University, 1977.

————. *Plantation Slavery on the East Coast of Africa*. New Haven: Yale University Press, 1977.

————. "The Problem of Slavery in African Studies." *Journal of African History* 20 (1979): 103–25.

Coupland, Sir Reginald. *The Exploitation of East Africa 1856–1890: The Slave Trade and the Scramble*. London: Faber & Faber, 1939.

Courtenay, P. P. *Plantation Agriculture*. London: Bell, 1965.

Craster, J. E. E. *Pemba, The Spice Island of Zanzibar*. London: Unwin, 1913.

Craton, Michael. *Sinews of Empire: A Short History of British Slavery*. Garden City, N.Y.: Doubleday, 1974.

Curtin, Philip D. *Two Jamaicas: The Role of Ideas in a Tropical Colony*. Cambridge, Mass.: Harvard University Press, 1955.

Dale, Godfrey. *The Peoples of Zanzibar*. London: Universities' Mission to Central Africa, 1920.

Davis, David Brion. *The Problem of Slavery in the Age of Revolution, 1770–1823*. Ithaca, N.Y.: Cornell University Press, 1975.

DeCanio, Stephen S. *Agriculture in the Postbellum South: The Economics of Production and Supply*. Cambridge, Mass.: MIT Press, 1974.

Derman, William. *Serfs, Peasants, and Socialists: A Former Serf Village in the Republic of Guinea*. Berkeley: University of California Press, 1973.

Dewey, Clive, and A. G. Hopkins, eds. *The Imperial Impact: Studies in the Economic History of Africa and India*. London: Athlone, 1978.

de Wilde, John C. *Experiences with Agricultural Development in Tropical Africa. Vol. I: The Synthesis*. Baltimore: Johns Hopkins University Press, 1967.

Drescher, Seymour. *Econocide: British Slavery in the Era of Abolition*. Pittsburgh: University of Pittsburgh Press, 1977.

Duncan, K., and I. Rutledge, eds. *Land and Labour in Latin America: Essays on the Development of Agrarian Capitalism in the Nineteenth and Twentieth Centuries*. Cambridge: Cambridge University Press, 1977.

Ehrlich, Cyril. "Building and Caretaking: Economic Policy in British Tropical Africa." *Economic History Review* 26 (1973): 649–67.

Eisenberg, Peter L. *The Sugar Industry of Pernambuco, 1840–1910: Modernization without Change*. Berkeley: University of California Press, 1974.

Eliot, J. A. G. "A Visit to the Bajun Islands." *Journal of the Africa Society* 25 (1925–26): 10–22, 147–63, 245–63, 338–58.

Eliot, Sir C. N. E. *The East Africa Protectorate*. London: Arnold, 1905.

Fei, J. C. H., and Gustav Ranis. *Development of the Labor Surplus Economy: Theory and Policy*. Homewood, Ill.: Irwin, 1964.

Fitzgerald, W. W. A. *Travels in the Coastlands of British East Africa and the Islands of Zanzibar and Pemba*. London: Chapman and Hall, 1898.

Forbes Munro, J. *Colonial Rule and the Kamba: Social Change in the Kenya Highlands 1889–1939*. Oxford: Clarendon, 1975.

Foster-Carter, Aidan. "The Modes of Production Controversy." *New Left Review* 107 (1978): 47–73.

Foucault, Michel. *Discipline and Punish: The Birth of the Prison*. Translated by Alan Sheridan. London: Lane, 1977.

Frucht, Richard. "A Caribbean Social Type: Neither 'Peasant' nor 'Proletarian.' " *Social and Economic Studies* 13 (1967): 295–300.

Frykenberg, Robert E., ed. *Land Control and Social Structure in Indian History*. Madison: University of Wisconsin Press, 1969.

Furedi, Frank. "The Kikuyu Squatters in the Rift Valley, 1918–29." *Hadith* 5. Edited by B. A. Ogot. Nairobi: East African Literature Bureau, 1975.

Gann, Lewis. "The End of the Slave Trade in British Central Africa: 1889–1912." *Rhodes-Livingstone Journal* 16 (1954): 27–51.

Geertz, Clifford. *Agricultural Involution: The Process of Ecological Change in Indonesia*. Berkeley: University of California Press, 1963.

Genovese, Eugene D. *Roll, Jordan, Roll: The World the Slaves Made*. New York: Pantheon, 1974.

———. *The World the Slaveholders Made*. New York: Pantheon, 1969.

Gershenberg, Irving. "Customary Land Tenure as a Constraint on Agricultural Development: A Re-evaluation." *East African Journal of Rural Development* 4, no. 1 (1971): 51–62.

Gerteis, Louis. *From Contraband to Freedmen: Federal Policy toward Southern Blacks, 1861–1865*. Westport, Conn.: Greenwood, 1973.

Glassman, Carla. "The Illegal East African Slave Trade, 1873–1900." Unpublished paper, Cambridge University, 1977.

Grace, John. *Domestic Slavery in West Africa*. London: Muller, 1975.

Gray, John. *A History of Zanzibar from the Middle Ages to 1856*. London: Oxford University Press, 1962.

Green, William. *British Slave Emancipation: The Sugar Colonies and the Great Experiment, 1830–1865*. Oxford: Clarendon, 1976.

———. "Caribbean Historiography, 1600–1900: The Recent Tide." *Journal of Interdisciplinary History* 7 (1977): 509–30.

Hall, Douglas. "The Flight from the Estates Reconsidered: The British West Indies 1838–42." *Journal of Caribbean History* 10–11 (1978): 7–24.

Hamilton, Robert W. "Land Tenure among the Bantu Wanyika of East Africa." *Journal of the Royal Anthropological Society* 20 (1920): 13–18.

Hardinge, Arthur. *A Diplomatist in the East*. London: Cape, 1928.

Harris, John H. *Africa: Slave or Free?* London: Student Christian Movement, 1919.

————. "Back to Slavery?" *Contemporary Review* 120 (1921): 190–97.

Harrison, Brian. *Drink and the Victorians: The Temperance Question in England, 1815–1872.* Pittsburgh, Pa.: University of Pittsburgh Press, 1971.

Hay, Douglas, et al. *Albion's Fatal Tree.* New York: Pantheon, 1975.

Higgs, Robert. *Competition and Coercion: Blacks in the American Economy 1865–1914.* Cambridge: Cambridge University Press, 1977.

Hildermeier, Manfred. "Agrarian Social Protest, Populism and Economic Development: Some Problems and Results from Recent Studies." *Social History* 4 (1979): 319–32.

Hobley, C. W. "Native Problems in Eastern Africa." *Journal of the Africa Society* 22 (1923): 189–202, 287–301.

Hollingsworth, L. W. *Zanzibar under the Foreign Office, 1890–1913.* London: Macmillan, 1953.

Hollis, A. C. "Zanzibar: Present Conditions and Interests." *Journal of the Africa Society* 28 (1929): 217–23.

Hopkins, A. G. *An Economic History of West Africa.* London: Longman, 1973.

Hyder Kindy. *Life and Politics in Mombasa.* Nairobi: East Africa Publishing House, 1972.

Iliffe, John. *A Modern History of Tanganyika.* Cambridge: Cambridge University Press, 1979.

Ingrams, W. H. "Native Industries and Occupations." *Zanzibar: An Account of Its People, Industries and History.* Zanzibar: Local Committee of the British Empire Exhibition, 1924.

————. *Zanzibar, Its History and Peoples.* London: Witherby, 1931.

Jackson, Frederick. *Early Days in East Africa.* London: Arnold, 1930.

Janmohamed, Karim K. "African Labourers in Mombasa, c. 1895–1940." In *Hadith 5*, edited by B. A. Ogot. Nairobi: East African Literature Bureau, 1975.

————. "A History of Mombasa, c. 1895–1939: Some Aspects of Economic and Social Life in an East African Port Town during Colonial Rule." Ph.D. dissertation, Northwestern University, 1977.

Jivanji, Yusufali Esmailjee. *Memorandum on the Report of the Commission on Agriculture 1923.* Poina: Aryabhushar, 1924.

Johnston, Bruce, F., and Peter Kilby. *Agriculture and Structural Transformation: Economic Strategies in Late-Developing Countries.* New York: Oxford University Press, 1975.

Kamarck, Andrew W. *The Economics of African Development.* Revised edition. New York: Praeger, 1971.

Katz, Friedrich. "Labor Conditions on Haciendas in Porfirian Mexico: Some Trends and Tendencies." *Hispanic American Historical Review* 54 (1974): 1–47.

Kay, Cristobal. "The Development of the Chilean *Hacienda* System, 1850–1973." *Land and Labour in Latin America: Essays on the Development of Agrarian Capitalism in the Nineteenth and Twentieth Centuries.* Edited by K. Duncan and I. Rutledge. Cambridge: Cambridge University Press, 1977.

Keegan, Tim. "The Restructuring of Agrarian Class Relations in a Colonial Economy: The Orange River Colony, 1902–1910." *Journal of Southern African Studies* 5 (1979): 234–54.

Kirk, John. "Agricultural Resources of Zanzibar." *Kew Bulletin* (1892), pp. 87–91.

Kjekshus, Helge. *Ecology Control and Economic Development in East African History: The Case of Tanganyika 1850–1950*. Berkeley: University of California Press, 1977.

Kloosterboer, Wilemina. *Involuntary Labour since the Abolition of Slavery*. Leiden: Brill, 1960.

Koffsky, Peter. "History of Takaungu, East Africa, 1830–1896." Ph.D. dissertation, University of Wisconsin, 1977.

Kolchin, Peter. *First Freedom: The Responses of Alabama's Blacks to Emancipation and Reconstruction*. Westport, Conn.: Greenwood, 1972.

Kuczynski, R. R. *Demographic Survey of the British Colonial Empire*. 3 vols. London: Oxford University Press, 1949.

Kuper, Leo. *Race, Class and Power*. Chicago: Aldine, 1975.

Lanchester, H. V. *Zanzibar: A Study in Tropical Town Planning*. Cheltenham, Eng.: Burrow, 1923.

Lee, J. M. *Colonial Development and Good Government: A Study of the Ideas Expressed by the British Official Classes in Planning Decolonization 1939–1964*. Oxford: Clarendon, 1967.

LeRoy, Alexandre. "Au Zanguebar anglais." *Missions Catholiques* 22 (1890): 435–37, 448–634

Lewis, W. Arthur. "Economic Development with Unlimited Supplies of Labour." *The Manchester School* 22 (1954): 139–91.

————. "Unlimited Labour: Further Notes." *The Manchester School* 26 (1958): 1–32.

————, ed. *Tropical Development 1880–1913: Studies in Economic Progress*. London: Allen & Unwin, 1970.

Leys, Colin. "Capital Accumulation, Class Formation and Dependency—The Significance of the Kenyan Case." *The Socialist Register 1978*. Edited by Ralph Miliband and John Saville. London: Merlin, 1978.

————. *Underdevelopment in Kenya: The Political Economy of Neo-Colonialism*. Berkeley: University of California Press, 1974.

Leys, Norman. *Kenya*. 4th edition. London: Cass, 1973. Originally published 1924.

Lipton, Michael. "Towards a Theory of Land Reform." *Peasants, Landlords, and Governments: Agrarian Reform in the Third World*. Edited by David Lehmann. New York: Holmes & Meier, 1974.

Litwack, Leon. *Been in the Storm So Long: The Aftermath of Slavery*. New York: Knopf, 1979.

Lofchie, Michael F. *Zanzibar: Background to Revolution*. Princeton: Princeton University Press, 1965.

Lonsdale, John, and Bruce Berman. "Coping with the Contradictions: The Development of the Colonial State in Kenya." *Journal of African History* 20 (1979): 487–506.

Lorimer, Douglas. *Colour, Class and the Victorians: English Attitudes to the Negro in the Mid-Nineteenth Century*. Leicester: Leicester University Press, 1978.

Low, D. A., and Alison Smith, eds. *History of East Africa, Vol. III*. Oxford: Clarendon, 1976.

Lugard, Frederick. *The Rise of Our East African Empire.* 2 vols. Edinburgh: Blackwood, 1893.

————. "Slavery under the British Flag." *Nineteenth Century* (February 1896), pp. 335–55.

Lyne, Robert Nunez. "Causes Contributing to the Success of the Zanzibar Clove Industry." *Bulletin of the Imperial Institute* 8 (1910): 143–44.

————. *Zanzibar in Contemporary Times.* London: Hurst & Blackett, 1905.

McClellan, F. C. "Agricultural Resources of the Zanzibar Protectorate." *Bulletin of the Imperial Institute* 12 (1914): 407–29.

McDermott, P. L. *British East Africa or IBEA.* London: Chapman & Hall, 1895.

McKay, William F. "A Precolonial History of the Southern Kenya Coast." Ph.D. dissertation, Boston University, 1975.

MacKenzie, Donald. "A Report on Slavery and the Slave Trade in Zanzibar, Pemba, and the Mainland of the British Protectorates of East Africa." *Anti-Slavery Reporter,* ser. 4, 15 (1895): 69–96.

MacKenzie, George. "British East Africa and the Mombasa Railway." *Fortnightly Review,* n.s. 51 (1892): 566–79.

Maini, Krishan. *Land Law in East Africa.* Nairobi: Oxford University Press, 1967.

Mandle, Jay R. "The Plantation Economy: An Essay in Definition." In *The Slave Economies,* edited by Eugene D. Genovese. New York: Wiley, 1973.

————. *The Roots of Black Poverty: The Southern Plantation Economy after the Civil War.* Durham, N.C.: Duke University Press, 1978.

Marglin, Stephen A. "What Do Bosses Do? The Origins and Functions of Hierarchy in Capitalist Production." *Review of Radical Political Economy* 6, no. 2 (1974): 33–60.

Marshall, Woodville K. "Notes on Peasant Development in the West Indies Since 1838." *Social and Economic Studies* 17 (1968): 252–63.

Martin, Esmond Bradley. *The History of Malindi: A Geographical Analysis of an East African Town from the Portuguese Period to the Present.* Nairobi: East African Literature Bureau, 1973.

Martinez-Alier, Juan. *Haciendas, Plantations and Collective Farms.* London: Cass, 1977.

Marx, Karl. *Capital.* Translated by Samuel Moore and Edward Aveling. 3 vols. New York: International Publishers, 1967.

Mbithi, Philip, and Carolyn Barnes. *The Spontaneous Settlement Problem in Kenya.* Nairobi: East African Literature Bureau, 1975.

Mbotela, James Juma. *The Freeing of the Slaves in East Africa.* London: Evans, 1956.

Meek, Charles. *Land Law and Custom in the Colonies.* London: Oxford University Press, 1949.

Meillassoux, Claude. *Femmes, greniers et capitaux.* Paris: Maspero, 1975.

————, ed. *L'Esclavage en Afrique pre-coloniale.* Paris: Maspero, 1975.

Memon, P. A. "Mercantile Intermediaries in a Colonial Spatial System: Wholesaling in Kenya, 1830–1940." Ph.D. dissertation, University of Western Ontario, 1974.

————, and Esmond B. Martin. "The Kenya Coast: An Anomaly in the Development of an 'Ideal Type' Colonial Spatial System." *Kenya Historical Review* 4 (1976): 187–206.

Middleton, John. *Land Tenure in Zanzibar.* London: Her Majesty's Stationery Office, 1961.

———, and Jane Campbell. *Zanzibar: Its Society and Its Politics.* London: Oxford University Press, 1965.

Miers, Suzanne. *Britain and the Ending of the Slave Trade.* London: Longman, 1975.

———, and Igor Kopytoff, eds. *Slavery in Africa: Historical and Anthropological Perspectives.* Madison: University of Wisconsin Press, 1977.

Migdal, Joel S. *Peasants, Politics, and Revolution: Pressures toward Political and Social Change in the Third World.* Princeton: Princeton University Press, 1974.

Miller, David. "Agricultural Change on the Lower Tana: Lower Pokomoni, c. 1870–1939." Staff seminar paper, Department of History, University of Nairobi, 1977.

Mintz, Sidney W. *Caribbean Transformations.* Chicago: Aldine, 1974.

———. "The Rural Proletariat and the Problem of the Rural Proletarian Consciousness." *Journal of Peasant Studies* 1 (1974): 291–325.

———. "Slavery and the Rise of Peasantries." *Historical Reflections* 6, no. 1 (1979): 213–43.

Moore, Barrington, Jr. *The Social Origins of Dictatorship and Democracy: Lord and Peasant in the Making of the Modern World.* Boston: Beacon, 1966

Morris, M. L. "The Development of Capitalism in South African Agriculture: Class Struggle in the Countryside." *Economy and Society* 5 (1976): 292–343.

Morton, Rodger Frederic. "Slaves, Fugitives, and Freedmen on the Kenya Coast, 1873–1907." Ph.D. dissertation, Syracuse University, 1976.

Mungeam, G. *British Rule in Kenya, 1895–1912.* Oxford: Clarendon, 1966.

Murray, Nancy Uhlar. "Nineteenth Century Kenya and the 'Imperial Race for Christ.'" Paper for the Annual Meeting of the Historical Association of Kenya, 1978.

Newman, Henry S. *Banani: The Transition from Slavery to Freedom in Zanzibar and Pemba.* London: Headley, 1898.

Oldham, Joseph H. *Christianity and the Race Problem.* London: Student Christian Movement, 1925.

Orde Browne, G. St. J. *The African Labourer.* London: Oxford University Press, 1933.

Paige, Jeffrey M. *Agrarian Revolution: Social Movements and Export Agriculture in the Underdeveloped World.* New York: Free Press, 1975.

Painter, Nell Irvin. *Exodusters: Black Migration to Kansas after Reconstruction.* New York: Knopf, 1976.

Palmer, Robin. *Land and Racial Domination in Rhodesia.* Berkeley: University of California Press, 1977.

———, and Neil Parsons, eds. *The Roots of Rural Poverty in Central and Southern Africa.* London: Heineman, 1977.

Pan American Union. *Plantation Systems of the New World.* Washington: Pan American Union, 1959.

Parkin, David J. *Palms, Wine, and Witnesses.* London: Intertext, 1972.
————. "The Politics of Ritual Syncretism: Islam among the Non-Muslim Giriama of Kenya." *Africa* 40 (1970): 217–33.
Pearce, F. B. *Zanzibar: The Island Metropolis of Eastern Africa.* London: Unwin, 1920.
Pease, Joseph. *How We Countenance Slavery.* London: British and Foreign Anti-Slavery Society, 1895.
Perham, Margery, ed. *The Diaries of Lord Lugard. Vol. 1: East Africa, November 1889 to December 1890.* London: Faber & Faber, 1959.
Ranger, Terence, "Growing from the Roots: Reflections on Peasant Research in Central and Southern Africa." *Journal of Southern African Studies* 5 (1978): 99–133.
Ransom, Roger, and Richard Sutch. *One Kind of Freedom: The Economic Consequences of Emancipation.* Cambridge: Cambridge University Press, 1977.
Rashid bin Hassani. "The Story of Rashid bin Hassani of the Bisa Tribe, Northern Rhodesia." Recorded by W. F. Baldock. In *Ten Africans,* edited by Margery Perham. London: Faber & Faber, 1963.
The Red Book, 1925–26. Nairobi: East African Standard.
Reid, Joseph D., Jr. "Sharecropping and Agricultural Uncertainty." *Economic Development and Cultural Change* 24 (1976): 549–76.
Rey, Pierre-Phillipe. *Les Alliances de classes.* Paris: Maspero, 1973.
Richards, A. I.; Forde Sturrock; and Jean M. Fortt, eds. *Subsistence to Commercial Farming in Present-Day Buganda.* Cambridge: Cambridge University Press, 1973.
Richards, Alan. "The Political Economy of *Gutswirtschaft:* A Comparative Analysis of East Elbian Germany, Egypt, and Chile." *Comparative Studies in Society and History* 21 (1979): 483–513.
Roark, James C. *Masters without Slaves: Southern Planters in the Civil War and Reconstruction.* New York: Norton, 1977.
Roberts, Richard, and Martin Klein. "The Banamba Slave Exodus of 1905 and the Decline of Slavery in the Western Sudan." *Journal of African History,* forthcoming.
Rollestone, I. H. O. "The Watumbatu of Zanzibar." *Tanganyika Notes and Records* 8 (1939): 85–97.
Ross, William McGregor. *Kenya from Within.* London: Cass, 1968. Originally published 1927.
Salim, A. I. *The Swahili-Speaking Peoples of Kenya's Coast, 1895–1965.* Nairobi: East African Publishing House, 1973.
Sandbrook, Richard, and Robin Cohen, eds. *The Development of an African Working Class: Studies in Class Formation and Action.* London: Longman, 1975.
Schultz, Theodore W. *Transforming Traditional Agriculture.* New Haven: Yale University Press, 1964.
Scott, James C. *The Moral Economy of the Peasant: Rebellion and Subsistence in Southeast Asia.* New Haven: Yale University Press, 1976.
Semmel, Bernard. *Imperialism and Social Reform.* London: Allen & Unwin, 1960.
————. *Jamaican Blood and Victorian Conscience: The Governor Eyre Controversy.* Boston: Houghton Mifflin, 1963.

Shanin, Teodor, ed. *Peasants and Peasant Societies*. Harmondsworth, Eng.: Penguin, 1971

Skocpol, Theda. *States and Social Revolutions*. Cambridge: Cambridge University Press, 1979.

Sorrenson, M. P. A. *The Origins of European Settlement in Kenya*. Nairobi: Oxford University Press, 1968.

Spear, Thomas. *The Kaya Complex: A History of the Mijikenda Peoples of the Kenya Coast to 1900*. Nairobi: Kenya Literature Bureau, 1979.

Spencer, I. R. G. "The Development of Production and Trade in the Reserve Areas of Kenya, 1895–1929." Ph.D. dissertation, Simon Fraser University, Burnaby, B.C., 1974.

Stedman Jones, Gareth. *Outcast London: A Study in the Relationship between Classes in Victorian Society*. Oxford: Clarendon, 1971.

――――. "Working-Class Culture and Working-Class Politics in London, 1870–1900: Notes on the Remaking of a Working Class." *Journal of Social History* 7 (1973–74): 460–508.

Stren, Richard. *Housing the Urban Poor in Africa: Policy, Politics, and Bureaucracy in Mombasa*. Berkeley: Institute of International Studies, University of California at Berkeley, 1978.

Strobel, Margaret. *Muslim Women in Mombasa, 1890–1975*. New Haven: Yale University Press, 1979.

Temperley, Howard. *British Anti-Slavery 1833–1870*. London: Longman, 1972.

――――. "Capitalism, Slavery and Ideology." *Past and Present* 75 (1977): 94–118.

Thomas, Roger G. "Forced Labour in British West Africa: The Case of the Northern Territories of the Gold Coast 1906–1927." *Journal of African History* 14 (1973): 79–103.

Thompson, E. P. *The Making of the English Working Class*. New York: Vintage, 1963.

――――. "Time, Work-Discipline and Industrial Capitalism." *Past and Present* 38 (1967): 56–97.

――――. *Whigs and Hunters: The Origins of the Black Act*. London: Penguin, 1975.

Tidbury, G. E. *The Clove Tree*. London: Lockwood, 1949.

Tignor, Robert L. *The Colonial Transformation of Kenya: The Kamba, Kikuyu, and Maasai from 1900 to 1939*. Princeton: Princeton University Press, 1976.

Tinker, Hugh. *A New System of Slavery: The Export of Indian Labour Overseas, 1830–1920*. London: Oxford University Press, 1974.

Tosh, John. "Lango Agriculture during the Early Colonial Period: Land and Labour in a Cash-Crop Economy." *Journal of African History* 19 (1978): 415–39.

Trapido, Stanley. "Landlord and Tenant in a Colonial Economy: The Transvaal 1880–1910." *Journal of Southern African Studies* 5 (1978): 26–58.

Tucker, A. R. *Eighteen Years in Uganda*. London: Arnold, 1908.

Uzoigwe, G. N. *Britain and the Conquest of Africa: The Age of Salisbury*. Ann Arbor: University of Michigan Press, 1974.

――――. "The Mombasa-Victoria Railway, 1890–1902: Imperial Necessity, Humanitarian Venture, or Economic Imperialism?" *Kenya Historical Review* 4 (1976): 11–34.

Vail, Leroy. "Ecology and History: The Example of Eastern Zambia." *Journal of Southern African Studies* 3 (1976): 129-55.

Van Hekken, P. M., and H. U. E. Thoden van Velzen. *Land Scarcity and Rural Inequality in Tanzania.* The Hague, 1972.

van Onselen, Charles. *Chibaro: African Mine Labour in Southern Rhodesia 1900-1933.* London: Pluto, 1976.

————. "Randlords and Rotgut, 1886-1903." *History Workshop Journal* 2 (1976): 33-89.

————. "Worker Consciousness in Black Miners: Southern Rhodesia, 1900-1920." *Journal of African History* 14 (1973): 237-55.

van Zwanenberg, Roger. *Colonial Capitalism and Labour in Kenya 1919-1939.* Nairobi: East African Literature Bureau, 1975.

Waller, Horace. *The Case of Our Zanzibar Slaves: Why Not Liberate Them?* London: King, 1896.

————. *Heligoland for Zanzibar, or One Island Full of Free Men for Two Full of Slaves.* London: Stanford, 1893.

Wallerstein, Immanuel. "The Three Stages of African Involvement in the World-Economy." In *The Political Economy of Contemporary Africa,* edited by P. C. W. Gutkind and Immanuel Wallerstein. Beverly Hills, Calif.: Sage, 1976.

Warmington, W. A.; E. Ardener; and S. Ardener. *Plantation and Village in the Cameroons.* London: Oxford University Press, 1960.

Weidner, Fritz. *Die Haussklaverei in Ostafrika.* Jena: Fischer, 1915.

Weiskel, Timothy C. "Labor in the Emergent Periphery: From Slavery to Migrant Labor among the Baule Peoples, 1880-1925." *The World-System of Capitalism: Past and Present.* Edited by Walter Goldfrank. Beverly Hills, Calif.: Sage, 1979.

Weston, Frank. *The Serfs of Great Britain.* London: Knott, 1920.

Wiener, Jonathan M. "Class Structure and Economic Development in the American South, 1865-1955." *American Historical Review* 84 (1979): 970-92.

————. *The Social Origins of the New South: Alabama 1860-1885.* Baton Rouge: Louisiana State University Press, 1978.

Wijeyewardene, G. E. T. "Some Aspects of Village Solidarity in Ki-Swahili Speaking Communities of Kenya and Tanganyika." Ph.D. dissertation, Cambridge University, 1961.

Williams, Eric. *Capitalism and Slavery.* Chapel Hill: University of North Carolina Press, 1944.

Williamson, Joel. *After Slavery: The Negro in South Carolina during Reconstruction, 1861-1877.* Chapel Hill: University of North Carolina Press, 1965.

Wilson, F. B. "Emergency Food Production in Zanzibar." *East Africa Agricultural Journal* 10 (1944): 93-100.

————, and G. E. Tidbury, "Native Paddy Cultivation and Yields in Zanzibar." *East Africa Agricultural Journal* 9 (1944): 231-35.

Wolf, Eric. *Peasant Wars of the Twentieth Century.* New York: Harper, 1969.

————. "Specific Aspects of Plantation Systems in the New World: Community Sub-Cultures and Social Classes." In *Plantation Systems of the New World.* Washington: Pan American Union, 1959.

Wolff, Richard D. *The Economics of Colonialism: Britain and Kenya, 1870–1930.* New Haven: Yale University Press, 1974.

Woodman, Harold. "Sequel to Slavery: The New History Views the Postbellum South." *Journal of Southern History* 43 (1977): 523–54.

Woodward, C. Vann. *Origins of the New South, 1877–1913.* Baton Rouge: Louisiana State University Press, 1951.

_____. "The Price of Freedom." *What Was Freedom's Price?* Edited by David S. Sansing. Jackson: University of Mississippi Press, 1978.

World Bank. *Kenya: Into the Second Decade.* Baltimore: Johns Hopkins University Press, 1975.

Wright, Gavin. *The Political Economy of the Cotton South: Households, Markets, and Wealth in the Nineteenth Century.* New York: Norton, 1978.

_____, and Howard Kunreuther. "Cotton, Corn and Risk in the Nineteenth Century." *Journal of Economic History* 35 (1975): 526–51.

Ylvisaker, Marguerite. *Lamu in the Nineteenth Century: Land, Trade, and Politics.* Boston: African Studies Center, Boston University, 1979.

Zarwan, John. "Indian Businessmen in Kenya: A Case Study." Ph.D. dissertation, Yale University, 1976.

Periodicals

Anti-Slavery Reporter
Central Africa
Church Missionary Intelligencer

Index